THE HOLY LAND IN AMERICAN RELIGIOUS THOUGHT, 1620-1948

The Symbiosis of American Religious Approaches to Scripture's Sacred Territory

Gershon Greenberg

UNIVERSITY
PRESS OF
AMERICA

Lanham • New York • London

THE AVRAHAM HARMAN
INSTITUTE OF
CONTEMPORARY JEWRY

THE HEBREW UNIVERSITY
OF JERUSALEM

Copyright © 1994 by
University Press of America®, Inc.
4720 Boston Way
Lanham, Maryland 20706

3 Henrietta Street
London WC2E 8LU England

Co-published by arrangement with
The Avraham Harman Institute of Contemporary Jewry,
The Hebrew University of Jerusalem

Library of Congress Cataloging-in-Publication Data

Greenberg, Gershon.
The Holy Land in American religious thought : 1620–1948 / by
Gershon Greenberg.
p.   cm.
"The Avraham Harman Institute of Contemporary Jewry, The Hebrew
University of Jerusalem."
Includes bibliographical references and index.
1. Palestine in Christianity—History of doctrines.   2. Palestine in
Judaism—History of doctrines.   3. Religious thought—United
States.   4. Judaism—Doctrines—History.   I. Title.
BT93.G74   1994   263'.0425694—dc20   93–37015 CIP

ISBN 0–8191–9237–6 (cloth : alk. paper)
ISBN 0–8191–9238–4 (pbk. : alk. paper)

 The paper used in this publication meets the minimum requirements of
American National Standard for Information Sciences—Permanence
of Paper for Printed Library Materials, ANSI Z39.48–1984.

Dedicated to my beloved parents
Morris and Lillian Berkson Greenberg
of blessed memory

The Avraham Harman Institute
of Contemporary Jewry
expresses its gratitude to
Samuel Rothberg
for his abiding commitment to
scholars and scholarship.

Research was done as part of the
American-Holy Land Project,
supported by the
Blaustein Fund for American Studies.

Table of Contents

Preface

This book explores the variety of religious consciousness in America pertaining to the sacred territory of Scripture, a territory that unites Jews, Christians, and Mormons even while it divides them. The Holy Land brings the religions of America together in union at the very moment they reject one another.

The idea for a monograph on American religious thought and the Holy Land came from Professor Moshe Davis of the Avraham Harman Institute of Contemporary Jewry (ICJ) of the Hebrew University of Jerusalem. The volume was written in the framework of the ICJ's America-Holy Land Project, whose ongoing research is generously assisted by the Jacob Blaustein Fund for American Studies. It is intended as a text for the Institute's continuing seminars on America and the Holy Land, and of course for American university and seminary study. In the process of preparing the book, I received generous advice from the members of the America-Holy Land "family": especially Moshe Davis and Robert Handy, along with Ron Aaronsohn, Ya'akov Ariel, Joseph Glass, Ruth Kark, Deborah and Abraham Karp, Menahem Kaufmann, David Klatzker, Franklin Littell, Jonathan Sarna, Lester Vogel, Bernard Wax, and the late Selig Adler and Nathan Kaganoff. Arnold Eisen and Timothy Smith also made helpful suggestions. I am grateful to the editor, Marc Beckwith, and to the manuscript typists, Linda Railey and Debora A. Flores.

I am indebted to the following for providing sources: Harry and Miriam Rosenthal Holy Land Resource Library, ICJ; the Hebraica Section and Rare Book Division of the Library of Congress; Archives of the Franciscan Monastery, Washington, D.C.; Houghton Library, Harvard University; Moorland-Spingarn Research Library, Howard University; American Jewish Historical Society, Waltham, Massachusetts; Archives of the Seventh-day Adventist Church World Headquarters, Silver Spring, Maryland; Harold B. Lee Library, Brigham Young University; and New York Historical Society. The reading room staff of the Library of Congress, Bruce Martin in particular, has been a reliable partner in my research.

I use the term "Land of Israel" or "Land" to refer to the geographic area within the pre-1948 boundaries of Palestine.[1] The term "Holy Land" is used interchangeably with "Zion" and refers to the sacred territorial reality of Scripture, whether in the Land of Israel, America, or the heavenly kingdom. The term "state" refers to the political entity before 1948 and "State of Israel" to that after 1948. "Israel" refers to the people of Israel. I use the term "restoration" to mean the rebuilding of the Land and the people in the Land.

Seventeenth- through nineteenth-century English usage is modernized, and I have decided against capitalizing many terms that in some contexts are customarily capitalized. Pronouns referring to the God of Israel or Christ, the names of holy places in the Land, "Holy Land," "Holy City" meaning Jerusalem, "Messiah" as Christ, and "Ten Lost Tribes" are all capitalized.

The footnotes contain the scriptural references of the respective authors as well as my own examples. Biblical quotations are from the Authorized Version, *Esdras* from the New Revised Standard.

G. G.

Notes

1.   See Gideon Biger, "The Names and Boundaries of Erets-Israel (Palestine) as Reflections of Stages in Its History," in Ruth Kark, ed., *The Land That Became Israel: Studies in Historical Geography* (Jerusalem 1989):1-22.

Introduction: The Holy Land in American Religious Thought

The history of religious America from 1620 to 1948 is bound up with the idea and reality of the scriptural Holy Land. The grand array of material on this connection between America and the Land reveals much common ground for Jew, Christian, and Mormon. From the perspective of the overall history of the relationship, those religions participated in the changing center of gravity, from America to the Land of Israel to both together. They had common experiences of the real versus the ideal sacred territory and of the endless elusiveness of the ideal. They invoked divine initiative in the America-Holy Land relation and the active and passive roles of man. They spoke of the concrete reality of Jerusalem, made it transcend geographic reality, and sublimated it into myth. In speaking of the restored or redeemed Holy Land, they involved America positively or expected her demise, sometimes both. They felt that the restored Land would either benefit or damage the rest of mankind. Their views of the indigenous Jewish population ranged from a sense that it was hopeless to a belief that it could benefit greatly from restoration of the Land. And the various religions shared apocalyptic expectations for the sacred territory.

Holy Land and America: A Changing Relation

From the seventeenth century through the beginning of the nineteenth, "Holy Land" or "Zion" meant America. The Puritans imported the Holy Land reality to America, as a transgeographical spiritual entity. Sephardic Jews found scriptural dimensions (i.e., hints of the Holy Land) in the American Revolution, although they also regarded American victory as a catalyst for the realization of Holy Land in the Land of Israel. Early American settlers projected the Holy Land onto the landscape of America, giving places scriptural names and onto American natives. Beginning with Roger Williams (1604-1683), American Indians were identified as descendants of the Ten Lost Tribes.

In the nineteenth century the spiritual territory returned to its geographical source, the Land of Israel. America's first (unofficial) consul to Jerusalem, Warder Cresson (1798-1860), went to the Land in 1844 to personally help bring about the millennium. Several pilgrims, such as William C. Prime (1855-1856), Herman Melville (1857), and Thomas de Witt Talmage (1880), sublimated their historical experiences in the Land into scriptural timelessness. In the early 1820s, Congregational missionaries Pliny Fisk (1792-1825), Levi Parsons (1792-1822), and Jonas King (1792-1869) went to the Land of Israel to convert Jews and make the onset of a Land-centered Christian millennium possible. American consuls with deep interests in the history and peoples of the Land included Victor Beauboucher (1865-1869), Frank S. de Hass (1874-77), Selah Merrill (1882-1907, with interruptions), and Edwin S. Wallace (1891-1893).

In the twentieth century, the dialectical thesis of Zion-as-America and the antithesis of Zion-as-the-Land-of-Israel were synthesized, both positions occurring together and sometimes implying each other (e.g., secular Zionism). Protestant liberals supported Jewish political sovereignty conditioned upon a Jewish-Arab rapprochement to satisfy American standards of freedom, democracy, and morality. Catholics tended to be anti-Zionist, believing that a modern Jewish state would threaten the existential experience of being with Christ in the scriptural Holy Land, implicitly reinforcing Jewish innocence of deicide. Twentieth-century Judaism, with some marginal exception within Reform and ultra-Orthodoxy, was Zionist. The Mormons crystallized the synthesis, speaking simultaneously of Zion in America and Zion in the Land of Israel.

Common Religious Concerns

Several common themes run through this history of the relationship between religious America and the Holy Land, with the responses varying from group to group and through time.

Human Initiative or Passivity under Divine Aegis

One common concern was the roles of God and man in the process of realizing Zion. Puritans believed that entry into Holy Land-America resulted from divine action. In 1646 the governor of Plymouth Colony, William Bradford (1588-1657), exhorted his followers in these words:

> Come let us declare in Zion the word of the Lord our God [*Jeremiah* 51:10] . . . Are not these Jebusites overcome that have vexed the people Israel so long, even holding Jerusalem till David's days? . . . The tyrannous bishops are ejected, their courts dissolved, their canons forceless, and all their super-stitious discarded, their service cashiered, their ceremonies useless and despised, their plots for popery prevented and returned to Rome from whence

they came . . . But who hath done it? Who, even He that sitteth on the white horse, is called faithful and true and judgeth and fighteth righteously [*Revelation* 19:11].[1]

Jewish Reformers who identified America with Zion spoke of divine leadership. When David Einhorn (1809-1879) arrived in America in 1855, he expressed gratitude to God for bringing him to the Promised Land of Canaan, where Tora principles would be fulfilled, Washington, D.C., would become the new Jerusalem, and the Capitol building would become the new temple sanctuary.[2]

Those who identified Zion with the Land of Israel also saw divine intervention. Orthodox Jews Abraham J. G. Lesser (1834-1925) and Barukh M. Klein (1873-1932), who retained a pre-Enlightenment concept of redemption, believed that Zion could be realized only through divine initiative. American Catholics were predisposed toward divine history, rejecting the notion of human, historical development of the Land since they saw that activity as a threat to reenacting Jesus' life and crucifixion there. The theme of the passive human role, complementing divine initiative, was enunciated by missionaries and colonists. Missionary Levi Parsons believed that he was called to convert Jews to share in the forward surge of Christian history toward the second coming. Colonist Clorinda S. Minor (1805-1855) of Philadelphia related in 1851 that she was led to Jerusalem—though she had no reason to expect "spiritual profit" there and would indeed suffer and lose everything—because "the conviction of my soul increased every hour, that God was calling me to go."[3]

Some spoke of an active human role in the realization of Zion within the divine context. While still a Christian—he later became a Jew—Cresson detected "signs" of the restoration and declared that it was time to "enter into the plans of divine providence [and] cooperate in accomplishing the prophecies" about restoring the Jews.[4] He worked actively to restore the Land through agriculture. In 1906 Orthodox Rabbi Joseph M. Levin (1870-1936) also spoke of human activity under divine aegis:

The truth is that authentic redemption will come only from God. For only He is the redeemer. But we are not to rely on miracles when we can save ourselves in a natural way. If we consolidate ourselves into one body and one soul, with one longing, if our views are harmonized without exception, we can hope that the authentic savior will come and bring authentic redemption upon His wings.[5]

Jerusalem Above and Below

Another common concern was this-worldliness and otherworldliness. One aspect focused on this-worldly American reality. Louis D. Brandeis (1856-1941) identified Zion in the Land of Israel with contemporary American society:

> Not since the destruction of the Temple have the Jews in spirit and in ideals been so fully in harmony with the noblest aspirations of the country in which they lived . . . Indeed, loyalty to America demands rather that each American Jew become a Zionist.[6]

Horace Kallen (1882-1974) also derived his Zion concept from American reality. He spoke of a "Hebraic" state with elements of Jewish history, ethnic solidarity, language, and religion, and of religion as reflecting the American principle that all men were created equal and with inalienable rights. In his 1918 Pittsburgh Program Kallen analyzed the Hebraic state in terms of social justice and securing individual life, liberty, and happiness. Natural resources would be controlled and there would be free public education in the name of economic and social democracy. The state would foster free expression, political and civil equality, and equality of opportunity.[7]

Others detached the Holy Land from this-worldly reality. The Zion of black American Christianity transcended both geographic America and Land of Israel, thereby locating it beyond the boundaries of this-worldly space. The editors of the *AME Church Review* in 1918, believing that the age for fulfilling prophecy had arrived, hoped that Jews would rejoice not in returning to Jerusalem to build the foundations for a Jewish state where David's throne once was but in the homecoming of their exiles to Christ, "Who opened in the house of King David a fountain for sin and all uncleanness." Christians should return to Jerusalem not "simply to cherish the sacred places, hallowed by the footprints of Jesus, but in neighborliness, in brotherhood, in justice, righteousness and peace."[8] The Mormons also spoke of a Zion that transcended geographical America and the Land of Israel. In the future, Jerusalem in the Land and "New Jerusalem" in America would serve as two "space-time capitals" of the universalized covenant community in a geographically transformed universe.[9]

Some believed that the Holy Land in the Land of Israel would sublimate the earthly reality into an ahistorical kingdom, a celestial Jerusalem.[10] Missionary Fisk wrote of his experience of the Holy Sepulcher:

> I looked at the dome which covers the Tomb, and thought of the death and resurrection of my Lord and burst into tears . . . It seemed then as if Jesus Christ the son of God had really suffered, died, and risen from the dead. The period of time that has elapsed since His death dwindled as it were to a moment.[11]

For Reform Jewish Zionist Abba H. Silver (1893-1963), the worldly Jewish state had mythic dimensions:

> What is really moving us toward Palestine, and why is our movement irresistible? Our Sages say [in *Mekhilta Beshallah* Pesikta 24b] that two arks led the children of Israel through the wilderness on to the promised Land: the ark wherein lay the dead body of Joseph, and the ark of the covenant. Two arks! The ark of death and the ark of faith.[12]

Sublimation can also be seen in the anti-Zionism of Hungarian-born Orthodox Rabbi Joel Teitelbaum (1888-1974), who stated in April 1948 that according to *Sanhedrin* 98a of the Babylonian Talmud,

> the son of David will not come until after even the slightest traces of sovereignty are removed. Anyone who participates in promoting sovereignty contributes to hindering the coming of the messiah. There is nothing worse. Stupid people call sovereignty redemption. No! It hinders redemption . . . Let us wait each day for the complete redemption. [It will occur] through the coming of the son of David as a manifestation of the creator's will. He is omnipotent. He can do everything in a single moment.[13]

Another view attributed a this-worldly quality to Jerusalem and the Land. In 1893 the Orthodox Hebrew writer Ralph B. Raphael set out plans for a vanguard of pioneers to restore the Land and a governmental structure under the Turks (who then ruled the Middle East) and Jews. Raphael urged mass immigration, with the goal of two million people by the early 1940s. Together with agricultural development this would assure de facto justification of Jewish sovereignty. After all these concrete steps were taken *teshuva* (repentant return to God) and redemption would begin.[14] Liberal Protestant Reinhold Niebuhr (1892-1971) wanted to establish a Jewish state in the Land immediately and unconditionally, in the name of freedom, social justice, and the right to national identity.[15]

Redeemed Land vis-à-vis the World

American religious thinkers deliberated about the ramifications of restoring and redeeming Zion in the Land of Israel in terms of effects on America and the rest of the world. The American factor in the process was regarded both negatively and positively. Some who hoped that America would be Zion were disappointed. They turned to the Land of Israel, where Zion originated and Holy Land ideals were first enunciated. Thus Congregationalist Clorinda S. Minor, of Puritan descent, wrote that her literal reading of Scripture concerning present duty and future promise was threatened by "a great discrepancy between the religion and the form of godliness in this age."[16] She thought Christ would precipitate the millennium in October 1844. When it failed to take place she concluded that a "day of preparation" had to precede Christ's coming. To her this meant restoring the Land of Israel, and by fall 1851 she was working the land at Artas, south of Bethlehem. Consul Cresson was offended by American materialism, self-indulgence, and slavery.[17] Herman Melville visited Palestine in 1857 "in an effort to recapture the true spirit of Christianity" that had disappeared from America.[18] Among Jews, Kallen looked to the "Hebraic" homeland to realize the ideals of a Jeffersonian, liberal, just, socialist democracy, unrealized in America.

America also served as a positive impetus for establishing Zion in the Land of Israel. For the eighteenth-century Sephardic congregants of Shearit Israel, the victory of American revolutionaries implied that the Jerusalem-centered redemption was imminent.[19] Following the Balfour Declaration in 1917, Orthodox Rabbi Haim Hirschensohn (1857-1935) wrote that democratic American institutions were indispensable models for developing a covenant-centered *halakha* (legal system) in the Holy Land.[20]

What effect would the restored Holy Land in the Land of Israel have on the world in general and the Jewish people in particular? Some envisioned only positive influences. Henry Pereira Mendes (1852-1937) of the historical (proto-Conservative) school of Judaism wrote in 1899 that it was more than necessary to establish a Jewish state for spiritual purposes: it was essential for the existence of society, for human liberty, and for humanity's progress. A Jewish state would be a spiritual center, radiating spirituality to the end of the world.[21] The liberal Protestant Adolf A. Berle, Sr. (1866-1961) spoke in a similar vein in 1918; establishing a Jewish "Social Commonwealth"

> will be a wonderful thing for Israel, but it will be not less wonderful for the rest of the world. Under the influence of the religionizing of the Jew himself there will also come an idealizing of his purposes, which will be one of the most serviceable agencies for world happiness and culture imaginable.[22]

Jewish Zionists, of course, foresaw a rebirth of the Jewish people the world over. But other Jewish thinkers predicted negative repercussions. In 1898 Leo Franklin (1870-1958), a Reform Jew, considered the conceived Jewish state as an historical regression into a "national hermitage." Pure, unmixed race was something for savages to boast about; in the "veins of civilized man" there "mingled the blood of such a multitude of races that purity is a reproach rather than a cause of self-laudation."[23] In 1900 another Reform Jew, Hyman G. Enelow (1877-1934), spoke of the Zionist rationale for a state as a theological regression. Outside its secular connotation, he said, Zionism was "a dogma of effete Jewish theology." It was rooted in the ancient religious limitation of the gods to specific physical environments.[24] From the Christian side, Protestant liberal Harry Emerson Fosdick (1878-1969) criticized Jewish nationalism per se in 1927:

It is rather discouraging that today, when nationalism has been shown to be a Caesar, a false God which we have been worshipping and magnifying past all reason, that this Jewish experiment should be started with nationalism as its fundamental basis.[25]

Redeemed Land and the Jews of the Land

Another common concern was the effect of a realized Zion in the Land of Israel on its residents and culture. Some spoke positively. In 1899 Orthodox Rabbi Simon I. Finkelstein (1861-1947) described the salutary and enlightening influence of the physical Land:

In every place where Rabbi Yohanan dwells in the Land he feels in his soul that God is present [*Rosh Hashana* 31a] . . . Rab Hiyya Bar Gamada kissed the sand of our Land [*Ketubot* 112b]. Only the Land has the source of Tora and an atmosphere of anticipating [its realization].[26]

In 1898 Consul Edwin S. Wallace (1864-1960), a Presbyterian, described how the restored Land could restore true Judaism. Christianity had the "real life" of spirit, a stage to which Judaism had yet to advance. Ultimately the "wall of partition" (*Ephesians* 2:14) would break down, an unprecedented union of religion nearer the divine ideal would take place, and Jews would be "Israelites indeed" (*John* 1:47-49), that is, spiritualized into Christians.[27]

Others spoke negatively. Consul Albert Rhodes (b. 1840) thought the Jews in the Land were pathetic and could become really human only after they abandoned Judaism:

When a Jew is converted, a transformation takes place in his appearance. The filthy gown, slatternly shoes, and furred caps are thrown aside, and the dangling frontlocks are shorn. From a thorough scouring, his complexion assumes a different hue. He is seen in clean linen and a good plain suit of European clothes. He has a more civilized air, and partly loses his excessive Jewish humility, which made him cringe and bow before every passer-by. He walks erect, and in short, recovers his lost manhood.[28]

Barukh M. Klein attacked secular Zionist Jews in the Land for separating Jewish nationality from Tora, for defying *mitsvot* (biblical commands) and eating prohibited foods even in Jerusalem.[29] Orthodox Rabbi Haim Hirschensohn wrote of negative aspects to the association between contemporary Jews and the Land:

It is not the Land, God forbid, that has lost its holiness. That lasts forever. There is another danger. Zionism attracts many materialists. If the sickness of [careerism] spread to the Land of Israel, we will all be lost. We will be, God forbid, like all the nations . . . It is our Land, the inheritance of our fathers. We must not end up murmuring in Israel itself, "Where, O where is the Holy Land? My spirit longs for it."[30]

Some thought that all life in the Land was bad. In 1857 Melville said that Jerusalem "looks at you like a cold gray eye in a cold gray man." The Holy Sepulcher was a sickening cheat, surrounded by the "least nameable filth of a barbarous city."[31] Presbyterian pilgrim Thomas de Witt Talmage, who journeyed to the Land in 1880, felt that "Christ-land" was withering under the accursed Turkish nation and prayed, "May God remove the curse of nations, that old hag of the centuries, the Turkish government! For its everlasting insult to God and woman, let it perish."[32]

Jews and the Apocalypse

Others spoke of the Land in terms of a cosmic drama of redemption, with negative or positive ramifications for the Jews. In 1858 James T. Barclay (b. 1806) of the American Christian Missionary Society (ACMS) envisioned an apocalypse in which the Antichrist would be destroyed, the Jews in the Land of Israel converted, and the salvation of the whole world ensue.[33] In 1888 Seventh-day Adventist leader Ellen G. White (1827-1915) described Jesus' return to earth at the millennium to battle Satan's forces:

In the fate of the chosen city we may behold the doom of a world that has rejected God's mercy and trampled upon His law. Dark are the records of human misery that earth has witnessed during its long centuries of crime. But a scene yet darker is presented in the revelation of the future . . . when the restraining spirit of God shall be wholly withdrawn from the wicked, no longer to hold in check the outburst of human passion and Satanic wrath! But in that day, as in the time of Jerusalem's destruction, God's people will be delivered . . . Then shall they that obey not the gospel be consumed with the spirit of His mouth and be destroyed with the brightness of His coming.[34]

In March 1945 a representative of the Lubavitch Hasidim described a nightmare in which all the filth of the world, including the murderers of the Jews and those who stood by while they were murdered, would be washed into the sea by a divine mop. Meanwhile, deserving Jews would be swept away to the Land of Israel:

Those who feel that they are being washed away from the earth as filth will drag along as many Jews as possible. But the cleaning-mop will slap them across the face, and they will not be able to carry out their planned evil, with God's help. One of the tasks of the cleaning-mop is to sweep the Jewish people away from exile and back toward the Land of Israel. This means that those who oppose Jewish liberation will become a part of the filth on the earth which will be swept away into the sea.[35]

Observations

In essence, the data through 1948 show that American religions shared remarkably similar concerns with sacred territory, scripturally defined. Together, they participated in the dialectical pattern from the initial Puritan stage until 1948. They were drawn toward specific religious themes: (1) Man's passive or active role under the aegis of God. (2) Jerusalem as this-worldly or otherworldly. (3) America's negative or positive role for the Land, and the restored Holy Land's negative or positive implications for the world and world Jewry. (4) The redeemed Land's negative and positive meaning for the residents and local culture. (5) The Jew's radically negative or positive status in the apocalypse.

These common themes point to and reflect a common source, the sacred territory of Scripture. The religions of America projected their absolute hopes into it, and from it they all drew spiritual sustenance. The territory functioned in an a priori way, as part of the collective consciousness of American religions, and in an a posteriori way, as generated by cultural experiences. The commonality also engendered conflict. Judaism, Christianity and their respective subdivisions were now situated within the same boundary. This forced them to sharpen their self-definitions and differences—even their mutual exclusivities. Only when the religious approach was emphatically universal and transcendental—notably the liberal Protestants and secular Zionists—did the conflict tend to disappear. The America-Holy Land relationship has been intensely symbiotic. The religions have been drawn as much into common values as into attacks upon one another.

Notes

1. William Bradford, *History of Plymouth Plantation, 1620-1647* (Boston 1912):15-16.

2. Gershon Greenberg, "David Einhorn's Conception of History," *American Jewish Historical Quarterly* 63 no. 2 (December 1973):160-184; Isaac M. Wise, *The End of Popes, Nobles, and Kings; or, The progress of civilization* (New York 1852):20; Max Lilienthal, "The Platform of Judaism," in David Philipson, *Max Lilienthal, American Rabbi* (New York 1915):457; Isaac W. Bernheim, *The Reform Church of American Israelites* (Buffalo, N.Y., 1921):6.

3.   Clorinda S. Minor and Charles Minor, *Meshullam! or, Tidings from Jerusalem from the journal of a believer recently returned from the Holy Land* (1851; reprint, New York 1977):vi-xi.

4.   Warder Cresson, *Jerusalem the Center and Joy of the Whole Earth* (Philadelphia 1844):7-8.

5.   Joseph M. Levin, "Sermon on Zion," in *The Lesson of Joseph* (New York 1906, Hebrew):76.

6.   Louis D. Brandeis, "The Jewish Problem—How to Solve It," *Jewish Frontier* 8 no. 10 (October 1941):23.

7.   Horace M. Kallen, "Constitutional Foundations of the New Zion," *Maccabean* (April 1918):97-100 and (May 1918):127-129.   See Sarah Schmidt, "Messianic Pragmatism: The Zionism of Horace M. Kallen," *Judaism* 25 no. 2 (April 1976):217-229; idem, "Toward the Pittsburgh Program: Horace M. Kallen, Philosopher of an American Zionism," *Herzl Yearbook* 8: *Essays in American Zionism, 1917-1948* (New York 1978):18-36.

8.   *AME Church Review* 34 no. 3 (January 1918):179-180, cited in Albert Raboteau, "Black Americans," in Moshe Davis, ed., *With Eyes toward Zion* (New York 1986):2:319.   See also Timothy I. Smith, "Slavery and Theology: The Emergence of Black Christian Consciousness in Nineteenth-Century America," *Church History* 41 no. 4 (December 1972):497-514.

9.   Truman G. Madsen, *The Mormon Attitude toward Zionism*, Haifa University Lecture Series on Zionism no. 5 (Haifa 1989).

10.   Yehoshua Prawer, "Jerusalem, Capital of the Crusader Kingdom," *Judah and Jerusalem, the Twelfth Archaelogical Convention* (Jerusalem 1957, Hebrew):92-93.

11.   Alvan Bond, *Memoir of the Rev. Pliny Fisk, A.M., Late Missionary to Palestine* (Boston 1828):286.

12.   Abba H. Silver, "The Conspiracy of Silence," in *Vision and Victory* (New York 1949):7.

13.   Joel Teitelbaum, "Concerning a Government for Israel—Before the Coming of the Messiah," in *The Words of Joel: Letters* (Brooklyn 1980-81, Hebrew):1:89.

14.   Ralph B. Raphael, *The Question of the Jews* (New York 1893, Hebrew).

15.   Reinhold Niebuhr, "Jews after the War," *Nation* (21 and 28 February 1942):214-216, 253-255; Franklin H. Littell, "Reinhold Niebuhr and the Jewish People," International Niebuhr Symposium, King's College, London, 20 September 1984.

16.   Minor and Minor, *Meshullam,* 3.

17. Warder Cresson, *A Humble and Affectionate Address to the Select Members of the Abington Quarterly Meeting* (Philadelphia 1827); idem, *Babylon the Great Is Falling! The morning star or light from on high. Written in defense of the rights of the poor and oppressed* (Philadelphia 1830); Frank Fox, "Quaker, Shaker, Rabbi: Warder Cresson, the Story of a Philadelphia Mystic," *Pennsylvania Magazine of History and Biography* 95 (April 1971):147-194.

18. William Braswell, *Melville's Religious Thought* (Durham, N.C., 1943):108-109.

19. [Jacob Cohen], "Prayer in Hebrew, Composed by Rabbi Hendla Yohanan van Oettingen," *Publications of the American Jewish Historical Society* (PAJHS) 27, *Lyons Collection* (1920):2:34-37.

20. Haim Hirschensohn, *My King into the Sanctuary* [*Psalms* 64:25], 6 vols. (St. Louis 1919, 1921, 1923, Hebrew). See Eliezer Schweid, "Democratic State Based on Halakha," *Democracy and Halakha* (Jerusalem 1978, Hebrew):59-89.

21. H. Pereira Mendes, "Should a Jewish State Be Established?" *American Hebrew* 64 (13 January 1899):392.

22. Adolph A. Berle, *The World Significance of a Jewish State* (New York 1918):45-46.

23. Leo Franklin, "A Danger and a Duty Suggested by the Zionist Agitation," *Hebrew Union College (HUC) Journal* 2 nos. 5 and 6 (March 1898):143-147.

24. Hyman Enelow, "Zionism as a Theologic Dogma," *HUC Journal* 5 nos. 5 and 6 (1900):111.

25. "Fosdick Sees Ruin Ahead for Zionism," *New York Times* (25 May 1927):8.

26. Simon I. Finkelstein, *Harvest of Grapes* (Chicago 1899, Hebrew):24.

27. Edwin S. Wallace, *Jerusalem the Holy: A brief history of ancient Jerusalem with an account of the modern city and its conditions political, religious, and social* (1898; reprint, New York 1977):359.

28. Albert Rhodes, *Jerusalem as It Is* (London 1865):458.

29. Barukh M. Klein, *Pray for the Peace of Jerusalem* [*Psalms* 122:6]: *Do Not Ruin Israel. A Serious Word amidst the Joyous Outbursts. An Explanation of the Ingathering of Exile and Onset of Redemption. Also, Why an Orthodox Jew Can Be Neither Zionist nor Mizrahi* (New York 1918, Yiddish):28.

30. Haim Hirschensohn, "Where, Where Are You, Land of Holiness? My Spirit Longs for You," *Yearbook of the Federation of Palestine Jews of America, Second Annual Convention*, 13-14 June 1931 (New York [1931?], Hebrew):20-23.

31. Herman Melville, *Journal of a Visit to Europe and the Levant, 11 October 1856-6 May 1857*, Howard C. Horsford, ed. (Princeton 1955):155-160.

32. Thomas de Witt Talmage, *Talmage on Palestine: A series of sermons* (Springfield, Ohio, 1890):10-11.

33. James T. Barclay, *The City of the Great King; or, Jerusalem as it was, as it is, and* as it is to be (1858; reprint, New York 1977):581.

34. Ellen G. White, "Destruction of Jerusalem," in *The Great Controversy between Christ and Satan* (Oakland, Calif. 1888):36-37. See also idem, "Salvation of the Jews," in *The Acts of the Apostles* (Mountain View, Calif., 1911):372-382.

35. "A Thousand Nightmares—One Explanation," *Ha'keriyya Veha'kedusha* 5 no. 54 (March 1945, Yiddish):4.

Part One

The Holy Land Comes to America

1 Puritans and Congregationalists: The Americanization of Zion

As a spiritual territory, the Zion of ancient Israel was brought to America by Puritan and Congregationalist Christians when they began to arrive in 1620.[1] The New World proved remarkably hospitable to the transplant.

The New Land of Scripture

Bradford and Winthrop

William Bradford, governor of the Plymouth Colony from 1621 through 1651, believed that his people were nearing the new Jerusalem. During the hardships of the Cape Cod winter he identified them with the Israelites who had endured the tribulations of the wilderness.* The present offered little consolation, but Bradford was sure that they would ultimately ascend Mount Pisgah with Moses to view the good country† and enter the new Jerusalem, where neither sun nor moon were needed for light, "for the glory of God did lighten it, and the lamb is the light thereof" (*Revelation* 21:23).[2]

How could the Puritans of the Cape Cod wilderness accelerate the transition from the harsh present to the glorious future? Bradford spoke of establishing the holy priesthood of the future kingdom then and there. That could be done by realizing that they, the Puritans, were actors in God's history just as the ancient Israelites were. Like them, they should "declare in Zion the work of the Lord

---

*See, for example, *Deuteronomy* 32:10: "He found him in a desert land, and in the waste howling wilderness; He led him about, He instructed Him, He kept him as the apple of his eye."

†"And Moses went up from the plains of Moab unto the mountain of Nebo to the top of Pisgah, that is over against Jericho. And the Lord showed him all the land of Gilead, unto Dan." *Deuteronomy* 34:1.

our God" (*Jeremiah* 51:10). They should realize that their own Jebusites had been overcome—the "tyrannical bishops, courts," and such of England.* Of course, now it was Christ rather than the God of the ancient Israelites who ordered history. Who, Bradford asked, liberated the people? The God of the apocalypse, riding a white horse, with garments dipped in blood and ruling with a rod of iron.† Bradford sought leaders for his holy priesthood, especially a Nehemiah to rebuild the city walls.‡ He sought the elimination of guilt and of sinfulness, of intoxication, fornication, and commercial selfishness. The transformation of desolation into the new Jerusalem involved dying and rising with Christ. In 1626 Bradford marveled at how his people overcame despair, how they rose again from their nadir. Human means exhausted, Christ on the cross sustained them as they went from death to life.[3]

In his later years Bradford despaired over the realization of the kingdom. He felt that the sacred bond, the "sweet communion" with Christ, had been lost. When his church applied in 1617 for permission to settle in the New World, the members had been knit together in a "strict and sacred bond and covenant of the Lord." Each was committed to it, in the interest of the whole body. Now, in his old age, he mourned the decay of fidelity: "I have been happy in my first times to see and with much comfort to enjoy the blessed fruits of this sweet communion, but it is now a part of my misery in old age to find and feel the decay and want thereof (in a great measure), and with grief and sorrow of heart to lament and bewail the same."[4] In 1650 Bradford responded to the loss by studying Hebrew, believing that it would bring him closer to the creation, revelation, and redemption of Scripture:

> Though I am grown aged, yet I have had a longing desire to see with my own eyes something of that most ancient language and holy tongue in which the law and oracles of God were written, and in which God and angels spoke to the holy patriarchs of old time; and names were given to things from the creation. And though I cannot attain to much herein, yet I am refreshed to have seen some glimpse thereof (as Moses saw the Land of Canaan afar off). My aim and desire is to see how the words and phrases lie in the holy text; and to discern somewhat of the same for my own content.[5]

---

*"And the king and his men went unto the Jebusites, the inhabitants of the land." *II Samuel* 5:6.

†"And I saw heaven opened, and behold a white horse; and He that sat upon him was called faithful and true, and in righteousness He doth judge and make war . . . And He was clothed with a vesture dipped in blood: and His name is called the word of God . . . And He shall rule them with a rod of iron." *Revelation* 19:11, 13, 15.

‡See, for example, *Nehemiah* 2:17: "Then I said unto them, Ye see the distress that we are in, how Jerusalem lieth waste, and the gates thereof are burned with fire. Come, and let us build up the wall of Jerusalem, that we be no more a reproach."

Bradford's biographers also saw him as a scriptural figure, one who had passed into Zion through Christ. Cotton Mather (1663-1728) wrote in 1702, "The leader of a people in a wilderness had need [of] a Moses. And if a Moses had not led the people of Plymouth Colony when this worthy person was their governor, the people with so much unanimity and importunity still called him to lead them."[6]   Two centuries later, George C. Blaxland wrote that Bradford solaced himself during his last days by contemplating the divine hopes and promises Moses received atop Pisgah, and he loved the Hebrew letters in which they were expressed in Scripture. At the beginning of this century, Bradford's writings were called a New England Old Testament, a *Genesis, Exodus,* and *Joshua* of the Plymouth Plantation.[7] A more recent biographer wrote in 1966 that for Bradford, the Lord's hand was on all things and in all history, often tangibly. For him the distant scriptural past prefigured the pilgrims' historic mission.[8]

In August 1629, shortly before he left England to become governor of the Massachusetts Bay Colony (on and off between 1630 and 1649), John Winthrop (1587-1649) addressed the scriptural dimensions of the experience. He believed that failure by England to reform had evoked divine displeasure and that "evil times" would follow. God provided New England as a refuge from the coming calamity, and it was up to Winthrop and his followers to establish "tabernacles" there. By going to the new land Winthrop was de facto chosen by God to find the way to overcome the prevailing sinfulness, a new Israelite:[*]

It may be God will, by this means, bring us to repent of our former intemperance, and so cure us of that disease which sends many among us untimely to our graves and others to hell. So He carried the Israelites into the wilderness and made them forget the fleshpots of Egypt, which was some [irritation] at first. But He disposed it to their good in the end.[†9]

Aboard the *Arabella* in early spring 1630, Winthrop delivered a sermon about a special "commission" awarded by God to the Puritans who journeyed with him. All divine commissions contained details which had to be implemented, e.g.,

---

[*]See, for example, *Hebrews* 11:9: "By faith he sojourned in the Land of promise, as in a strange country, dwelling in tabernacles with Isaac and Jacob, the heirs with him of the same promise."

[†]"And He humbled thee, and suffered thee to hunger, and fed thee with manna, which thou knewest not, neither did thy fathers know; that He might make thee know that man doth not live by bread only, but by every word that proceedeth out of the mouth of the Lord doth man live." *Deuteronomy* 8:3.

Saul's commission to smite Amalek lest the recipients be punished.* If the Puritans endeavored "to do justly, to love mercy and to walk humbly before God" (*Micah* 6:8), then God "will delight to dwell among us as His own people and will command a blessing upon us in all our ways, so that we shall see much more of His wisdom, power, goodness and truth than formerly." They would become a "city upon a hill" (*Matthew* 5:14) for all to view. But if they failed to carry out their commission, their prayers would be turned into curses and they would be "consumed out of" that good land toward which they were headed. Like the ancient Israelites, the Puritans had both a privileged task and a radical choice. If they loved God, followed His laws, fully participated in the covenant with Him, and loved one another, He would bless the new land. But if they turned from God they would perish there. Like ancient Israelites, the *Arabella* pilgrims were enjoined to "choose life."†[10]

Cotton Mather reaffirmed Winthrop's scriptural perception of himself. He said that Winthrop was selected as "the Moses" when the colony of chosen people set out for the American wilderness. Only a "Mosaic spirit" could have endured the temptation to remain in his homeland instead of traveling to a strange land. Winthrop was the "New-English Nehemiah" who could manage "American Jerusalem's" public affairs—even with the Tobiahs" and "Sanballats" there to vex him (*Nehemiah* 6).[11]

The Second Generation

Subsequent writers amplified the scriptural references. In 1658 John Norton (1606-1663), pastor of the Church of Christ in Boston, said that the flight of Congregationalist John Cotton (1585-1652) from England was a manifestation of God's "shutting up the door of service in England and on the other hand opening it in New England." Cotton was guided by God's word and eye. As David once yielded to the persuasion of his men to remove himself from danger, so Cotton was persuaded by his friends to retreat from his persecutors in order to preserve—as Jacob, Moses, and Christ Himself had done—a precious light in Israel.[12]

In 1679 Increase Mather (1639-1723) wrote that God's ways with the Puritans resembled those with ancient Israel. The first Puritans had ventured across the turbulent ocean in order to follow the Lord into America, just as

---

*"Now go and smite Amalek, and utterly destroy all that they have, and spare them not." *I Samuel* 15:3. "For the Lord hath rent the kingdom out of thine hand, and given it to thy neighbour, even to David: Because thou obeyedst not the voice of the Lord, nor executedst His fierce wrath upon Amalek, therefore hath the Lord done this thing unto thee this day." *I Samuel* 28:17-18.

†"I have set before you life and death, blessing and cursing: therefore choose life, that both thou and thy seed may live." *Deuteronomy* 30:19.

Abraham left Ur and his seed left Egypt. The same God Who appeared to ancient Israel was "upon the head" of the Puritans in America and "planted a vine—having cast out the heathen, prepared room for it, and caused it to take deep rooting and to fill the land." Mather dwelt on the sins of early Puritans, and he warned New England Christians to follow God lest they suffer dreadful consequences:

> It is a solemn thought, that the Jewish church had (as the churches in New England have this day) an opportunity to reform (if they would) in Josiah's time. But because they had not heart unto it, the Lord quickly removed them out of His sight. What God out of His sovereignty may do for us, no man can say. But according to His wonted dispensations, we are a perishing people if we reform not.

Mather called for the new people of Israel to be strong, secure in the fact that God was with them just as He was with those who left Egypt.*[13]

In 1673 Urian Oakes (1631-1681), who would serve as president of Harvard (1679-1681), also compared God's care for the Puritans and "New-English" Israel with His care for ancient Israel. The earlier Puritans who came to America demonstrated great love for communion with God, and so the Lord showed them the "pattern of His house and the true scriptural way" for church governance. First, the Congregational church in America inherited the divine bounty of those who followed Him into the American wilderness; it shared in the blessing once given to Joseph.† Second, God had assigned Canaan to the children of Israel for their habitation; now He brought the Puritans over the ocean from their native land, to a place of rest for enjoying special mercies. He had decreed that the American wilderness be a Canaan for the Puritans, and what "He thought in His heart He has fulfilled with His hand." Third, as God had given Israel Moses, so He provided pious and prudent magistrates to the Puritans with "men of Nehemiah's spirit" who did not seek things for themselves but were intent upon the welfare of the people.‡ God in His goodness, no matter the offenses against Him, saw that the magistrates stood against sin and immorality, Sabbath-breaking

---

*"Be strong, all ye people of the land, saith the Lord, and work: for I am with you, . . . according to the word that I covenanted with you when ye came out of Egypt, so My spirit remaineth among you: fear ye not." *Haggai* 2:4-5.

†See, for example, *Genesis* 39:2: "And the Lord was with Joseph, and he was a prosperous man."

‡"Now that which was prepared for me daily was one ox and six choice sheep; also fowls were prepared for me, and once in ten days store of all sorts of wine: yet for all this required not I the bread of the governor, because the bondage was heavy upon this people." *Nehemiah* 5:18.

and the like. The character of leadership expressed God's love for "our Israel."[*] Church councils ministered according to the mind of God. God instructed the Puritans as He had instructed Israel in the wilderness.[†] Fourth, as with ancient Israel, God had found the Puritans in the desert: "God's people followed Him into this wilderness for Himself, and for His kingdom and righteousness." He kept them as the apple of His eye and brought evil upon those who sought to devour them as He once did with the adversaries of Israel.[‡]

Oakes believed the Puritans had a special relationship with God. They relied on God's mercy; God was there for them, and His power gave them the land.[#] It was ultimately God Who had touched their hearts, so they willingly chose to leave the pleasant land of their fathers' sepulchers,

> and to cast, not their bread, but themselves and their families upon the great waters, to venture all upon the mere mercy of God (who called them to His foot, as He did the righteous man who He raised from the east).[**] And to follow Him into a wilderness, a land that was not sown [see *II Esdras*], a place of great hardships and difficulties.

God alleviated their wilderness condition, He led them as with a pillar of cloud and fire (*Exodus* 13 and 14), He protected them from the many threatening dangers and directed them.[††] It was God Who chased out the growing spirit of error and heresy threatening to subvert both civil and sacred institutions, Who vanquished the Pequot Indians, "and put the dread and terror of you into the

---

[*]"Blessed be the Lord thy God, which delighted in thee to set thee on His throne, to be king for the Lord thy God: because thy God loved Israel, to establish them forever, therefore made He thee king over them, to do judgment and justice." *II Chronicles* 9:8.

[†]"If there be among you any man, that is not clean by reason of uncleanness, that chanceth him by night, then shall he go abroad out of the camp, he shall not come within the camp." *Deuteronomy* 23:10.

[‡]See *Deuteronomy 32:10*, supra. "Israel was holiness unto the Lord, and the first fruits of his increase: all that devour him shall offend; evil shall come upon them, saith the Lord." *Jeremiah* 2:3.

[#]"In the day that I lifted up mine hand unto them, to bring them forth of the land of Egypt into a land that I had espied for them, flowing with milk and honey, which is the glory of all lands." *Ezekiel* 20:6.

[**]"Who raised up the righteous man from the east, called him to His foot, gave the nations before Him and made him rule over kings?" *Isaiah* 41:2.

[††]"For the Lord God is a sun and a shield: the Lord will give grace and glory." *Psalms* 84:11.

hearts of the natives" so the Puritans could dwell in safety.* God acted ferociously on their behalf: "Has not the same hand of the most high broken the head of many a leviathan in pieces, and given him to be meat to (the faith of) His people inhabiting this wilderness?"† The new Israel was unique:

Happy art thou, O New-England-Israel! Who is like unto thee, O people saved by the Lord, the shield of thy help, and who is the source of thy excellence! And thine enemies have been found liars unto thee, as Moses speaks upon consideration of the condition of that Israel.‡ So that as [David] says, Bless ye God . . . from the fountain of Israel# . . . So, let the successors and seed of [Jacob and Israel] that laid our foundations bless the Lord . . . We may say with wonderment (almost) as in the words of Moses. Ask now of many of the ages that are past, and ask from one side of heaven unto the other, whether there has been any such thing as this great thing is, or has been heard like it, for many generations?** Has God essayed to go and take Him a part of a nation from the midst of a nation, by temptations, by signs, by wonders, by a mighty hand and by outstretched arm, according to all that the Lord your God has done for you before your eyes? God has shown us almost unexampled, unparalleled mercy.[14]

For Oakes, Puritan America was the onset of God's kingdom. He believed that "our commonwealth seems to exhibit to us a specimen, or a little model of the kingdom of Christ upon earth." Subsequently, "this work of God, set on foot and advanced to a good degree here" in America, will "spread over the face of the earth, and perfected as to greater degrees of light and grace and gospel glory, will be (as I conceive) the kingdom of Jesus Christ so much spoken of":††

---

*"And I will make with them a covenant of peace, and will cause the evil beasts to cease out of the land: and they shall dwell safely in the wilderness, and sleep in the woods." *Ezekiel* 34:25.

†"Thou brakest the heads of leviathan in pieces, and gavest him to be meat to the people inhabiting the wilderness." *Psalms* 74:14.

‡"Happy art thou, O Israel: who is like unto thee, O people saved by the Lord, the shield of thy help, and who is the sword of thy excellency! and thine enemies shall be found liars unto thee; and thou shalt tread upon their high places." *Deuteronomy* 33:29.

#"Bless ye God in the congregations, even the Lord, from the fountain of Israel." *Psalms* 68:26.

**"For ask now of the days that are past, which were before thee, since the day that God created man upon the earth, and ask from the one side of heaven unto the other, whether there hath been any such thing as this great thing is, or has been heard like it?" *Deuteronomy* 4:32.

††"The kingdoms of this world are become the kingdoms of our Lord, and of His Christ: and He shall reign forever and ever." *Revelation* 11:15.

You have been as a city upon a hill (though in a remote and obscure wilderness), as a candle in the candlestick that gives light to the whole house. You have to a considerable degree, enlightened the whole house (world, I mean) as to the pattern of God's house, the form and fashion and ongoing and incoming thereof . . . God has been doing (in my apprehension) the same thing for the substance of it here, that shall be done more universally and gloriously when Israel shall blossom and bud and fill the face of the world with fruit."*

As Jacob's remnant was to be in the midst of many people and fructify the world, so the Puritans, separated from the rest of Christianity, would be the center from which the universal kingdom would arise.† But Oakes also warned about the consequences of sin:

And truly methinks I hear the Lord speaking these very words of New England at this day: "O that they were wise, that they understood this, that they would consider their latter end." As Christ sometimes stood weeping over Jerusalem and said, "O that thou had known that even thou, at least in this thy day, the things which belong unto thy peace."‡ So methinks the Lord Jesus is this day standing above, beholding us from the height of His glory, and saying, "O that my dear people in New England (whom I have peculiarly loved and pitied and protected and blessed) were wise, and would consider understandingly and rationally what the end of their sinful deportments before Me will be at last." I hope He does not add: "But now this wisdom is hid from their eyes."[15]

In 1697 John Higginson (1616-1708), pastor in Salem, Massachusetts, wrote that Jesus Christ stirred up the spirits of thousands of His servants to leave their pleasant native England and cross the ocean into the "desert land" in America. They were motivated by "pure religion," not knowing the source for their daily bread but trusting in God, searching for the kingdom of God. God granted His presence to them and blessed their undertakings, so that within a few years the

---

*"He shall cause them that come of Jacob to take root: Israel shall blossom and bud, and fill the face of the world with fruit." *Isaiah* 27:6.

†"And the remnant of Jacob shall be in the midst of many people as a dew from the Lord, as the showers upon the grass, that tarrieth not for man, nor waiteth for the sons of men." *Micah* 5:7.

‡"And when He was come near, He beheld the city, and wept over it, saying, If thou hadst known, even thou, at least in this thy day, the things which belong unto thy peace! but now they are hid from thine eyes." *Luke* 19:41-42.

wilderness would be tamed.*[16] In 1702 Cotton Mather (1663-1728) wrote that Jesus Christ had carried thousands of reformers into the "American desert" in order for His faithful servants to have the opportunity to enjoy the liberty of their ministry. In America Christ would provide them with "many good things" to which His churches elsewhere would aspire.[17] Mather wrote that the journey from oppression to freedom, through Christ, was prefigured in the ancient exodus: "When the God of heaven had carried a nation into a wilderness, upon the designs of a glorious reformation, He there gave them a singular conduct of His presence and spirit in a certain pillar, which by day appeared as a cloud and by night as a fire before them."† Now, "more than a score of years after the beginning of the age which is now expiring, our Lord Jesus Christ, with a thousand wonders of His providence, carried into an American wilderness a people persecuted for their desire to see and seek a reformation of the church, according to the Scripture.[18]

In sum, the early Puritans and Congregationalists raised their contemporary reality into the mythic eternity of Scripture. They viewed themselves as the new Israelites, this time under Christ. They risked their lives as they trusted in God, and under God they entered the Promised Land to implant scriptural reality. On an existential level, they became a collective Christ, separable from yet the same as Him, passing through dark suffering into a new life. "The root and rise of the Plymouth settlement lies in the crises related in Scriptures and the writings of the church fathers. Cain and Abel, children of Israel's wanderings, Jeremiah, incarnation of Christ, sufferings and triumph of the early church—all prefigured the Puritan errand in the wilderness."[19]

God's Holy Commonwealth

The new Israelites under Christ endeavored to bring even the polity of the ancient Israelite Holy Land into the present. Richard Mather (1596-1669), pastor of Dorchester Congregational Church, spoke of the American polity in terms of the covenantal theocracy of ancient Israel:

When Jehoiada [contemporary clergy] made a covenant between the king [contemporary magistrates] and the people [contemporary Americans], that covenant was but a branch of the Lord's covenant with them all, both king

---

*"This is the Lord's doing; it is marvellous in our eyes." *Psalms* 118:23. "So didst Thou lead Thy people, to make Thyself a glorious name." *Isaiah* 63:14.

†See, for example, *Exodus* 14:20: "And was a cloud and darkness to them, but it gave light by night to these: so that the one came not near the other all the night."

and people.[*] For the king promised to rule the people righteously, according to the will of God, and the people to be subject to the king so ruling. Now these duties of the king to them, and of them to the king, were such as God required in His covenant of Him and them . . . Whatsoever ordinance of the Old Testament is repealed in the New Testament, as peculiar to the Jewish pedagogy, but was of moral and perpetual equity, the same binds us in these days, and is to be accounted us the revealed will of God in all ages.[20]

John Norton wrote that when the American commonwealth was ready "in respect of civil and church-estate to walk with God according to the precept of His work," John Cotton was sent by God to help lead the way, to be the "eyes in the wilderness." Cotton had drawn up an abstract of the judicial laws concerning moral equity which God had delivered through Moses, advising the people "to persist in their purpose of establishing a theocracy (i.e., God's government) over God's people."[21] Cotton's posthumously published *Abstract of Laws and Government* contained "the very marrow and sum of all or most of those laws which Jesus Christ, the eternal wisdom of the Father, thought necessary for the administration of His kingdom in righteousness and peace." It would demonstrate "the complete sufficiency of the word of God alone, to direct His people in judgment of all causes, both civil and criminal."[22]

In the desired holy commonwealth of Christ, the civil and church powers coincided under God. In 1636 Cotton cited the view of William Perkins (1558-1602) that God's word contained a platform not only for theology but for other sacred sciences such as economics and politics.[23] For Cotton, God's omniscience prescribed the right way for the commonwealth insofar as it was subordinated to spiritual ends. Church and civil government had independent spheres of interest, but both existed ultimately under God. He cited the words of Thomas Cartwright (1535-1603), as quoted by Thomas Hooker (1586-1647), the Congregational pastor of Hartford, Connecticut: "No man fashions his house to his hangings [but] his hangings to his house." Cotton did not approve of democracy:

Democracy, I do not conceive that ever God did ordain as a fit government, either for church or commonwealth. If the people be governors, who shall be governed? As for monarchy and aristocracy, they are both of them clearly approved and directed in Scripture, yet so as refers the sovereignty to Himself, and sets up theocracy in both, as the best form of government in the commonwealth, as well as in the church.[24]

---

[*]"And Jehoiada made a covenant between the Lord and the king and the people, that they should be the Lord's people; between the king also and the people." *II Kings* 11:17.

In 1644 Cotton provided various guidelines:

1. The church was to submit to civil authority in such matters as the disposition of man's goods or land, lives or liberties, tributes, customs, worldly honors and inheritances.*
2. When religion was corrupted there would be civil conflict; when it thrived the state would flourish.†
3. Civil power was not to compel in matters of religion, and religion did not belong to the civil power. For example, civil authorities could not compel men to sit at the Lord's table, nor enter the communion of the church, unless they were prepared to do so themselves.
4. The church would not oppose the civil magistrate regarding spiritual administrations which advanced the civil state's public good according to God's word. For example, in the time of a public calamity the magistrate could lawfully proclaim a fast.‡
5. The church would accept even unjust persecution by the civil magistrate and not revolt. If the church were to take up the sword in self-defense, it would ultimately threaten its own preservation.#

In essence, for Cotton the church was subject to the magistrate in matters of civil peace, while the Christian magistrate was subject to the church in matters of conscience and the kingdom of heaven.**25

In 1645 John Winthrop tied civil to divine government. "Natural liberty," which tolerated no authority, produced in man "that wild beast which all the

---

*"Jesus answered, My kingdom is not of this world: if My kingdom were of this world, then would my servants fight, that I should not be delivered to the Jews: but now is My kingdom not from hence." *John* 18:36.

†See, for example, *Judges* 5:8: "They chose new gods; then was war in the gates: was there a shield or spear seen among forty thousand in Israel?" and *Haggai* 2:18-19: "Consider now from this day and upward, from the four and twentieth day of the ninth month, even from the day that the foundation of the Lord's temple was laid, consider it. Is the seed yet in the barn? yea, as yet the vine, and the fig tree, and the pomegranate, and the olive tree, hath not brought forth: from this day will I bless you."

‡"And Jehoshaphat feared, and set himself to seek the Lord, and proclaimed a fast throughout all Judah." *II Chronicles* 20:3.

#"And, behold, one of them which were with Jesus stretched out his hand, and drew his sword, and struck a servant of the high priest's, and smote off his ear. Then said Jesus unto him, Put up again thy sword unto his place: for all they that take the sword shall perish with the sword." *Matthew* 26:51-52.

**"And kings shall be thy nursing fathers, and their queens thy nursing mothers: they shall bow down to thee with their face toward the earth, and lick up the dust of thy feet; and thou shalt know that I am the Lord: for they shall not be ashamed that wait for me." *Isaiah* 49:23.

ordinances of God bent against to restrain." "Civil" or "federal" liberty, which involved authority, was moral, just, and honest as defined by man's covenant with God.[26] The Congregational Cambridge Platform, drafted by Richard Mather in 1648, enunciated the plan of government agreed upon by New England churches. It stipulated that church government was unopposed to civil government, that it was unlawful for church officers and magistrates to meddle in the affairs of each other. But it was "the duty of the magistrate to take care of matters of religion and to improve his civil authority for the observing of duties." The magistrate's office had as its end "not only the quiet and peaceable life of the subject in matters of righteousness and honesty, but also in matters of godliness."[27]

In 1659 John Eliot composed a program for government based upon Scripture, a "divine institution of civil government": Christ was king and sovereign lawgiver, and His people were to be ruled by Him in all things. It was the "mind of the Lord," Eliot explained, that nations should be governed by scriptural institutions. Indeed, the time had come when the Lord was about "to shake all the earth and throw down that great idol of humane-wisdom in governments, and set up scriptural government in the room thereof." The people were to receive God in the platform of their government and its laws such that Christ would reign over them in all things.* The substance of God's rule, Eliot specified, consisted in acknowledging natural corruption and free divine grace, in redemption by Christ and God's entry into the soul, and in surrendering to God in love and obedience. Eliot expected the people to receive

> from the Lord both the platform of their civil government as it is set down (in the essentials of it) in the Holy Scripture; and also all their laws, which they resolve through His grace to fetch out of the word of God, making that their only *Magna Charta*; and accounting no law, statute or judgment valid, further than it appears to arise and flow from the word of God.[28]

In 1679 Increase Mather urged the civil magistrate to cooperate with positive religious reformation. Neither Scripture nor history evidenced reformation which took place without encouragement from the civil magistrate. For example, the sermons of Haggai and Zechariah† would not have built the Temple unless the

---

*"For the Lord is our judge, the Lord is our lawgiver, the Lord is our king, He will save us." *Isaiah* 33:22.

†"And the Lord stirred up the spirit of Zerubbabel the son of Shealtiel, governor of Judah, and the spirit of Joshua the son of Josedech, the high priest, and the spirit of all the remnant of the people; and they came and did work in the house of the Lord of hosts, their God." *Haggai* 1:14. "The hands of Zerubbabel have laid the foundation of this house; his hands shall also finish it; and thou shalt know that the Lord of hosts hath sent me unto you." *Zechariah* 4:9.

magistrates Zerubbabel and Shealtiel had offered support. At the same time, Mather considered beneficent civil authority to be under God.*[29]

The End of History and God's Kingdom

The new Israel had eschatological ramifications. John Cotton distinguished between resurrection where souls and bodies dead from sin arose (either because the church returned from idolatry and superstition or the House of Israel returned from ignorance and apostasy) and resurrection of bodies forever.[†] The first meant resurrection to spiritual life, the second to physical life. Spiritual resurrection applied to churches which died under the tyranny of Antichrist and arose with the Reformation of Luther, Calvin, Zwingli, and Butzer in the sixteenth century.

In America some were properly and positively affected by the English Reformation while others undermined it. Cotton urged Christians to take the opportunity to "strike in with Christ" so that God would bear with them through the imminent apocalypse, in which Rome would be destroyed. If the unaffected were not "brought in," God would cast them into the bottomless pit and set a seal on it; they would be "condemned for destruction."[‡] They would not recover for a thousand years, and because they would not live a thousand years they would die in that condition, with their posterity and all their spirit—just as Jews, having rejected Christ's truth, remained dead until today. God would temporarily bear with Christians while they tolerated the "vanity of episcopacy" and "usurpation of the sons of men." But

if we be not brought on to this resurrection when we see [God's destructive acts] before our eyes, and have all stumbling blocks removed out of our ways that may hinder our reformation and regeneration; if we do not now strike

---

*See, for example, *II Kings* 25:24: "And Gedaliah sware to them and to their men, and said unto them, Fear not to be the servants of the Chaldees: dwell in the land and serve the king of Babylon; and it shall be well with you."

†"Awake thou that sleepest, and arise from the dead, and Christ shall give thee light." *Ephesians* 5:14. "For if the casting away of them be the reconciling of the world, what shall the receiving of them be, but life from the dead?" *Romans* 11:15. "The hand of the Lord was upon me, and carried me out in the spirit of the Lord, and set me down in the midst of the valley which was full of bones." *Ezekiel* 37:1. "Marvel not at this: for the hour is coming, in which all that are in the graves shall hear His voice." *John* 5:28.

‡"And cast him into the bottomless pit, and shut him up, and set a seal upon him, that he should deceive the nations no more, till the thousand years should be fulfilled: and after that he must be loosed a little season." *Revelation* 20:3. "And a stone was brought, and laid upon the mouth of the den; and the king sealed it with his own signet, and with the signet of his lords; that the purpose might not be changed concerning Daniel." *Daniel* 6:17.

a fast covenant with our God to be His people; if we do not now abandon whatsoever savors of death in the world, of death in lust and passion, then we and ours will be of this dead-hearted frame for a thousand years. We are not likely to see greater encouragements for a good while than now we see.[30]

Beginning with the Reformation in Europe, Cotton explained, there was resurrection on the individual level but not in the collective church, a phenomenon that continued in America. New Englanders, Cotton related, had not resurrected themselves from carnal self-love, oppression, and hypocrisy to exalt Christ and have His word rule homes and hearts. Using the image of refining sugar from maple sap, Cotton declared that the "syrup" of reformation had not yet "boiled up" to its full "consistency," and the churches were flittering up and down as if incompletely "boiled."[31]

Cambridge pastor Jonathan Mitchel (1624-1668) identified the purpose of the "people of God" in New England as the profession and practice of the word of God commanded to the ancient Israelites.* This required reformation, such as that enunciated by Thomas Hooker in *Survey of the Sum of Church Discipline* (1648).[32] The reformation that had begun in Europe could be fulfilled in America if the people would "clear the rights of Christ's kingly office" and actually "set up His kingdom." Christ's enduring inner kingdom on earth, within the hearts and words of men, had been growing toward "the general conversion of Jews and gentiles [to become] the inlet of the greatest glory of God's kingdom on earth," and now should be established on an outward, public level:

Erecting of Christ's kingdom in whole societies (whereby Christ is seen ruling all in a conspicuous and open, in a prevailing and peaceable manner), was our design and our interest in this country . . . The public setting up of Christ's kingdom, and enjoyment of those ordinances and ways of His which can only be enjoyed in whole societies, and that with purity and liberty, was our end in coming hither. And this also is Christ's design in these latter days. To set up His kingdom in a public and openly prevailing manner, in all parts and ways thereof.[33]

In the kingdom of God, completed inwardly and outwardly, all civil laws would be brought into the religious context. In Mitchel's "commonwealth of Christ's

---

*"That He may incline our hearts unto Him, to walk in all His ways, and to keep His commandments, and His statutes, and His judgments, which He commanded our fathers." *I Kings* 8:58. "And let these my words, wherewith I have made supplication before the Lord, be nigh unto the Lord our God day and night, that He maintain the cause of His servant, and the cause of His people Israel at all times, as the matter shall require." *I Kings* 8:59.

kingdom," laws and civil administrations would be established to "most fitly and effectively advance, promote, and maintain religion and reformation."[34]

Urian Oakes, for whom God's kingdom in America would begin the universal kingdom, explained in 1673 that the Reformation, beginning with King Edward VI (1547-1553) in England and Calvin in Geneva, continued in America with the "Congregational way of the first immigrants." Its substance was identical to primitive Christianity; it promoted liberty, omitted oppressive authority, and reconciled liberty with the authority of elders. It fostered a church government which reflected Christ's wisdom, one devoid of political and human contrivance. Upon this foundation contemporary Puritans could build in the spirit of Christ.[35] In 1679 Increase Mather explained that the Puritan fathers did not seek great things for themselves or come into the wilderness to see "a man clothed in soft raiment"* but sought the kingdom of God and His righteousness.[36]

Langdon's Holy Land of Christian America

Samuel Langdon (1723-1797) was minister at the Congregational north Church of Portsmouth, New Hampshire (1747-1773), president of Harvard College (1774-1780), and pastor in Hampton Falls, New Hampshire (1781-1797). Ezra Stiles (1727-1745), the future president of Yale College who succeeded him at Portsmouth in 1777, said Langdon believed that had Adam obeyed God he would have been exempted from natural death. By missing the opportunity he became responsible for man's staying in the natural mortal state and "in Adam all die." But God was disposed to show mercy, and He did so through Christ. Christ testified to God's abhorrence of sin, and because His sufferings transcended the bodily pains of crucifixion, they covered the entire elected people. Now men could again live forever.[37] Langdon's religious center, Christ on the cross, was reflected in his view of Holy Land-America.

On 13 May 1775, shortly after the outbreak of hostilities in Lexington on 19 April, Langdon spoke before the Congress of the Massachusetts Bay Colony. To comprehend the English brutalities he looked to God's supreme government, how He established and destroyed kings, let excellent human government become degenerate and corrupt, and restored decayed political constitutions by reviving public virtue and religion.† Thus, Isaiah had prophesied about decline, and the

---

*"And as they departed, Jesus began to say unto the multitudes concerning John, What went ye out into the wilderness to see? A reed shaken with the wind? But what went ye out for to see? A man clothed in soft raiment? behold, they that wear soft clothing are in kings' houses." *Matthew* 11:7-8.

†"And I will restore thy judges as at the first, and thy counselors as at the beginning: afterward thou shalt be called, The city of righteousness, the faithful city." *Isaiah* 1:26.

kingdom of Israel was subsequently destroyed because of failure to reform. When the people were exiled in 586 B.C.E. there were barely any remnants of the "original excellent civil polity" left, although the people would persist until the messiah came.* Langdon regarded the original Jewish polity as a perfect civil republic. Based upon a constitution given by God through Moses, the government was divinely established. Tribal heads and city elders were counselors and judges; the assemblies took the advice of the people and managed public affairs according to the general voice. The polity was so excellent that he thought some of its principal laws could be copied in the present. But it became corrupted. Common justice and humaneness were disregarded in the courts. Oppression and violence were so severe that Isaiah looked forward to the point when they would become extreme enough to precipitate desolation and captivity.† Indeed, in His righteous judgment, God had allowed the people to perpetrate enough vice to destroy themselves. Had they returned to revealed religion, He would have restored them to their Land to build their state.

The Israelite destruction, Langdon believed, prefigured contemporary decay.‡ England warred against her children in the Colonies solely out of lust for power and luxury. At the same time, the Colonists sinned by abandoning the Christian spirit of the first Puritan immigrants, so God employed England—herself sinful—for His righteous judgment. Because God distinguished the first Puritans with "signal favors of providence when they fled from tyranny and persecution into this western desert," the sins of the successors were the more grievous: "The sins of a people who have been remarkable for the profession of godliness are more aggravated by all the advantages and favors they have enjoyed, and will receive more speedy and signal punishment."# The American Christians were supposed to promote the "Redeemer's kingdom" but had not. Just as Israel still had a messianic future, Langdon hoped that calamity in the form of the war would bring religious revival, whereupon God's blessings would be manifest. The fact that God had already given the Colonists victories indicated that a positive process toward the "city of righteousness" for a "holy people" was

---

*"The scepter shall not depart from Judah, nor a lawgiver from between his feet, until Shiloh come; and unto him shall the gathering of the people be." *Genesis* 49:10.

†"Ah sinful nation, a people laden with iniquity, a seed of evil-doers, children that are corrupters: they have forsaken the Lord, and they have provoked the Holy One of Israel unto anger." *Isaiah* 1:4.

‡"Because there is no truth, nor mercy, nor knowledge of God in the land. By swearing, and lying, and killing, and stealing, and committing adultery, they break out, and blood toucheth blood." *Hosea* 4:1-2.

#"You only have I known of all the families of the earth: therefore will I punish you for all your iniquities." *Amos* 3:2.

underway. Langdon concluded with a plea to the God of Jacob to strengthen the Christians in their new Zion.[*38]

While serving in Hampton Falls, Langdon represented the town at the New Hampshire convention for ratifying the federal Constitution at the end of June 1788. After reviewing ancient Israel's decline from model government, he emphasized his hope for restoring that ancient democratic institution as a Christian reality in America. He recalled that Moses called upon Israel to observe the divine commandments, civil and religious, which expressed Israel's special tie to God.[†] The commandments provided an exemplary constitution of government, covering civil and military institutions, a judicial system, a minutely prescribed form of worship, and system of morals. It was thoroughly democratic; all people had a voice in public affairs; laws were rooted in rational principles, in justice, and in social virtue; and common interests of the tribes were addressed. For example, tribal representatives were chosen by constituents, and the senate was established upon consultation with the people. Each tribe had its elders and princes who acted upon the constituency's consent, just as the Constitution provided for a president and a senate.[39] But democracy was no sooner established than the people sought a king like other nations, eliminating the divine basis to government.[‡] David (1010-970 B.C.E.) and Solomon (967-928 B.C.E.) restored the impaired religious establishment, but the national senate which was required for democracy was missing. During the reigns of King Rehoboam (928-911 B.C.E.) and King Jeroboam (928-907 B.C.E.) a despotic atmosphere prevailed which precluded the administration of justice, judges were corrupt, and idolatry and vice spread. King Jehoshaphat (866-833 B.C.E.) attempted to restore democracy, but by then the educational system required for inculcating the principles of divine law was irretrievably ruined. The decline continued until the exile in 586 B.C.E.

---

[*]"The Lord hear thee in the day of trouble; the name of the God of Jacob defend thee: send thee help from the sanctuary and strengthen thee out of Zion." *Psalms* 20:1-2.

[†]"Behold, I have taught you statutes and judgments, even as the Lord my God commanded me, that ye should do so in the Land whither ye go to possess it. Keep therefore and do them; for this is your wisdom and your understanding in the sight of the nations, which shall hear all these statutes, and say, Surely this great nation is a wise and understanding people. For what nation is there so great, who hath God so nigh unto them, as the Lord our God is in all things that we call upon Him for? And what nation is there so great, that hath statutes and judgments so righteous as all this law, which I set before you this day?" *Deuteronomy* 4:5-8.

[‡]"But the thing displeased Samuel, when they said, Give us a king to judge us. And Samuel prayed unto the Lord. And the Lord said unto Samuel, Hearken unto the voice of the people in all that they say unto thee: for they have not rejected thee, but they have rejected Me, that I should not reign over them." *I Samuel* 8:6-7.

When Israel returned from Babylon, attempts were made to restore the original Mosaic principles, religious and political. The zeal for divine law was reinstilled, idolatry purged, worship institutionalized, and the Sanhedrin and supreme magistrate instituted. But the government again grew corrupt, while religion deteriorated into formalism and hypocrisy in place of true fear of God. Finally, the people of Israel "filled up the measure of their sins by crucifying the Lord of glory and rejecting His gospel, for which they have been made monuments of divine displeasure until this day." In Langdon's mind, the ultimate collapse of the model Israelite government coincided with the sin of deicide.

Christian America was Langdon's arena for the proper restoration of ancient Israel's government—as well as for the undoing of Israel's ultimate sin. He looked to America for a Mosaic constitution synthesized with the word of Christ. The Constitution recaptured the Mosaic spirit. Founded upon rational, equitable and liberal principles, it empowered the people to make righteous laws and promote public order and good morals. It would be implemented along with Christ's revealed truths:

> He has moreover given you by His son Jesus Christ, who is far superior to Moses, a complete revelation of His will and perfect system of true religion, plainly delivered in the sacred writings. It will be your wisdom in the eyes of the nations and your true interest and happiness to conform your practice in the strictest manner to the excellent principles of your government, adhere faithfully to the doctrines and commands of the gospel, and practice every public and private virtue. By this you will increase in numbers, wealth, and power, and obtain reputation and dignity among the nations. Whereas the contrary conduct will make you poor, distressed, and contemptible.[40]

For Langdon the Constitution was God given. Although American Christians did not witness God's glory as Israel did at Sinai, and God did not write American civil laws with His own finger, the new legal system did exhibit "signal interpretations of divine providence" and divine favor. This explained the recent miracles: God had provided George Washington as military leader, He guided the Revolutionaries to victory and escape from English vengeance, He granted peace and independence. Langdon thought there was "an heavenly charter for these United States . . . We cannot but acknowledge that God has graciously patronized our cause, and taken us under His special care, as He did His ancient covenant people." The supreme ruler of the universe, Langdon believed, had once again provided a government completed under His direction. Langdon warned his fellow American Christians not to squander the opportunity as Israel once had. He urged them to believe in Christ the crucified as the new, second Moses for the new Israel in the new Holy Land of Scripture:

If you neglect or renounce that religion taught and commanded in Holy Scriptures, think no more of freedom, peace and happiness; the judgments of heaven will pursue you. Religion is not a vain thing for you, because it is your life. It has been the glory and defense of New England from the infancy of the settlements. Let it be also our glory and protection. I mean no other religion than what is divinely prescribed, which God himself has delivered to us, with equal evidence of His authority, and even superior to that given to Israel. And which He has as strictly commanded us to receive and observe . . . We are now no more at liberty to draw up schemes of religion for ourselves, according to our own deceitful reasoning and vain imaginations and commands of men.

Nor were American Christians free to fall in with "the refinements of human wisdom and the fashionable sentiments of the world" any more than Israel was to substitute modes of serving God different from those He had expressly required.[41]

The Language of the Holy Land

The identification of America with (Christian) Zion by the early Puritans and Congregationalists was expressed further by the spread of Holy Land literature and its language. Under the Articles of Confederation (1781) Congress allocated funds for importing 20,000 Bibles from England. The first printed book of the Massachusetts Bay Colony was the *Bay Psalm Book of Hebrew Words and Letters* (1640). Colonists inscribed important dates and events in their family Bibles. Biblical personal names were used widely—even animals had them, and over one thousand biblical names would appear on the American map. When Thomas Jefferson delivered his second inaugural address (4 March 1805) he spoke with biblical resonance: "I shall need, too, the favor of that being in whose hands we are, who led our forefathers as Israel of old from the native land and planted them in a country flowing with all the necessaries and comforts of life; who has covered our infancy with His providence and our riper years with His wisdom and power."[42]

As to the language of the ancient Holy Land, Hebrew, the 12 May 1680 Reforming Synod in Boston agreed as follows:

The Old Testament in Hebrew (which was the native language of the people of God of old) and the New Testament in Greek (which at the time of the writing of it was most generally known to the nations) being immediately inspired by God, and by His singular care and providence kept pure in all ages, are therefore authentic. In all controversies of religion the church is finally to appeal unto them. But these original tongues are not known to all the peoples of God who have right unto and interest in the Scriptures and are commanded in the fear of God to read and search them. Therefore, they are to be translated into the vulgar language of every nation unto which they come, that the word of God dwelling plentifully in all, they may worship Him in an acceptable manner, and through patience and comfort of the Scriptures may have hope.[43]

Hebrew was required of students at Columbia and Yale. Increase Mather's son Nathaniel (d. 1688) delivered a commencement address in Hebrew at Harvard in 1685. Nathaniel's older brother, Cotton, said that "the Hebrew language has become so familiar with him, as if he had apprehended it should quickly become the only language which he should have occasion for."[44] The college seals of Yale, Columbia and Dartmouth have Hebrew mottos.[45]

John Cotton knew the language, and when he was examined at Cambridge University in the exceptionally difficult text of *Isaiah* 3:16 he handled its "construction and resolution" with ease.[*46] Ezra Stiles decided to study Hebrew when he was 40; Isaac Touro, serving as *hazan* (cantor) in Newport, Rhode Island, taught him letters and vowels. Stiles worked by himself on the *Psalms*, and beginning with *Psalm* 19 he read ten pages every morning before breakfast. He translated them into Latin and English and then translated *Genesis* and *Exodus*.[47]

Bela B. Edwards (1802-1852), a graduate of Andover Theological Seminary, became assistant secretary of the American Board of Commissioners for Foreign Missions (ABCFM) and editor of its *Missionary Herald* in 1828, professor of Hebrew at ATS in 1837, of Hebrew literature in 1838, and of biblical literature in 1848. Soon after he arrived at the seminary he wrote of his joy in Hebrew biblical study:

My principal study is the Hebrew Bible, and a most delightful study it is. I never saw the book of *Genesis* in so interesting a light. I never knew before how benevolent God is represented to be in that book. Many persons associate an unbending strictness with His character, as it is exhibited in the Old Testament. They do not remember that from the time Adam fell, we have had a dispensation of mercy. How nobly was the kindness of the Sovereign displayed in His appearing at various times to Abraham, conversing with him, enlightening his mind, lifting up the veil of futurity, and giving to the venerable patriarch a glory which was to endure, even down to the universal reign of the mediator. The more I study the books of Moses, so much the more fully I am convinced that they came from the inspiration of

---

*"Moreover the Lord saith, Because the daughters of Zion are haughty, and walk with stretched forth necks and wanton eyes, walking and mincing as they go, and making a tinkling with their feet." *Isaiah* 3:16.

God. He has put the seal of unerring truth on the pages of the Pentateuch. And if we are satisfied of this, we have almost the evidence of sense that there is an almighty being who reigns above these heavens. Or we almost see Him on the plains of Mamre, making the rainbow a pledge of safety to Noah, walking among the trees of Eden. It is true, there is hidden glory on the leaves of God's word. And the deeper our search, so much the more yellow is the discovered gold.

On 18 December 1825 Edwards resolved to acquire a thorough knowledge of Hebrew and to dedicate two and a half hours every morning to its study and at least one every evening.[48] In his inaugural address of 18 January 1838 he recited instances of early Hebrew usage in America. Twenty of the original settlers of the Massachusetts Bay Colony studied Hebrew at Cambridge or Oxford.[49] The first and second presidents of Harvard, Henry Dunster (1612-1659) and Charles Chauncy (1592-1672), were trained at Cambridge.[50] Chauncy—who also taught Hebrew at Cambridge—expounded on the Bible at morning prayer at Harvard and had the students read the Hebrew text. His student Thomas Thacher (1620-1678), first minister of the Old south Church in Boston, compiled a Hebrew lexicon.[51] Judah Monis (1683-1764), a Jew and a regular Hebrew instructor at Harvard (1722-1760), was praised for his Hebrew by biblical scholar Benjamin Colman (1633-1647)—standing in for Increase Mather—at Monis's baptism in Cambridge in 1722:

[Monis] is truly read and learned in the Jewish Kabbala and [Sages], and a master and critic in the Hebrew. He reads, speaks, writes and interprets it with great readiness and accuracy, and is truly *didaktikos*, apt to teach. His diligence and industry, together with his ability, are known unto many who have seen his grammar and nomenclature Hebrew and English, his translation of the Creed and the Lord's Prayer, the thirty-nine Articles of the Church of England and the Assembly's Shorter Catechism into Hebrew.[52]

Monis's student Stephen Sewall (1733-1804) succeeded Monis as Hancock professor of Hebrew and other Oriental languages (1765-1785).[53] The second rector of Yale College, Timothy Cutler, according to Ezra Stiles, was a "great Hebrician and Orientalist." During the first 50 years of settling New England, Edwards observed, the flame of sacred Hebrew learning, kept alive at Oxford University by John Selden (1584-1654) and John Lightfoot (1602-1675), was rekindled on American shores. One parish minister of a new settlement read so much Hebrew that he became blind; he consoled himself with the thought that his eyes would be opened at the resurrection of the just.

Edwards offered various reasons for the great interest. Knowing the text in the simplicity and freshness of the Hebrew original compelled recognition that it was inspired, strengthening faith. Knowing Hebrew provided direct access to the real source of faith, and given the universal implications of Scripture, demonstrated the unity of the human race. Finally, knowledge of Hebrew was indispensable in missionary work for a number of reasons:

1. It strengthened the student's faith in the divine authority of the Scriptures. The Hebrew of the old Testament

   has the signature of a simplicity and freshness, which no translation can fully copy unless it be itself inspired. It is the freshness of Eden on the seventh morning of the creation; it is the simplicity of patriarchs and prophets; it is the innocent guilelessness of angels. Our translation is faithful to the sense of the original and it will be an everlasting monument of the powers of the English language, especially in its Anglo-Saxon features. But it is no disparagement to the version to assert that it does not give us all the vitality and beauty of the original. In reading the latter, we cannot but feel that we have passed into the holy of holies; the proofs of divinity are thick around us. We do not simply know that our faith in these records is firm, we feel that it is.

2. Since translation was necessarily confined,

   the translator must, in many cases, select *one* word, the best which he can find, to express the senses of the original word. He cannot employ amplification, paraphrase, circumlocution. He must take a single substantive, or a single epithet; else he weakens, or obscures the passage. He very properly renders the verb *davar* by its fifth signification, *to speak.* He cannot even allude to the other, and more primary meanings—to arrange, to guide, to follow and to be in wait. He rightly translates the noun *derekh* by *path* or *road*, without even hinting that it has also the meaning of act of going, journey, mode of living, conduct toward God and man, religion, destiny or the way in which it goes with any one . . . thus with many other terms which might be mentioned. The sight of the original word will suggest to the reader, not simply the substantial signification of it in the passage, but all the related significations near or remote.

3. Knowledge of the Hebrew original provided "a vivid apprehension" of the passage:

   The characters of the revelation will stand out in bold relief. The student will feel that he is no longer dealing with shadows . . . He will gain, not faith in its lower forms, but a living and enduring impression of the great realities which are couched beneath the terms which are daily coming under his eye.

4. Knowing Hebrew helped to evaluate the original unity of mankind:

This language or family of languages is the Indo-Germanic or Indo-European. By further researches, it appears to be established that this family is connected with the Semitic, of which the Hebrew is a dialect, not by a few verbal coincidences, but linked together, both by points of actual contact, and by the interposition of the Coptic, grounded on the essential structure and most necessary forms of the three. In the common Hebrew lexicon now used in [ATS], whole families of biliteral roots are illustrated by analogies from the Indo-Germanic tongues, proving that the Hebrew in its primary elements approaches much nearer both to the European and the southern Asiatic languages than has been generally supposed.

Edwards drew this conclusion: "In the labors which are to be entered into for the conversion of the five or six million of Jews, scattered over the world, the necessity of the Hebrew Bible is too obvious to need the briefest allusion. In respect to familiarity with its pages, the missionary himself must become a Jew."[54]

Observations

The idea and spiritual reality of the Holy Land entered America with the first Puritans and Congregationalists from England. Bradford and Winthrop viewed themselves as Israelites who came to the Promised Land within salvational history. In order to fulfill that history, however, great obstacles had to be overcome; their followers needed to pass with Christ from despair to hope. In this way, Christianity became ingrained in the original soil of the American Holy Land. The religious thinkers of the next generation—John Norton, Increase Mather, Urian Oakes, John Higginson, and Cotton Mather—reaffirmed the scriptural aspect of the entry into America. They brought the ancient myth of exodus, liberation, and entry into wilderness and Promised Land into a new time and new space. Whether parallel, similar, or coincident, the two expressions of the single myth were intimately related and equally evocative of the Holy Land experience. Again, Christianity was written into the American Holy Land; the journey was made possible and overseen by Christ and would hopefully culminate with a complete Christian community.

The transfer of the Holy Land into American time and space implied the restoration of the ancient theocracy, in the form of a holy commonwealth where civil law would be sublimated to one degree or another into religious law. Further, it brought history closer to its culmination, its *eschaton*: the Reformation was made more complete, a model Christian kingdom was expected which would reverberate around the world, the apocalyptic scenes of *Revelation* were anticipated. That is, the renewal of the ancient Holy Land in America involved the ultimate sacred territory. Samuel Langdon spelled out the failure of ancient

Israel to realize the potential of the Holy Land polity, and the new opportunity presented by America. The key was the recognition of Christ, the integration of Christianity into American law. If properly pursued, the new opportunity could be used to establish a new, complete Zion of righteousness.

The transfer of the Holy Land into American space and time was reflected in and simultaneously reinforced by the currency of Hebrew Scripture. As could be expected, scriptural language was used in the new Land of the Bible—and use of Hebrew in turn deepened the presence of scriptural myth. The Christian succession to Judaism, and the pivotal role of Christianity in bringing the Holy Land to America, were captured by using Hebrew for the purpose of converting Jews to Christianity.

The Puritans and Congregationalists who came to America in the seventeenth and early eighteenth centuries saw themselves within a scriptural context. For them, Moses, Nehemiah, wilderness, sin, and resurrection had reality in the present. Early Americans were part of the mythic eternity provided by the scriptural past; only the location had changed, from the ancient Near East to America. The spatial shift involved another change, one that enabled the transfer: Israel was passing from Judaism to Christ. The Jewish tradition became a ladder for Christianity to ascend. Thus the expected kingdom of God was in Christ. The Puritan and Congregationalist interest in Hebrew had missionary ramifications; indeed, the first university instructor in Hebrew converted from Judaism to Christianity. Ancient Israelite history and Hebrew Scripture became transformed into preludes for Christian Israel and the New Testament. The wilderness of ancient Israel's experience became open space for a holy territory which was Christian, ultimately a kingdom of God in Christ. This sacred Christian territory preserved the Holy Land in America, where it became implanted in religious consciousness. In terms of America's collective memory, it was there to be drawn upon later by Jewish "Israelites" (Reformers) and Conservative and Orthodox Jews—many of whom would seek to return the Holy Land to its original soil.

Notes

1. On Puritans, Congregationalists, and Zion, see Robert T. Handy, *A Christian America: Protestant Hopes and Historical Realities* (New York 1971), ch. 1 and 2; R. Fingerhut, "Were the Puritans Hebraic?" *New England Quarterly* 40 no. 4 (December 1967):521-531; Richard B. Morris, "Civil Liberties and the Jewish Tradition," *Publications of the American Jewish Historical Society (PAJHS)* 46 nos. 1-4 (September 1956-June 1957):20-39; Clifford K. Shipton, "The Hebraic Background of Puritanism," *PAJHS* 47 no. 3 (March 1958):140-153; Mark A. Noll, "The Image of the United States as a Biblical Nation, 1776-1865," in Nathan A. Hatch and Mark A. Noll, eds., *Bible in America* (New York 1982):39-58; Truman Nelson, "The Puritans of Massachusetts: From Egypt to the Promised Land," *Judaism* 16 no. 2 (Spring 1967):193-206.

2.   Jesper Rosenmeier, "With My Own Eyes: William Bradford's *Of Plymouth Plantation*," in Sacvan Berkovitch, ed., *The American Puritan Imagination* (London 1974):82-83, 106.

3.   Rosenmeier provides examples of how Christ's passion was grafted onto the experience of Bradford's Pilgrims.

4.   William Bradford, *Bradford's History of Plymouth Plantation*, 1606-1646, William Davis, ed. (New York 1908):29, 54-55.

5.   Cited in David de Sola Pool, "Hebrew Learning among Puritans," *PAJHS* 20 (1911):32.   See Isidore S. Meyer, "The Hebrew Exercises of Governor William Bradford," in Charles Berlin, ed., *Studies in Jewish Bibliography, History, and Literature in Honor of I. Edward Kiev* (New York 1971):237-288; idem, "The Hebrew Preface to Bradford's *History of the Plymouth Plantation,*" *PAJHS* no. 38 part 4 (June 1949):289-293.

6.   Cotton Mather, "*Galeacius Secundus* (The Second Shield-bearer).   The life of William Bradford, esq., Governor of Plymouth Colony," in *Magnalia Christi Americana; or, The ecclesiastical history of New England from its first planting in the year 1620 unto the year of our Lord 1698 (MCA).   Ecclesiarum Clypel (The Shields of the Churches): The second book of the New-English history: Containing the lives of the governors and the names of the magistrates that have been shields unto the churches of New England until the year 1686* (1702; reprint, Hartford 1853):113.

7.   George C. Blaxland, *"Mayflower" Essays on the Story of the Pilgrim Fathers as Told in Governor Bradford's Ms. "History of the Plymouth Plantation"* (1896; reprint, New York 1972):129; "Round about Scrooby," *New England Magazine* n.s. 1 no. 1 (September 1889):31-40; James Shepherd, *Governor William Bradford and His Son Major William Bradford* (New Britain 1900):43.

8.   Peter Gay, *A Loss of Mastery: Puritan Historians in Colonial America* (Berkeley 1966):26-52.

9.   John Winthrop, "Reasons to be Considered for Justifying the Undertaking of the Intended Plantation in New England and for Encouraging Such Whose Hearts God Shall Move to Join with Them in It," in Robert C. Winthrop, ed., *Life and Letters of John Winthrop* (New York 1971):1:309-317.

10.   Winthrop, "A Model of Christian Charity, Written Aboard the *Arabella* on the Atlantic Ocean, 1630," in *Winthrop Papers* ([Boston] 1931):2:282-295.

11.   Cotton Mather, *"Nehemias Americanus* (The American Nehemiah): The life of John Winthrop, esq., Governor of the Massachusetts Colony," in *MCA Antiquities: The first book of the New-English history. Reporting the design whereon, the manner wherein, the people whereby, the several colonies of New England were planted*, 118-131.

12.   John Norton, *Abel Being Dead Yet Speaketh; or, The life and death of that deservedly famous man of God, Mr. John Cotton, late teacher of the Church of Christ at Boston in New England* (London 1658):21-22.

13. [Increase Mather], Epistle Dedicatory, *The Necessity of Reformation: With the expedients subservient thereunto asserted. In answer to two questions: (1) What are the evils that have provoked the Lord to bring His judgments on New England? (2) What is to be done that so these evils may be reformed? Agreed upon by the elders and messengers of the churches assembled in the synod of Boston in New England, 10 September 1679* (Boston 1679):i-iv.

14. Urian Oakes, *New England Pleaded With, and Pressed to Consider the Things Which Concern Her Peace at Least in This Her Day; or, A seasonable and serious word of faithful advice to the churches and people of God (primarily those) in the Massachusetts Colony, musingly to ponder and bethink themselves, what is the tendency and will certainly be the sad issue, of sundry unchristian and crooked ways, which too too many have been turning aside unto, if persisted and gone on in. Delivered in a sermon preached at Boston in New England, 7 May 1673, being the day of election there. By Urian Oakes, Pastor of the Church of Christ in Cambridge* (Cambridge, Mass., 1673):17-24. See Increase Mather, "Urian Oakes," in William B. Sprague, *Annals of the American Pulpit; or, Commemorative notices of distinguished American clergymen of various denominations, from the early settlement of the country to the close of the year 1855* (New York 1857):1:141-143; and Cotton Mather, *"Drusius Nov-Anglicanus; or, The life of Mr. Urian Oakes," in MCA Sal Gentium (The Salt of the Nations): The fourth book of the New-English history. Containing an account of the university, from whence the churches of New England (and many other churches) have been illuminated. Its laws, its benefactors, its vicissitudes, and a catalogue of such as have been therein educated and graduated. Whereto are added the lives of some eminent persons who were plants of renown growing in that nursery,* 114-118.

15. Oakes, *New England Pleaded With*, 17-24.

16. John Higginson, "An Attestation to This Church-History of New England," in Cotton Mather, *MCA Antiquities*, 13-18. See John Higginson, *Our Dying Savior's Legacy of Peace to His Disciples in a Troublesome World: From John 14:27. "My peace I give unto you," etc. Also a discourse on the two witnesses showing that it is the duty of all Christians to be witnesses unto Christ, from Revelation 11:3. "I will give my two witnesses," etc. Unto which is added some help to self-examination* (Boston 1686). See John Dunton and Cotton Mather, "John Higginson," in Sprague, *Annals of The American Pulpit*, 1:91-99.

17. Cotton Mather, General Introduction, in *MCA Antiquities*, 25-38.

18. Cotton Mather, *MCA Polybius: The third book of the New-English history. Containing the lives of many reverend, learned, and holy divines, arriving such from Europe to America, by whose evangelical ministry the churches of New England have been illuminated,* 248-249.

19. Gay, *Loss of Mastery*, 26-52.

20. Richard Mather, *An Apology of the Churches in New England for Church-Covenant; or, A discourse touching the covenant between God and men, and especially concerning church-covenant. That is to say, the covenant which a company does enter into when they become a church, and which a particular person enters into when he becomes a member of a church* (London 1643):8. See Perry Miller, *The New England Mind in the Seventeenth Century* (New York 1939):415; and Cotton Mather, "The life of Mr. Richard Mather," in *MCA Polybius*, 443-458.

21. Norton, *Abel Being Dead*, 21-22.

22. William Aspinwall, "To the Reader," in *An Abstract of Laws and Government: Wherein as in a mirror may be seen the wisdom and perfection of the government of Christ's kingdom. Accommodable to any state or form of government in the world that is not antichristian or tyrannical. Collected and digested into the ensuing method by that godly, grave, and judicious divine Mr. John Cotton of Boston and New England in his lifetime, and presented to the General Court of the Massachusetts. And now published after his death by William Aspinwall* (London 1655):i-vi.

23. William Perkins, Preface to *A Golden Chain; or, The description of theology, containing the order of the causes of salvation and damnation according to God's word* (London 1591).

24. John Cotton, "Letter from Mr. Cotton to Lord Say and Seal in Year 1636," Appendix 3 in Lawrence S. Mayo, ed., *History of the Colony and Province of Massachusetts Bay* (Cambridge, Mass., 1936). See George E. Ellis, "The Biblical Commonwealth," in *Puritan Age and Rule in the Colony of the Massachusetts Bay, 1629-1685* (New York 1970):167-199.

25. Cotton, *The Keys of the Kingdom of Heaven: And the power thereof according to the word of God* (1644; reprint, Boston 1843):95-100.

26. Robert C. Winthrop, *Life and Letters*, 2:340-341.

27. Cotton Mather, "Of the Civil Magistrates' Power in Matters Ecclesiastical: A platform of church discipline. Gathered out of the word of God and agreed upon by the elders and messengers of the churches assembled in the synod at Cambridge in New England. To be presented to the churches and General Court for their consideration and acceptance in the Lord, the 8th month, anno 1649," in *MCA Acts and Monuments: The fifth book of the New-English history*, 235-236.

28. John Eliot, Preface to *The Christian Commonwealth; or, The civil poli[t]y of the rising kingdom of Jesus Christ. Written before the interruption of the government by Mr. John Eliot, teacher of the church of Christ at Roxbury in New England* (London 1659):1-3.

29. [Increase Mather], "Epistle Dedicatory."

30. Cotton, *The Church's Resurrection; or, The opening of the fifth and sixth verses of the twentieth chapter of the Revelation* (London 1642):15-16. Cotton experienced an eschatological "fever":

> There is a certain kind of warmth by which the soul does not only affect the ordinances of God, but by which it does in some measure digest them . . . even made his soul to break within him [*Psalms* 119:20], and so to pant after God's Word [*Psalms* 42:1], and His presence in His ordinances. There was a kind of panting, and longing, and eager desire after God, by which it comes to pass that the soul of a Christian closes with God in His ordinances, and turns them into nourishment within himself and so is more strongly and inwardly bent towards God in the ways of His grace.

Cotton, *Christ the Fountain of Life; or, Sundry choice sermons on part of the fifth chapter of the first Epistle of Saint John* (London 1651):148. See Alan Simpson, "The Covenanted Community," *Puritanism in Old and New England* (Chicago 1955):19-38.

31. Cotton, *The Church's Resurrection*, 15-16.

32. Thomas Hooker, *Survey of the Sum of Church Discipline: Wherein the mercy of the churches of New England is warranted out of the Word, and all exceptions of weight which are made against it answered. Whereby also it will appear to the judicious reader that something more must be said than yet has been, before their principles can be shaken or they should be unsettled in their practice* (London 1648).

33. [Jonathan Mitchel], "The Great End and Interest of New England: Stated by the memorable Mr. Jonathan Mitchel, extracted from an instrument of his which bears the date 31 December 1662," in Samuel Mather, *An Apology for the Liberties of the Churches of New England: To which is prefixed a discourse concerning Congregational churches* (Boston 1738): 200-203. See Cotton Mather, *"Ecclesiastes* (The Preacher): The life of the reverend and excellent Jonathan Mitchel, a pastor of the church and a glory of the college in Cambridge, New England," in *MCA Sal Gentium,* 114-118.

34. [Mitchel], "The Great End and Interest of New England," 200-203.

35. Oakes, *New England Pleaded With,* 114-118.

36. [Increase Mather], "Epistle Dedicatory."

37. Ezra Stiles, diary entry of 31 July 1777, in Franklin B. Sanborn, *President Langdon: A Biographical Tribute* (Boston 1904):9-10. See Samuel Langdon, *The Excellency of the Word of God, in the Mouth of a Faithful Minister: A sermon delivered at the ordination of the Reverend Mr. Samuel McClintock, colleague with the Reverend Mr. William Allen, in the pastoral care of the church in Greenland in the province of New Hampshire, 3 November 1756* (Portsmouth, N.H., 1756); idem, *The Duty and Honor of a Minister of Christ: A sermon preached at Windham, near Casco Bay, at the ordination of the Reverend Mr. Peter Thatcher Smith, to the work of the gospel ministry, and the pastoral care of the church there, 22 September 1762* (Portsmouth, N.H., 1762); idem, *A Summary of Christian Faith and Practice: Being an attempt to exhibit the doctrines and precepts of the New Testament in a concise and easy view, chiefly in Scriptural language, for the assistance of Christians of all denominations in recollecting the main articles of*

their common profession (Boston 1768); idem, *An Impartial Examination of Mr. Robert Sandeman's Letters on Theron and Aspasio. In three parts: (1) Some general remarks on the spirit and leading nations of the author of those letters. (2) A particular consideration of the character of the Pharisee, and of Jesus, as drawn by Mr. Sandeman—Remarks upon his conversion of Jonathan. (3) The principle sentiments in the letters collected into order, distinctly examined, and shown in several instances to be inconsistent with one another, and with the sacred oracles, and the whole to be an unhappy mixture of truth with absurdity and falsehood* (Boston 1769); idem, *A Rational Explication of Saint John's Vision of the Two Beasts in the Thirteenth Chapter of The Revelation: Showing that the beginning, power, and duration of popery are plainly predicted in that vision, and that those predictions have hitherto been punctually verified* (Portsmouth, N.H., 1774). See also idem, *Observations on the Revelation of Jesus Christ to Saint John: Which comprehend the most approved sentiments of the celebrated Mr. Mede, Mr. Lowman, Bishop Newton, and other noted writers on this book; and cast much additional light on the more obscure prophecies. Especially those which point out the time of the rise and fall of Antichrist* (Worcester, Mass., 1791). On the last, see Ethan Smith, *A Dissertation on the Prophecies Relative to Antichrist and the Last Times: Exhibiting the rise, character, and overthrow of that terrible power and a treatise on the seven apocalyptic vials* (Charleston, Mass., 1811):327.

38. Langdon, *Government Corrupted by Vice and Recovered by Righteousness: A sermon preached before the honorable congress of the colony of the Massachusetts Bay in New England, assembled at Watertown on Wednesday, 31 May 1775* (Watertown 1775).

39. Langdon did not cite sources. They may be pursued by consulting Haim Hirschensohn, *These Are the Words of the Covenant,* 2 vols. (Jerusalem 1926-1928, Hebrew) or Daniel Elazar, *Covenant as the Basis of Jewish Political Tradition* (Ramat Gan 1983).

40. Langdon, *A Sermon Preached at Concord in the State of New Hampshire, before the Honorable General Court at the Annual Election, 5 June 1788* (Exeter, N.H., 1788). Sanborn said that the sermon reflected Langdon's belief in Old Testament infallibility and that Mosaic laws and the Israelite experience should be "guides to permanence and prosperity in the new republic." Sanborn, *President Langdon,* 27.

41. Langdon, *A Sermon Preached at Concord.*

42. Thomas Jefferson, *Works* (Washington, D.C., 1903):3:383. See also Charles V. LaFontaine, "God and Nation in Selected U.S. Presidential Inaugural Addresses, 1789-1955: Part one," *Journal of Church and State* 18 no. 1 (Winter 1976):39-60; Moshe Davis, "Historical Perspective on the America-Erets Israel Relationship," in *The House of Israel in America* (Jerusalem 1970, Hebrew):343-402; idem, "The Holy Land Idea in American Spiritual History," in Moshe Davis, ed., *With Eyes toward Zion* (New York 1977):1:3-33; Lottie Davis, "Old Names, New Names," *Land of the Bible Newsletter* 1 no. 5 (May 1959):1, and 1 no. 7 (August-September 1959):1-2; John Leighly, "Biblical Place-Names in the United States," *Names: Journal of the American Name Society* 27 no. 1 (March 1979).

43. *A Confession of Earth Owned and Consented Unto by the Elders and Messengers of the Churches Assembled at Boston in New England, 12 May 1680: Being the second session of that Synod* . . . (Boston 1680), cited in Williston Walker, *The Creeds and Platforms of Congregationalism* (Boston 1960):369.

44. See Cotton Mather, "The Life and Death of Mr. Nathaniel Mather," *MCA Sal Gentium,* 156-176.

45. Pool, "Hebrew Learning." See Ezra Stiles, "Further Progress in Semitics and the Study of Hebrew at Yale," in George A. Kohut, *Ezra Stiles and the Jews* (New York 1902):99-107; Shalom Goldman, "Biblical Hebrew in Colonial America: The Case of Dartmouth," *American Jewish History* 79 no. 2 (Winter 1989-1990):173-180; idem, "Hebrew at the Early Colleges: Orations at Harvard, Dartmouth, and Columbia," *American Jewish Archives* 42 no. 1 (Spring/Summer 1990):23-26.

46. Norton, *Abel Being Dead,* 21-22.

47. Abiel Holmes, *The Life of Ezra Stiles, D.D., LL.D.: A fellow of the American Philosophical Society, of the American Academy of Arts and Sciences, of the Connecticut Society of Arts and Sciences, a corresponding member of the Massachusetts Historical Society, professor of ecclesiastical history, and president of Yale College* (Boston 1798):129-130.

48. Edward A. Park, "Course of Theological Study," in *Writings of Professor Bela B. Edwards: With a memoir by Edward A. Park* (Boston 1853):1:48-49.

49. See Fingerhut, "Were the Puritans Hebraic?" and Pool, "Hebrew Learning," 31-85.

50. See Henry Dunster and Richard Lyons, eds., *The Psalms, Hymns, and Spiritual Songs of the Old and New Testament, Faithfully translated into English Meter,* cited in Perry Miller and Thomas H. Johnson, *The Puritans* (New York 1938):556. During Dunster's presidency, students read the Scriptures "out of Hebrew into Greek from the Old Testament in the morning, and out of English into Greek from the New Testament in the evening." Jeremiah Chaplin, *Life of Henry Dunster, First President of Harvard College* (Boston 1872):65. See Cotton Mather, *"Psaltes:* The Life of Mr. Henry Dunster," in *MCA Polybius,* 405-408; Isidore Meyer, "Hebrew at Harvard, 1636-1760: A Résumé of the Information in Recent Publications," *PAJHS* 35 (1939):145-170.

51. Edwards cited Benjamin B. Wisner, *The History of the Old south Church in Boston: In four sermons, delivered 9 and 16 May 1830, being the first and second Sabbaths after the completion of a century from the first occupancy of the present meeting house* (Boston 1830):11-12, 84-85. According to Cotton Mather, Thacher "was not unskilled in the tongues, especially in the Hebrew, whereof he did compose a lexicon; but so comprised it, that within one sheet of paper he had every considerable word of the language." Cotton Mather, "The Life of Mr. Thomas Thacher," in *MCA Polybius,* 488-497.

52. Judah Monis, *Dikduk Leshon Ivrit: A grammar of the Hebrew tongue. Being an essay to bring the Hebrew grammar into English, to facilitate the instruction of this primitive tongue by own studies. In order to their more distinct acquaintance with the sacred oracles of the Old Testament, according to the original. And published more*

especially for the use of the students of Harvard College at Cambridge, in New England (Boston 1735). A translation of the Lord's Prayer and the Apostle's Creed was offered on p. 94. See Lee M. Friedman, "Judah Monis: First instructor in Hebrew at Harvard University," *PAJHS* 22 (1914):1-24. I have been unable to identify Monis's translation of the Articles or Shorter Catechism. Benjamin Colman, *A Discourse had in the College Hall at Cambridge, 27 March 1722, before the Baptism of R. Judah Monis. To which are added three discourses written by Mr. Monis himself: [1] The Truth. Being a discourse which the author delivered at his baptism. Containing nine principal arguments the modern Jewish rabbis do make to prove the messiah is yet to come. With the answers to each, not only according to the Orthodox opinion, but even with the authority of their own authentic rabbis of old, and likewise with the confession of his faith at the latter end . . . Prefaced by Increase Mather. [2] The Whole Truth. Being a short essay wherein the author discovers what may be the true reason why the Jewish nation are not as yet converted to Christianity. Besides what others have said before him. And likewise, he proves the divinity of Christ not only with the authority of the sacred oracles, but even by the common of the Jewish authors of old. And answers all the objections that the discourse brings forth out of Isaiah 9:6-7. Concluding with a word of exhortation [3] Nothing but the Truth. Being a short essay wherein the author proves the doctrine of the ever blessed and adorable trinity. Both out of the Old Testament and with the authority of the Kabbalistic Rabbis, ancient and modern. And that said doctrine is not a novelty, as his countrymen do think, but as ancient as the Bible itself* (Boston 1722). In 1760 Thaddeus M. Harris wrote of Monis:

> This aged incumbent was a Jew of Algiers. Becoming a convert to the Christian religion, and publicly baptized at Cambridge in 1722, he was appointed to teach a language which, though he perfectly understood himself as a grammarian and philologist, he was not happy in enabling others to understand. He retained, moreover, a great fondness for rabbinical lore and his criticisms were so abstruse, and his conversation and manners so uncourteous, that he did not conciliate the respect of his pupils, and attendance on his teaching was deemed a disgusting requisition.

Lee M. Friedman, "Miscellanea," *PAJHS* 38 pt. 2 (December 1948):146-151.

53. Monis's grammar proved unsatisfactory, and Sewall was requested to prepare a new one. Stephen Sewall, *An Hebrew Grammar Collected Chiefly from Those of Mr. Israel Lyon, Teacher of Hebrew in the University of Cambridge, and the Rev. Richard Grey, D.D., Rector of Hinton, in northhamptonshire. To which is subjoined a praxis, taken from the sacred classics, and containing a specimen of the whole Hebrew language. With a sketch of the Hebrew poetry, as retrieved by Bishop Hare* (Boston 1763). See Friedman, "Miscellanea"; Clifford K. Shipton, *Sibley's Harvard Graduates XV, 1761-1763* (Boston 1970):105-114.

54. Bela B. Edwards, "Reasons for Study of the Hebrew Language," *American Biblical Repository* 12 no. 31 (1838):113-130.

2 Sephardic Jewry: Present and Future Zion

The Sephardic Jews in America in the eighteenth and early nineteenth centuries established various concrete connections to Zion in the Land of Israel.[1] In Charleston, south Carolina, they used earth from the Land in burials.[2] In New York, Isaac Pinto (1720-1791) urged the congregants of Shearit Israel to use Hebrew to prepare themselves for the eventual revival of the Land.[3] *Meshullahim*, emissaries from the Land of Israel, were well received during their fundraising tours of America. They included Moses Malki from Safed (1759); Raphael Haim Isaac Karigal from Hebron (1772), who preached about restoring the Land and messianic redemption; and Samuel Ha'cohen from Hebron (1775).[4] The Sephardic Jews' ideology brought the Puritan theme of Zion in America a step further, regarding America as a stop on the way toward messianic Zion in Jerusalem.

The American Revolution under God

The identification of Zion with America appeared in the Sephardic interpretation of the American Revolution through Hebrew Scripture: King George III was the oppressive King Rehoboam (*I Kings* 11-14 and *II Chronicles* 10-13). On 15 July 1790 President Jacob Cohen of Bet Elohim Congregation in Charleston, south Carolina, wrote the new president, George Washington:

> While historians of this and every age shall vie with each other in doing justice to your character and in adorning their pages with the splendor of your endowments, and of your patriotic and noble achievements; and while they cull and combine the various good and shining qualities of the pagan and modern heroes to display your character, we and our posterity will not cease to chronicle and commemorate you, with Moses, Joshua, Othniel, Gideon, Samuel, David, Maccabees, and other holy men of old, who were raised up by God, for the deliverance of our nation, His people, from their oppression.

May the great being, our universal Lord, continue propitious to you and to the United states; perfect and give increase and duration of prosperity to the great empire which He has made you so instrumental in producing.

When Washington responded to Levi Sheftall's (1739-1809) congratulatory letter on behalf of the Hebrew Congregation of Savannah, Georgia, he invoked Scripture:

May the same wonder-working deity, who long since delivered the Hebrews from their Egyptian oppressors, planted them in a promised land, *whose providential agency has lately been conspicuous in establishing these United States as an independent nation*, still continue to water them with the dews of heaven and make the inhabitants of every denomination participate in the temporal and spiritual blessings of that people whose God is Jehovah.[5]

The congregants of Shearit Israel used scriptural language to assure the welfare and victory of the Revolution's leaders and soldiers:

May the supreme king of kings, through His infinite mercies, save and prosper the men of these United States who are gone forth to war; the Lord of hosts be the shield of those who are armed for war by land, and for those who are gone in ships to war on the seas. May the Lord fight for them. May they, their rulers, their leaders and all their allies joining them in battle, equally experience Thy goodness; and may Thy angels have them in charge, and save them from death and all manner of distress. May the supreme king of kings implant among them amity, brotherly love, peace and sociableness. Let not their lips speak evil, nor their tongues utter deceit. May their troops go forth without duplicity when they have taken counsel together, to war against those that seek their injury. May the supreme king of kings through his infinite mercies, impart His divine wisdom, to the rulers of these United States, and grant them a spirit of just council and true valor, so that they may be enabled to support their determinations with wisdom and judgment. And may a permanent peace subsist between them and the kings and the potentates in alliance with them and establish them a covenant of peace, until time shall be no more, so that nation shall not lift up their sword against nation, neither shall they combat or make war anymore, Amen. Grant it thus O Lord, for the sake of Thy great and ineffable name, and for the sake of Thy people, and Thine inheritance, who offereth up their supplications to Thee, whose seat is in heaven.[6]

On 15 July 1773 Yale College President Ezra Stiles discussed the contemporary expectations for the messiah with Karigal:

I asked whether the rabbis of this age thought themselves to have any particular reasons for expecting the messiah immediately. He said, no; but he thought it was high time for him to come. He added that if all nations were in war and universal tumult and confusion, then he should expect him immediately, but this not being more the case now than in every current age.

Historian Raphael Mahler has observed that the Jews of the time were expecting redemption. When the Revolution broke out in 1775 and Jews became fully involved, their national consciousness and messianic hopes were sharpened. They recalled their ancestors' independence in the ancient homeland; the aims for reordering political structures were reminiscent of messianic visions. Moreover, numerical calculations (*gematria*) over the previous decade specified that 5543 (1783) was the year for messianic revelation, and on 3 September 1783 the Treaty of Paris recognized American independence. After victory the children of Jacob would naturally ask the patriarch's question: "And now when shall I provide for mine own house also?" (*Genesis* 30:30).

Sephardic spokesmen believed that since God participated in Revolutionary history and victory, as He once did in ancient Israel's history, a process was underway that would culminate in the liberation of Israel. The present became an instance of redemptive history, the beginning of a return to the Land and establishment of the messianic kingdom. The history of ancient Israel, Sephardim believed, prefigured the Revolution, while it in turn prefigured the messianic future. Dutch Rabbi Hendla Yohanan van Oettingen, Shearit Israel Congregation's *shohet* (ritual slaughterer), expressed this belief in the prayer he composed when the congregants returned to New York after hiding in Philadelphia from the Tories.[7] It begins with an affirmation of God's role in history in general and in the American victory in particular:

> King eternal, to Him is kingship and He causes monarchs to reign. He it is Who implanted peace in the heart of kings so that they may return the sword to its sheath. The Lord has said peace to those afar and to those near. We will praise the Lord as a congregation for His lovingkindnesses which He has benevolently bestowed upon us. We cried unto the Lord from our straits and from our troubles He brought us forth. And for us, a weak people, inhabiting the land, He in His goodness prospered our warfare. Thou hast restored us our inheritance from the hands of aliens and strangers and given us back the joy of our heart.

God is then asked to bestow welfare, honor, and wisdom upon American rulers as He once did with the leaders of ancient Israel. As He gave His glory to David and wisdom to Solomon, He should now grant the same to the rulers of the thirteen states, and to Governor George Clinton of New York and his staff. The prayer asks God to make the governor "as the fresh olive tree, and blossom as the lily of the valley, as the rose of Sharon." As God gave strength to Samson, so He should "strengthen and support the saving shield of our Lord and commanding general George Washington . . . In Thine own time Thou wilt subdue the people beneath his feet." The peace to follow the war will emulate Scripture:

> O how goodly, how beautiful might it be wouldst Thou confirm the peace that Thou hast planted on the hearts of kings and rulers that they should beat their swords into plowshares, their spears into pruning hooks, that nation should not lift up sword against nation, nor should they any more learn war [*Isaiah* 2:4]. "And I will give peace in the land, and ye shall lie down and none shall make you afraid" [*Leviticus* 26:6].

America is the paradigm for the redemption of Israel in the Land of Israel:

> As Thou hast granted to these thirteen States of America everlasting freedom, so mayst Thou bring us forth once again from bondage into freedom, and mayst Thou sound the great horn for our freedom [*Isaiah* 27:13] . . . Hasten our deliverance at the day of retribution, for Thou art our redeemer. Then shall we sing a new song to the Lord God of Israel, and there we shall serve Him with reverence as in the former days of old. May He show us wonders as in days of old, and may He the holy one, blessed be He, restore the presence of Zion and the order of service to Jerusalem. And may we be granted to gaze on the beauty of the Lord and to behold His sanctuary. May He send us the priest of righteousness who will lead us upright to our Land. May the beauty of the Lord be upon us, and may the redeemer come speedily to Zion in our days. O that they may be Thy will, and let us say Amen.[8]

God's apparent entry into American history allowed the believer to draw the redemption of Israel nearer from the indefinite future: if America had achieved liberation, so could the people of Israel enjoy it in the future. In contrast to Europe, where Emancipation upset the belief in restoring the Land, in America liberation from England provided new impulse for that belief.[9]

Gershom M. Seixas

Gershom M. Seixas (1746-1816) was another who connected American history, especially the Revolution, with the redemption of Israel. He said that Israel's history was not subsumed into America's; to the contrary, American history was a prelude to Israel's redemption. In November 1789 he declared that God's providence was wonderfully displayed in the course and outcome of "the late War", in its happy consequences for public liberty, and in the new Constitution's benefits to the states. He expressed gratitude to the Supreme Ruler because Jews shared equally in all the benefits. They could not adore God enough for manifesting His care over Israel. Still, Jews were in exile, even in America, and redemption and return to their own Land was their overwhelming hope:

> And we are still at this time in captivity among the different nations of the earth; and though we are, through divine goodness, made equal partakers of the benefits of government by the Constitution of these states with the rest of the inhabitants, still we cannot but view ourselves as captives in comparison to what we were formerly, and what we expect to be hereafter, when the outcasts in the land of Assyria, and the outcasts in the land of Egypt, shall come and worship the Lord in the holy mount of Jerusalem.

Captivity resulted from sin, and Seixas hoped for the repentance which redemption required.[10]

On 9 May 1798, a day of fasting and prayer called by President John Adams to end the economically destructive strife between France and England, Seixas spoke of the imminence of redemption and of the particular role of American Jews in the process. He explained the concept "punishment comes into the world only on Israel's account" (*Yebamot* 63a) to mean that historical trouble had religious significance for Israel. As God said, "I have cut off the nations: their towers are desolate; I made their streets waste . . . I said, Surely thou wilt fear Me, thou wilt receive instruction" (*Zephaniah* 3:6-7). The contemporary troubles meant that the birth pangs of the messianic arrival were underway, that God would soon "restore us to our own Land." Seixas thought of the current wars, of worldwide depravity, and of the corrupted state of human nature all in terms of premessianic suffering, and he believed that the period of redemption when God would carry out His intention to collect the scattered remnant of Israel was near. God would soon establish Israel in her Land as promised—provided the people acted rightly, for "what doth the Lord require of thee, but to do justly, and to love mercy, and to walk humbly with thy God?" (*Micah* 6:8). Seixas expected Zechariah's prophecy would soon be fulfilled: "Thus saith the Lord of hosts; In those days it shall come to pass, that ten men shall take hold out of all languages of the nations, even shall take hold of the skirt of him that is a Jew, saying, We will go with you: for we have heard that God is with you" (*Zechariah* 8:23).

What was the particular role of American Jewry during the passage from suffering to redemption? Seixas believed that American Jewry held a privileged position in the divine scheme of history: "It has pleased God to have established us in this country, where we possess every advantage that other citizens of these states enjoy, and which is as much as we could in reason expect in this captivity." The privileged position entailed responsibility, overcoming sin, repentance, loving one's neighbor as oneself, and peaceful existence within the community of Israel.

The Jews of America were also responsible for their behavior as Americans. Indeed, the recent divine punishment was related to Israel's trespasses within the American community. Conversely, peace in America would help end exile and enable redemption.* There were also international ramifications, for America was a gathering place for people from all lands, and American actions had worldwide significance. Once the special role of American Jewry was fulfilled, with its reverberations for America and the world, redemption could be expected. The people of Israel would be gathered in from among the heathens into their own land.† The Land would be restored and the Temple rebuilt.‡[11]

In December 1805 Seixas expressed his commitment to the reality of God's role in American history, specifically the present government:

> We humbly beseech Thee, O Lord, to look down upon us from thine holy habitation and grant us Thine all-powerful protection . . . Bless and protect the president of the Union, with the administrators of the general government, in their respective departments—the governor and rulers of this State—judges and counselors—and the magistrates of this city. Impart to them an emanation of Thy divine wisdom that they may know to judge distinctly between that which would prove beneficial to the United States and that which might be injurious—let no party schisms in state affairs prevail, so as to destroy the principles of the Constitution, which is for the security of person and property, and sworn to be observed by the administrators of government.
>
> May the Congress assembled, act in unison with each other to promote the welfare of all—and may they be able to deliberate and decide on all laws proposed for the advantage of their constituents. May agriculture flourish, and commerce be prosperous; may the seminaries of education be continued under the direction of able teachers and professors—that the succeeding generations may gain the knowledge of freedom without licentiousness, and the usefulness of power without tyranny.
>
> May the people be convinced of the fidelity of their representatives, and may no cause of jealousy subsist among the different states of the Union—may the blessing of peace attend their councils; and finally may the land [and] earth be filled with knowledge as waters cover the seas.[12]

---

*"They shall beat their swords into plowshares, and their spears into pruning hooks." *Isaiah* 2:4.

†"I will take the children of Israel from among the heathen, whither they be gone, and will gather then on every side, and bring them into their own Land." *Ezekiel* 37:21.

‡"But, The Lord liveth, which brought up and which led the seed of the house of Israel out of the north country, and from all countries whither I had driven them; and they shall dwell in their own Land." *Jeremiah* 23:8.

Seixas interwove the themes of God's presence in American history and of imminent redemption in the Land of Israel in his sermon on private charity delivered in January 1807. He asked God to protect the president, vice-president, senators, congressmen, officers and administrators of the federal government, the governor of New York, and the magistrates of New York City. He asked that God "deal kindly with us and with all Israel, in their day and ours, Judah be saved, and Israel dwell in safety, and may the redeemer come to Zion." Seixas urged his audience to scrutinize its moral behavior and attention to God's law in anticipation of the eschatological events.* Why had Israel been afflicted for nearly 20 centuries, subjected to every imaginable evil, driven from the Land of promise to be expelled from one country after another? Seixas traced all this to sin: "What was it that brought death in the world? Sin. What was the cause of our captivity? Sin. And what continues us in this deplorable state? Sin. Are we not sinners in the sight of God? Ought we not to repent us of our sins? . . . 'For, behold, the day cometh, that shall burn as an oven; and all the proud, yea, and all that do wickedly, shall be stubble'" (*Malachi* 4:1). In the meantime, Jewish welfare in America depended upon pleasing God:

> For although we are, through divine mercy, in favor with the people of these States, we can not boast of what may be hereafter. Much, nay all, depends on ourselves. It has pleased God to have cast our lot in this happy land, and we deserve the blessing of His providential care, we need not be afraid of what men can do to us.

Seixas thought that the Napoleonic Sanhedrin in Paris qualified as the kind of event predicted by the prophets to take place before Israel was restored to her former glory. After a lapse in liberty and self-respect for nineteen centuries, the most powerful potentate in Europe had convened the most learned rabbis of his country. Seixas prayed that the emperor, "under the influence of divine grace, be a means to accomplish our re-establishment. If not as a nation in our former territory, let it only be as a particular society, with equal rights and privileges of all other religious societies." Seixas had no doubt that the prophecies of Scripture about Israel's ultimate future would be fulfilled. Their truth was evidenced by Israel's preservation as a distinct body, and "we should not admit a doubt of the entire fulfillment of every sentence relative to our situation—we must entirely depend on the word of God, who will in His own good time complete what He has promised." The Sanhedrin, in Seixas's mind, signified the imminent fulfillment of God's promise, but Israel's behavior had to be appropriate:

---

*"For lo, I will command, and I will sift the house of Israel among all nations, like as corn is sifted in a sieve, yet shall not the least grain fall upon the earth." *Amos* 9:9.

If we observe His law in all things, He will not abandon or forsake us. But if we obey not His law, and persist in the spirit of disobedience, profaning His holy name, breaking of the Sabbath, polluting the body with things prohibited, and setting His denunciations as defiance, what can we expect? Misery and desolation! Continuance of captivity! And the oppression of man. Now, now is the time to strive, try to be virtuous, be wise and be happy.

Seixas expressed both gratitude for equal citizenship in America and a commitment to restoration and redemption, praising God for the blessings enjoyed in the "land of peace" while noting that those blessings were enjoyed "in a captive state." Despite the equal rights and privileges, "we are but strangers and sojourners, as all our fathers were" (*I Chronicles* 29:15). He admonished his listeners to keep in mind the sacred promise in Scripture about restoration as a nation and redemption before the end of time. He pointed to the signs of the *eschaton*:

Examine the sacred pages, study them with attention, compare them with the present position of things, and judge if they are not applicable. There is not a prophet from Moses to Malachi (with the rest of the inspired writers), but what takes notice of the remarkable events that have attended us, from the commencement of our general captivity even unto the present day. Twice have we been redeemed, according to the sacred history. We have every reason to expect the third time is nearly (and rapidly) approaching, when we shall be established forever, as it is said, "After two days He will revive us: in the third day he will raise us up, and we shall live in his sight" [*Hosea* 6:2].[13]

Observations

After the Puritans introduced the sacred reality of the Holy Land into American history and geography, the Sephardim both brought the process forward and reversed it. They saw the events of American history as new expressions of eternal Hebrew Scripture. The central concern was the American Revolution, which revalidated the ancient truth of divine participation in history and assured that it would continue and reach fulfillment in the messianic future. Paradoxically, the same American landscape which brought salvational history into the present provided assurance that the people of Israel would leave exile (including America) and return to their own Land. Puritans and Sephardim both thought of America in scriptural terms, but for Christians it was the last stage in redemptive history, while for Jews it was the next to last.

Seixas brought these ideas into an apocalyptic framework. He spoke of the American Revolution as the transitional midpoint between biblical past and messianic future and identified it with the sufferings which were to precede the redemption. There was an existential counterpart to the apocalyptic transition. American Jews, provided by God with as much as could be expected in captivity, were responsible for leading America—and through America the world—in eliminating sin. God was closely and specifically involved in the welfare of America and its Jews, while Jews remained obliged to fulfill their role in the ontological change from worsening exile to redemption. Seixas viewed the entire process in scriptural terms.

Notes

1. David de Sola Pool, "Early Relations between Palestine and American Jewry," *The Brandeis Avuka Annual of 1932* (Boston 1932):536-548.

2. See Lou Silberman, *The American Impact: Judaism in the United States in the Early Nineteenth Century* (Syracuse 1964). The Charleston Freemasons eliminated references to the Holy Land from the *Ahavat Olam* prayer. See Moshe Davis, *The House of Israel in America* (Jerusalem 1970, Hebrew):393-94.

3. *Prayers for Shabbat, Rosh Hashana, and Yom Kippur, or the Sabbath, the Beginning of the Year and the Day of Atonement: With the Amida and Musaf of the Mo'adim or solemn seasons. According to the order of the Spanish and Portuguese Jews,* Isaac Pinto, trans. (New York [1766?]).

4. On the *meshullahim*, see Moshe Davis, "A Highway of Nations: A Chapter in Nineteenth-Century American-Erets Israel Activities," in *In the Time of Harvest: Essays in honor of Abba Hillel Silver,* Daniel J. Silver, ed. (New York 1963):136-145. Haim I. Karigal, *A Sermon Preached at the Synagogue in Newport, Rhode Island, called "The Salvation of Israel," On the Day of Pentecost, or Feast of Weeks, the 6th Day of the Month of Sivan, the Year of the Creation 5533; or 28 May 1773: Being the anniversary of giving the law at Mount Sinai* (Newport 1773).

5. Lee M. Friedman, *Jewish Pioneers and Patriots* (Philadelphia 1945):15-30. See Charles A. Beard, *History of American Civilization* (Boston 1937):1:259-260; Raphael Mahler, "American Judaism and the Idea of *Shivat Tsiyon* in the Period of the American Revolution," *Tsiyon* 15 (1950, Hebrew):107-134.

6. "Items Relating to Gershom M. Seixas: Prayer for Peace during the American Revolution," *PAJHS* 27, *Lyons Collection* (1920):2:126-127. Compare the prayer "God, guard my tongue from evil," following the Eighteen Benedictions.

7. Morris Jastrow, "Chapters from the Diary of Ezra Stiles," *PAJHS* 10 (1902):30; Mahler, "American Judaism."

8. "Items Relating to Congregation Shearit Israel," *Lyons Collection,* (1920):2:35-37.

10. Gershom M. Seixas, *A Religious Discourse Delivered in the Synagogue in This City, on Thursday the 26th of November, 1789. Agreeable to the proclamation of the President of the United States of America to be observed as a day of public thanksgiving and prayer* (New York 1977).

11. Seixas, *A Discourse, Delivered in the Synagogue in New York, on the Ninth of May, 1798, Observed as a Day of Humiliation, etc., etc., Conformably to a recommendation of the President of the United States of America,* summarized in Mahler, "American Judaism."

12. Seixas, "Discourse Delivered in the Synagogue by G. Seixas on Thursday the 18th of Tevet 5565 and 20 December 1805. By appointment of the direction of the fund appropriated to private charities. Being the same day recommended by the corporation of the City of New York at the instance of the reverend clergy, to be observed a day of public thanksgiving and prayer," American Jewish Historical Society, Waltham, Mass.

13. Seixas, "A Charity Sermon Preached in the Synagogue in New York by G. Seixas. In compliance with the request of the trustees, for the benefit of the institution of the funds of the Tsedaka Mattan Ba'seter (the fund appropriated to private charity) on Sunday the 2nd of Shevat 5567 and the 11th of January 1807," American Jewish Historical Society. Excerpts are printed in Seixas, "A Charity Sermon," *Lyons Collection,* (1920):2:140-143. On the Napoleonic Sanhedrin, see Richard H. Popkin, "Mordecai Noah, the Abbé Grégoire, and the Paris Sanhedrin," *Modern Judaism* 2 no. 2 (May 1982):133-148.

3 American Indians: Ten Lost Tribes and Christian Eschatology

American Indians have long been identified as descendants of the Ten Lost Tribes of Israel. The tribes of the northern kingdom of Israel were exiled when the kingdom fell in 722 B.C.E., leaving those of Judah and Benjamin in the Holy Land; they went eastward and then disappeared.* The notion that their descendants ended up in America was considered systematically as early as 1569 in Venice and achieved prominence with the work of Menasseh ben Israel in Amsterdam and English Puritan clergymen John Dury and Thomas Thorowgood (1650-1660).[1] In America the belief was enunciated by Christians, Jews, and Mormons, beginning with Roger Williams in 1635 and continuing still in the Mormon church. It reflected the sentiment that America had characteristics of the Holy Land, connected the original Americans genealogically to the ancient people of Israel, and drew America into Holy Land eschatology.

Original Christian Views

On 20 December 1635 the Puritan Roger Williams, who had arrived in America four years earlier, wrote Thorowgood that he thought the Indians were Jewish:

Three things make me yet suspect that the poor natives came from the southward and are Jews or Jewish to an extent, and not from the northern barbarous [lands] as some imagine: [1] Themselves constantly affirm that their ancestors came from the southwest, and thither they all go dying. [2] They constantly and strictly separate their women in a little wigwam by

---

*"In the ninth year of Hoshea, the king of Assyria took Samaria and carried Israel away into Assyria, and placed them in Halah and in Habor by the river Gozan, and in the city of the Medes." *II Kings* 17:6.

themselves in their feminine seasons. [3] And beside their god "Kuttand" to the southwest, they hold that Nanuwitnawit (a god overhead) made the heavens and the earth. [I have also found] some taste of affinity with the Hebrew.[2]

Cambridge University graduate John Eliot (1604-1690), who also arrived in 1631, translated the Bible into Algonquian in 1661 to teach "the posterity of the dispersed and rejected Israelites, concerning whom our God has promised, that they shall yet be saved by the deliverer coming to turn ungodliness from them."[3] In 1649, this "apostle" to the American Indians detailed the lineage of the Ten Lost Tribes, from Shem through Ever (*Genesis* 10:24) and Abraham, and asserted that the Ten Lost Tribes were the Hebrew (*Ivri*) people who had gone to the "lands beyond (*me'ever*) the rivers" and ended up in America.* They were to go to the "farthest east," which meant America. Eliot believed that this "multitude of nations" would be dispersed into America until the culmination of history, the *eschaton*, when they would be gathered back to their Land:† God "will gather the scattered and lost dust of our bodies at the resurrection, can and will find out these lost and scattered Israelites, and in finding them, bring in with them the nations among whom they were scattered, and so shall Jacob's promise extend to a multitude of nations indeed."[4]

In 1660 Eliot explained that when the descendants of Ever brought religion into the "eastern world," their "national" identity excluded those outside Abraham's line. But Christ initiated a universal policy whereby at the *eschaton* God's glory would be manifested throughout the world. On account of their sins which remained unspecified, the Ten Tribes were "scattered to the utmost ends of the eastern world"—and that meant "assuredly into America, because that is part of the eastern world and peopled by eastern inhabitants." The process of manifesting God's glory would begin in the east as well; in Ezekiel's vision of the Temple the eastern gate was measured first (40:6), God's glory entered the Temple at the eastern gate (43:1-3), the precious waters of the sanctuary issued eastward, and the forefront of the Temple faced the east (47:1). Eliot anticipated "a glorious church in all the eastern world. And God grant that the old bottles of the western world be not so incapable of the new wine of Christ, His expected kingdom, that the eastern bottles be not the only [vessels] thereof for a season." The Ten Tribes suffered less in their dispersion than Judah and Benjamin because

---

*"Woe to the land shadowing with wings, which is beyond the rivers of Ethiopia: That sendeth ambassadors by the sea, even in vessels of bulrushes upon the waters, saying, Go, ye swift messengers, to a nation scattered and peeled, to a people terrible from their beginning hitherto; a nation meted out and trodden down, whose land the rivers have spoiled!" *Isaiah* 18:1-2.

†"And God said unto him, I am God Almighty: be fruitful and multiply; a nation and a multitude of nations shall be of thee, and kings shall come out of thy loins." *Genesis* 35:11.

they were innocent of the sin of crucifixion.* For example, when the Ten Tribes arrived in America, other descendants of Shem and Ever were already there to receive them, and the Ten Tribes could understand the spoken language. Eliot thought "the grammatical frame of our Indian language nearer to the Hebrew than the Latin or Greek." The people of Judah and Benjamin, dispersed after 70 C.E. to the "uttermost ends of the western world," went among strange people with strange languages—presumably in Europe.

Further, since the Ten Tribes were the first to be sent, they would be the first to receive God's grace and return to the Land to join Christ's kingdom.† In the final days Christ would find Israel both in the east and west and bring her into His kingdom; He Who could resurrect dead bodies, Eliot reasoned, could find those who were lost. Through Christ, God's free grace would return the Ten Tribes—the Indians—from dispersion, restore them and bring them into the Christian kingdom.[5]

In 1683 the Quaker William Penn (1644-1718) offered his reasons for concluding that the Indians were the Ten Lost Tribes:

> I am ready to believe them of the Jewish race, I mean of the stock of the Ten Tribes, and that for the following reasons: First, they were to go to a "land not planted or known," which to be sure Asia and Africa were, if not Europe; and He that intended that extraordinary judgment upon them, might make the passage not uneasy to them, as it is not impossible in itself from the easternmost of America.‡ In the next place, I find them of like countenance, and their children of so lively resemblance, that a man would think himself in Dukes Place or Berry Street in London, when he sees them. But this is not all. They agree in rites, they reckon by moons, they offer their first fruits, they have a kind of feast of tabernacles, they are said to lay their altar upon twelve stones, their mourning [lasts] a year. Customs of women, many things that do not now occur [are agreed].[6]

---

*"And the Lord shall scatter thee among all people, from the end of the earth even unto the other." *Deuteronomy* 28:64. "And thine elder sister is Samaria, she and her daughters that dwell at thy left hand: and thy younger sister, that dwelleth at thy right hand, is Sodom and her daughters." *Ezekiel* 16:46.

†"When thy sisters, Sodom and her daughters, shall return to their former estate . . . then thou and thy daughters shall return to your former estate." *Ezekiel* 16:55. "Say unto them, Thus saith the Lord God; Behold, I will take the stick of Joseph, which is in the hand of Ephraim, and the tribes of Israel his fellows, and will put them with him, even with the stick of Judah, and make them one stick, and they shall be one in Mine hand." *Ezekiel* 37:19.

‡For a possible example, see *II Esdras* 13, infra, or *Jeremiah* 2:2: "I remember thee, the kindness of thy youth, the love of thine espousals, when thou wentest after Me in the wilderness, in a land that was not sown."

In 1758 missionary Jonathan Edwards (1745-1801) considered linguistic similarities between Mohegan and Hebrew:

> Besides what has been observed concerning prefixes and suffixes, there is a remarkable analogy between some words in the Mohegan language, and the correspondent words in the Hebrew . . . How far the use of prefixes and suffixes, together with these instances of analogy, and perhaps other instances which may be traced out by those who have more leisure, go toward proving that the north American Indians are of Hebrew, or at least of Asiatic extraction, is submitted to the judgment of the learned. The facts are demonstrable; concerning the proper inferences, everyone will judge for himself.[7]

The Irish trader James Adair (1709-1783), who lived among the Indians, primarily Cherokee and Chickasaw, from 1735 to 1768, was "forced to believe them lineally descended from the Israelites, either while they were a power or soon after the general captivity; the latter, however, is the most probable." Adair offered detailed reasons for his belief:

1. Indian society was structured according to tribal divisions defined by linear descent. Each tribe had its special symbol which, like the biblical cherubim, was an animal.*
2. The Indians regarded their deity as the direct head of state.
3. The Indians regarded themselves as unique and chosen from among the rest of mankind. They were the beloved and holy people, while whites were contemptible and accursed people. God was ever present to them and offered direction through prophets, while the whites were alienated, outlaws to the Indian covenant with god. The conviction of chosenness "alike animates both the white Jew and the red American with that steady hatred against all the world except themselves."
4. Indians divided the year into spring, summer, autumn and winter, and they began the year with the first new moon of the vernal equinox. Like the Israelites before 70 C.E., the Indians designated months with numbers. The Israelites called the seventh month *Aviv*, which also meant unripened corn; and the Indians had a Passover-like celebration known as the "green corn dance."†

---

*"And every one had four faces: the first face was the face of a cherub, and the second face was the face of a man, and the third the face of a lion, and the fourth the face of an eagle. And the cherubims were lifted up." *Ezekiel* 10:14-15.

†See, for example, *Deuteronomy* 16:1: "Observe the month of Abib, and keep the Passover unto the Lord thy God: for in the month of Abib the Lord thy God brought thee forth out of Egypt by night."

5. The Indians had prophets, priests, and a sanctum sanctorum housing consecrated vessels which the laity could not approach. The priestly order, called *Ishtoallo* (a corruption of *Ish Ha'elohim*, *II Kings* 4:16ff.), possessed a divine spirit enabling its members to foretell the future and control the course of nature. The spirit was transmitted to their children, who kept sacred laws. When the high priest made a holy fire for the yearly atonement ceremony, he wore a white ephod and breastplate of white conch shell with two bored holes for attaching buckhorn buttons fastened to straps of skin.*

6. The Indian god was a great supreme holy spirit, the "Great Yohewah" who dwelt above the clouds but also with the good people. No tribe attempted to form an image of this god. The Indians had a mysterious name for the Great Spirit which, like the tetragrammaton, was not to be employed in common speech. When they used it to invoke god in a solemn hymn, they spent a full breath on each of the two first syllables of the awesome divine name.

7. According to Indian tradition, their forefathers came from a distant country in remote ages and moved eastward until they settled east of the Mississippi. How did they cross the water between the continents? According to Plato's *Timaeus*, Atlantis was originally torn asunder from the eastern continent. Atlantis was America, and the crossing was made over islands in the narrow strait between northeast Asia and northwest America.

8. The surviving brother of a man who died childless was to marry the widow and raise seed for his brother. A widow was bound to mourn the death of her husband for at least three years, unless the brother of the deceased husband wished to take her. In that case she was released from the law as soon as the brother made love to her.

9. The Indians had a sacred ark of the covenant, which they never placed directly on the ground but rather on stones or logs. They carried it when they went into battle. Only the chieftain could handle it, and it was deemed dangerous even for sanctified warriors to touch it.

10. The Indians obliged women in the "lunar retreats" to separate themselves, and remain at a distance at the risk of their lives. "It conveys a most horrid and dangerous pollution to those who touch, or go near them, or walk anywhere within the circle of their retreats; and are in fear of thereby spoiling the supposed purity and power of their holy ark."[8]

---

*"And they shall make the ephod of gold, of blue, and of purple, of scarlet, and fine twined linen, with cunning work." *Exodus* 28:6. "And thou shalt make upon the breastplate chains at the ends of wreathen work of pure gold. And thou shalt make upon the breastplate two rings of gold." *Exodus* 28:22-23.

In 1768 minister Charles Beatty (1715-1772) concluded, after a two-month tour "westward of the Allegheny Mountains," that several customs among many of the Indians so much resembled those of the Jews "that it is a great question with me, whether we can expect to find among the Ten Tribes (wherever they are) at this day, all things considered, more of the footsteps of their ancestors, than among the different Indian tribes":

1. At the "first appearance of the catamenia" a young woman was separated from others, and placed in an isolated hut some distance from town for the seven days of her "disorder." The person who brought her food was not to touch her, and she herself used sticks and ladles so as not to touch her food. At the end of the period she bathed in water, washed her clothes, and cleaned the vessels used "during her menses."
2. The feast of firstfruits was observed. Venison and corn baked into cakes were divided into portions for twelve old men. The celebrants raised the venison and corn and prayed with their faces to the east to acknowledge the goodness and bounty of heaven and elicit a blessing from god for the firstfruits.
3. An evening festival resembled the Passover. A great portion of venison was prepared and distributed. The remainder was thrown into the fire and burned so that none remained by sunrise. No bone of the venison could be broken.
4. Once a year twelve men gathered, constructed a tent, and placed hot stones inside. They burned the fat of deer-innards or tobacco on an altar made of the stones and prayed and cried out, making a sound similar to "Hallelujah."
5. Upon extraordinary occasions, sickness, or death, they consulted "Pow-waas," just as the ancient Jews' consulted prophets.
6. Some Indians did not eat the hollow of the thigh of the deer.
7. The Indians had a high sense of liberty, many preferring death to captivity or slavery. In war they were exceptionally courageous; they proved their bravery by bringing the scalps and prisoners of their enemies home: "Were not the Jews of old remarkable for their courage and high sense of liberty? And was it not customary, in the days of Saul and David, to bring home testimonies of the number they had slain in battle?"
8. A "Christian Indian" who had died 40 years earlier said "that circumcision was practiced long ago . . . but that their young men, at length, making a mock of it, brought it into disrepute, and so it came to be disused."
9. There was a tradition that water once overflowed all the land. All but a few, who made a great canoe and survived, drowned.
10. According to another tradition, a long time ago the people tried to build "a high place to reach up a great way." While they were building it they

lost their language and could not understand one another. From that time on the Indians began to speak different languages.

11. An Indian asked an English trader whether he had a book, meaning the Bible, with him. When told that he had, the Indian explained that long ago the same book was theirs; that as long as they kept it and acted according to it, their god was kind to them and they prospered. The white people bought it from the Indians, learned much from it and they prospered. From that point onward, the Indians began to decline or other nations persecuted them. God was angry because they parted with the book and he left them, but finally he took pity and "brought or directed them to this country America." When they reached a great body of water, "God made a bridge over the water in one night, by which they passed over safe; and that next morning, after they were over, god took away the bridge."

12. At death, good Indians went after one or two days to a pleasant place. Those who did bad things went to a disagreeable place where they had nothing to eat or drink and did not sleep.[9]

Derivative Christian Views

Like Eliot, Charles Crawford (1752-1815) had theological interests in the similarities between Jews and Indians. Ultimately, he hoped his fellow Americans would "tame" and "incorporate" the Indians and "mate" them—along with Negros and Jews—to Christianity. As to the Jews themselves, that "afflicted but once-glorious nation," Christ Himself asked that they be forgiven, so they were not to be reproached.[*10]

In 1799 Crawford said the globe split during the days of Peleg, and Noah's descendants through Ever ended up in a land divided from Asia, which included America.[†11] Subsequently, the Ten Tribes captured by Assyrian King Shalmeneser (*II Kings* 17:2) left "the multitude of nations to go to a more distant region."[‡] This meant over the Afghan and Tartar territory of Ararat, through

---

*"Father, forgive them; for they know not what they do." *Luke 23:34.*

†"And unto Eber were born two sons: the name of one was Peleg; for in his days was the earth divided; and his brother's name was Joktan." *Genesis* 10:25.

‡"And as for your seeing him gather to himself another multitude that was peaceable, these are the ten tribes which were led away from their own Land into captivity in the days of King Hoshea, whom Shalmeneser the king of the Assyrians, made captives; he took them across the river, and they were taken into another land. But they formed this plan for themselves, that they would leave the multitude of the nations and to a more distant region, where no human beings had ever lived, so that there at least they might keep their statutes which they had not kept in their own land. And they went in by the narrow passages of the Euphrates river. For at that time the Most High performed signs for them, and stopped the channels of the river until they had crossed over. Through that region there was a long way to go, a journey of a year and a half; and that country is

Asia and over the Bering Straits to America.[12] The descendants of Judah and Benjamin would end up in Europe.

Crawford added new similarities between ancient Israelites and Indians. He thought that the practice of scalping might have originated with the former because they were instruments of God's vengeance and as such capable of such acts.* He also said that "a person of information, whose appointments led him to be frequently in the country of the Indians," told him that some Indians had the custom, "in imitation of the Jews, to carry the amputated part [of the enemy's body] in triumph."† Crawford wanted Jews and Indians to become aware of their tie. Some Jews already were:

> There was a learned Jew, the son of a Jewish rabbi or a rabbi himself, who was converted to Christianity and who preached with some applause in various parts of Great Britain sometime before the year 1787.[13] About this time he came over to Philadelphia, where the religious people were considerably struck with the decency of his behavior. He said that many of the Indians in America were the descendants of the Ten Tribes. He said his design was to go and live among them (he went first among the Chickasaws, I believe) to learn their language, that he might teach them the gospel and proceed with them in person to Jerusalem . . . He died a natural death, it is supposed, some little time after being among the Indians.

Crawford hoped there would be a missionary who spoke the Indian language to "excite their curiosity and admiration" about their legacy. He would tell them that they were descended from the Almighty's favorite nation, "the greatest people on earth," that their forefathers were delivered from Pharaoh's tyranny, and that the Great Spirit" descended upon Mount Sinai to give the Ten Commandments, which He wrote with His own finger. The missionary would share Paul's views that the faith of the people of Israel had determined their history.‡ He would speak of the prophecies about the great Savior of the world, the promised messiah of the Jews, and of their exact fulfillment. Once the Indians became aware of all this, they would receive the Christian message and convert.[14] For

---

called Arzareth. Then they dwelt there until the last times; and now, when they are about to come again, the Most High will stop the channels of the river again, so that they may be able to pass over. Therefore you saw the multitude gathered together in peace." *II Esdras* 13:39-47.

*"But God shall wound the head of his enemies, and the hairy scalp of such an one as goeth on still in his trespasses." *Psalms* 68:21.

†"Wherefore David arose and went, he and his men, and slew of the Philistines two hundred men; and David brought their foreskins, and they gave them in full tale to the king, that he might be the king's son-in-law." *I Samuel* 18:27.

‡"By faith they passed through the Red Sea as by dry land: which the Egyptians assaying to do were drowned. By faith the walls of Jericho fell down, after they were compassed about seven days." *Hebrews* 11:29-30.

their part, once Americans became aware of the origins of the tribes, they would "treat the Indians with as much lenity and forbearance as possible."

Crawford anticipated both Jews and Indians converting "before a very great length of time" and that around 1900 the converted Jews and Indians would be gathered from the dispersion and restored to the Land of Israel:

> It is probable, when the time arrives foretold by the prophets, that the Jews will be gathered from their dispersion among all nations. Many of the Indians will pass over in tribes, at Bering's or Cook's Straits, into Asia. It is said of the Almighty by the prophet, "For lo, I will command, and I will sift the House of Israel, like as corn is sifted in a sieve, yet shall not the least grain fall upon the earth" [*Amos* 9:9]. And Isaiah says, "I will bring thy seed from the East, and gather thee from the West. I will say to the north, give up; and to the south, keep not back. Bring My sons from far, and My daughters from the ends of the earth" [*Isaiah* 43:5-6].

Once the Indians left America, the remaining Christians would inherit the vacated lands:

> We reason "from the sure word of prophecy" [*II Peter* 1:19], according to the expression of the apostle, when we say that all the descendants of the House of Israel, among which are many Indians, will be restored to the Land of their forefathers. The time is not far distant when this restoration will be affected. Many of the Indians will then relinquish their land to the white people. Upon the restoration of the Jews, it is said that the Land of their forefathers will be too small to contain them, and they will wish its borders to be enlarged. "For thy waste and thy desolate places and the land of thy destruction, shall even now be too narrow by reason of the inhabitants" (*Isaiah* 49:19).[15]

In 1803 Crawford wrote that the contemporary condition of the Jews provided living evidence for the truth of Scripture. They were "scatter[ed] among all people, from one end of the earth to the other" (*Deuteronomy* 28:64). They have become "a curse and an astonishment, a hissing and a reproach" (*Jeremiah* 29:16-18) the world over, while "Jerusalem is trodden down of the gentiles" (*Luke* 21:24). The Romans indeed "besieged Jerusalem in all her gates" (*Deuteronomy* 28:49). The Jewish condition verified Christian revelation:

> It is not possible with the least appearance of reason to ascribe the prophecy of the dispersion of the Jews, or any of these prophetic descriptions, to chance. Such an extraordinary, such a singular event, as the dispersion of a nation without their extinction, had never happened before the prophecy that the Jews would be dispersed, yet not extinguished. Moses and the other prophets . . . could only have altered these prophecies through the particular

inspiration of Him who foresees all events. If these prophecies therefore have been uttered through the inspiration of God, it is part of reason to believe that those who uttered them came from God, that their writings are holy, and in short, it will naturally follow from hence that Christianity is a true and certain revelation.[16]

The French Huguenot Elias Boudinot (1740-1821), president of the Continental Congress, founding president of the American Bible Society, and a member of the ABCFM, also subscribed to the view that the Ten Tribes' descendants were in America.[17] He believed they would participate in the initial stages of establishing the Christian messianic kingdom, which was imminent.

Boudinot explained that Judah and Benjamin ended up in Europe (the "East") and the Ten Tribes in America (the "West"). The Ten Tribes would end up in a country northwest of Judea, indeed at the ends of the earth.[*] It would be a country where the sun went down; a land without inhabitants, free of heathens, and beyond the seas from Palestine.[†] Upon the culmination of history, the Israelites would gather in from east and west. Boudinot felt that Judah and Benjamin suffered more than their brethren. After returning from Babylon "they perversely put [the Messiah] to death on the cross, and voluntarily imprecated that His blood might rest on them and their children." As their subsequent history of dispersion and misery verified, their request was fulfilled. The Ten Tribes, however, had no hand in that "impious transaction" and so were exempted from the misery. Thus, soon after the crucifixion the Romans drove Judah and Benjamin as slaves and criminals into Assyria, Egypt, and Persia while the Ten Tribes were banished to the frontiers of Persia and Media and lost. But they carried God's promise of return.[‡] At the fulfillment of history Israelites would gather from the east and the west.[#]

---

[*]"In those days the House of Judah shall walk with the House of Israel, and they shall come together out of the land of the north to the land that I have given for an inheritance unto your fathers." *Jeremiah* 3:18. *Isaiah* 43:5-6, supra. "Behold, these shall come from far: and lo, these from the north and from the West; and these from the land of Sinim." *Isaiah* 49:12.

[†]"And it shall come to pass in that day, saith the Lord God, that I will cause the sun to go down at noon, and I will darken the earth in the clear day." *Amos* 8:9. See *II Esdras* 13:41, supra. "Surely the isles shall wait for me, and the ships of Tarshish first, to bring thy sons from far, their silver and their gold with them, unto the name of the Lord thy God, and to the Holy One of Israel, because He hath glorified thee." *Isaiah* 60:9.

[‡]"Turn, O backsliding children, saith the Lord; For I am married unto you: and I will take you one of a city, and two of a family, and I will bring you to Zion." *Jeremiah* 3:14.

[#]"Thus saith the Lord of hosts; Behold, I will save my people from the east country, and from the west country." *Zechariah* 8:7.

Insofar as America was the scene for the onset of the eschatological drama of return, she shared in the sacred history of salvation: "Who knows, but God has raised up these United States in these latter days for the very purpose of accomplishing His will in bringing His beloved people to their own Land?" The natives of America became part of the history of salvation, "subjects of God's protection and gracious care." It was a matter of "utmost consequence" in these "latter times" to identify the Lost Tribes, presumably because awareness would help precipitate the series of eschatological events. Boudinot did not think that the Indians themselves were capable of discovering their past: "The Indians have so degenerated, that they cannot at this time give any tolerable account of the origin of their religious rites, ceremonies and histories."

Boudinot was confident about the Christian identity with the *eschaton*. The Jewish plight demonstrated the validity of divine threats about the consequences of sin and about Israel's blindness until the end of time. Nevertheless, the persecution of the Jews was a matter of the degeneracy of natural man, and since it was not for God's glory the persecutors would be punished. At the end of history the "veil" would be removed from their eyes and Jews would convert.* As to the Indians, when those "children of God's watchful providence shall be manifestly discovered," they will be converted to Christianity and assisted in returning to Jerusalem and their own Land.[18]

In 1823 Ethan Smith (1762-1849), a pastor in Hopkinton, New Hampshire and Poultney, Vermont, spoke of American natives as scattered remnants of Scripture.[19] The indications of the Hebrew origins of Indians "seem almost like finding, in the various regions of the wilds of America, various scraps of an ancient Hebrew Old Testament; one in one wild; another in another; inscribed in some durable substance in evident Hebrew language and character, though much defaced by the lapse of ages." Smith had his own list of similarities, drawn from earlier writers:

1. One supreme god: Mohegan Indian preacher Samson Occom related that Long Island (Montauk) Indians believed in one great and good god above all other gods, and that the Great Spirit made a covenant with their fathers. They said that the white Americans who injured them were outside the covenant and worthy of extermination.

2. Reverence for one particular tribe: In this respect the Mohawks resembled the tribe of Levi.† New England Indians fled from the Mohawks rather than fight them; Mohawk advice was much sought after, and neighboring nations paid them annual tributes. *Mohawk* came from

---

*See, for example, *Isaiah* 35:5: "Then the eyes of the blind shall be opened, and the ears of the deaf shall be unstopped."

†See, for example, *Deuteronomy* 10:8: "At that time the Lord separated the tribe of Levi, to bear the ark of the covenant of the Lord, to stand before the Lord to minister unto Him, and to bless in His name, unto this day."

Mhhokek (i.e., *Mehokek*), signifying an interpreter of the law with superior status.

3. Drunkenness:* According to Samuel Williams:

     No sooner had the Indians tasted of the spirituous liquors brought by the Europeans, than they contracted a new appetite, which they were wholly unable to govern. [The Europeans found it the most lucrative branch of the Indian trade, to gratify this inclination. With an avidity of desire altogether uncontrolled, the Indians fell in the snare. The first object of inquiry with them was whether the trader had brought any brandy or rum; and no considerations would restrain them in the use of it.] The old and the young, the sachem, the warrior, and the women, wherever they can obtain liquors, indulge themselves without moderation and without decency, till universal drunkenness takes place. All the tribes seem to be under the dominion of this appetite, and unable to govern it.[20]

4. Refuge cities: According to William Bartram, Apalachucla, the mother town of the Creek Confederacy, was sacred to peace. No captives were put to death and no human blood was spilled there.[21]

5. Vengeance: It was a "well-known trait of Indian character" to pursue anyone who killed a friend, no matter the distance or time required to avenge the blood which was shed.†

6. Crossing a great body of water (*II Esdras* 13:40): According to Alexander Mackenzie, the Chipewyans of the northwest believed they had wicked ancestors who left their homeland, passed through a great lake over a shallow stretch of islands, and suffered from the ice and snow.

7. Deluge: According to Beatty and Mackenzie, the Chipewyans believe that their ancestors survived a great deluge by perching atop mountains.[22]

8. Passover: Jedidiah Morse reported about a feast to the Great Spirit. After each participant ate his portion of food, the bones were collected in a separate bowl and burned. Anyone who did not finish the portion passed it to the neighbor with a piece of tobacco. Those who prepared the feast gave their entire portions to the Great Spirit.‡

---

*"Woe to the crown of pride, to the drunkards of Ephraim, shall be trodden under feet . . . For all tables are full of vomit and filthiness, so that there is no place clean." *Isaiah* 28:1, 8.

†See, for example, *Deuteronomy* 32:42: "I will make Mine arrows drunk with blood, and My sword shall devour flesh; and that with the blood of the slain and the captives, from the beginning of revenges upon the enemy."

‡"And they shall eat the flesh in that night, roast with fire, and unleavened bread; and with bitter herbs they shall eat it. Eat not of it raw, nor sodden at all with water, but roast with fire; his head with his legs, and with the purtenance thereof. And ye shall not let nothing of it remain until morning; and that which remaineth of it until the morning

9. Separation of females: Morse reported that during menstrual periods women lived in specially built lodges without furniture or flint to make fires, and men could not approach.*

10. The creation of man: Morse reported a Sioux belief that the Great Spirit created two men from the dust of the earth and took a rib from each and made two women. Their descendants constituted one nation. At some point they misbehaved, and the Great Spirit talked in different languages to them and separated them into different nations.²³

11. Tribal division: Each tribe was symbolized by an animal, such as a wolf, tiger, panther, buffalo, bear, deer, raccoon, or eagle.†

Smith believed that the physical land of the Indians would participate in the Christian eschatological drama. As the Judean wilderness rejoiced and blossomed when John the Baptist ministered there, so the solitary wilderness of the "vast continent containing the Lost Tribes of the House of Israel will, on a most enlarged scale, rejoice and blossom as the rose, when the long Lost Tribes shall be found there and shall be gathered to Zion."‡ As to the native Americans, Smith followed in the tradition of his predecessors. The Ten Tribes, he explained, had been largely civilized when they first arrived in America, but savagery eventually prevailed: "As a holy, vindictive providence would have it, and according to ancient denunciation, all were left in an outcast, savage state."# Christian "heralds of salvation" could draw them into the final events. Toward that end, Christians should teach the savages about their history, from Abraham through America. They should explain the early blessings, ejection from the Land and promise of return. The Indians should be told that "the time" was drawing near, and "they must now return to the God of their salvation". The "Great Spirit above the clouds" was now about to call them "to come and receive his grace by Christ, the true star from Jacob, the Shiloh Who has come, to Whom the people must be gathered."** For Smith, the *eschaton* was imminent. It

---

ye shall burn with fire." *Exodus* 12:8-10.

*See *Leviticus* 18:19: "Also thou shalt not approach unto a woman to uncover her nakedness, as long as she is put apart for her uncleanness."

†"Dan shall be a serpent by the way, an adder in the path, that biteth the horse heels so that his rider shall fall backward." *Genesis* 49:17. "Benjamin shall ravin as a wolf: in the morning he shall devour the prey, at night he shall divide the spoil." *Genesis* 49:27.

‡"The wilderness and the solitary place shall be glad for them; and the desert shall rejoice, and blossom as the rose. It shall blossom abundantly, and rejoice even with joy and singing." *Isaiah* 35:1-2.

#"And He shall set up an ensign for the nations, and shall assemble the outcasts of Israel, and gather together the dispersed of Judah from the four corners of the earth." *Isaiah* 11:12.

**Genesis 49:10, supra.

involved the final destruction of Antichrist in the "last days." The event was prefigured by Jerusalem's destruction 40 years after Christ's ascension, fulfilling His wrathful denunciations of His persecutors. Without specifying them, Smith thought that the "signs of the times" had been in place for some 30 years and soon would issue in "the battle of that great day of God almighty and in the millennial kingdom of Christ."[24]

In 1811 Smith spoke of the anticipated return of the Jews and Ten Tribes in the "latter day" as described in *Zechariah* 9. Their return from Babylon partially fulfilled the prophecy, but God had yet to "fill His bow with Ephraim." "Ere long" the blood of the covenant with Abraham would be fulfilled, and the return would be completed. The Jews were "prisoners in a dry pit" but also "prisoners of hope." God had promised to recover them and would fulfill His promise. Entry into the Land was bound together with accepting Christ; the "seventh vial" of the apocalyptic drama would not be poured out until the Jews both returned and converted.*[25] In 1823 Smith wrote that

> The Jews became carnal; crucified the Lord of glory; and they fell under the denunciations, and the full execution of His wrath. Their lawgiver Moses and their prophets had long thundered against them, that when they should become of the character finally assumed, the most tremendous judgments of God will cut them off. And the Messiah uttered against them, in consequence of their rejecting Him, a new edition of these fatal denunciations.†

But still Isaiah's prophetic eye "evidently rested with signal pleasure on a literal restoration of his long-lost brethren."[26] Indeed, Smith spoke in 1833 of Jews becoming missionaries: "The converted Jews, taking pre-eminent stand in the church of Christ, might be expected to burn with a holy zeal, to promote that cause of their Messiah, Whom they have so long trampled under foot."[27]

In 1823 Barbara A. Simon of New York dedicated her *Evangelical Review of Modern Genius; or, Truth and Error* to the Board of the American Society for Meliorating the Condition of the Jews (founded in 1816 as the American Society for Evangelizing the Jews). She called upon "those who owe their salvation to the heaven-appointed mediator, [to] arise and shine in that light, which is reason's glory to derive from revealed truth." She attributed the destruction of Jerusalem and the exile of Jerusalem's "family" to "unbelief in the divine character of the 'word made flesh'" (*John* 1:14). For eighteen centuries this unbelief made Israel

---

*"And the seventh angel poured out his vial into the air." *Revelation* 16:17.

†See, for example, *Luke* 19:43-44: "For the days shall come upon thee, [Jerusalem] that thine enemies shall cast a trench about thee, and compass thee round, and keep thee in on every side. And shall lay thee even with the ground, and thy children within thee; and they shall not leave in thee one stone upon another; because thou knewest not the time of thy visitation."

into "a monument bearing to every nation under heaven an unwilling testimony to the truth of the *divinity* of their rejected Messiah."

Still, as a nation beloved of God, once the people of Israel looked upon the one they pierced and mourned they were destined to be "reunited to their own olive."* Simon expressed the theme poetically:

O! *Why so long* trodden in dust-like disgrace,
Those *else* who had shone like the stars of their race?
What makes them unsham'd—in each land of their shame,
Grown gray without wisdom—dishonor their name?

Ah! *Unbelief* ruin'd, and drown'd thee in woes—
This scattered thy children—*this* gather'd thy foes—
Nor shall thou arise, or thy tribes be restor'd,
Till *this* which hath pierced Him, is *faith in the Lord.*[†28]

In 1825 she dedicated *A View of the Human Heart* to the chiefs of native Indian tribes, from one "affectionately desirous of seeing your tribes *united in love to the Redeemer*":

Chiefs of the forest! whose sun-setting glory
To morning awaketh the orient earth,
Tribes of a secret, but heaven-whispered story!
Lords of the land which gave freedom her birth:

To you would a stranger this tribute of feeling
Inscribe—for its spirit no fetters confine.
Great Spirit! the truth of thy record revealing.
Arise on the tribes who are destined to shine!

Long have you wandered as outcasts forsaken—
Been driven by the lawless to ocean's wild shore;
But now shall your spring-time of promise awaken,
As vines yield their blossoms when winter is o'er.

---

*"And I will pour upon the house of David, and upon the inhabitants of Jerusalem, the spirit of grace and of supplications: and they shall look upon me whom they have pierced, and they shall mourn for him, as one mourneth for his only son, and shall be in bitterness for him, as one that is in bitterness for his firstborn." *Zechariah* 12:10. See, for example, *Romans* 11:24: "For if thou wert cut out of the olive tree which is wild by nature, and wert grafted contrary to nature into a good olive tree: how much more shall these, which be the natural branches, be graffed into their own olive tree?"

†*Zechariah* 12:10, supra.

Your free-born spirits, unquell'd by oppression
Have tower'd o'er the wrongs that would smother their flame—
Untutor'd by art—unsubdu'd by depression,
Have nobly defended your dear native claim.

Illumin'd by truth, that pure light of the holy!
How bright its reflection shall lighten from you.
O say not salvation to you hath mov'd slowly—
"The last" it o'ertakes *"shall be first"* to pursue.*[29]

Simon identified American Indians as the descendants of the Ten Tribes in *The Hope of Israel* (1829), whose title page speaks of Israel's sin and punishment, and in *The Ten Tribes of Israel* (1836), whose title page describes the gathering of lonely and scattered Israel.† In both she reiterated the observations of Adair, Beatty, Bartram, and Boudinot and offered some qualifications. For example, Bartram said that the "busk or feast of first fruits" was the principal festival and began the new year; but it was the great feast on the day of expiation and harvest, not the spring firstfruits feast.[30]

In 1830 Calvin G. Colton (1789-1857) reported on Indians of the northwest Territory. He contended that the burning sacrifice of the dog was the remnant of the ancient Israelite sacrifice of the lamb and that Indian "prophets" were descended from those of ancient Israel. The Indians chanted the names "Yah-ho-he-wah" and "A-loh-heem," celebrated the feast of firstfruits, used a portion of food as a tithe devoted to religious use (they threw a piece of fat into the fire "very religiously"), used a "sacred vessel" of the nature and design of the ark of the covenant, believed in the immortality of the soul and in reward and punishment after death, and avenged the death of a relative according to the principle of blood for blood.[31]

Mordecai M. Noah

In 1818 the statesman and Jewish leader Mordecai M. Noah (1785-1851) advocated Jews' taking advantage of the equal rights granted them in America, but only until they could recover their own ancient Land and take their position among the governments of the world.[32] In 1825 he established an anticipatory Jewish commonwealth, Ararat, on Grand Island, New York. At its inauguration Noah pointed out similarities between Indians and ancient Hebrews—Seneca Chief

---

*"But many that are first shall be last; and the last shall be first." *Matthew* 19:30.

†"Comfort ye, comfort ye my people, saith your God. Speak ye comfortably to Jerusalem, and cry unto her, that her warfare is accomplished, that her iniquity is pardoned: for she hath received of the Lord's hand double for all her sins." *Isaiah 40:1-2. Isaiah 49:21,* supra. "He that scattereth Israel will gather him, and keep him, as a shepherd doth his flock." *Jeremiah* 31:10.

Red Jacket was present—and encouraged Indians to join their Jewish brethren on the island.[33]

In Noah's proto-Zionist statements of 1837 he spoke of Indians living in the restored Land of Israel. He was convinced that American Indians were descended from the Lost Tribes that went into Assyria, citing the usual proofs: (1) Belief in one God, (2) time-computation according to new moon ceremonies, (3) division of the year into four seasons, (4) parallels to the Day of Atonement and Feast of the Tabernacles, (5) temple, ark of the covenant, and altars, (6) division of the nation into tribes headed by a chief or grand sachem, (7) laws of sacrifices, (8) ablutions, (9) linguistic affinities, (10) transmission of everlasting covenant in circumcision as a seal in the flesh.

Noah, however, introduced a new idea: America would be the scene of the onset of the Jewish, not the Christian, *eschaton*. The Indians would return to the Land of the Jews—but as Jews:

Firmly as I believe the American Indian to have been descended from the tribes of Israel, and that our continent is full of the most extraordinary vestiges of antiquity, there is one point, a religious as well as a historical point, in which you may possibly continue to doubt amidst almost convincing evidences!

If these are the remnants of the nine and a half tribes which were carried to Assyria,* and if we are to believe in all the promises of the restoration, and the fulfillment of the prophecies, respecting the final advent of the Jewish nation, what is to become of these our red brethren, who we are driving before us so rapidly, that a century more will find them lingering on the borders of the Pacific Ocean?

Possibly, the restoration may be near enough to include even a portion of these interesting people. Our learned rabbis have always deemed it sinful to compute the period of restoration; they believed than when the sins of the nation were atoned for, the miracles of their redemption would be manifested. My faith does not rest wholly in miracles—Providence disposes of events, human agency must carry them out.[34]

In 1844 Noah wrote a treatise on the restoration of the Holy Land and America's assistance in that undertaking. There was, he believed, a natural sympathy between America and its Jews traceable to the Puritan adoption of Mosaic law from which this mutual activity could draw.[35]

---

*"By lot was their inheritance, as the Lord commanded by the hand of Moses, for the nine tribes, and for the half tribe." *Joshua* 14:2.

Mormons

The Protestant and Jewish writers on the American Indians and the Ten Tribes invested the original inhabitants of America with a Holy Land pedigree—they were the posterity of the Land's people—and these writers envisioned America becoming involved in the sacred drama at the end of history, which centered on the Land of Israel.[36] The Mormons went further and invested the land of America itself with holy quality.[37] They believed in the Lost Tribe-American Indian tie and anticipated American Indian conversion to Christianity at the end of history, when America would be transformed into Zion. The Tenth Article of Mormon faith reads as follows: "We believe in the literal gathering of Israel and in the restoration of the Ten Tribes; that Christ will reign personally upon the earth."[38]

In the *Book of Mormon* (1829) Joseph Smith (1804-1844) says the American Indians, or Lamanites, had Hebrew ancestors. Christ himself once appeared in America to the Ten Tribes of Israel—they were never lost to the Father even outside the Land of Israel—and ultimately they would convert to Christ in anticipation of His second coming (*II Nephi* 30:507; *III Nephi* 15:2, 14, 15, 20; *III Nephi* 17:1-4). In April 1831 missionary Oliver Cowdery, one of the witnesses to the gold plates on which the *Book of Morman* was based, wrote Smith that Delaware Chief Anderson was part of a larger process in which God was redeeming His ancient convenantal people and leading them to His holy hill of Zion.[39]

Smith may have drawn from the work of Ethan Smith, which was itself derivative. Oliver Cowdery was in Poultney, Vermont, when Ethan Smith preached there. Numerous similarities can be drawn between the *Book of Mormon* and *View of the Hebrews; or, The tribes of Israel in America (VH)*:

1. Nephi says that after reading *Isaiah* 49 his brethren asked if it was to be interpreted spiritually (*I Nephi* 22:1); *VH* debates the mystical meaning of the text (64).
2. Nephi says that the text's spiritual terms also have temporal ramifications (*I Nephi* 22:2), *VH* that mystical texts often have literal fulfillment (258-259).
3. Nephi says that the House of Israel would be scattered over the earth (*I Nephi* 22:3), *VH* that Judah would be strewed over the face of the earth (233, 247).
4. Nephi says that many (Jews) lost the knowledge once held by those of Jerusalem (*I Nephi* 22:4), *VH* that a special branch of the ancient (Hebrew) people lost the knowledge of the known descendants of Abraham (71).

5. Nephi states that most tribes were scattered upon the isles of the sea (*I Nephi* 22:4), *VH* that the isles of the sea were among the places from which Judah and Ephraim would be restored (232-233).*

6. Nephi speaks of prophecies about those who were led away (*I Nephi* 22:5), *VH* of predictions about "dispersed" Jews and the "outcast" Ten Tribes (70).†

7. Nephi attributes the scattered state to the Jews' hardening their hearts against the Holy One of Israel (*I Nephi* 22:5); *VH* says that Jews received dreadful judgments because they rejected their Savior (67-68, 253-254).

8. Nephi says the Jews were nursed by the gentiles (*I Nephi* 22:6); *VH* refers to Christian efforts to improve the condition of the Jews and to prepare their way to restoration, for example the ABCFM Palestine mission and Joseph Wolff (1792-1892), missionary to Palestine (68-69).

9. Nephi says that the Lord set the gentiles "up for a standard" (*I Nephi* 22:6), *VH* that "an apostrophe is made by the most high to all nations, to stand and behold the banner of salvation now erected for His ancient people" (241-242).‡

10. For Nephi the elements of *Isaiah* 49:22 that refer to the days to come and the House of Israel are of temporal character (*I Nephi* 22:6);# *VH* states that upon their restoration to the Land of their fathers Jews would dwell in temporal prosperity (26, 64).

11. Nephi speaks of "our seed" being scattered among the gentiles (*I Nephi* 22:7); *VH* dwells on the wrongs done by whites against the Indians (133-134, 227).

12. Nephi states that God would do marvelous, nourishing things for "our seed" which is scattered among the gentiles (*I Nephi* 22:8), *VH* that American Christians must save American natives from extinction, have pity on them and restore them (227-230).[40]

---

*"Surely the isles shall wait for me, and the ships of Tarshish first, to bring thy sons from far." *Isaiah* 60:9.

†*Isaiah* 11:12, supra. "The Lord God which gathereth the outcasts of Israel saith, Yet will I gather others to him, beside those that are gathered unto him." *Isaiah* 56:8.

‡"Thus saith the Lord God, Behold, I will lift up mine hand to the gentiles, and set up my standard to the people: and they shall bring thy sons in their arms, and thy daughters shall be carried upon their shoulders." *Isaiah* 49:22. "All ye inhabitants of the world, and dwellers on the earth, see ye, when he lifteth up an ensign on the mountains; and when he bloweth a trumpet, hear ye." *Isaiah* 18:3.

#*Isaiah* 49:22, supra.

Some Protestant writers (Williams, Penn, Edwards) confined themselves to general observations about similarities between the Ten Tribes and American Indians and to conjectures about a probable genealogical tie. Adair presented exhaustive evidence. Several (Eliot, Beatty, Crawford, Boudinot, Ethan Smith, Simon) integrated the data with Christian triumphalist interpretations of Jewish history. Dwelling on the Jewish sins against God, crucifixion, and ultimate conversion, they brought the issue into an eschatological and apocalyptic framework. The land of America would be the scene of the onset of the universal messianic kingdom, and its native inhabitants would participate, as newly converted Christians, in the ingathering of the people of Israel in their ancient Holy Land. These writers identified the tribes of Judah and Benjamin with the act of crucifixion and consequently saw them as subject to greater punishment than the Ten Lost Tribes. The land to be abandoned by the converted Indians would revert to Christians living in America. The triumphalists thought that American Christians were obliged to convince the Indians of their special heritage—even if the Indians would find it difficult to understand. Convinced of the Indian-Lost Tribe tie and its eschatological import, they wrote excitedly about living at a crucial point in history, the threshold of the messianic kingdom. The increasingly numerous discoveries of the sacred origins of the Indians went hand in hand with intensified apocalyptic concern. M. M. Noah's radical transformation of the issue into a Jewish drama was striking; he used the arguments for the Christian *eschaton* as rationale for a Jewish homeland in the Land of Israel. The Mormons were part of the tradition described here, but they felt the Ten Lost Tribes would convert to the Mormon religion, and they had two ultimate Zion centers, the old Jerusalem and the new Jerusalem.

In the sense that religious consciousness is collective and develops historically, it could be said that these writers were indebted to the Puritan and Congregationalist belief in the holiness of the land and purity of America. They added the sanctity of the land's natives, their pivotal role in eschatology—and their expected departure to Jerusalem at the end of history.

Notes

1. Johannes F. Lumnius, *De extremo dei Judicio et Indorum vocatione* II (Venice 1569). On the discussion of the notion at the time of Columbus's discovery of America, see John L. Phelan, *The Millennial Kingdom of the Franciscans in the New World*, 2nd ed. (Berkeley, Calif., 1970):24-28. An extensive analysis of the connection between the Ten Lost Tribes and Mexican Indians was made by Edward King, Viscount Kingsborough (1795-1837); see Edward King Kingsborough, "Arguments to Show that the Jews in Early Ages Colonized America," in *Antiquities of Mexico* (London 1831):6:232-420; idem, Note 31, *Antiquities of Mexico* (London 1848):8:3-268.

   The idea circulated in Jerusalem after it faded in America. In 1845 longtime Palestine resident Joseph Schwarz (1805-1865) thought it would be a "truly ludicrous assumption to pretend to find [the Ten Tribes] among the Americans . . . for no better reason than that people suppose they have discovered some traces of Jewish customs among them, and to argue thence that the Israelites had been entirely lost and mixed up with them." Joseph Schwarz, "The Latest Accounts Concerning the Ten Lost Tribes," in *A Descriptive Geography and Brief Historical Sketch of Palestine*, Isaac Leeser, trans. (Philadelphia 1850):518. In 1873 Joseph Pollack of Turawitsch referred to Menasseh ben Israel's *Mikve Israel*, to William Penn's observations about physical similarities between Indians and Jews and about European influences that destroyed Indian ethical quality, and to James Adair's forty years among the Indians. Joseph Pollack, "The Exile of the Ten Tribes," *Pirhe Havatselet* 3 no. 7 (Jerusalem November-December 1873, Hebrew):55-56. Belief in the connection remained alive among English writers at least through 1843. See Israel Worsley, *A View of the American Indians: Their general character, customs, language, public festivals, religious rites and traditions. Showing them to be the descendants of the Ten Tribes of Israel. The language of prophecy concerning them, and the course by which they traveled from Medea into America* (London 1828). See also George Jones, *An Original History of Ancient America: Founded upon the ruins of antiquity. The identity of the aborigines with the people of Tyrus and Israel. And the introduction of Christianity by the apostle Saint Thomas* (London 1843); Jones (1810-1879) planned to publish a second volume, "The Israel Era of the Original History of Ancient America," arguing that "the aborigines of the north are Israelites and of the house of Jeroboam, not Jews, i.e., of the house of Judah" and thus not involved with the crucifixion (pp. 18, 463); cf. idem, *Tecumseh and the Profit of the West: An historical Israel-Indian tragedy, in five acts* (London 1844).

   For refutations of the theory see Haman L'Estrange, *America: No Jews; or, Improbabilities that the Americans are of that race* (London 1652); William Hubbard, *A General History of New England: From the discovery to 1680* (1680; reprint, Cambridge, Mass., 1815); John D. Baldwin, "Ancient America," in *Notes on American Archaeology* (New York 1876). For a survey of the literature see Samuel F. Haven, "General Opinions Respecting the Origin of Population in the New World," *Archaeology of the United States; or, Sketches, historical and bibliographical, of the progress of information and opinion respecting vestiges of antiquity in the United States. Smithsonian Contributions to Knowledge* 8 (Washington, D.C., 1856):3-6; and William Hart Blumenthal, *In Old America. Random chapters on the early aborigines*, foreword by George A. Kohut (New York 1931).

Menasseh ben Joseph ben Israel, *The Hope of Israel (Mikve Israel)* . . . *In this treatise is showed the place wherein the Ten Tribes at this present are proved partly by the strange relation of one Anthony Montezinus, a Jew, of what befell him as he traveled over the mountains Cordillaere, with divers other particulars about the restoration of the Jews* (London 1650), originally *Esperança de Israel* (Amsterdam 1650). See Peter Toon, "The Question of Jewish Immigration," in *Puritans, the Millennium, and the Future of Israel: Puritan Eschatology, 1600 to 1660* (Cambridge, 1970):115-125.

John Dury, "An Epistolical Discourse to Mr. Thorowgood Concerning His Conjecture that the Americans are Descended from the Israelites," in Thomas Thorowgood, *Jews in America; or, Probabilities that the Americans are of that race. With the removal of some contrary reasonings, and earnest desires for effectual endeavours to make them Christian* (London 1650):28-43; another edition bearing the same date includes correspondence between Dury and Menasseh ben Israel; a decade later an expanded version bore the subtitle *Probabilities that those Indians are Judaical. Made more probable by some additionals to the former conjectures. An accurate discourse is premised of Mr. John Eliot (who first preached the Gospel to the natives in their own language) touching their origination, and his vindication of the planters* (London 1660).

2. It is unclear why southern rather than northern origins should have persuaded Williams that Indians were to some extent Jewish. Roger Williams to Thomas Thorowgood, 20 December 1635, in *The Correspondence of Roger Williams*, Glenn W. LaFantasie, ed. (Hanover, N.H., 1988):1:30-31. Williams subsequently modified his view; see *A Key into the Language of America; or, A help to the language of the nations in that part of America called New England* (London 1643):19-21.

3. Cotton Mather, *MCA Polybius: The third book of the New-English history. Containing the lives of many reverend, learned, and holy divines, arriving such from Europe to America, by whose evangelical ministry the churches of New England have been illuminated* (1702; reprint, Hartford 1853):560.

4. I have been unable to trace the term "farthest east." John Eliot to Mr. [Edward] Winslow, 8 May 1649, in *The Light Appearing More and More towards the Perfect Day; or, A farther discovery of the present state of the Indians in New England concerning the progress of the Gospel among them* (London 1651):14-18. Eliot cited Hugh Broughton (1549-1612): "It seemeth to me probable that these people are Hebrews, of Ever, whose sons the Scripture sends farthest east (as it seems to me) and learned Broughton put some of them over into America, and certainly this country was peopled eastward from the place of the ark's resting, seeing the finding of them by the west is but of yesterday." See Hugh Broughton, *A Consent of Scripture* ([London] 1620); idem, *A Treatise of Melchitsedek: Proving him to be Shem, the father of all the sons of Ever* (London 1591); Cotton Mather, "The Triumphs of the Reformed Religion in America; or, The life of the renowned John Eliot," in *MCA Polybius*, 526-583; and Sidney H. Rooy, "John Eliot: The establishment of the mission," in *The Theology of Missions in the Puritan Tradition* (Delft 1965):230-235.

5. Eliot, "The Learned Conjectures of Rev. Mr. John Eliot Touching the Americans, of New and Notable Consideration, Written to Mr. Thorowgood," in Thorowgood, *Jews in America*, 1-22.

6. [William Penn], "A Letter from William Penn, Proprietor and Governor of Pennsylvania in America, to the Committee of the Free Society of Traders to that Province Residing in London: Containing a general description of the said province, its soil, air, water, seasons, and produce, both natural and artificial, and the good increase thereof. With an account of the natives, or aborigines," in *A Collection of the Works of William Penn* (London 1726):2:699-706. On Penn, see Elias Boudinot, *A Star of the West; or, A humble attempt to discover the long lost Ten Tribes of Israel. Preparatory to their return to their beloved city, Jerusalem* (1816; reprint, Freeport, N.Y., 1970):205-206.

7. Jonathan Edwards, *Observations on the Language of the Indians: In which the extent of that language in north America is shown; its genius is grammatically traced; some of its peculiarities and some instance of analogy between that and the Hebrew are pointed out* (New Haven 1758):14. The Mohegan Indian clergyman Samson Occom (1723-1792) studied Hebrew at Dartmouth College. See Goldman, "Biblical Hebrew."

8. Lewis and Clark offered this response to Adair's work:
    Notwithstanding Mr. Adair has asserted that the nations among whom he resided observed with very little variation all the rites appointed by the Mosaic law, I own I could never discover among those tribes that lie but a few degrees to the northwest, the least traces of the Jewish religion, except it be admitted that one particular female custom and their divisions into tribes carry with them proof sufficient to establish this assertion.
    Meriwether Lewis and William Clark, *New Travels among the Indians of north America: Being a compilation taken partly from the communications already published by Captains Lewis and Clark to the President of the United States and partly from other authors who traveled among the various tribes of Indians* (Philadelphia 1812):112; see also 219-222. Adair apparently drew the account of Atlantis from Plato's *Timaeus*. James Adair, *The History of the American Indians: Particularly those nations adjoining to the Mississippi, east and west Florida, Georgia, south and north Carolina, and Virginia. Containing an account of their origin, language, manners, religious and civil customs, laws, form of government, punishments, conduct in war and domestic life, their habits, diet, agriculture, manufactures, diseases, and method of cure . . .* (London 1775):13-17, 19, 32-34, 74-76, 80-84, 123-124, 131, 159-161, 194-195, 219. See Charles Hudson, "James Adair as an Anthropologist," *Ethnohistory* 24 no. 4 (Fall 1977):311-328. A critical edition is Samuel C. Williams, *Adair's History of the American Indians* (New York 1930).

9. See Charles Beatty, *The Journal of a Two Months' Tour: With a view of promoting religion among the frontier inhabitants of Pennsylvania, and of introducing Christianity among the Indians to the westward of the Allegheny Mountains. To which are added remarks on the language and customs of some particular tribes among the Indians, with a brief account of the various attempts that have been made to civilize and convert them, from the first settlement of New England to this day* (London 1768):84-92; and Charles Beatty, *Double Honor Due to the Laborious Gospel Minister: Represented in a sermon preached at Fairfield in New Jersey 1 December 1756. At the ordination of Mr. William Ramsey. Published at the desire of the hearers* (Philadelphia 1757). See Guy S. Klett,

Introduction, in *Journals of Charles Beatty, 1762-1769*, Guy S. Klett, ed. (University Park, Pa., 1962):xiii-xxix.

10. Charles Crawford, "An Address to the People of America," in *The Christian: A poem in four books. To which is prefixed a preface in prose in defense of Christianity. With an address to the people of America* (Philadelphia 1783):v-vi. See his *Observations upon Negro Slavery* (Philadelphia 1784) and *Liberty: A Pindaric ode. To the honorable Congress of the United States of America and to his excellency General Washington, the following ode is humbly inscribed by the author, a disciple of Locke, an ardent assertor of the liberties of mankind from the deliberate conviction of his understanding* (Philadelphia 1783):13-15.

11. Crawford also drew from the *Timaeus*:

> We read in Scripture that the division of the globe was made in the days of Peleg, who was the seventh son of Noah (see *Genesis* 10:25). The Hebrew word Peleg signifies a division. It is a strong argument in favor of the division of the earth being a fact of great notoriety, that a man of eminence obtained his name from the circumstance. From the *Timaeus* of Plato it appears that the Greeks had some idea of this event.

He cited James Beattie, *The Minstrel; or, The progress of genius* (London 1771-1774).

12. Crawford cited Williams Jones, *Dissertations and Miscellaneous Pieces Relating to the History and Antiquities, the Arts, Science, and Literature, of Asia* (Dublin 1793), and Aaron Hill, *A Full, Just Account of the Present of the Ottoman Empire in All Its Branches* (London 1709).

13. I have been unable to identify the "learned Jew." Crawford referred to another conversion reported in London. See "Extract of a Letter From Rev. Mr. Pearsall of Taunton, Containing a Remarkable Relation: Sent to him by the Rev. Dr. Doddridge," *The Gentleman's Magazine and Historical Chronicle* 20 (London, July 1750):313.

14. Some Indians may have accepted the notion. See also Daniel O. Morton, *Memoir of Rev. Levi Parsons, Late Missionary to Palestine* (Poultney, Vt., 1824):217.

15. Crawford, *An Essay upon the Propagation of the Gospel* (Philadelphia 1799):17, 33-35, and *Essay on the Propagation of the Gospel: In which there are numerous facts and arguments adduced that many of the Indians in America are descended from the Ten Tribes*, 2nd ed. (Philadelphia 1801):4-8, 18, 25-29, 120-121. Crawford drew from Pierre Charlevoix. According to Charlevoix's findings among the Huron and Iroquois, a widower married his deceased wife's sister and a widow married her deceased husband's brother (he cites *Deuteronomy* 25); there was memory of a universal deluge; and blood was avenged as among ancient Jews. Charlevoix, *Journal of a Voyage to north America: Undertaken by order of the French King. Containing the geographical description and national history of that country, particularly Canada. Together with an account of the customs, characters, religion, manners, and traditions of the original inhabitants* (London 1761):2:48-49, 144. See also Crawford, *Observations upon the Fall of Antichrist and the Concomitant Events* (Philadelphia 1786); *A Dissertation on the "Phaedon" of Plato; or, Dialogue of the immortality of the soul. With some general observations about the writings of that philosopher. To which is annexed a psychology,*

or an abstract investigation of the nature of the soul in which the opinions of all the celebrated metaphysicians on the subject are discussed (London 1773); and idem, *An Essay on the Eleventh Chapter of Saint John: In which is shown that the words "and in the same hour was there a great earthquake, and the tenth part of the city fell, and in the earthquake were slain of men, seven thousand" relate to Jerusalem and not to Rome or France* (Philadelphia 1800). Also *Three Letters to the Hebrew Nation* (London 1817), which evoked a critical response: Salomon Bennett, "Kritische und theologische Erwiederung auf das von Lord Crawford erschienene Sendschreiben an die hebräische Nation," in *Israels Beständigkeit. Eine unbegangene Beleuchtung mehrerer wichtiger Bibelstellen, insbesondere sogenannte messianische Weissagungen: In kritischer Erwiederung auf das von Lord Crawford erschienene öffentliche Sendschreiben an die hebräische Nation nebst einen kurzen Abriss der jüdischen Geschichte und Nachrichten über den Zustand der heutigen Juden in Europa. Aus dem englischen [The Constancy of Israel*, London 1809] *übersetzt* (Darmstadt 1835):1-79.

16. Crawford, Preface to *The Christian: A poem in six books*, 5th ed. (London 1803):1:5-6. See Lewis Leary, "Charles Crawford: A Forgotten Poet of Early Pennsylvania," *Pennsylvania Magazine of History and Biography* 83 (July 1959):293-306.

17. George A. Boyd, *Elias Boudinot: Patriot and Statesman, 1740-1821* (Princeton 1952); *Report of ABCFM: 21st Annual Meeting* (Boston 1830):5.

18. Elias Boudinot, *A Star in the West; or, A humble attempt to discover the long lost Ten Tribes of Israel, preparatory to their return to their beloved city, Jerusalem* (1816; reprint, Freeport, N.Y., 1970):iii, 27, 43-50, 75, 87, 297. For an analysis of Boudinot, see Calvin Colton, "Origin of the American Indians," in *Tour of the American Lakes and among the Indians of the northwest Territory in 1830: Disclosing the character and prospects of the Indian race* (London 1833):2:1-29. In contemplating the second advent, Boudinot said of the Jews:

> The present hour bears witness to its divine origin, as well as the generations that are past.—Jerusalem is trodden down of the gentiles—its walls are beaten down distinct and separate from all;—afflicted, but not forsaken;—reviled as a proverb and a bye word, yet numerous and generally opulent, enriched with the spoil of their enemies;—they abide without a king, and without a priest; and without a sacrifice; a conspicuous monument of the truth of prophecy to every people among whom they dwell.

Boudinot, *The Second Advent; or, The coming of the messiah in glory, shown to be a scripture doctrine and taught by divine revelation from the beginning of the world. By an American layman* (Trenton, N.J., 1815):542-543.

19. Ethan Smith, *A Dissertation on the Prophecies Relative to Antichrist and the Last Times: Exhibiting the rise, character, and overthrow of that terrible power. And a treatise on the seven apocalyptic vials* (Charleston, Mass., 1811):332, says the Ten Tribes ended up in Afghanistan. He had changed his mind by the time he wrote *View of the Hebrews; or, The tribes of Israel in America exhibiting: (1) The destruction of Jerusalem. (2) The certain restoration of Judah and Israel. (3) The present state of Judah and Israel. (4) An address of the prophet Isaiah to the United States, relative to*

their restoration (Poultney, Vt., 1825):271-272. Cf. Boudinot, *A Star in the West,* 33-31.

20. Samuel Williams, *The Natural and Civil History of Vermont,* 2nd ed. (Burlington, Vt., 1809):1:190. I have added in brackets the sentences Smith omitted.

21. William Bartram, *Travels through north and south Carolina, Georgia, East and West Florida: The Cherokee country, the extensive territories of the Muscogulges or Creek Confederacy and the Country of the Choctaws* (Philadelphia 1792):387-391.

22. I have been unable to find the source: See [Alexander Mackenzie], *A Narrative or Journal of Voyages and Travels through the northwest Continent of America, in the years 1789-1793* (London 1802); and idem, *Voyages from Montreal on the River Saint Lawrence through the continent of north America to the frozen and Pacific Oceans, in the years 1789 and 1793* (London 1801).

23. Jedidiah Morse, *A Report to the Secretary of War of the United States, on Indian Affairs: Comprising a narrative of a tour performed in the summer of 1820, under a commission from the President of the United States, for the purpose of ascertaining, for the use of the government, the actual state of the Indian tribes in our country* (New Haven 1822):136-137. See Payson Williston, Isaac Hurd, John Todd and S.F.B. Morse, "Jedidiah Morse, D.D.," in Sprague, *Annals of the American Pulpit,* 2:247-256.

24. Smith, *View of the Hebrews: Exhibiting the destruction of Jerusalem, the certain restoration of Judah and Israel, the present state of Judah and Israel, and an address of the prophet Isaiah relative to their restoration* (Poultney, Vt., 1823):iii, 6, 66, 158-161, 167, and idem, *View of the Hebrews* 1825):172, 247-250. See Abraham Burnham, "Ethan Smith," in Sprague, *Annals of the American Pulpit,* 2:296-300; and William Miller, "A Review of Ethan Smith's and David Campbell's Exposition of the Little Horn, and Return of the Jews," in *Views of the Prophecies and Prophetic Chronology: Selected from manuscripts of William Miller. With a memoir of his life by Joshua V. Himes* (Boston 1881): 172-181.

25. Smith, *A Dissertation on the Prophecies,* 199-231, 336-350.

26. Smith, *View of the Hebrews* (1823), 6, 7, 158-160.

27. Smith, *Key to the Revelation: In thirty-six lectures, taking the whole book in course* (New York 1833):381-383.

28. Barbara A. Simon, Dedication and "'Jerusalem,' Addressed to the Unbelieving Sons of Abraham," in *Evangelical Review of Modern Genius; or, Truth and error contrasted* (New York 1823):106-116.

29. Simon, *A View of the Human Heart: A series of allegorical designs, representing the human heart from its natural to its regenerated state, with explanatory addresses, meditations, prayers, and hymns, for the instruction of youth* (New York 1825):5-6.

30. Bartram, *An Account of the Persons, Manners, Customs, and Government of the Muscogulges or Creeks, Cherokees, Choctaws, etc., Aborigines of the Continent of north America* (Philadelphia 1791):509; Simon, *The Hope of Israel: Presumptive evidence that the aborigines of the western hemisphere are descended from the ten missing tribes of Israel* (London 1829); idem, *The Ten Tribes of Israel: Historically identified with the aborigines of the western hemisphere* (London 1836). There is some confusion whether the same Barbara Simon wrote the works of 1823, 1825, 1829, and 1836. I am following the National Union and British Museum catalogs, which identify Barbara Anne Simon with Barbara Allan Simon. There is an intriguing reference in this regard by missionary Joseph Wolff (see Chapter 5): "With regard to the Indians being the Ten Lost Tribes, Wolff does not believe that such is the case, for they themselves know nothing about it; nor does he feel inclined to assist gentlemen and ladies in America and England, in their attempt to force the Indians to believe that they are the Ten Tribes. Besides this, he saw some of the Indian tribes at Washington, who also have a resemblance to the Tartars in their countenance, as well as in their language. Wolff asked one of the Indians, 'Whose descendants are you?' She replied, 'We are Jews.' Wolff asked her, 'Who told you so?' She replied, 'Mrs. Simons, from Scotland, a few years ago.'." Joseph Wolff, *Travels and Adventures of the Rev. Joseph Wolff, D.D., LL.D* (London 1861):518.

31. Calvin Colton, *Tour of the American Lakes and among the Indians of the northwest Territory in 1830: Disclosing the character and prospects of the Indian race* (London 1833):2:18-23.

32. See Jonathan Sarna, *Jacksonian Jew: The Two Worlds of Mordecai M. Noah* (New York 1951). Mordecai M. Noah, *Discourse Delivered at the Consecration of the Synagogue K. K. Shearit Israel, in the City of New York on Friday, 10 Nissan 5578, Corresponding with 17 April 1818* (New York 1818). See Frederick Marryat, *Diary in America: With remarks on its institution* (Philadelphia 1840):258.

33. [Noah], "Address of Mordecai M. Noah: From the *New York Evening Post* no. 7241 (September 1825)," *PAJHS* 21 (1913):230-52.

34. Noah, *Discourse on the Evidence of the American Indians Being the Descendants of the Lost Tribes of Israel: Delivered before the mercantile library association, Clinton Hall* (New York 1837):8-9, 37-39. See Sarna, *Jacksonian Jew*, 205 n. 47.

35. Noah, *Discourse on the Restoration of the Jews Delivered at the Tabernacle, 25 October and 2 December 1844* (New York 1845):46-51. See Sarna, *Jacksonian Jew*, 135-37, 153-58.

36. While Catholics had missions to the Indians, and the Ten Tribe connection was of much concern for the church in the context of Columbus (see Phelan, *Millennial Kingdom*), I do not find any subsequent attention to it in America. See, for example, John D. G. Shea, *History of the Catholic Missions among the Indian Tribes of the United States, 1529-1892* (New York 1969); Eugene Vetromile, *Indian Good Book* (New York 1857); Amleto G. Cicognani, *Sanctity in America* (Paterson, N.J., 1939).

37. On Mormons and the Indians, see Lynn Glaser, "American Eschatology and the Mormons," in *Indians or Jews* (Gilroy, Calif., 1973):60-74.

38. James F. Talmage, *A Study of the Articles of Faith* (Salt Lake City 1960):2

39. Donna Hill, *Joseph Smith: The First Mormon* (Garden City, N.Y., 1977):123.

40. David Persuitte, *Joseph Smith and the Origins of the Book of Mormon* (Jefferson, N.C., 1985):143-147. Persuitte (105 and 277n) and Glaser ("American Eschatology," 74 n. 15) note that Mormon scholar Brigham H. Roberts published similarities in the *Rocky Mountain Mason* (January 1956). On Wolff, see Chapter 5.

Part Two

Nineteenth-Century Individual
Ties to the Holy Land

4 Protestant Pilgrims: Disjunctions between Expectation and Reality

An important expression of the attachment to the Holy Land of Israel was individual pilgrimage to the scene of Jesus' life. Protestant pilgrims wished to relive the events in the life of the Lord, to merge present reality with biblical past. Often the process was interrupted, because the contemporary reality of the Holy Land contrasted sharply with the romantic biblical image.

William C. Prime

William C. Prime, LL.D. (1825-1905), son of Presbyterian minister Nathaniel S. Prime, journeyed to the Holy Land in 1855-1856 and wrote a book about it, returning in 1869-1870.[1] For Prime, temporal events were interspersed with transtemporal realities. As a young student of Scripture he had experienced the intermingling of time and eternity, existential experience and eternal Scripture:

> My father's head was white with the snows of three-score years and ten, but his footstep was as firm as mine. But, though I—I—yes, it was even so—I know it not—I was on the borders of Canaan, my footsteps were entering Holy Land on earth, and his, far away from me, were on the borders of the promised Land! I was close to the Jerusalem of the cross, he already close to the Jerusalem of the crown—I was going to lave my weary limbs in the Jordan, he was to lie down on the banks of the river of life—I was to go wearily to Gethsemane and the place of death and the Sepulcher, he was passing swiftly to the presence of the risen Lord.

After actually reaching the Holy Land and climbing the mountains of Lebanon, Prime felt his father was ascending into the sublime and solemn company of the Hebrew patriarchs and prophets "of all time." At Jaffa he could imagine what the tanneries must have been like two thousand years ago.* But the reality of the Land also interrupted the blending. Indeed, present conditions devalued the eternal myth, pushed it away. "The desolation of the Land of Israel could scarcely be more total and complete." Christianity in the Holy Land had a "stunted growth." Muslims perversely considered their mosques polluted because Christians looked at them.

In the end, however, the disjunction between scriptural myth and present reality dissolved. Prime took pleasure in seeing that wildflowers could bloom amidst the desolation, "extract from that ancient soil the delicate food of the bees, and grow as if only to assert the former richness of the Land of promise." The Land remained a refuge from the sinful world: "I visited the sacred soil, as a pilgrim, seeking mine own pleasure. I went where it pleased me, I acted as it pleased me, yielding with delicious license to the whim of every passing hour. I prayed or laughed, I knelt or turned my back. I wept or I sang." There was nothing to be ashamed of, Prime said, in weeping in Palestine: "I wept when I saw Jerusalem, I wept when I lay in the starlight of Bethlehem, I wept on the blessed shores of Galilee." Weeping did not mean he ignored reality: "My hand was no less firm on the rein, my finger did not tremble on the trigger of my pistol when I rode with it in my right hand along the shore of the blue sea. My eye was not dimmed by those tears, nor my heart in might weakened." The disjunction resolved, Prime hoped that other Americans would join him, even though the fatigue and excitement of travel in the Holy Land had become so intense for some that they were led to their graves in the very soil they venerated.

Harmony between scriptural myth and present reality pervaded Prime's report: "Every step that I advanced on the soil of Palestine offered some new and startling evidence of the truth of the sacred story.[2] Every hour we were exclaiming that the history must be true, so perfect was the proof before our eyes. The Bible was a new book, faith in which seemed to have passed into actual sight, and every page of its record shone out with new, and a thousandfold increased luster." At Mount Moriah, the site of Solomon's Temple, Prime read about "a river, the streams whereof shall make glad the city of God, the holy place of the tabernacles of the most High" (*Psalms* 46:4). He observed a beautiful fountain with springs under mountain rocks, and learned that they were the source for the Siloam pool.† When they descended into the Valley of Jehoshaphat he thought about Ezekiel's vision of divine salvation and the river

---

*"And it came to pass, that he tarried many days in Joppa with one Simon a tanner." *Acts* 9:43.

†Jesus "said unto him, Go, wash in the pool of Siloam (which is by interpretation, Sent). He went his way therefore, and washed, and came seeing." *John* 9:7.

flowing eastward out of a sanctuary, giving life even to the Dead Sea.* Standing outside St. Stephen's Gate and looking into the Valley of Kidron and across to the steep slope of the Mount of Olives, the Mount of Ascension, Prime understood why the psalmist compared the guardianship of the father to the watch kept on the mountains around Jerusalem.† Jerusalem, set on a hill, was commanded on the north, east, south and west by higher hills, "over whose summits the blue sky curves downward, with that close embrace that one might well expect from the heavens above the City of the Sepulcher."

The discontinuity between myth and present behind him, Prime ventured into the eternal level of Christian Scripture. One morning, while looking across the Valley of Kidron toward the holy Mount of Ascension, he saw a faint halo above the mountain:

> The flush became a gleam, a glow, an opening heaven of deep, strong light that did not dazzle nor bewilder. I looked into it and was lost in it, as one is lost that gazes into the deep loving eyes of the woman he worships. It seemed as if I had but to wish and I should be away in the atmosphere that was so glorious. Strong cords of desire seemed drawing me thither. I even rose to my feet and leaned forward over the carved turban on a tomb. I breathed strong, full inspirations as if I could breathe in that glory.

He contemplated the buried Jews in the valley:

> The glory did not reach down to their low graves; yet I thought almost aloud that if that radiance could but once touch those stones, heavy as they were, the dead would spring to life, even the doubly dead who lie in that valley of tombs . . . Also for the dead whose grave the morning radiance from the mountain of the Lord's ascension will never reach! Alas for the sealed lips of earth that will never be kissed to opening those rays.

At the Garden of Gethsemane, at the base of the Mount of Olives, Prime imbibed the reality of Christ's passion, from the agony in the Garden through His death at Calvary. The whispering leaves of the olive trees, the winds over Mount Moriah, the blue sky above the Mount of Olives which Christ clove with His

---

*"Then he said unto me, These waters issue out toward the east country, and go down into the desert, and go into the sea: which being brought forth into the sea, the waters shall be healed. And it shall come to pass, that everything that liveth, which moveth, withersoever the rivers shall come, shall live: and there shall be a very great multitude of fish, because these waters shall come thither: for they shall be healed; and everything shall live whither the river cometh." *Ezekiel* 47:8-9.

†"As the mountains are round about Jerusalem, so the Lord is round about his people henceforth even for ever." *Psalms* 125:2.

departing glory—from all these Prime heard the story of His suffering for others, and he was moved to recite:

Tu Tu, mi Jesu, totum me
Amplexus es in cruce!
Tulisti clavos, lanceam,
Multamque ignominiam,
Innumeros dolores,
Sudores et angores,
Ac mortem! et haec propter me,
Ac pro me peccatore!

You, You my Jesus
Embraced all of me,
In being on the cross.
You bore the nails, the lance,
And much shame,
Countless sorrows,
Sweating and pain
And death! And this because of me,
Because of me, a sinner.[3]

The Garden before him passed beyond time and space:

But no voice of human grief or human joy reached the deep valley to disturb the profound stillness of the Garden of the Passion. The olives on the mountain waved their flashing branches in the gentle breeze, but those within the enclosure scarcely moved. The lavender that bloomed with the utmost profusion made the atmosphere heavy with perfume, as we sat down on the ground and endeavored to realize the midnight scene of the agony and the betrayal.

Throughout his stay in Jerusalem Prime went to the Garden daily to sit under the ancient olive trees and read the accounts of Christ's agony (*Mark* 14:32-42, *Matthew* 26:36-46, *Luke* 22:40-46). He discussed its actors and contemplated especially the betrayal of Judas: Did Judas betray his master, hoping to compel Him to acknowledge His heavenly power and summon His angels to conquer the throne and kingdom and share it with the traitor? As the sun descended behind Mount Moriah and the moon rose over the Mount of Olives, Prime entered scriptural drama:

Did the moon shine on that last night of the life of the Lord before the sacrifice? Did the full moon, in whose light young maidens love to hear the words of young love, behold that love which would not put away the cup of agony, though countless angels stood ready to seize the chalice and dash it down to hell?

I never thought of it before. In all the scene of all the centuries that I have imagined the moon beholding: and of which I have striven sometimes to gather some intelligence in those cold calm rays, I never before imagined that on that still orb in the blue sky of Judea the tear-dimmed eyes of the Lord gazed through the rustling leaves of Gethesemane.

At the Wailing Wall Prime shared in the sacred history of triumphalist Christianity. One Friday he saw men, women, and children of all ages crowd around, pressing their throbbing foreheads against the beloved stones; a man of noble features stood still for half an hour with his face to the Wall, reading *Isaiah* with a grief beyond expression. When the Sabbath commenced at sundown,

Still some old men lingered, and still we lingered too, for the scene was not one not to be witnessed elsewhere on all the earth, the children of Abraham approaching as nearly as they dared to the holy of holies and murmuring in low voices of hushed grief, and sobs of anguish, their prayers to the great God of Jacob. Some kissed the rocky wall with fervent lips, some knelt and pressed their foreheads to it, and some prayed in silent, speechless grief, while tears fell like rain-drops before them.

I was deeply moved as one might be in the presence of this sad assembly; the last representatives, near the site of their ancient Temple, of those who once thronged its glorious courts and offered sacrifices to the God Who has so long withdrawn His countenance from the race.

A more abject race of men can hardly be imagined than are the downtrodden children of Israel in the city of their fathers, except when they assemble here where the majesty of their grief demands respect from every human heart.[4]

Prime continued to sublimate space and time into sacred, scriptural eternity after he left the Holy Land. In 1865 he recalled that one morning, as his horse picked its way up a dangerous rocky ridge to the north of Jerusalem, he began to sing an old hymn about the mythic Jerusalem, the "sacred city, queen and wife of Christ eternally." When, he sang, could he come to "mother" Jerusalem, where his sorrows would turn to joy, where he could join God's saints and walk upon the sweet and pleasant soil? "Lord . . . take me to Thy Jerusalem and place me with Thy saints who there are crowned with glory great and see God face to face." In that Jerusalem there were no sorrows, sickness, or death, "every soul as the sun, for God Himself [is] light." It was a city of God wherein resided the light of God's Lamb. Jerusalem was pure of all filth, devoid of grief. It was the garden of paradise: "Thy gardens and thy goodly walks continually are green.

There grow such sweet and pleasant flowers as nowhere else are seen. There cinnamon and sugar grow, there nard and balm abound." The figures of Scripture provided glorious music: David played the harp, Mary sang the Magnificat (*Luke* 1:46-55), even Mary Magdalene "left her moan and cheerfully doth sing."* As long as he was outside Jerusalem, Prime felt abandoned: "But we that are in banishment continually do moan. We sigh, we mourn, we sob, we weep—perpetually we groan. Our sweetness is mixed with gall, our pleasure is but pain." Prime could barely wait to leave the temporal world outside the city: "Come quickly Lord and end my grief and take me home to Thee! O print Thy name in my forehead and take me hence away, that I may dwell with Thee in bliss and sing Thy praises aye!"⁵ Viewing Jerusalem from its surrounding mountaintops, Prime shared its eternal, sanctified reality in a longing that removed him from the profane world outside.

Herman Melville

Herman Melville journeyed to Palestine in 1857 in search of the ideal Holy Land that industrialization had suppressed in America.⁶ He kept a journal from which he drew to express his hopes and disappointments in the Land of Israel in the epic poem *Clarel.*⁷

In the poem, Clarel travels to Jerusalem to find the answers that eluded him as a divinity student in America. There he falls in love with Ruth. Her mother, Agar, is homesick for America, while her father, Nathan, a Puritan zealot turned Jew, seems content to cultivate the soil to restore the Holy Land. Nathan is murdered by Arabs, and Clarel is denied access to the mourners because he is not Jewish. He reacts by going on a pilgrimage to the holy places. His companions include Margoth, a born Jew who mocks religion in the name of science and thinks of Palestine as simply a geographical location; the aged, saintly millennialist Nehemiah, who characterizes Margoth as a "sinful son of Judah"; and the priest Derwent, who criticizes Jews because they have pursued gentile professional aims.⁸ After the pilgrimage, Clarel returns to Jerusalem on Ash Wednesday and finds Ruth and Agar dead. He is convinced their death was foretold when Nehemiah and another traveler, Celio, wandered at night into the Dead Sea in an apocalyptic vision. Jerusalem is filled with despair for Clarel, a city tragically without the light or glory that Isaiah had proclaimed, old and blighted:

Oppressive roofed with awful skies
Whose stars like silver nailheads gleam

---

*See, for example, *Luke* 7:37-38: "A woman . . . stood at His feet behind Him weeping, and began to wash His feet with tears, and did wipe them with the hairs of her head, and kissed His feet, and anointed them with the ointment."

Which stud some lid over lifeless eyes.[9]

In his *Journal* Melville dwells on the darker side. A dung heap serves as a lepers' park. Nature and man are indifferent to the sacred spots. The Holy Sepulcher is a sickening cheat surrounded by the "least nameable filth of a barbarous city . . . The color of the whole city is gray and looks at you like a cold gray eye in a cold gray man." His dismay over the Land, however, did not kill Melville's expectation of the second coming, and while opposed to zealous missionaries, he still expected Jews to convert in preparation for it.[10]

The longest canto in *Clarel* is about Nathan, a figure said to be modeled after Jerusalem Consul Warder Cresson. Nathan was brought up a devout Puritan but after reading Paine's *Age of Reason* developed doubts about religion.[11] Those doubts are confirmed by the savageries of nature, and he turns to pantheism and then, after meeting Agar, converts to Judaism, the ultimate source of his Puritan heritage. They marry and have Ruth and another child. Disappointed with the religious life of America, Nathan channels his vigor and enterprise toward renewing ancient Zion, taking the family to the Land of Israel to work the soil. There they are robbed by Arabs—just as Algonquian Indians attacked New England settlers. Agar wants Nathan to leave, but neither she nor the death of the younger child persuade him. Time and fate, however, soon sever Nathan's tie to the Land.[12]

The canto begins by describing the austere stock from which Nathan came. His forefathers

> Hewed their way from sea-beat rock
> Wherever woods and winter be.
> The pilgrim-keel in storm and stress
> Had erred, and on a wilderness.

The "landing patriarchs" bear inland to the White Mountains of New Hampshire and then westward until they reach the rich midwestern plains:

> To Illinois—a turf divine
> Of promise how auspicious spread,
> Ere yet the cities rose thereon.

Nathan's father dies, leaving him to care for their farm:

> A stripling but of manful ways
> Hardy and frugal, oft he filled
> The widow's eyes with tears of praise.

He begins to doubt the Christian orthodoxy of his parents but continues to observe it for his mother's sake. He cannot, however, lock out the thoughts of death which disturb the beauty of nature around him:

> Three Indian mounds
> Against the horizon's level bounds
> Dim showed across the prairie green
> Like dwarfed and blunted mimic shapes
> Of pyramids at distance seen
> From the broad Delta's planted capes
> Of vernal grain. In nearer view
> With trees he saw them crowned which drew
> From the red sagamores of eld
> Entombed within the vital gum
> Which green kept each mausoleum.

The dead assume a Christ-like character:

> Lambs had he known by thunder killed
> Innocents—and the type of Christ
> Betrayed.

Nathan is overcome by thoughts of nature's ravages in the worst storm in White Mountain history. On 28 August 1826 a landslide buries several people, including his uncle:

> The Saco and Ammonoosuc's fount;
> Where, in September's equinox
> Nature hath put such terror on
> That form his mother man would run—
> Our mother, Earth: the founded rocks
> Unstable prove: the Slide! the Slide!
> . . . .
> Somewhere his uncle slept; no mound.
> Since not a trace of him was found,
> So whelmed the havoc from the heaven.
> This reminiscence of dismay,
> These thoughts unhinged him.

The response to death and the ravages of nature emerge some time later when Nathan chances upon *The Age of Reason*:

> A book all but forsaken now

For more advanced ones not so frank.
Nor less in vogue and taking rank;
And yet it never shall outgrow
That infamy it first incurred,
Though viewed in light which moderns know—
Capricious infamy absurd.

He is impressed with its blunt, straightforward language, its clean and sincere thoughts, and it provides a solid basis for his religious doubts. He takes it home, although its Scottish owner tries to dissuade him:

Fearing for Nathan even him
So young, and for the mill, may be,
Should his unspoken heresy
Get bruited so.

By now, the farmwork has become a burden:

Sullen he tilled, in Adam's frame
When thrust from Eden out to dearth
And blest no more, and wise in shame.
The fall!

The fire of Paine's deism takes its toll; God is expelled and replaced with pantheism:

How frequent when Favonius low
Breathed from the copse which mild did wave
Over his father's sylvan grave,
And stirred the corn, he stayed the hoe,
And leaning, listening, felt a thrill
Which heathenized against the will.

The sectarians around him made belief in God offensive:

To believe,
Belief to win nor more to grieve!
But how? a sect about him stood
In thin and scattered neighborhood;
Uncanny, and in rupture new;
Nor were all lives of members true
And good.

Full of doubt, Nathan finally discovers his religious identity through the Jewess Agar, with whom he falls in love:

> He wrestled with the pristine forms
> Like the first man. By inner storms
> Held in solution, so his soul
> Ripened for hour of such control
> As shapes, concretes. The influence came,
> And from a source that well might claim
> Surprise. 'Twas in a lake-port new,
> A mart for grain, by chance he met
> A Jewess.

As the dry plains of Rephaim are grateful for rain, so is Nathan for Agar's love. But before he can win her she asks that he become a Jew:

> "Wilt join my people?" Love is power;
> Came the strange plea in yielding hour.

Nathan realizes that in his crumbling faith he can find security in the religion which preceded Christianity:

> Nay, and turn Hebrew? But why not?
> If backward still the inquirer goes
> To get behind man's present lot
> Of crumbling faith; for rear-wall shows
> Far behind Rome and Luther—what?
> The crag of Sinai.

Full of life, Nathan is caught up in Judaism, the glamour of Zion, love for eternal Jerusalem, the "mitered race," the psalms of David. He recognizes the tie between his own Puritan background and the Hebrew source from which it diverted. Once earnest in disbelief, Nathan now returns to faith with more intensity than ever:

> Distance therefrom but gave career
> For impetus that shot him sheer
> Beyond.

Agar and Nathan marry, "one in heart and creed," and bear two children. Ever active, Nathan soon becomes restless. He looks to the Land of Israel, where he can cultivate the soil and help return the Land to its former glory:

The mind infertile of the Jew.
His northern nature, full of pith.
Vigor and enterprise and will,
Having taken thus the Hebrew bent
Might not abide inactive so
And but the empty forms fulfill:
Needs utilize the mystic glow—
For nervous energies find vent.
The Hebrew seers announce in time
The return of Judah to her prime;
Some Christians deemed it then at hand.
Here was an object: Up and do!
With seed and tillage help renew—
Help reinstate the Holy Land.

Unlike the "zealous Jews on alien soil" who only dream about "next year in Jerusalem" and recite that phrase on Passover, Nathan wants action. Full of faith, he and Agar sell their possessions and journey to the Holy Land with Ruth and "a young child in arms."

They settle on the Plains of Sharon, build a shed surrounded by a defense wall, and begin to work the earth. Tragedy soon strikes, when wandering Arabs attack and rob them. The family finds refuge in Jerusalem, "the stronghold town of Zion," and Nathan and three companions set out after the attackers—as once New England settlers set out against Algonquians, or Israelites against the Hittites:

Himself and honest servants three
Armed husbandmen became, as erst
His sires in Pequod wilds immersed.
Hittites—foes pestilent to God
His fathers old those Indians deemed;
Nathan the Arabs here esteemed
The same—slaves meriting the rod.

Agar pleads with him not to go, to remain in Jerusalem:

Serve God by cleaving to thy wife,
Thy children.

But neither her pleading nor the nursling's death stops him. He is killed by the Arabs he hunts; time and fate "doomed him and cut short his date." Before his death he even loses Agar's love:

But first was modified the lien
The husband had on Agar's heart;
And next a prudence slid athwart
After distrust.

Melville's Nathan, like Clarel, seeks in the Holy Land a religious identity that was inaccessible to him in America. This, his Hebrew identity, is intimately related to his American self with its Puritan legacy and New Hampshire spirit. In the Holy Land the ultimate source for his Puritan self can be found and his New England vitality, courage and action expressed. But his hopes are dashed, reality intervenes, and in trying to cope with it he loses the very love of Agar through which he first recovered his religious faith.[13]

Mark Twain

While Melville turned to the Land of Israel in a religious way and with scriptural ideals in his heart, Mark Twain (1835-1910) went there in 1868 as a tourist with grand images of the Land from his childhood.[14] His accounts appeared in the New York *Tribune*, the New York *Herald*, and the San Francisco *Alta Californian*. They were published in 1869 as *The Innocents Abroad; or, The New Pilgrim's Progress*.[15]

Twain experienced a disjunction between image and reality. The descendants of the ancient Israelites in the Holy Land looked like any other savages. The contemporary Jacob was a foolish-looking donkey rider making barbarous sounds. Palestine was desolate and filthy, its inhabitants ignorant and lazy. The women of Nazareth, reputed to be beautiful, were ugly. Some natives were disgusting. In Baniyas he met a woman riding a little donkey with a small child:

Honestly, I though the child had goggles on as we approached, and I wondered how the mother could afford so much style. But when we drew near, we saw that the goggles were nothing but a camp meeting of flies assembled around each of the child's eyes, and at the same time there was a detachment prospecting its nose. The flies were happy, the child was contented, and so the mother did not interfere.

The difference in scale between what Twain had expected from his biblical education and what he saw caused another disjunction. The celebrated Sea of Galilee was nowhere near as large as Lake Tahoe. As for beauty, the Sea was "no more to be compared to Tahoe than a meridian of longitude is to a rainbow." The whole Land was disappointingly small. It astonished him that the "flourishing plant" of Christianity could have sprung form such an "exceedingly small portion of the earth." The longest journey the Savior took, from Capernaum to Jerusalem, was no more than 120 miles, that from Capernaum to Sidon no more than 70. Twain saw things from an American's point of view: "Instead of being wide apart—as American appreciation of distances would naturally suggest—the places made most particularly celebrated by the presence of Christ are nearly all right here in full view, and within cannon shot of Capernaum." Aside from a few short journeys, the Savior spent His whole life, preached His gospels and performed His miracles in an area no larger than an ordinary American county. The difference between the grandeur of scriptural history and reality was incomprehensible: "It is as much as I can do to comprehend this stupefying fact. How it wears a man out to have read up a hundred pages of history every two or three miles—for verily the celebrated localities of Palestine occur that close together. How wearily, how bewildering they swarm about your path." Sunday school images had to be reduced if he was to understand what he saw: "I must begin a system of reduction . . . I must try to reduce my ideas of Palestine to a more reasonable shape." All those kings in *Joshua* lost their grandeur when Twain looked at petty chiefs whose "kingdoms" were considered large if they were five miles square with a population of two thousand.* All the 30 monarchies destroyed by Joshua (*Joshua* 12) would fit into four American counties.

While other pilgrims reconciled reality with their preconceptions of holiness, for Twain travel in the Holy Land sent any sense of the sacred he brought with him into oblivion. He recalled how one of his party, Dr. G. B. Birch, treated a child's eyes. The mother told everyone and a crowd gathered. Twain drew a parallel to Jesus' success:

She went off and started the whole nation, and it was a sight to see them swarm! The lame, the halt, the blind, the leprous—all the distempers that are bred of indolence, dirt, and iniquity—were represented in the congress in ten minutes, and still they came! Every woman that had a sick baby brought it along, and every woman that hadn't, borrowed one. What reverent and what worshipping looks they bent upon that dread, mysterious power, the doctor . . . I believe they thought he was gifted like a god. When each individual got his portion of medicine, his eyes were radiant with joy—notwithstanding by nature they are a thankless and impassive race—and upon his face was written the unquestioning faith that nothing on earth could prevent the patient from getting well now. Christ knew how to preach to these simple, superstitious, disease-tortured creatures. He healed the sick. They flocked to our poor human doctor this morning when the fame of what he had done to the sick child went abroad in the Land, and they worshipped him with their eyes, while they did not know as yet whether there was virtue in his simples or not. The ancestors of these—people precisely like them in color,

---

*"And when all these kings were met together, they came and pitched together by the waters of Merom, to fight against Israel." *Joshua* 11:5.

dress, manners, customs, simplicity—flocked in vast multitudes after Christ and when they saw Him make the afflicted whole with a word, it is no wonder that they worshipped Him.

As to the "sacred birthplace" of Jesus in the underground grotto of the Church of the Nativity, Twain chose to recall how priests and members of the Latin and Greek churches had to enter by different avenues, to avoid fighting on that "holiest ground on earth." In place of holiness, he found nothing:

I have no "meditations," suggested by this spot where the very first "Merry Christmas" was uttered in all the world, and from whence the friend of my childhood, Santa Claus, departed on his first journey, to gladden and continue to gladden roaring firesides on wintry mornings in many a distant land forever and forever. I touch, with reverent finger, the actual spot where the infant Jesus lay, but I think—nothing.

For Twain, the ground on which Jesus walked was not sacred. He felt no intermingling of Christ's sacred presence and the earth:

It seems curious enough to us to be standing on ground that was once actually pressed by the feet of the Savior. The situation is suggestive of a reality and a tangibility that seem at variance with the vagueness and mystery and ghostliness that one naturally attaches to the character of a god. I cannot comprehend yet that I am sitting where a god has stood, and looking upon the brook and the mountains which that God looked upon, am surrounded by dusky men and women whose ancestors saw Him, and even talked with Him, face to face, and carelessly, just as they would have done with any other stranger. I cannot comprehend this; the gods of my understanding have been always hidden in clouds and very far away.[16]

Twain concluded that his Sunday school picture of the ancient Israelites was simply "too holy" for the "coarse earth."

The offensiveness and tininess of the Land versus biblical expectations and the absence of the sacred left Twain in despair:

Palestine sits in sackcloth and ashes. Over it broods the spell of a curse that has withered its fields and fettered its energies. Where Sodom and Gomorrah reared their domes and towers, that solemn sea now floods the plain, in whose bitter waters no living thing exists—over whose waveless surface the blistering air hangs motionless and dead—about whose borders nothing grows but weeds, and scattering tufts of cane, and that treacherous fruit that promises refreshment to parching lips, but turns to ashes at the touch.

He responded with satiric humor, as if to make it all profane. For example, when he looked at the Land from the Lebanese hills he observed that the distances were so small that "a cannon ball would carry beyond the confines of the Holy Land and light upon profane ground three miles away." The Bashan Valley amounted to a "respectable strip of fertile land . . . There is enough of it to make a farm."[17] He mocked those who cried in awe about the Land:

> I have read all the books on Palestine, nearly, that have been printed, and the authors all wept. When Mr. Prime was here, before he wrote his curious *Tent Life in the Holy Land*, he wept and his party all wept and the dragoman wept and so did the muleteers and even a Latin priest and a Jew that came straggling along. It would have been just as cheap to believe that the camels and asses wept also, and fully as likely; and he might as well have added them to the water company likewise. Prime got such a start then that he never could shut himself off; and he went through Palestine and irrigated it from one end to the other. No man was ever so easily affected as he, probably. Whenever he found a holy place that was well authenticated, he cried; whenever he found one that was not well authenticated, he cried anyhow and took the chances; whenever he could not find any holy place at all, he just cried "for a flyer," as the worldly say. No man ever enjoyed a funeral as Prime did his sentimental journey through the Holy Land.
>
> How his horse ever kept his health, being exposed to these periodical showers all the time, is a wonder. I never will believe anybody again that says he cried over Jerusalem; the bookmakers have created within me a bitter animosity against these boastful Jerusalem-weepers and also a lack of faith in them. If ever a party were peculiarly liable to tears under such circumstances, it is our pilgrims. They are the very bodies to go into sentimental convulsions at the merest shadow of a provocation, yet they wept not over Jerusalem.[18]

Thieving Bedouins reminded him of Jews who stole everything in sight before they "vamoosed the Egyptians ranch." The golden calf must have been a "pleasant free lunch." Twain laughed over the story—freely interpreted by him—of Yael driving a ten-penny spike into Sisera's brain after inviting him to bed (*Judges* 4 and 5). He enjoyed recalling the two Samarian women who agreed to boil and eat their sons during a famine, one of them reneging (*II Kings* 6).

Twain's disenchantment was reinforced by the 40 refugees of George Adams' Jaffa Colony who ended up aboard with the *Quaker City* with Twain in September 1867:

> Our forty were miserable enough in the first place, and they lay about the decks seasick all the voyage, which about completed their misery, I take it. However, one or two young men remained upright, and by constant

persecution we wormed out of them some little information. They gave it reluctantly and in a very fragmentary condition, for having been shamefully humbugged by their prophet, they felt humiliated and unhappy. In such circumstances people do not like to talk. The colony was a complete *fiasco*. I have already said that such as could get away did so, from time to time. The prophet Adams—once an actor, then several other things, afterward a Mormon and a missionary, always an adventurer—remains at Jaffa with his handful of sorrowful subjects.[19]

Twain must have been pleased to return to America, where there were no romantic biblical visions to conflict with reality, no investment in the sacred to turn sour.

John Fulton

Scottish-born John Fulton (1834-1907) was an Episcopal priest in New Orleans, Mobile, and St. Louis; lecturer on canon law at the Philadelphia School of Divinity; and in 1878 editor of two Episcopal journals, *The Living Church*, published in Chicago, and *The Church Standard*, published in Philadelphia. He received honorary doctorates from the universities of Georgia, Alabama, and The south. Fulton visited the Land of Israel sometime in the 1880s, and after his return to New York he wrote about it in *The Beautiful Land*.[20]

In his introduction, Bishop Henry C. Potter (1834—1908) of New York related that Fulton had asked himself, "What do I really know about Jerusalem? I am constantly talking of the great events which occurred there, but if I were set down in one of its streets, what should I really know about the place?" Travel guides, such as those by Edward Robinson, James T. Barclay, or William M. Thomson, did not satisfy his quest for knowledge, but they did allay his fears about going to the Holy Land, and he was ready to follow the Savior without a guide. Once he made the trip, Fulton was "satisfied from his own experience that every Christian man who does any part of it will find some part of the gospel story lit up before his mind's eye with a new and wondrous light."[21]

Like the other pilgrims, Fulton experienced a disjunction in the Land between what "it was" according to Scripture and what "it is." He spoke of the naked children and filthy residents in the pathetic huts of Magdala on the Sea of Galilee, the garbage along the Via Dolorosa, the vermin and mosquitos of Tiberias. He found many local rituals offensive. The Church of the Holy Sepulcher was "desecrated by the blood of Christians shed by Christian hands; and to this day the supposed scene of Christ's resurrection yearly profaned by a pretended miracle" of the descent of God upon the Holy Tomb during the Greek Easter celebration. Fulton was repelled by the Greek Orthodox Easter at the Chapel of the Holy Sepulcher (reported by Arthur P. Stanley, Dean of Westminster). Inside the Chapel a heaving sea of heads roared in expectation of the visible descent of the Holy Ghost. The Bishop of Petra, for the moment "Bishop of the fire," inserted flame through a hole in the north side of the Chapel, a flame passed hand to hand to light thousands of candles and then rushed to a Greek church in Bethlehem. In the streets of Jerusalem onlooking pilgrims rubbed their faces and breasts against the lighted tapers to demonstrate their harmlessness. As far as Fulton was concerned, the only real miracle would be for the stones of the Chapel to "cry out against the wild fanaticism without, and wretched fraud within, by which it is at that hour desecrated." He cited Stanley: "'Such is the Greek Easter—the greatest moral argument against the identity of the spot which it professes to honor—stripped, indeed, of some of its most revolting features, yet still, considering the place, the time, and the intention of the professed miracle, probably the most offensive imposture to be found in the world.'"[22]

Fulton responded to the disjunction by concentrating on authentic rituals. For example, he appreciated Jews coming to Jerusalem to atone, study the law with intensity, and enjoy Passover and *Simhat Tora*. He was impressed by their remorse over the loss of their ancient world. On the last day of the year—presumably *Erev Rosh Ha'shana*—they arose three hours before sunrise and received 39 lashes. He could imagine how they felt, dwelling as they did in their filthy quarter, strangers in the Land of their forefathers, as they recited the litany at the Wall.[*23] Fulton did not dwell on either Jewish guilt for crucifixion as the source for Jewish woe or upon conversion, as did some fellow Episcopalians.[24]

Thomas de Witt Talmage

Thomas de Witt Talmage was a Presbyterian minister in Brooklyn and author of popular studies of the Bible. In 1889-1890 he led a group of pilgrims to "Christland." It was a dream come true: "For a long while I had cherished the dream that I might some day visit the Holy Land, to see with my own eyes the sky, the fields, the rocks, and the sacred background of the divine tragedy."[25]

Like the others, Talmage was distressed at what he actually saw. The Land was withering under Turkish control. He resented Islam, which he considered opposed to modern civilization and free thinking, a dark power rejecting other religions from the Holy Land because it could not stand their light.

Talmage confronted the disjunction. On a practical level, in order to increase the number of Christian pilgrims, he suggested building a train bridge over the Bering Straits. He hoped that Jews would leave those lands where they were

---

*"*Rabbi:* For the palace that lies waste. *People:* We sit in solitude and weep! *R:* For the Temple that is overthrown. *P:* We sit in solitude and weep! *R:* For the walls that are cast down. *P:* We sit in solitude and weep! *R:* For the mighty stones that are turned to dust. *P:* We sit in solitude and weep! *R:* For our glory that is clean and vanished away. *P:* We sit in solitude and weep."

persecuted to settle in the Holy Land, and he believed in God's promise that the Jews would ultimately gather there:

> God will gather in that distant Land, those of that race who have been maltreated and He will blast with the lightnings of His omnipotence those lands on either side of the Atlantic, which have been the instruments of annoyance and harm to that Jewish race to which belonged Abraham and David, and Joshua and Baron Hirsch and Montefiore and Paul the Apostle, and Mary the Virgin, and Jesus Christ the Lord.

On a spiritual level Talmage responded to the disjunction by bridging contemporary events and scriptural reality, continually shifting between the two. Like Prime he left the present—"we have lost our hold of the nineteenth century and we are clear back in the ages"—and entered into the timelessness of the Bible:

> Christ-like Abrahamic, Mosaic, Davidic, Solomonic, and Herodic histories overlap each other with such power that by the time I took my feet out of the stirrups at the close of the journey, I felt so wrung out with emotion that it seemed nothing else could ever absorb my feelings again.

The Bible was "newer than any book that yesterday came out of any of our great printing houses." At Golgotha Talmage was enveloped by scriptural reality. As he recited *John* 19 on the crucifixion and burial of Christ, a chill blast struck the hill. Talmage saw raging mobs gnashing their teeth and shaking their clenched fists at Christ. Horses pawed the earth and snorted at the smell of carnage. A group of gamblers pitched up to decide who would have the Savior's coat. "There are women almost dead with grief among the crowd, His mother and His aunt, and some whose sorrows He had comforted and whose guilt He had pardoned. Here a man dips a sponge into sour wine and by a stick lifts it to the hot and cracked lips. The hemorrhage from the five wounds has done its work." Overcome by the scriptural events, he broke down and cried but was consoled by anticipation of another crusade for Jerusalem.

Another shift from the present time into timelessness took place at Jaffa. Standing on the balcony of his hotel, Talmage looked out upon miles of black waters filled with logs fastened together. They were for him the cedars of Lebanon which King Hiram had furnished to King Solomon for the Temple.* The king floated them down to Jaffa, whence they were taken 41 miles over the

---

*"Now Hiram the king of Tyre had furnished Solomon with cedar trees and fir trees, and with gold, according to all his desire, that then king Solomon gave Hiram twenty cities in the land of Galilee." *I Kings* 9:11.

Plains of Sharon to Jerusalem on wagons pulled by oxen. Those rough cedars, would become carved pillars, beautiful altars, exquisite harps and kingly chariots. Talmage contemplated the vast numbers who had built the Temple and the similar numbers presently building the wider, higher and grander Christian temple of righteousness. For generations Christians had given their sweat and tears for it. In Solomon's day everybody helped—some cut down trees in Lebanon, some rode the rafts at sea, some pulled the load across the land, and some heaved up the rafters. Now all Christians should join together from all parts of the world:

One will bind a wound and another will wipe away a tear and another will teach a class, and another will speak the encouraging word, and all of us will be ready to pull and lift and in some way help on the work until the millennial morn shall gild the pinnacles of that finished temple and at its shining gates the world shall put down its last burden, and in its lavers wash off its last stain, and at its altars the last wanderer shall kneel.

Talmage saw the history of the Holy Land pass before him, its different eras moving through an eternal moment. In Jerusalem he heard the crashes of the sieges upon the city. He thought of the pools of Hezekiah and Siloam reddened with human gore.* He envisioned the towers and walls of Jerusalem falling over and over again; he saw David taking the throne at Hebron and going on to capture Jerusalem.† He could see Sennacherib, Nebuchadnezzar, Pompey, Titus, the Crusaders, and finally Saladin all take Jerusalem. "For the last four hundred years it has been in possession of cruel and polluted Mohammedanism!" He contemplated the future:

Another crusade is needed to start for Jerusalem, a crusade in this nineteenth century greater than all those of the past centuries put together. A crusade in which you and I will march. A crusade without weapons of death, but only the sword of the spirit. A crusade that will make not a single wound, nor start one tear of distress, nor incendiarize one homestead. A crusade of gospel peace! And the cross will again be lifted on Calvary, not as once an instrument of pain, but a signal of invitation. And the Mosque of Omar shall give place to a Church of Christ. And Mount Zion become the dwelling place not of David, but of David's Lord. And Jerusalem, purified of all its idolatries, and taking back the Christ once cast out, shall be made a worthy

---

*"This same Hezekiah also stopped the upper watercourse of Gihon, and brought it straight down to the west side of the city of David. And Hezekiah prospered in all his works." *II Chronicles* 32:30. *John* 9:11, supra.

†"And the time that David was king in Hebron over the house of Judah was seven years and six months." *II Samuel* 2:11.

type of that heavenly city which Paul styled "the mother of us all" and which Saint John saw, "the holy Jerusalem descending out of heaven from God."* Through its gates may we all enter when our work is done and in its Temple, greater than all the earthly temples piled in one, may we worship.

Back in the present, Talmage described Russian pilgrims walking hundreds of miles to reach Jerusalem. One old, exhausted woman begged her fellow pilgrims not to let her die until she entered the Holy City. She was carried through the gate with her head held up, crying out, "Now I die content. I have seen it!" He was sure that the angels of mercy would help, that one "glimpse" of God's temple and the lamb, one "look" at the "king in His beauty" would compensate for all the tears and heartbreaks of the journey.† For Talmage, the pilgrimage to Jerusalem sublimated time into eternity.[26]

Observations

The American Protestant pilgrims of the nineteenth century set out to integrate their lives with ancient Scripture by experiencing the sacred religious context, in particular the life and death of Jesus of Nazareth. For some pilgrims—for example, Philip Schaff (1819-1893) in 1877—expectations coincided with reality:

At last I have fulfilled a long-cherished desire to see with my own eyes and to tread with my own feet the most sacred and the most classical Land in the world . . . I found the country and the people pretty much as I expected, but I trust I understand both better than before. My faith in the Bible has not been shaken, but confirmed. Many facts and scenes which seem to float ghost-like in the clouds to a distant reader, assume flesh and blood in the Land of their birth. There is a marvelous correspondence between the Land and the book. The Bible is the best handbook for the Holy Land, and the Holy Land is the best commentary on the Bible.[27]

For J. W. Greenwood, an Episcopal priest who visited the Holy Land in 1884, the sacred was inseparable from what he saw in the night at the Sea of Galilee:[28]

---

*"But Jerusalem which is above is free, which is the mother of us all." *Galatians* 4:26. "And I John saw the holy city, new Jerusalem, coming down from God out of heaven, prepared as a bride adorned for her husband." *Revelation* 21:2.

†"Thine eyes shall see the king in His beauty: they shall behold the land that is very far off." *Isaiah* 33:17.

A solemn and precious hour, a night whose holy and far-reaching thoughts will go with us beyond the grave to recall our earthly vision of a region stamped with our incarnate master's footprints and where we read the gospel written on nature's varied page. Christ, Peter, James, John, saints, and apostles had been there before us, looking on the same hills and little sea which things at least, have never changed. [The following night we] saw several men engaged in fishing and many women toiling beneath their black goatskin sacks of water up the difficult hill—weary workers, such as those upon whom Christ was doubtless looking when, somewhere in this very region, He graciously said, "Come unto Me, all ye that labor and are heavy laden, and I will give you rest" [*Matthew* 11:28]. But neither the elements of that peaceful scene, nor the feelings of its pilgrim spectators, can I properly describe. To attempt the one would be a forlorn hope; to speak too freely of the other would be sheer irreverence.[29]

But the predominant experience was that reality upset religious expectations. Prime resolved the disjunction and ascended into the sacred outside time and space. Melville blended his disappointment in the Land with the tragic religious experience of Clarel but retained the scriptural indices to Clarel's tribulations and his own messianic hopes. Twain resolved the disjunction by separating scriptural myth and its sacred content from Holy Land reality; he felt disappointed and was happy to go back to America. Fulton solved the problem by focusing on religious rituals, in which both empirical and nonempirical factors worked themselves out. Talmage blended present reality with Scripture by dwelling on religious history, sacred or otherwise, as it moved into the messianic future. Altogether, the idea of the Holy Land survived its journey with the pilgrims to the actual Holy Land of Israel; its power endured the vagaries of time and space.

Notes

1. William C. Prime, *Tent Life in the Holy Land* (New York 1857). The Scottish pastor Horatius Bonar, D.D. (1808-1889), publisher of the *London Quarterly Journal of Prophecy*, traveled with Prime, his wife, and other Americans. See Horatius Bonar, *The Land of Promise* (London 1858):342, 359, 423, and Isaac C. Wellcome (1818-1895), *History of the Second Advent Message and Mission, Doctrine and People* (Yarmouth, Me., 1874):553. On Bonar and Cresson, see Chapter 6. On American Protestants in general, see Robert T. Handy, ed., *The Holy Land in American Protestant Life* (New York 1981)

2. Some years later, in *Holy Cross: A history of the invention, preservation, and disappearance of the wood known as the true cross* (New York 1877):9-10, Prime made clear that scientific reasoning about empirical reality did not determine faith:
[This] is only the story of two or three pieces of old wood; pieces of wood which

the blind, unquestioning faith of men made the wood of the cross on which their savior died.

The ardor of religious controversy leads many now to look on that faith with contempt. No faith is contemptible. Faith is worthy of more or less respect, even if it seems to be faith in a falsehood. For faith is power. Faith is what leads to work and produces results. Faith in a lie will sometimes accomplish more than reason in support of truth . . .

If it will help the reader to dismiss prejudice from his mind in reading the story, I will at the outset, say that I have never found reasonable grounds sufficient for the faith whose results I describe, and therefore I do not believe that these fragments of wood were the very cross; but I am bound to add that there is nothing to prove the contrary. They may have been so. Whether they were or were not the wood men believed them to be is not the question in this story, and has no importance in reference to its object, which is not so much to give the history itself as to furnish an illustration of the effect of faith on anything in the history of man and of the world. The wood of the cross, which faith made an object of passionate affection and reverence to all the Christian world, was one of the most important objects in history.

3.   Edward Bodner of Georgetown University translated the Latin. I have been unable to identify the source.

4.   Prime, *Tent Life*, frontispiece, 22-23, 59-67, 99-100, 138-140, 315, 497.

5.   Prime, "'The New Jerusalem; or, The soul's breathing after her heavenly country,'" in *O Mother Dear, Jerusalem: The old hymn, its origin, and genealogy* (New York 1865):35-41.   The book deals with a church hymn translated by David Dickson of Scotland in the seventeenth century.

6.   See Franklin D. Walker, *Irreverent Pilgrims: Melville, Browne, and Mark Twain in the Holy Land* (Seattle 1974); Nathaniel Wright, *Melville's Use of the Bible* (New York 1974); William Braswell, *Melville's Religious Thought* (Durham, N.C., 1943):108-109.

7.   Herman Melville, *Journal of a Visit to Europe and the Levant, 11 October 1856-6 May 1857*, ed. Howard C. Horsford (Princeton 1955); Herman Melville, *Clarel: A Poem and Pilgrimage in the Holy Land*, Walter E. Bezanson, ed. (New York 1960). See Vincent S. Kenny, *Herman Melville's Clarel: A Spiritual Autobiography* (Hamden, Conn., 1973).

8.   See *Clarel* I.8.23-29, I.16.78, and III.21.278 for Melville's ambivalent attitudes towards Jews. Cf. Jay A. Holstein, "Melville's Stereotypical Treatment of Jews," *Journal of Reform Judaism* 28 no. 4 (Fall 1981):40-51.

9.   Melville, *Clarel*, IV.29.153-155.

10.   Melville, *Journal*, 140-153, 155-160.

11.   Thomas Paine, *The Age of Reason* (London 1794-1795).

12. See Horsford's comments on Melville's *Journal*, 143, and Bezanson's comments on Melville's *Clarel*, 542-543. On Cresson, see Chapter 6.

13. Melville, *Clarel*, I.17.

14. See Allison Ensor, "To the Holy Land," in *Mark Twain and the Bible* (Lexington, Ky., 1969):15-28; John Q. Hays, *Mark Twain and Religion: A Mirror of American Eclecticism* (New York 1989):49-55.

15. Mark Twain, *The Innocents Abroad; or, The new pilgrim's progress* (Hartford 1871):ch. 42-58. The chapters contain a number of sarcastic remarks about Prime, called "Grimes." See also Bernard de Voto, ed., *Mark Twain in Eruption* (London 1940):349.

16. Twain, *Innocents Abroad*, 472-475, 486, 502, 507, 601.

17. Twain, *Innocents Abroad*, 478, 480, 607.

18. Twain, "A Curious Remnant of the Past," in *Traveling with the Innocents Abroad: Mark Twain's Original Reports from Europe and the Holy Land*, Daniel M. McKeithan, ed. (Norman, Okla., 1958):265.

19. Twain, *Innocents Abroad*, 613. On the Adams Colony see Chapter 9.

20. I am indebted to David L. Holmes for his advice on this section. I have been unable to determine the date of Fulton's journey. *The Living Church: A weekly record of its news, its work, and its thought* (*LC*) published 1879-1885, did not mention it, though it did record his serving at Saint George's Church in St. Louis (*LC* 3 no. 40/144 [6 August 1881]:5) and his recovering from a serious illness (*LC* 6 no. 44/304 [30 August 1884]:1). *The Living Church Quarterly* (Milwaukee) 6 no. 1 (1 December 1890):222. John Fulton, *The Beautiful Land: Historical, geographical, and pictorial. Described and illustrated as it was and it is now. Along the lines of our Savior's journeys* (New York 1891), reprinted as *Palestine: The Holy Land as It Was and as It Is* (Philadelphia 1900). Variants of the phrase "as it was and it is" were used by James T. Barclay, George W. J. Adams, Albert Rhodes, and Israel P. Warren, *Jerusalem, ancient and modern: Outlines of its history and antiquities, with descriptions of its topography, and the principal points of interest in both the ancient and modern city, including the Temple as it was in the time of Christ and the recent explorations and excavations, illustrated by plans and wood cuts and by the key plates of Selous's two great pictures of Jerusalem as it was and as it is* (Boston 1873). Fulton also wrote *Index Canonum: Containing the canons called apostolical, the canons of the undisputed general councils, and the canons of the provincial councils of Ancyra, Neo-Caesarea, Gangra, Antioch, and Laodicea* (New York 1872; Philip Schaff wrote a preface for the 1883 edition); *The Laws of Marriage: Containing the Hebrew law, the Roman law of the New Testament, and the canon law of the universal church. Concerning the impediments of marriage and the dissolution of the marriage bond* (New York 1883); and *Christian Unity and Christian Faith* (New York 1885).

21. Henry C. Potter, Introduction to Fulton, *Beautiful Land*, vii. Cf. Edward Robinson, *Biblical Researches in Palestine, Mount Sinai, and Arabia Petra* (Boston 1841); James T. Barclay, *City of the Great King; or, Jerusalem as it was, as it is, and as it is to be* (1858; reprint, New York 1977); and William M. Thomson, *The Land and the Book* (New York 1859). Potter's own journey to the Holy Land took place in 1875-1876. He too experienced disjunction:

> And one needs something exhilarating to sustain him amid the inevitable disappointment of the first days in Jerusalem. For, familiar as one's reading may have made him with all in the Holy City that is incongruous with its consecrated associations, the actual contact with those incongruities is inexpressibly shocking—I had almost written sickening . . . When in the Holy Land, I was pained, as many others have been, with the often dismal incongruity between its traditions and its people, and still more between its most holy places and the moral and religious atmosphere that surrounds them. It is impossible that this should be otherwise unless one has ceased to feel at all.

Potter, *The Gates of the East: A winter in Egypt and Syria* (New York 1877):191, 249.

22. Arthur P. Stanley, *Sinai and Palestine* (London 1856):464. The Catholic pilgrim William H. Bergan recalled that on his 1874 visit,

> Our time did not allow us to be present at the Holy Sepulcher for the great Greek jugglery, the drawing down fire from heaven—the "miraculous fire"—on the Holy Saturday of the Greeks.
>
> This blasphemous and wicked imposition upon the ignorant Greek clergy and people was, however, described to us in a lively manner by Count Kapoga whom we visited by invitation, and who on a later occasion called on us at our headquarters.

William H. Bergan, *Notes of Hand: Drawn at sight by William H. Bergan. Busy thoughts of a traveler in the Orient. A record of observations, impressions, and feelings, simply and candidly expressed in his correspondence to "The Catholic Standard" of Philadelphia. Experiences began with departure from the city of Trieste at the head of the Adriatic Sea, on 28 February 1874* (Philadelphia 1908):66-67. On Bergan see Chapter 12.

23. Fulton, *Beautiful Land*, 601-603, 616, 644, 647. I have been unable to verify the practice of 39 lashes. Schaff said that the elegy at the Wall

> keeps alive the memory of deepest humiliation and guilt, and the hope of final deliverance. The scene at the Wailing Place was to me touching and pregnant with meaning. God has no doubt reserved this remarkable people, which, like the burning bush, is never consumed, for some great purpose before the final coming of our Lord.

Philip Schaff, *Through Bible Lands: Notes of travel in Egypt, the desert, and Palestine* (New York 1871):251-252. See also Potter, "Literal Translation of the Jewish Lamentations at the Place of Wailing at Jerusalem," in *Gates of the East*, 254-259. See Hugh Nibley, "Christian Envy of the Temple," *Jewish Quarterly Review* 50 no. 2 (October 1959):97-123, and 50 no. 3 (January 1960):229-240.

On prayers at the Wall see Cyrus Adler, *Memorandum on the Western Wall: Submitted to the Special Commission of the League of Nations on Behalf of the*

Rabbinate, the Jewish Agency for Palestine, the Jewish Community of Palestine, and the Central Agudat Israel of Palestine (Jerusalem 1930). The early collection of prayers at the Wall, Gershon ben Asher of Scarmela, *The Lineage of the Pious* (Mantua 1601; reprint, *Jerusalem* 1896, Hebrew), does not contain the elegy. Titus Tobler, *Topographie von Jerusalem und seinen Umgebungen* (Berlin 1853—1854):1:629—630, says that the text, reminiscent of *Lamentations*, was recited by the Karaites. He cited Joseph Wolff in *Basler-Missionsmagazin* (1823):255. Cf. Joseph Wolff, "Extracts from the Journal of Mr. Wolff [Jerusalem 5 April 1822]," *Jewish Expositor and Friend of Israel: Containing monthly communications respecting the Jews and the proceedings of the London Jewish Society (JEFI)* (November 1822):461-468. See also Baron August von Haxthausen, "Liturgy of the Karaim Jews," in *Transcaucasia: Sketches of the nations and races between the Black Sea and the Caspian* (London 1854):139.

24. In March 1885, for example, Brad Courtland published "Via Dolorosa," *LC* 7 no. 22/334 (28 March 1885):1, on the front page of *LC*:
"Ecce Homo!" said the Roman prelate Pilate, stern and loud;
Answered back with fierce revilings all the rabble Jewish crowd;
Come Thou from the grand Praetorium with head thorn-crowned and bowed
The royal victim stately, and behold: a pallid cloud
Shadowed Via Dolorosa, as the Roman prelate proud
Washed his hands before the rabble, and in trumpet tones and loud
Said the ban on every Jewish child and parent in the crowd.

The royal victim, bending underneath His weight of woe,
Climbed the Via Dolorosa, eighteen hundred years ago,
Left behind the glorious city bathed on richest Syrian glow,
While the branching limes and olives swaying gently to and fro
Kissed the heated brow of Him whose faltering steps and slow
Climbed up Via Dolorosa fainting 'neath that weight of woe
Jeered by the Jewish rabble, eighteen hundred years ago.

Let us veil our Christian faces, we the Christians of to-day.
"Crucify Him, crucify Him," did the Jewish rabble say!
Does no other human rabble catch the note from far away,
As it comes down through the ages of the dimming centuries gray,
Lo! the warm Egyptian lilies blooming now as blossomed for aye;
And the mellow Syrian sunset gathering jewels from the day!
Hear again the wandering echoes: "Crucify Him," do they say.

Floating down the tide of ages comes again the muffled strain—
"Crucify Him, crucify Him! on our children be the stain."
Drooped the gorgeous Syrian lilies, nestling in the golden grain—
On the Via Dolorosa did the kingly victim drain
All that bitter cup of anguish; till the solemn, sad refrain
Is sent back through all the ages: "He is crucified again."
And alike on Jew and gentile rests the seal of His blood stain.

Fulton was not involved with his church's missionary work in the Holy Land. For example, see "Evangelization of the Jews," *LC* 7 no. 17/329 (21 February 1885):137, and "Church Society for Promoting Christianity among the Jews," *LC* 5 no. 8/216 (23 December 1882):9. He did deal with the view of Jews in the "primitive church" in *Index Canonum*.

25. [Eleanor M. Talmage], *Thomas de Witt Talmage as I Knew Him* (New York 1912):211.

26. Talmage, *Talmage on Palestine,* 6, 7, 19, 20-21, 25, 41, 50-51.

27. Schaff, *Through Bible Lands,* 383-384. On Schaff see James E. Smylie, "Protestant Clergymen and American Destiny: Prelude to Imperialism, 1856-1900," *Harvard Theological Review* 56 (1963):297-311.

28. This was so, even though he felt that "Christianity nowhere appears at a greater disadvantage than in its head-center, Jerusalem." J. W. G[reenwood], "Phases of Religious Belief in the Holy City [Jaffa 18 January 1884]," *LC* 6 no. 18/278 (1 March 1884):1.

29. Greenwood, "Days in the Holy Land: The Sea of Galilee," *LC* 7 no. 10/322 (3 January 1885):81. Cf. Greenwood, "Days in the Holy Land," *LC* 6 no. 52/312 (25 October 1884):425; 7 no. 2/314 (8 November 1884):9-10; 7 no. 3/315 (15 November 1884):21; 7 no. 4/316 (22 November 1884):31; 7 no. 5/317 (29 November 1884):39; 7 no. 6/318 (6 December 1884):47; 7 no. 8/320 (20 December 1884):59; 7 no. 10/322 (3 January 1885):81.

5 Protestant Missionaries: Jewish Conversion and Christ's Return

American Christian missionaries of the nineteenth century paid special attention to the Holy Land and its Jewish residents. The second coming, which was to be centered there, was thought imminent. Because the people of Israel were the ultimate testimony against Jesus' truth, Jews in the Land constituted living testimonies against the advent. It was imperative, therefore, that they become Christians.[1] The occupants of the sacred space must not be allowed to defy theological reality; they had to be converted. In 1853 the Corresponding Secretary of the Disciples of Christ's American Christian Missionary Society (ACMS) observed that since the Lord's law went forth eighteen hundred years ago from the Land of Israel (the real point of origin of Christians), the restoration of primeval Christianity sought by the Disciples would also take place there. As part of the restoration, the Jews of the Land had to become Christians. Christians had to bring this about because these Jews were so degraded and ignorant that they could not acquire divine knowledge by themselves. Moreover, since the Land of Israel was the geographic center of the world, bridging Asia and Africa, what happened there would reverberate around the globe, and so it was crucial that Christian truth reign there.[2]

Fisk, Parsons, and King

Before Departure

The first American missions to the Holy Land were sponsored by the Congregational American Board of Commissioners for Foreign Missions (ABCFM).[3] Following promising reports about missionary work in Smyrna and Madras, ABCFM decided in 1818 to establish a mission in Palestine despite danger and the power of Catholics and Muslims. Two graduates of the Andover

Theological Seminary (Congregational) were chosen, Pliny Fisk and Levi Parsons.[4]

On 11 September 1819 Parsons asked "God for a more perfect knowledge of His revealed will in regard to the Jews." He found many predictions, many precious promises, yet his "mind remained in darkness."[5] Six weeks later, when he delivered his farewell address—on Sunday afternoon, 31 October 1819, in Boston's Park Street Church—his mind had cleared. He described the desolation of the Jews on account of murdering Christ and how history was surging forward to the second coming. During this, the eve of the *eschaton*, the Jews had to convert and be restored to their Land.

Parsons recalled that 40 years after Jewish hands were bloodied by the murder of the Son of God, Jerusalem was demolished by heavenly judgment. The Temple lay in ruins, its sacrifices over. As the Savior had predicted, every stone was cast down.* Mount Zion, as Jeremiah had predicted, was plowed like a field.† Just as Lot had fled Sodom, so the followers of Christ fled Jerusalem. As to the Jews, "the Holy Spirit departed from the maddened people forever." The God of their fathers forsook them. "The door of hope was closed, the day of probation past, and these wretched beings were shut up in the darkness of an eternal night." The remnant that escaped was completely dispersed, politically annihilated. Those who remained in Judea were enslaved and physically punished. They were prohibited from treading the soil of Jerusalem and from shedding tears upon the ground where they crucified the Lord. Since that time the Jews had awaited the messiah, but in vain. Jews the world over "remain the objects of abhorrence and contempt. Thus the blood of Jesus has been upon them and upon their children; thus for ages they have been suffering the vengeance of an incensed judge."‡ Like the bush of Horeb, they have continued to burn without being consumed.

Throughout this entire history of desolation, Parsons continued, the Jews have sought to return to the Land of their fathers and restore it. In his mind the return would coincide with conversion to Christianity: when the Jews came to Zion they would look upon the One Whom they pierced and mourn. They would declare that they had now found the One of Whom Moses and the prophets spoke.

---

*"And Jesus went out, and departed from the temple: and His disciples came to Him for to show Him the buildings of the temple. And Jesus said unto them, See ye not all these things? Verily I say unto you, There shall not be left here one stone upon another, that shall not be thrown down." *Matthew* 24:1-2.

†"Thus saith the Lord of hosts; Zion shall be plowed like a field, and Jerusalem shall become heaps, and the mountain of the house as the high places of a forest." *Jeremiah* 26:18.

‡"Then answered all the people, and said, His blood be on us and on our children." *Matthew* 27:25.

The return of the Jews would bring rejoicing in heaven and earth.* The saints of the world would sit at the Lord's table with the "outcasts of Israel" and exclaim, "This our brother was dead, and is alive again; and was lost, and is found".† Parsons believed that Jews were already converting in increasing numbers and that many more were ready.[6] Jews were concentrating on Jerusalem, where they expected the messiah to arrive imminently. If the Savior did indeed come, the Jews "might renounce their fatal delusion, and receive Him who was crucified on Calvary, as the Lamb of God who taketh away the sins of the world."

How could the complete return and conversion of the Jews be brought about? First by sharing the Christian message with them: "As they gave the gospel to us, we are to give it to them, and how great is the privilege of reflecting back a part of that glory, which has so long beamed upon us from the holy of holies!" Second, by having Christians pray for Jews, as Saint Paul and Jesus himself did.‡ Parsons emphasized the theme of reciprocity:

> They toiled and suffered, and died in defense of our holy religion. *Our* God was *their* God, *our* heaven is *their* heaven. This *Holy Bible* they faithfully handed down to us secure from the assaults of infidelity. All our seasons of communion with God, all our hopes of glory, are come to us through the instrumentality of the Jewish saints. *Gratitude* demands a suitable return for these invaluable favors.

When Parson's listeners died and entered the new Jerusalem they would be reprimanded by the patriarchs and prophets, by Peter and Paul, for the continued degeneracy of the Jewish children: "We toiled and suffered for you, but our children have been left to famish for the bread of life." The first Jewish Christians "brought their substance and laid it at the apostles' feet." As the original missionaries of the cross, Jewish Christians had to relinquish every earthly interest for the salvation of the gentiles. Jews were the first teachers of those very gentiles and pagans from whom Parsons and his listeners descended. "When shall we repay this unmeasured benevolence, when be as faithful to them as they were to us? . . . He who now intercedes for you before the throne of God, as concerning the flesh, is a Jew. And His last command was "Go ye into *all* the world, and preach the gospel to every creature" (*Mark* 16:15).

---

*"For if the casting away of them be the reconciling of the world, what shall the receiving of them be, but life from the dead?" *Romans* 11:15.

†*Isaiah* 11:12, supra. *Luke* 15:32.

‡"Brethren, my heart's desire and prayer to God for Israel is, that they might be saved." *Romans* 10:1. *Luke* 23:34, supra.

Parsons asked his listeners to be resolved about the Christian future of the Holy Land, and to pray together: "If I forget thee, O Jerusalem, let my right hand forget her cunning. If I do not remember thee, let my tongue cleave to the roof of my mouth; if I prefer not Jerusalem above my chief joy" (*Psalms* 137:5-6).[7]

In the evening of that same Sunday Pliny Fisk spoke in Boston's Old south Church. He talked of rekindling the flames of primitive piety "on the crumbling altars of long corrupted Christianity" in the Holy Land.[8] He was going there himself to "besiege a great empire of sin, where Satan from ancient times has held undisputed possession of his strongholds."[9]

The Sacred Land

The two friends departed America on 3 November 1819.[10] They arrived on Malta the day after Christmas, then went to Smyrna (Izmir, Turkey) and Cyprus. In January 1821 Parsons went alone to the Holy Land to survey the conditions for missionary work to "take possession of the Land of promise."[11] He experienced the sacred reality of Christianity blending with the present. On 22 February 1821 he climbed the Mount of Olives and thought of David weeping as he ascended.[*] The Mount was filled with the sacredness of Christ:

> On the east side of it our blessed Savior raised Lazarus from the grave; and on the west, He endured the agony of Gethsemane. Here He beheld the city, and wept over it. From this mount He was at one time conducted to Jerusalem with shoutings of "Hosanna to the son of David."[†] And at another with the cry of "Crucify Him, crucify Him."[‡] From this spot He gave His last commission, "Go into all the world, and preach the gospel," and then ascended, and sat down on the right hand of the majesty on high.[#]

Parsons participated in a Catholic Easter ritual which drew Scripture into the present. On Friday, 20 April 1821, at the spot on Mount Calvary where the Savior was nailed to the cross and then raised, he saw a cross erected with a figure about three feet long in the posture of a person crucified upon it. Then two men, representing Nicodemus and Joseph, ascended the cross, drew out the

---

[*]"And David went up by the ascent of Mount Olivet, and wept as he went up, and had his head covered, and he went barefoot." *II Samuel* 15:30.

[†]"And the multitudes that went before, and that followed, cried, saying, Hosanna to the son of David: Blessed is He that cometh in the name of the Lord; Hosanna in the highest." *Matthew* 21:9.

[‡]See, for example, *Luke* 23:21: "But they cried, saying, Crucify Him, crucify Him."

[#]*Mark* 16:15, supra.

nails, took down the body, and laid it in a napkin. The body was taken to the Stone of Unction, where it was anointed. The superior of the adjacent convent delivered a sermon in Arabic. He began by clasping his hands and raising his eyes to heaven, as if to say, "All is lost." The body was then deposited in the Church of the Holy Sepulcher.[12]

Parsons was repelled by some of Jerusalem's ritual. At the Greek Orthodox Easter celebration, which started on the evening of Saturday, 21 April 1821, about five thousand Jews, Turks, Christians, and "people from every nation under heaven" assembled around the Church of the Holy Sepulcher "to witness the supposed miraculous descent of the Holy Spirit, under the similitude of fire":

About 12 o'clock we witnessed scenes of a very extraordinary nature, and highly derogatory to the Christian profession. A body of Arab Christians, natives of Palestine, were admitted to perform their part in the duties of the Holy Week. They began by running around the Holy Sepulcher, with all the frantic air of madmen;—clapping their hands, throwing their caps into the air, cuffing each other's ears, walking half-naked upon the shoulders of their companions hallooing, or rather shrieking, to the utmost extent of their voices . . . Every eye was fixed as the time approached. As we stood waiting, suddenly there darted from the Sepulcher a flaming torch, which was carried almost instantaneously to a distant part of the assembly. I stood among the first to receive the fire, and to prove that as to its power of burning it contained no extraordinary qualities. The zeal of the fire, before the superior qualities departed (as they say it burns like other fire in a few minutes), endangered the lives of many. Several were well nigh crushed to death. Some lighted candles . . . with a view to preserve part of its influence. Some held their faces in the blaze, saying "It does not burn." Others said, "Now Lord, I believe. Forgive my former unbelief." After this the pilgrims returned, abundantly satisfied with what they had seen and heard.[13]

Earlier, Parsons had ascended the hill west of Jerusalem, turned to view "the dearest spot on earth," and thought of David's hope that he would find favor in God so that God would return him to Jerusalem.*[14] He worked in Jerusalem for most of the year—Procurator General Procopius of the principal Greek monastery reported that Parsons visited Jews daily.[15] Then he went to Alexandria to meet Fisk, report favorably about missionary prospects, and return together. But he fell ill and died in Egypt on 10 February 1822.[16]

---

*"If I shall find favor in the eyes of the Lord, He will bring me again, and show me both it and His habitation." *II Samuel 15:25.*

The editor of *The Missionary Herald* hoped that Parson's death would not discourage his readers about the missionary effort in Palestine:

He to whom all power in heaven and on earth is committed, has certainly more regard for Zion and for the attempts, however feeble, which are made in obedience to His command to render her the joy of all lands, than the most holy of His saints can ever have; and will by no means suffer a permanent injury to befall her. In this truth we find the common refuge of God's people in every age when the church has been afflicted.[17]

Parsons was replaced, at Fisk's request, by Jonas C. King, another Andover seminarian.[18] He and Fisk arrived in Jerusalem 15 April 1823 and joined Joseph Wolff, a converted Jew and well-known missionary.[19] As it had been for Parsons, travel in the Holy Land for Fisk and King was a journey within the sacred time and space of the mythic drama of Scripture. They related their ascent towards Jerusalem as follows:

Each step is so fastened into the "everlasting hills" as to show you that it was placed there by the hand of Him who existed "before the mountains were brought forth."* On these steps, which are sometimes three or four rods wide and sometimes only a few feet, you will see soil which produces shrubs and when cultivated, vines, figs, and olives. The country continued the same till we were within half an hour of Jerusalem, when all at once Mount Olivet and the Holy City opened to our view. Thus it is often with the last hours of the Christian. He is obliged to pass over a rough and wearisome way while he is continually exposed to the attacks of enemies, till near the close of life—till his feet are about to stand within the gate of the new Jerusalem, and then he is favored with some bright visions of the place he is soon to enter.

As we drew near the city we remembered how our dear brother Parsons, when wars and rumors of wars obliged him to leave the place, turned back his eyes as he ascended the hill west of Jerusalem and wept, and said, "If I shall find favor in the eyes of the Lord, he will bring me again, and show me both it and his habitation" [*II Samuel* 15:5]. Alas for us! These words were fulfilled in a much higher sense than he anticipated. We cannot for a moment doubt that he did find favor in the eyes of the Lord, and though he was not permitted to return to the earthly Jerusalem, yet his divine Savior has

---

*"He stood, and measured the earth: He beheld, and drove asunder the nations; and the everlasting mountains were scattered, the perpetual hills did bow: His ways are everlasting." *Habakkuk* 3:6. "Before the mountains were brought forth, or ever Thou hadst formed the earth and the world, even from everlasting to everlasting, Thou art God." *Psalms* 90:2.

given him an infinitely higher felicity, even that of seeing and enjoying the bliss of that eternal city in which the divine glory dwells.[20]

The history of Israel and Christianity was a palimpsest; in the Land where time blended into eternity the entire past streamed into the present:

> With feelings not easily described, about 4:00 we entered *Jerusalem*. The scenes and events of 4,000 years seemed to rush upon our minds; events in which heaven and earth and hell had felt the deepest interest. This was the place selected by the Almighty for His dwelling and here His glory was rendered visible. This was the "perfection of beauty" and the "glory of all lands."* Here David sat and tuned his harp and sang the praise of Jehovah. Hither the tribes came up to worship. Here enraptured prophets saw bright visions of the world above and received messages from high for guilty man. Here our Lord and Savior came in the form of a servant and groaned and wept and poured out His soul unto death, to redeem us from sin, and save us from the pains of hell. Here too, the wrath of an incensed God has been poured out upon His chosen people and has laid waste His heritage.[21]

On 28 April 1823 King visited the Garden of Gethsemane, sat under an olive tree, and read *Isaiah* 53 and gospel texts about "that sorrowful night when the Son of Man was betrayed into the hands of sinners." He was brought closer to Jesus when some fierce-looking armed Bedouins on horseback suddenly appeared, seemed ready to attack him, and then passed by. "The momentary fear which this excited brought to my mind more impressively the scene when Jesus was betrayed and taken by a multitude, who 'came out against Him with swords and staves.'"†

Two days later Fisk and King rode along the rocks and cliffs between Nazareth and Bethlehem and thought of the son of David making His appearance there. When they suddenly came upon a green valley they imagined a multitude of the heavenly host descending from heaven, hovering over the verdant spot where the flocks were resting, and praising God.‡[22] On 5 May 1823 Fisk and

---

*"Out of Zion, the perfection of beauty, God hath shined." *Psalms* 50:2. *Ezekiel* 20:6, supra.

†"And while He yet spake, lo, Judas, one of the twelve, came, and with him a great multitude with swords and staves, from the chief priests and elders of the people." *Matthew* 26:47.

‡See, for example, *Luke* 2:9: "And lo, the angel of the Lord came upon them, and the glory of the Lord shone around about them: and they were sore afraid." "And suddenly there was with the angel a multitude of the heavenly host praising God, and saying, Glory to God in the highest, and on earth peace, goodwill toward men." *Luke* 2:13-14.

King visited the Mount of Olives; they bowed before Him Who ascended from there to glory and "sat down on the right hand of the majesty on high."* There the Lord first commissioned His disciples to go and preach the gospel to every creature, promising to be with them unto the end of the world, and Fisk and King were "permitted to look up toward heaven and plead with Him to hasten His second coming." When they descended into the Valley of Jehoshaphat, with Mount Zion and Mount Moriah towering above, they felt they were inside "a frightful chasm in the earth," and they experienced the force of the prophecies of Joel.† They sensed the Almighty sitting in His holy temple or on the summit of Zion, judging the multitudes in the valley beneath Him and executing His judgments. The sun, moon and stars were darkened. God spoke from Jerusalem, and the heavens and the earth shook. The confused idolaters and the true Israel both witnessed God dwelling in Zion, His holy mountain, and the hope and strength of His people Israel.[23]

The intermingling of sacred reality and empirical experience is also reflected in King's 7 May 1823 report on Mount Calvary:

My feet now stand on that awful hill, where our dear Lord and Savior poured out His soul unto death and finished the work of man's redemption! Here the arms of everlasting love were extended on the cross, and here the meek and tender heart of the son of God was pierced with a spear! Here flowed that precious blood in which our polluted souls must be cleansed or be lost forever.

I suffered much in the wilderness from scorching winds which were, sometimes, indeed dreadful to bear, and also from want of pure water. All this however I as it were forgot, the moment my feet entered within the limits of Canaan. Thus will the soul redeemed from sin forget all the trials of its earthly pilgrimage as soon as it enters the heavenly Canaan.[24]

A month later in Jerusalem King expressed the transspatial character of the journey: "I am a pilgrim, a traveler, a stranger; I have no home on earth." At the Jordan River he felt the intermingling between daily experience and Scripture in the Holy Land:

I swam across the river and took a walk in the plain of Moab in the inheritance of Reuben "on the other side of Jordan, toward the rising of the

---

*"Who being the brightness of His glory, and the express image of His person, and upholding all things by the word of His power, when He had by Himself purged our sins, sat down on the right hand of the Majesty on high." *Hebrews* 1:3.

†See, for example, *Joel* 3:12: "Let the heathen be wakened and come up to the Valley of Jehoshaphat: for there will I sit to judge all the heathen round about."

sun."* After this I sat on the bank and read the third chapter of *Joshua*. I also read *Matthew* third, and offered a prayer in Greek with two Greeks while Mr. Wolff read in German to the Germans who were with us. I do not suppose a prayer is any more acceptable to God for being offered in a particular place. Yet shall I never envy the man who could read these two chapters and pray on the shores of the Jordan without any particular emotions.[25]

Fisk said he traveled with "unconditional surrender to divine will." He compared the rugged terrain of the Mount of Olives to the inevitable hardships of life. Within Jerusalem he found time and space transformed into sacred eternity. He experienced Christ's suffering, death, and resurrection: "The period of time that has elapsed since His death, dwindled as it were to a moment." When Fisk looked at the dome over Christ's tomb and thought of the death and resurrection, he burst into tears: I "kneeled by the marble which is supposed to cover the spot where the body lay. My tears flowed freely, and my soul seemed to be moved in a way I cannot describe."

For the missionaries, the Jews in the Land were a painful element within the sacred experience. The Christian identity of the Land was interrupted by those who, according to Christian Scripture, were responsible for deicide. Fisk considered the physical Land cursed because three-fourths of Jerusalem's inhabitants remained "enemies of the faith" who out of "hardness of heart" denied the divinity of Jesus. Any Christian walking the ground rendered sacred by the ashes of prophets and apostles and the blood of Jesus' atonement "would not grudge any sacrifices they might make to redeem it from the reign of error." Jews who resisted conversion hated the very name of Christ; mention of it caused them to "almost gnash upon you with their teeth."[26] On 19 May 1823 King wrote that "The Jews here have generally all the blindness and stubbornness and stiff-neckedness of their fathers."[27] He believed that opposition to conversion was so fierce that converts were putting their lives in danger. One Sabbath (i.e., Sunday) two Jews—Avraham ben David Schleifer Iskavitch of Shklov (b. 1805) and a certain Yitshak—visited Fisk and King for prayer and instruction. Iskavitch was satisfied that Jesus of Nazareth was the messiah. They prayed that he might have the courage to confess this fact, even though it meant risking his life: someone was liable to poison him.[28] On Friday, 20 June 1823, Fisk and King visited the Wall a little past noon and reflected on the Jews' act of deicide and its consequences:

---

*See, for example, *Numbers* 21:11: "And they journeyed from Oboth, and pitched at Ijeabarim, in the wilderness which is before Moab, toward the sunrising."

The Jews go on Friday to lament over the destruction of the Temple . . . We found about thirty of them sitting on the ground near the Wall, and reading from their Hebrew books. It was deeply affecting to see these lineal descendants of Abraham, most of them poor and ragged, sitting in the dust and paying for the privilege of weeping where their fathers sung and rejoiced; miserable slaves on the very spot where their fathers were mighty kings. A Jew accompanied us. In the market a Turk, too lazy to light his own pipe, called on the Jew to do it for him. The Jew refused, and the Turk was rising in a rage to pursue him when, perceiving that the Jew was accompanying us, he desisted. Soon after this a Turkish peasant, who was carrying a sack of water, called to the Jew in a very domineering manner to assist in emptying the water into a vessel. We interfered, and nothing more was said. Poor Jews. When will they learn the true cause of their oppression and repent, and turn to God?[29]

On 12 November 1823 Fisk visited with the leader of the Safed Ashkenazim—presumably Israel ben Shmuel Ashkenazi of Shklov (1770-1839) of the *Kollel Perushim*—his wife Devora, and his "agent" Barukh. Fisk said he loved the Old Testament names but longed "for the time when the Jews unite in their families, names from the New and Old Testament, the names of the apostles with the names of the prophets."[30]

Debates with the Rabbis of Jerusalem

As part of their effort at conversion, the Christian missionaries regularly debated Jewish scholars.[31] According to the missionaries' reports, these traditional Jews were prepared to consider and argue various aspects of Christianity's claim to superiority over Judaism: premonitions of Christ in *Isaiah*, Jewish sinfulness, Jesus' messianic significance for Israel, and the New Testament as successor to Hebrew Scripture. The details of the encounters reveal a willingness to discuss each other's concerns on one level and an embedded antagonism between Jew and Christian on another.

The debating pattern and mood were set by Wolff in Jerusalem well before he teamed up with the Americans in April 1823. For example, as Wolff reported, on 14 March 1822 he explained to Karaite rabbis Saadia and Berakha that *Isaiah* 13 made sense only as applied to Jesus the Lord; Berakha responded by inviting Wolff to study Hebrew with him every Sabbath. On 18 March 1822 Wolff spoke with the Sephardi Moshe Secot, "one of the divines (*hakham*) of the Talmudist Jews, a Pharisee by persuasion" who read the Talmud "day and night."[32] Secot agreed to give Wolff lessons in Hebrew and Spanish and assured him that the Jews of Jerusalem would receive him well and show him their colleges and synagogues. Wolff lamented the fall of Jerusalem, citing *Jeremiah*, and Secot responded with other citations from the prophet.* The next day Secot told Wolff that New Testament citations about the messiah were correct; that when Isaiah said "Behold a virgin" he meant the Messiah; that there were messianic prophecies which were unfulfilled, for example about transforming the sun and moon.† Instead of arguing, Wolff cited *Isaiah* 53 and Stephen's sermon in *Acts* 7, thereby bringing Secot "rather more to the knowledge of Christ."[33]

On 27 March Wolff met with Menahem Mendel ben Barukh Bendet of Shklov (d. 1827), disciple of the Vilna Gaon Eliahu ben Shlomo Zalman (1720-1797).[34] Menahem Mendel came to Palestine in 1808, lived in Tiberias and Safed. In 1812 and in Jerusalem founded the messianically disposed Vilna Gaon circle, the *Kollel Perushim*.[35] After affirming that Jesus of Nazareth was the Messiah who came to suffer for human sin and would return to redeem Israel, Wolff asked him to interpret *Genesis* 3:15.‡ The rabbi explained that before Adam's fall, men and beasts were in God's paradise and endowed with glorified bodies. After Satan persuaded Eve to eat of the tree of knowledge and thereby transgress God's commandment, their bodies became sinful. God set enmity between Satan and Eve so that Satan could lead her astray despite her resistance, between passions or bad men and the messiah or the beloved people. Satan would also bruise the messiah's head and heel. This messiah was Jeroboam. Initially pious and good, he caused Israel to sin and ultimately was pierced and killed.# Satan would also bruise the people of Israel, inducing them to sin and forcing them into isolation, but they would be redeemed.** When? Daniel

---

*"She that was great among the nations, and princess among the provinces, how is she become tributary!" *Lamentations* 1:1. "Judah is gone into captivity, because of affliction." *Lamentations* 1:3. "The ways of Zion do mourn." *Lamentations* 1:4. "O Lord, though our iniquities testify against us, do Thou it for Thy name's sake: for our backslidings are many; we have sinned against Thee." *Jeremiah* 14:7.

†"Therefore the Lord Himself shall give you a sign; Behold, a virgin shall conceive and bear a son, and shall call his name Immanuel." *Isaiah* 7:14. "Moreover the light of the moon shall be as the light of the sun, and the light of the sun shall be sevenfold, as the light of seven days, in the day that the Lord bindeth up the breach of His people, and healeth the stroke of their wound." *Isaiah* 30:26.

‡"And I will put enmity between thee and the woman, and between thy seed and her seed; it shall bruise thy head, and thou shalt bruise his heel." *Genesis* 3:15.

#"And the man Jeroboam was a mighty man of valor; and Solomon seeing the young man that he was industrious, he made him ruler over all the charge of the house of Joseph." *I Kings* 11:28. "And he shall give Israel up because of the sins of Jeroboam, who did sin, and who made Israel to sin." *I Kings* 14:16. See for example, *Psalms* 60:7: "Ephraim also is the strength of mine head." "This alludes to Jeroboam, a descendant of Ephraim." *Sanhedrin* 104b. "For thus Amos saith, Jeroboam shall die by the sword." *Amos* 7:11.

**"The envy also of Ephraim shall depart, and the adversaries of Judah shall be cut off: Ephraim shall not envy Judah, and Judah shall not vex Ephraim." *Isaiah* 11:13.

spoke of 1290 days at the end of time, and 1290 (*elef, mata'im, tishim*) stood for truth (*emet: alef, mem, tav*).* Ultimately all gentiles would join in the flow toward the mountain of the Lord and learn the ways of God.[†36]

Menahem Mendel added his own identification of Jesus. One Jesus lived 172 years before the destruction of the Second Temple, a disciple of Yehoshua ben Perahia of the Sanhedrin. While playing with a ball near the Temple gate he accidentally hit the king of Jerusalem. Threatened with death, Jesus and Joshua ben Perahia managed to escape. They returned to Jerusalem after the king died. Subsequently, Yehoshua excommunicated Jesus for eyeing a woman too closely. After unsuccessfully seeking a pardon, He formed a party which induced others to sin and was ultimately stoned to death. The second Jesus, an illegitimate child, lived after the destruction of the Second Temple. Jesus of Nazareth was both men. Wolff responded that the New Testament was not written by impostors; it was improbable that words of good men were put into the mouth of a wicked person.[37]

On 29 March 1822 Wolff asked Menahem Mendel to interpret *Isaiah* 9:6 and 7:14.‡ The rabbi referred to discussion by the Sages of the rabbinic era about Hezekiah as the messiah.# Hezekiah was "mighty" because his confidence in God was strong and he destroyed the places of idol worship. He was "everlasting father" because he protected the people so they could read the Tora in safety, and he was "prince of peace" because he established peace. The rabbi added that the messiah would remove sorrow from poor Jews and rebuild the walls of Jerusalem. While Jews should serve God even in affliction, the rabbi prayed "that the glory of the Lord shall be revealed" (*Isaiah* 40:5).[38]

On 26 April 1823 Wolff was back in Jerusalem with Fisk and King. He met by himself with Menahem Mendel; Shlomo Zalman Shapira, a student of the

---

*"And from the time that the daily sacrifice shall be taken away, and the abomination that maketh desolate set up, there shall be a thousand two hundred and ninety days." *Daniel* 12:11.

†"And many people shall go and say, Come ye, and let us go up to the mountain of the Lord, to the house of the God of Jacob; and He will teach us of His ways, and we will walk in His paths: for out of Zion shall go forth the law, and the word of the Lord from Jerusalem." *Isaiah* 2:3.

‡"For unto us a child is born, unto us a son is given: and the government shall be upon his shoulder: and his name shall be called Wonderful, Counsellor, The Mighty God, The Everlasting Father, The Prince of Peace." *Isaiah* 9:6. See also *Isaiah* 7:14, supra.

#"The Holy One, blessed be He, wished to appoint Hezekiah as the messiah, and Sennacherib as Gog and Magog [*Ezekiel* 37-39]; whereupon the Attribute of Justice said before the Holy One, blessed be He, Sovereign of the universe! If Thou didst not make David the messiah, who uttered so many hymns and psalms before Thee, wilt Thou appoint Hezekiah as such, who did not hymn Thee in spite of all these miracles which Thou wrought for him?" *Sanhedrin* 94a [on *Isaiah* 9:7].

Vilna Gaon's most famous disciple, Haim ben Yitshak of Volozhin (1749-1821), and a leader of the Jerusalem *Kollel Perushim*; Shmuel of Namzi, Poland, who lived in Hebron; and Natan Neta the son of Menaham Mendel, who had come to Palestine with his father in 1808. Shmuel observed that Christians of Jewish origin, such as Wolff, had more sense than gentile Christians. He included Martin Luther in the category of sensible Christians, but Wolff corrected him. They discussed justification, Shmuel maintaining justification by works of law and Wolff speaking of grace. The next day Wolff and Iskavitch, who had "professed his conviction in Christ" in 1822, visited Fisk and King. They prayed (Wolff in "Jewish German" so Iskavitch would understand) and read Scripture together.[39] The same day Wolff cited "excellent doctrines" of the gospel to Menahem Mendel, Avraham Meir ben Yirmiyahu (whose father had come to Palestine with Menahem Mendel), and Tsevi Hirsch ben Zerah from Safed. According to Wolff, Menahem Mendel treated the information with respect.

On 28 April 1823 Wolff introduced King and Fisk to Menahem Mendel, who received them kindly, only regretting that he could not communicate directly in English. King hoped that Israel would soon be gathered into the Land, and Menahem Mendel added that when it would go well for the Jews it went well for all nations. According to the Sage Simeon bar Yohai Jews were the "root" and should govern; when they did, Isaiah's prophecy about the nations streaming toward the "house of God of Jacob" would be fulfilled.* When Israel governed in fear of the Lord all went well with her, and it would go well for her again when she became convinced of her sins and returned to the Lord. According to Wolff, Menahem Mendel thought King's answer a good one. King added that Christians in America were praying for Israel's restoration, for the Holy Spirit to be poured out upon her and that Israel feel her sinfulness and need for the "great sacrifice" to expiate her sins—a sacrifice foreshadowed by ancient sacrifices and the blood that Moses sprinkled upon the people after he read the book of the covenant.† When Menahem Mendel asked for the meaning of the "great sacrifice," King said it referred to Jesus of Nazareth, and the rabbi demurred. Fisk turned to the subject of America and said it was the only place where Jews enjoyed equal privileges and were not persecuted. Menahem Mendel responded that it was not good for Jews to enjoy too many privileges, lest

---

*"And it shall come to pass in the last days, that the mountain of the Lord's house shall be established in the top of the mountains, and shall be exalted above the hills; and all nations shall flow unto it." *Isaiah* 2:2. *Isaiah* 2:3, supra. I have been unable to find the source for the Simeon ben Yohai quote.

†King mistakenly said the blood was sprinkled on the book of the law. "And he took the book of the covenant, and read in the audience of the people: and they said, All that the Lord hath said will we do, and be obedient. And Moses took the blood, and sprinkled it on the people." *Exodus* 24:7-8.

Jeshurun wax fat and kick.* King added that "there were not many Jews among us who waxed fat, but that they sometimes kick." Wolff chose not to translate this for the rabbi, lest it offend him, but when he told him later "he seemed to be very much pleased, and remarked that Mr. King must have been himself a Jew." Wolff, Fisk and King then visited Menahem Mendel's "rival," Shlomo Mendel Shapira. When King asked Shapira what it took to be saved, the rabbi cited Hillel's identification of the entire contents of Tora with "Love thy neighbor as thyself."† King asked whether Shammai or Hillel kept the rule more closely.[40]

On 29 April 1823 King debated Yitshak ben Shlomo Pah of the Jerusalem *Kollel Perushim*. King regretted that Pah rejected Jesus, the king of the Jews and Lord of heaven and earth. If Pah realized the sinfulness in his heart he would recognize the need for a savior, believe in Jesus Christ and find evidence for this belief within himself and in history. But Pah replied, "If Jesus of Nazareth were the messiah, God would have poured out His holy spirit upon the whole Jewish nation and they would have believed." King explained that this did not happen because God hardened the hearts of His people for 1800 years, as He once hardened the heart of Pharaoh. Pah said there was a difference: God hardened Pharaoh's heart to display His power and demonstrate mercy for His chosen people to the world. King thought that God's motives with the Jews were the same. He broke them off so they could be grafted together with gentiles and brought together to Christ so that God's name would become glorious in all the world.‡[41]

On 1 May Pah and Yosef Marcovitz of Poland (b. 1745)—the latter not a member of the *Kollel Perushim*—called upon King, Fisk, and Wolff.[42] Fisk asked Marcovitz when the Messiah would come, and the latter replied it was not lawful to inquire about this subject, that even Daniel, supremely wise, declared that the time was sealed up.# Marcovitz conceded that some Jews did try to ascertain the time, but they were wicked. The missionaries asked whether the term "Shiloh" referred to the Messiah.** Pah affirmed that it did; when it

---

*"But Jeshurun waxed fat, and kicked: thou art waxen fat, thou art grown thick, thou art covered with fatness." *Deuteronomy* 32:15.

†"A certain heathen came before Shammai and said to him, Make me a proselyte, on condition that you teach me the whole Tora while I stand on one foot. Thereupon, he repulsed him with the builder's cubit which was in his hand. When he went before Hillel he said to him, What is hateful to you, do not do to your neighbor, that is the whole of Tora, while the rest is the commentary thereof; go and learn it." *Shabbat* 31a.

‡"Thou wilt say then, The branches were broken off, that I might be graffed in." *Romans* 11:19. *Romans* 11:25, supra.

#"And he said, Go thy way, Daniel: for the words are closed up and sealed till the time of the end." *Daniel* 12:9.

**Genesis* 49:10, supra.

referred to a place it was spelled differently.* The discussion was interrupted by a report that the wife of Tsevi Hirsch ben Zerah, whom Marcovitz had tried to cure with the ineffable name, had just died.⁴³

A few days later the three missionaries visited the site of the court of Jeremiah's prison (*Jeremiah* 32), where a blind and lame old man was brought daily because he wanted to die there. Wolff wished that Christ's light would enter his soul, so that on the day of resurrection his cured and glorified body would rise to meet Christ in the air. Since the man was unable to see the broken walls of Jerusalem below, Wolff hoped that Christ would enable him to see the jasper walls of Jerusalem above. On 7 May 1823 Wolff and Marcovitz discussed *Sukka* 52b.† Wolff thought the text exemplified the labyrinth in which Jews were caught and from which only Christ's truth could liberate them. The same day Shlomo Mendel Shapira begged Wolff to believe in the Talmud: "For even if you believe in Christ and transgress the whole law of Moses, still if you believe in the *Gemara*, you will finally be saved." Then he and Sephardic Rabbi Yitshak Abulafia referred to a passage in *Yalkut Reubeni*, and Wolff said the belief that God would permit the eating of prohibited flesh in the world to come meant that when the messiah arrived all ceremonial and political laws of Moses would be abolished.‡ Marcovitz also provided a rabbinic citation identifying the messiah with Shiloh.#

The following morning three young rabbis called upon Wolff and blasphemed him and Jesus Christ. He chased them out; they were "humbled and mortified" and then reentered for a calm discussion of Wolff's belief in Christ. In the end however, Wolff reported that the rabbis said "the holy congregation of Israel would undoubtedly put me to death if they were in power; for the rabbis at

---

*See *Joshua* 18:1, 8-10; 19:15; 21:2, 9, 12. *Judges* 18:31; 21:12, 19, 21. *I Samuel* 1:3, 9, 24; 2:14; 3:21; 4:3-4, 12; 14:3. *I Kings* 2:27; 14:2, 4. *Psalms* 78:60. *Jeremiah* 7:12, 14; 26:6, 9; 41:5.

†"'And the Land shall mourn, every family apart; the family of the house of David apart, and their wives apart' [*Zechariah* 12:12]. What is the cause of the mourning? Rabbi Dosa and the rabbis differ on the point. One explained, The cause is the slaying of messiah the son of Joseph, and the other explained, The cause is the slaying of the evil inclination." *Sukka* 52b. Wolff's version of the text: "Why are there so many lamentations? Answer: There are disputes between Dosa and the rabbis. The one says, They are on account of messiah the son of Joseph, who shall be killed. For this reason, it is written, They shall look on me, whom they have pierced, and mourn. The other says that the mourning is on account of the bad principle."

‡"'Speak unto the children of Israel, saying, These are the beasts which ye shall eat among all the beasts that are on the earth' [*Leviticus* 11:2]. The phrase *ha'matir asurim* (*Psalms* 146:7) means that all the unclean animals will be permitted by God in the world to come." Reuben ben Hoschke, *Yalkut Reubeni*. *II Shemini* (Warsaw 1882):34.

#"What is [the messiah's] name? The school of Rabbi Shila said: His name is Shiloh, for it is written, 'Until Shiloh come' [*Genesis* 49:10]." *Sanhedrin* 98b.

Jerusalem have made the observation that I have already excited feelings and sentiments among the Jews at Jerusalem, which never existed before."

On 10 May Menahem Mendel told Wolff that without *Gemara* the Pentateuch and prophets were "mere history, a mere tale." Wolff responded that he found divine wisdom in Scripture without *Gemara* and that it led him to the wisdom of Jesus' gospel. Two days later Shlomo Mendel Shapira again tried to convince Wolff to believe in Talmudic wisdom, and this time Wolff cited Paul's decision for the life of the spirit in Christ over the life of the flesh in law.* Wolff also recited *Acts* 9:4 to Pah and Avraham Meir ben Yirmiyahu and asked why they persecuted Jesus by their infidelity.† Wolff prayed that "the light of His grace may suddenly shine round about you, and make you sensible that it will be hard for you to kick against the pricks, and that you also may ask, 'What wilt thou have us do?'" The rabbis responded, "Do you think that all our great wise men here, and so many millions of Jews, can be in error, and that you alone are in the right way?" Wolff retorted, "All your wise men, and millions of Jews are wrong as those were who bowed their knees before Baal."[44]

On 15 May Wolff told Marcovitz about his visit to the grave of Zechariah, killed by his fellow Jews: "Thus our ancestors also put to death unjustly Jesus Christ, the Son of God."‡ Marcovitz observed to Fisk that Wolff loved Jesus too much for any argument to change him. The next day, Menahem Mendel refused Wolff's request to join the study to take place through the night of *Shavuot* (*Tikkun Lel Shavuot*) because he would not join in the Talmud reading. Wolff tried to instill fears about the afterlife, telling Marcovitz, "You must die; and if the doorpost of your soul is not sprinkled with the blood of Jesus Christ, you will not enter the heavenly Canaan, whether you be buried at Jerusalem or at Safed. I preach to you forgiveness of sins by Jesus Christ; by Him all that believe are justified from all things, from which they could not be justified by the law of Moses."

Wolff visited Yitshak Abulafia on 17 May 1823 and asked if Abulafia thought he would inherit eternal life once he read the Talmud completely. The rabbi told him that eternal life came to the one whose heart was fixed on God, and Wolff

---

*"For the law of the Spirit of life in Christ Jesus has made me free from the law of sin and death. For what the law could not do in that it was weak through the flesh, God sending his own Son in the likeness of sinful flesh, and for sin, condemned sin in the flesh." *Romans* 8:2-3.

†"And he fell to the earth, and heard a voice saying unto him, Saul, Saul, why persecutest thou me?" *Acts* 9:4.

‡"And they conspired against him, and stoned him with stones at the commandment of the king in the court of the house of the Lord." *II Chronicles* 24:21.

agreed, citing *John.** They discussed the messiah, with Wolff pointing out that according to *Sanhedrin* not David but a "Vice-David" would be the messiah.† Several sons of prominent rabbis arrived at this point and challenged Wolff's disbelief in their fathers' words. Wolff retorted that he did so because they followed "those who murdered and betrayed Jesus Christ," because they taught lies and were hypocrites. "Tell your rabbis in my name, that they must undoubtedly go to hell, if they do not bow their knee before Jesus Christ."

On 21 May 1823 Wolff told "several young and aged rabbis of the Spanish and Polish denominations" how he wept over Jerusalem's Jews because, like their ancestors, they were not only obstinate but boastful about being so. They were "liars, unmerciful toward each other; deceitful, covetous, vindictive, and despising other nations—crying always 'Temple of the Lord' and never 'Lord of the Temple'—boasting themselves to be descendants of those who crucified the Lord of glory." As once the brightness of the face of Moses could not be seen, the rabbis now could not see the glory of God in the face of Jesus Christ.‡ This was the Jesus who sorrowed unto death to remove the veil so Jews could repent and believe that He poured out His blood on the cross for them. Wolff pleaded with Jesus, "Give to my brethren who now hear my prayer, give them Thy holy spirit, that they may wash Thy feet with their tears; and wash Thou them with Thy holy blood!" That same day Pah showed Wolff *Baba Batra* on the pleasures Jews would enjoy when the messiah came.# On 22 May 1823 Shlomo Mendel Shapira accused Wolff of trying to entice Jews away from the Talmud; Wolff denied that he was enticing Jews to go after other gods.**45

---

*"Jesus answered and said unto him, Verily, verily, I say unto thee, Except a man be born again, he cannot see the kingdom of God. Nicodemus saith unto him, How can a man be born when he is old? can he enter the second time into his mother's womb, and be born? Jesus answered, Verily, verily, I say unto thee, Except a man be born of water and of the Spirit, he cannot enter into the kingdom of God." *John* 3:3-7.

†"Rabbi Papa said to Abbaye, It is written, 'And My servant David shall be their prince forever' [*Ezekiel* 37:25], by which is meant the Vice-David; just as one speaks of a Vice-king." *Sanhedrin* 98b.

‡"And when Aaron and all the children of Israel saw Moses, behold, the skin of his face shone; and they were afraid to come nigh him." *Exodus* 34:30.

#"Rabbah b. bar Hana further related, We were once traveling in the desert and saw geese whose feathers fell out on account of their fatness, and streams of fat flowed under them. I said to them: Shall we have a share in your flesh in the world to come? One lifted up its wing, the other lifted up its leg. When I came before R. Eleazar he said unto me: Israel will be called to account for the sufferings of these geese." *Baba Batra* 73b.

**"If thy brother . . . entice thee secretly, saying, Let us go and serve other gods, which thou hast not known, thou, nor thy fathers; Namely, of the gods of the people which are round about you, nigh unto thee, or far off from thee, from the one end of the earth even unto the other end of the earth; Thou shalt not consent unto him, nor hearken

On 21 June 1823 Fisk, King, and Wolff visited the Western Wall. Wolff mentioned a corner where Jews believed the *shekhina* (divine presence perceptible as light) could sometimes be seen. When a Jew asked Wolff why he did not remove his shoes, he responded that the time was coming for true worship: "These walls will not be built up again, until ye believe that Jesus of Nazareth is the Messiah."[*46]

On 16 January 1824 a Samaritan priest at Shechem ("Sychar" in *John* 4) asked King if there were Samaritans in America. King had heard that the Indian natives, who believed in one Great Spirit, were the Ten Tribes. He described them as living like Bedouins, roaming the forests, catching fish, and killing birds and wild beasts for their food. They had no books and could not read or write but had a "natural understanding."[47] The Samaritan priest said he knew "from books" that after the "separation" in 722 B.C.E. some tribes, including Samaritans, went eastward. They crossed a river, wandered about, and went to Moscobia (Russia), which was contiguous with America.[†] King could not deny that Indians were Samaritans, but found it doubtful.[48]

James T. Barclay

When Warder Cresson reached Jerusalem in 1844 he found the ABCFM mission empty—it had been transferred to Beirut—and thought of the missionaries' belief in an absolute decree that one half of mankind was elected to eternal salvation and the other to eternal damnation. If this were unalterable fact, he wondered why anyone would travel all the way from America to Jerusalem to try to convert the poor Jews, eternally damned as they were.[49]

In 1851, with the entry of the Disciples of Christ and the ACMS, a new chapter in Holy Land missionary work was opened. In *The Millennial Harbinger*, the Disciples' periodical edited by their founder, Alexander Campbell (1788-1866), Campbell pointed to the desolate character of the Holy Land. He cited the observations of Egyptologist Dr. William H. Yates (b. 1802) in his lectures at the Syro-Egyptian Society of London about the Holy Land (Palestine and Syria): "We behold her now in the days of her desolation. She is groaning under the yoke of a hard master; and we can form no idea, by what we now see, of what

---

unto him; neither shall thine eye pity him, neither shalt thou spare, neither shalt thou conceal him." *Deuteronomy* 13:6-8.

*"Jesus saith unto her, Woman, believe me, the hour cometh, when ye shall neither in this mountain, nor yet at Jerusalem, worship the father . . . But the hour cometh, and now is, when the true worshippers shall worship the Father in spirit and in truth: for the Father seeketh such to worship Him." *John* 4:21, 23.

†*Esdras* 13:39-47, supra.

she once was, and of what we have the strongest assurance, she will again become." Campbell also referred to the London *Jewish Chronicle*:

> The history of the Jews, after the final destruction of Jerusalem, is an almost unbroken tale of misery; the faint and temporary gleams of light resting upon the fortunes of the fallen race only adding to the predominant gloom of the picture. Nor is it easy to arrange their subsequent history satisfactorily. Their political existence as a separate kingdom was annihilated, Judea was the portion of strangers, the capital was destroyed, the royal race nearly extinct, the temple utterly demolished, and the high priesthood buried beneath its ruins.[50]

But the Jews also "were designed to be a standing miracle, or an unbroken series of miracles spanning the entire arch of time, from Abraham to the resurrection of the dead." The survival of the Jews as a separate race was God's work, and it testified to God's concern for the human race. In the course of their history Jews had entered the gentile world of sin and shut themselves out of Christ's kingdom. They ultimately left that world, converted to Christ, and replaced the covenant of flesh and blood with the spiritual faith of Christ's atonement, fulfilling the purpose of their miraculous survival. Campbell anticipated the imminent restoration of the desolate Land in connection with the restoration of the people to the true faith:

> But the end is not yet. A new series is soon to commence, and the signs of the times indicate that it is not far distant. The God of Abraham has said—"Though I make a full end of all the nations that afflicted Jacob, I will never make a full end of you" [*Jeremiah* 30:11]. Millions of Jews, known and proved to be such, yet exist, while not a remnant of their oppressors, known as such, is found in the four quarters of the globe.
>
> But God has not kept them these many ages for nothing. He will use them again, and yet again bless all the nations of the earth by the seed of Abraham his friend. "If the casting of them away has been the reconciling of the gentile world, what shall be the redemption of them but life from the dead" [*Romans* 11:15]. We hear a rattling in the valley of dry bones. The Jews are intent on rebuilding their city and their Temple, and in returning to their own Land. We intend to notice the Jews, and especially the converted Jews of this our own day, and their efforts to convert their nation to the belief of Him, as the true and long promised Messiah, whom their fathers repudiated and persecuted to death.[51]

The Disciples of Christ acted upon their commitment to restoration and conversion by calling for a mission in 1850 and appointing physician James T. Barclay as ACMS representative. He arrived with his family in February 1851, carrying the religious mindset that the destruction of Antichrist and world salvation depended upon the Jews' conversion. He considered the Jews and Muslims in the Land religiously sensitive and was optimistic about their accepting Christ. He even hoped that the converted Jews would become missionaries. Jews were so cosmopolitan and so successful in so many different fields—Rothschild in finance, Disraeli in politics, Moses Montefiore in philanthropy, August Neander in Church scholarship, John Braham in music—that they undoubtedly would be successful missionaries as well.

But Barclay managed to convert only 31 "poor, blinded Jews and benighted gentiles." He said there might have been more converts but he feared for the lives of Muslims if they left Islam, and he would have no part of those whose motives were impure. He criticized his predecessors, presumably of the London Society for Promoting Christianity amongst the Jews (more familiarly known as the London Jews' Society, or LJS), for using ecclesiastical pressure, threats, and entreaties. By 1858 Barclay had become quite bitter. He thought the rabbis of Jerusalem incomparably despotic, and he accused them of diverting charity for the poor to increase their personal power. The Holy City was a "camping ground" of the "father of lies and author of evil." After three and a half years he concluded that no missionary ground could be worse.[52]

Seven years later Barclay changed his mind. There were "symptoms of the events we desire," namely the coming kingdom. Visitors from all over the world were arriving in the Land. Beautiful buildings were being erected, there were new roads, a telegraph between Jerusalem and European cities, and an influx of north African Jews who had fled "for protection to the city of their fathers." The Jews themselves were open to Christian truths; light and knowledge of the truth were spreading increasingly among the Jews of the Land.[53]

Observations

Missionaries of the nineteenth century helped replant the sacred territory of Scripture from America to the Land of Israel, including its eschatological ramifications.[54] The Jews of the Land were regarded as an obstacle to the ultimate holiness of the Land but, through conversion, as a potential instrument for the Jerusalem-centered second coming of Christ.

The travels of Parsons, Fisk, and King in the Land were guided by Scripture. Scriptural reality filled their time and space: time passed into eternity and space intermingled with the myths of ancient Israel and primitive Christianity. The Jews had to be restored to the Land and converted in order for Christ to return, and the way to do that was to expose them to the truths of Christianity. Out of gratitude for what the children of Israel gave to original Christianity, the missionaries made every effort to impart those truths.

The missionaries debated reputable scholars, most of them members of the *Kollel Perushim*, which was vibrant with messianic and eschatological expectation. The issues discussed, as reported by the missionaries, were Christ-centered: continuity between Hebrew Scripture and the New Testament and the discontinuity between Hebrew Scripture and Talmud; Jewish rejection of Jesus and the need to recognize Him; Christian implications of *Isaiah*; Adam's sin, Satan and the messiah; Jewish sin and the destruction of Jerusalem; the messiah's identity (Shiloh, son of Ephraim, descendant of Jeroboam, Hezekiah, Jesus); the timing of the messianic age; Israel's material and religious condition during the onset of the messiah; and truth and ingathering during the messianic age. The rabbis were open to learning about Christian Scripture, the missionaries to postbiblical Hebrew literature, and there were moments of cordiality. But as Fisk's biographer recorded, while some inroads were made, Christian truth was generally resisted. He wrote that in the May 1823 debates Fisk

> was principally occupied in discussing religious subjects with Jews, Turks, Catholics and Greeks. He constantly appealed to Scripture, and they in some instances appeared to manifest a conviction at the time that he was right and they wrong. More frequently, however, truth was opposed by the authority of the Talmud, the tradition of popery, and the strong prejudices of a darkened understanding and depraved heart. A prevalent vice observed was profaneness. Almost every assertion made was accompanied with an oath.[55]

As the differences deepened, the confrontations led to verbal abuse, condemnations, and death threats. In pinning theological destiny upon Jewish submission to Christ, the missionary precipitated a no-win choice for the Jew—either join Christianity or provoke enmity. The American factor was present, in allusions to American Jews, the Ten Lost Tribes and American Indians. There was nothing specifically American-Christian in the missionaries' theological positions. But the Congregational missionaries presumably had imbibed the Holy Land atmosphere brought to America, along with its eschatological ramifications, and carried that with them as they went about their work in the Land of Israel.

Notes

1. Joseph L. Grabill, speaking of Andover Theological Seminary (ATS), ABCFM, and Fisk and Parsons in particular, observed that "Puritan pre-millennial thought believed that non-Christians in the sacred region of the Holy Land would soon bow to the Protestant revelation—a submission which would then lead to the final kingdom of God on earth." Joseph L. Grabill, *Protestant Diplomacy and the Near East* (Minneapolis 1971):6.

2. *The Jerusalem Mission under the Direction of ACMS* (Cincinnati 1853):19-25.

3.   Shaul Sapir, "Contribution of English Missionary Societies toward the Development of Jerusalem at the End of the Ottoman Empire" (thesis, Hebrew University, 1979, Hebrew); David H. Finnie, *Pioneers East: The Early American Experience in the Middle East* (Cambridge, Mass., 1967); Clifton J. Phillips, *Protestant America and the Pagan World: The First Half Century of the ABCFM, 1810-1860* (Cambridge, Mass., 1969); Isaac Bird, *Bible Work in Bible Lands; or, Events in the history of the Syria mission* (Philadelphia 1872). See Rufus Anderson, *History of the Missions of the ABCFM to the Oriental Churches*, 2 vols. (Boston 1873); *Report of the ABCFM: Thirteenth annual meeting, held at New Haven, Conn., 12-13 Sept. 1822* (Boston 1822).

4.   On ATS, see James K. Morse, *Jedidiah Morse: A Champion of New England Orthodoxy* (New York 1939), and Henry K. Rowe, *History of ATS* (Newton, Mass., 1933).

5.   Levi Parsons, *Memoir of Rev. Levi Parsons*, Daniel A. Morton, ed. (Poultney, Vt., 1824):251.

6.   On the actual number of converts, see Mel Scult, "English Missions to the Jews—Conversion in the Age of Emancipation," *Jewish Social Studies* 35 no. 1 (January 1973):3-17.

7.   Parsons, *The Dereliction and Restoration of the Jews: A sermon, preached in Park Street Church, Boston, Sabbath 31 Oct. 1819, just before departure of the Palestine mission* (Boston 1819):5-20 *passim*. Parsons does not identify the "Jewish Christians" and the Jewish "first teachers" of the gentiles.

8.   Pliny Fisk, *The Holy Land: An interesting field of missionary enterprise. A sermon, preached in the Old south Church, Boston, Sabbath evening 31 October 1819. Just before departure of the Palestine mission* (Boston 1819).

9.   Alvan Bond, *Memoir of the Rev. Pliny Fisk, A.M., Late Missionary to Palestine* (Boston 1828):v.

10.   On 6 November 1818 Fisk and Parsons signed a covenant of friendship: "We will never separate, unless duty very evidently require it; and then it must be by mutual counsel, and with Christian attachment." [Parsons], "Biography: Memoir of Rev. Levi Parsons, late missionary to Palestine," *Missionary Herald (MH)* 21 no. 9 (September 1825):265-268.

11.   [Parsons], "Palestine Mission: Extract of a letter from the Rev. Levi Parsons to the Treasurer of the ABCFM [Cyprus 7 June 1820]," *Panoplist and Missionary Herald* 16 no. 12 (December 1820):575-576.

12.   The text is ambiguous as to whether a real corpse was involved.

13.   William Jowett of Cambridge, England, a representative of the Church Missionary Society who often traveled with Fisk and King, referred to the accounts of the holy-fire ritual in Henry Maundrell, *A Journey from Aleppo to Jerusalem, 1697*, 5th ed. (Oxford 1732), in *Christian Researches in Syria and the Holy Land in 1823 and 1824 in*

Furtherance of the Objects of the Church Missionary Society, 2nd ed. (London 1826):216.

14. [Parsons], "Palestine Mission: Extracts from the journal of Mr. Parsons," *MH* 18 no. 1 (January 1822):16-19.

15. Joseph Wolff, "Extracts from the Journal of Mr. Wolff [Jerusalem 12 March 1822]," *JEFI* 7 (September 1822):381-388.

16. See Pliny Fisk, "Letter from Mr. Fisk to the Corresponding Secretary [of ABCFM], Respecting the Sickness and Death of Mr. Parsons," *MH* 18 no. 7 (July 1822):218-219.

17. Ibid., "Letter from Mr. Fisk."

18. See F. E. E. H. Haines, *Jonas King: Missionary to Syria and Greece* (New York 1879); "The Journal of Rev. Jonas King, Covering 1824-1825," Houghton Library, Harvard University, Cambridge, Mass.

19. Jonas King, "Account of Mr. Wolff's Labors in Jerusalem: In a letter from Rev. J. King, American missionary [to Henry Drummond, Jerusalem 12 May 1823]," *JEFI* 8 (September 1823):483. Wolff, King, and Fisk had worked together in Egypt; see [Wolff], "Extracts from the Journal of Mr. Wolff: On the Nile 21 January 1823," *JEFI* 8 (July 1823):263-286, and ibid., "Extracts . . . Cairo 24 March 1823," *JEFI* 8 (September 1823):359-371. See Jonas King, "Letter from Rev. J. King, American Missionary to Palestine [to Henry Drummond]: Malta 25 December 1822," *JEFI* 8 (April 1823):157. On Wolff and the Millerites, see Isaac C. Wellcome, *History of the Second Advent Message and Mission, Doctrine, and People* (Yarmouth, Me., 1874):146--160.

20. [Fisk and King], "American Board of Foreign Missions: Palestine mission. Journey of Messrs. Fisk and King from Cairo to Jerusalem through the desert," *MH* 20 no. 2 (February 1824):33-42.

21. Ibid. The sense of the sacred was communicated to King's biographer in 1879:
The sacred places in and about the Holy City are perhaps best unvisited, would one retain in full the charm with which a sanctified imagination cannot fail to invest them. Dr. King, however, in his journal, gives place to reflections such as must after all crowd upon the mind and heart of every true believer. The scenes of four thousand years rushed upon him. Here God had rendered His glory visible; hither the tribes came up to worship, here David had tuned his harp to the praise of Jehovah. Here Jesus, our Lord and God, had poured out His soul unto death, and heaven and earth seemed to approach each other. It was fitting that special prayer should be offered, that the name of Christ should be here honored and the work of the Lord revived.
Haines, *Jonas King*, 109.

22. [Fisk and King], "American Board of Foreign Missions: Palestine mission. Journal of Messrs. Fisk and King at Jerusalem," ("Fisk-King Journal") *MH* 20 no. 3 (March 1824):65-71.

23. Ibid.

24. King, Letter to S. V. S. Wilder 7 May 1823, *MH* 20 no. 1 (January 1824):31-32.

25. [Fisk and King], "Fisk-King Journal," *MH* 20 no. 4 (April 1824):97-101.

26. Bond, *Memoir of Fisk,* 24-25, 280-301.

27. Haines, *Jonas King,* 122-123. The view that Jews were naturally resistant was an ABCFM motif. Historian S. C. Bartlett wrote:

> And the Jews, in addition to their proverbial bigotry, are dependent on foreign Israelites for support, and are thus by their daily bread pledged to resist the truth. But in the midst of this thick-ribbed ice the fire was hopefully kindled, and in spite of every species of extinguisher has been made to burn. As to method, indeed, man has proposed but God has disposed. The Board originally had the Jews prominently in mind. Jerusalem as the center of operations, and Levi Parsons and Pliny Fisk, as their first, their chief agents. Yet thus far almost nothing has been done there directly for the Jews. Jerusalem, after a lingering experiment, was given up to others, and Parsons and Fisk were early removed by the hand of providence.

S. C. Bartlett, *Sketches of the Missions of the American Board* (Boston 1872):101-102.

28. Haines, *Jonas King,* 125-126.

29. [Fisk and King], "Fisk-King Journal," *MH* 20 no. 4 (April 1824):97-101.

30. Ibid., *MH* 20 no. 10 (October 1821):305-311.

31. I was unable to identify several of the rabbis whom the missionaries encountered. Nor could I find any corroboration of the debates from the side of the rabbis. See Israel Bartal, "The 'Old' and the 'New' Yishuv—Image and Reality," *Cathedra* 2 (November 1976, Hebrew):3-19; idem, "Further Evidence on Contact Between Protestant Missionaries and *Kollel Perushim* in Jerusalem in the 1820s," *Cathedra* 28 (June 1983, Hebrew):158-160; idem, "Messianic Concepts and Their Place in the Realities of History," *Cathedra* 31 (April 1984, Hebrew):159-171; Arye Morgenstern, *Messianism and the Settlement in the Land of Israel,"* in Richard I. Cohen, ed., *Vision and Conflict in the Holy Land* (Jerusalem 1985):141-162, 182-189; idem, "Messianic Concepts and Settlement of Erets Israel in the First Half of the Nineteenth Century," *Cathedra* 24 (July 1982, Hebrew):52-70; idem, "Historical Reality or Heartfelt Wish in Researching the 'Old Yishuv,'" *Cathedra* 31 (April 1984, Hebrew):172-181; Arye L. Frumkin, *History of the Scholars of Jerusalem* III (Jerusalem 1929, Hebrew); Joseph J. Rivlin and Benjamin Rivlin, eds., *Letters of the Pekidim and Amarkalim of Amsterdam,* 3 vols. (Jerusalem 1970, Hebrew); Jeff Halper, *Between Redemption and Revival: The Jewish Yishuv of Jerusalem in the Nineteenth Century* (Boulder 1991); Sherman Lieber, *Mystics and Missionaries: The Jews in Palestine, 1799-1840* (Salt Lake City, 1992):157-201.

32. Wolff considered Moshe Secot, along with Yitshak Abulafia, Shlomo Mendel Shapira, and Menahem Mendel ben Barukh Bendet of Shklov, "liberally" minded rabbis of Jerusalem. Wolff, "Palestine: Letters from the Rev. J. Wolff," *Monthly Intelligence of the Proceedings of the London Society for Promoting Christianity amongst the Jews* (*MI*) 1 (January 1830):13.

33. [Wolff], "Extracts from the Journal of Mr. Wolff [Jerusalem 12 March 1822]," *JEFI* 7 (September 1822):381-388.

34. See Menahem Mendel ben Barukh Bendet, *Sefer Yetsira with Commentaries* (Grodno 1806, Hebrew); idem, *Mighty Waters: A valuable and wonderful interpretation of Idra Zutra* (Warsaw 1886, Hebrew).

35. See Arye Morgenstern, "Messianic Conception and the Settlement of Erets Israel"; Menahem Friedman, "Messianism of the Disciples of the Gaon of Vilna in the Light of Contemporary Sources"; Ya'akov Katz, "1840 as a 'Year of Redemption' and the Perushim"; Yeshaiah Tishbi, "The Redemption of the *Shekhina* as a Motive for Immigration to Erets Israel," *Cathedra* 24 (July 1982, Hebrew):51-78; Halper, "Ashkenazi Days of Trial," in *Between Redemption,* 37-51.

36. [Wolff], "Extracts from the Journal of Mr. Wolff [Jerusalem 5 April 1822]," *JEFI* 7 (November 1822):461-468.

37. Ibid.

38. [Wolff], *Missionary Journal and Memoir of the Rev. Joseph Wolff, Missionary to the Jews,* John Bayford, ed. (New York 1824):251-252.

39. See [Wolff], "Extracts from the Journal of Mr. Wolff [Jerusalem 12 March 1822]," *JEFI* 7 (October 1822):417-427.

40. [Wolff], "Proceedings of the London Society: Palestine. Mr. Wolff's journal," *JEFI* 9 (March 1824):99-108. Wolff could preach in Arabic, Hebrew, Italian, Persian, and German, Fisk was responsible for sermons in Greek, and King in French. H. Sengelmann, *Dr. Joseph Wolff: Ein Wanderleben* (Hamburg 1863):59.

41. ABCFM records of 29 April 1823, Houghton Library, Harvard University.

42. Marcovitz claimed authorship of *Blessing of Joseph: Commentary to Sefer Yetsira* (Salonica 1831, Hebrew), which has been attributed to Edels Ashkenazi. J[ohn] Nicolayson, "Jerusalem Journal of Rev. J. Nicolayson," *MI* 5 (September 1834):137-152. On Marcovitz, see Morgenstern, "Historical Reality," and [Wolff], "Proceedings," *JEFI* 9 (March 1824):99-108, (June 1824):219-227, (July 1824):266-271, (August 1824):291-295.

43. [King], "ABCFM: Palestine mission. Journal of Messrs. Fisk and King at Jerusalem," *MH* 20 no. 3 (March 1824):65-71. [Wolff], "Proceedings," *JEFI* 9 (March 1824), 141-145.

44. [Wolff], "Proceedings," *JEFI* 9 (March 1824), 141-145.

45. Ibid., (June 1824):219-227.

46. Ibid., (August 1824):291-295.

47. As an ATS graduate, King would have been exposed to the theme. According to his biographer, Daniel O. Morton, Parsons in fact was:
Mr. Parsons had for years desired an opportunity of preaching to the American natives. This desire was granted. On the 7th of April [1819], agreeably to a request and appointment previously made, he visited the Stockbridge Indians under the care of the Rev. John Sergeant. Great preparations were made to receive him. It was at a late hour when he arrived, and though worn down with excessive fatigue, the sight of Indian blankets excited unusual animation. Never probably did he preach with more fervor; and the thought that his audience might be the descendants of Abraham inspired an ardor entirely unexpected. After sermon, the Indian chief, a large man of princely appearance, delivered an address to Mr. Parsons in the true style of Indian oratory. He thanked God that he had sent his servant among them, and that they had been permitted to hear "a great and important talk." He expressed his gratitude and that of his people for the good counsel of the missionary, and hoped that they should long bear in remembrance his faithful admonitions. Having delivered his speech, which by gentlemen present was considered excellent, he then read a "talk" in Indian and in English, which he desired Mr. Parsons to deliver to "the Jews, their forefathers in Jerusalem." Then the Indians contributed in money $5.87, and two gold ornaments. Next he was invited to the mission house, and presented with several small baskets curiously wrought and ornamented; and with an elegant pocket lantern, as a present to himself, containing on the bottom of it the following inscription:

This to illumine the streets of Jerusalem.
Jerusalem is my chief joy [*Psalms* 137:6].

At the close of this interview the Indians flocked around Mr. Parsons, and caught him by the hand, saying, "We understand you." Referring to this season Mr. Parsons says in a letter to his father, "Never did I rise so high above my ordinary course as when preaching Jesus to these once miserable pagans." The chief said, "I thank God that he has put it into your heart to visit Jerusalem; I hope he will bless you, and enable you to turn many unto the Lord." While he was delivering his address, I could from my heart call him brother. The events of this day will be held in pleasing remembrance through life. Degraded as are the wandering tribes, many of them will come to glory, and sit with Christ on his throne. The Lord make this season salutary to the kingdom of Christ.
Daniel O. Morton, *Memoir of Rev. Levi Parsons, Late Missionary to Palestine* (Poultney, Vt., 1824):217.

48. [King], "American Board of Foreign Missions: Palestine mission. Journal of Mr. King," *MH* 20 no. 10 (October 1824):311-315. In 1825 Menahem Mendel was arrested and put in chains by the Turks, who also tried to extort money. King helped gain his release. [George E. Dalton], "Proceedings of the London Society: Journal of Dr. Dalton," *JEFI* 11 (February 1826):133-140; [Mendel and Solomon Mendel Shapira], "Proceedings of the London Society: Letter from rabbis Mendel and Shapira," *JEFI* 10 (March 1825):108-109; Bartal, "Further Evidence." On subsequent ABCFM missionaries

and their debates, see Bird, *Bible Work; MI* and *JEFI* throughout; Lieber, *Mystics and Missionaries,* 292-317.

49. Warder Cresson, *The [London Jewish] Society Formed in England and America for Promoting Sawdust, Instead of Good Old Cheese, amongst the Jews of Jerusalem* (Philadelphia 1847):521n.

50. I have been unable to verify the *Chronicle* source. Cf. "The Jews in the Holy Land," *Jewish Chronicle* 5 no. 15 (London 19 January 1849):117-119, 5 no. 16 (26 January 1849):125-127. The essay included Mordecai M. Noah, "M. M. Noah's Address: Delivered at the Hebrew Synagogue in Crosby Street on Thanksgiving Day, to aid in the erection of the Temple in Jerusalem. Reprinted *verbatim* for the *New York Tribune,*" which responded to missionary activity in the Land of Israel.

51. Alexander Campbell, "The Present State of Palestine," *Millennial Harbinger,* series 3 vol. 6 (1849):85-88. For the ACMS attitude on conversion, see "The Future Circumstances of the Jews as published in *London Jewish Herald,*" ibid., *146-149, and "Mission to the Jews,"* ibid., *257-261.*

52. James T. Barclay, *The City of the Great King; or, Jerusalem as it was, as it is, and as it is to be,* (1858; reprint, New York 1977:581-587. On Barclay's activities in Jerusalem, see Vivian D. Lipman, *Americans and the Holy Land through British Eyes, 1820-1917: A Documentary History* (London 1989):99-115.

53. Barclay, "Missions: Significant signs in the Holy Land. The November [1864] number of the *Jewish Intelligence* contains striking facts from a letter of J. Barclay," *STHP* 3 no. 7 (Indian River, Me., 1 September 1865):7.

54. The ABCFM did not, however, surrender the notion that America was Zion. In his 14 September 1836 sermon to the Twenty-Seventh ABCFM annual meeting, John Codman, pastor of the Second Congregational Church in Dorchester, Mass., stated,

> The American churches have, within the last twenty years, been remarkably blessed with the effusions of the Holy Spirit. Divine influence has descended upon our Zion, "like rain upon the mown grass, as showers that water the earth" [*Psalms* 72:6] . . . A missionary spirit has been awakened in our colleges and theological schools, which promises incalculable good to the church and the world. In these miseries of Zion, numbers of holy, self-denying, devoted young men are now preparing to go far hence unto the gentiles, and are only waiting for the increased liberality of American Christians, to send them forth.

John Codman, *The Duty of American Christians to Send the Gospel to the Heathen: A sermon preached at Hartford, 14 September 1836, before the ABCFM at their twenty-seventh annual meeting* (Boston 1836):13-14.

55. Bond, *Memoir of Fisk,* 301.

6 Consuls: Jews and Holy Land History

The American consuls assigned to Jerusalem in the nineteenth century were motivated not by money (they were, in effect, unsalaried) but by interest in the history, people and religious life of the Land.[1] Consul Frank S. de Hass's

> object in accepting an appointment under the United States Government, and making his home for several years in Palestine, was not the honor or emoluments of office, but a desire to visit the lands of the Bible, that he might examine and see for himself how far the manners, customs and traditions of the people and topography of those countries, agreed with the inspired word.[2]

There was a variety of religious attitudes involved. Warder Cresson, who served unofficially from 1844 to 1848, threw himself into what he believed was the onset of the redemption. Victor Beauboucher (1865-1870) was initially concerned with the welfare of the postmillennialist Adams colonists. De Hass (1874-1877) was a pilgrim who was also interested in the welfare of American Jews and the overall religious life in the Land. Selah Merrill, who served intermittently from 1882 to 1907, was negatively disposed toward the indigenous religious life. He regarded Jews as unfit for, and uninterested in, building the Land. Henry Gillman (1886-1891) viewed the poor condition of Jews and Jerusalem as testimony to the wages of sin—but he also helped protect American and Russian Jewish immigrants. Edwin S. Wallace (1893-1898) hoped that the Land would be restored by and for the Jews and envisaged their being ultimately sublimated into a spiritual religion of Christian character.

Warder Cresson

Warder Cresson, a prosperous Philadelphia farmer, was successively a Quaker, a Shaker, a Mormon, a Millerite, a Campbellite, and finally a Jew.[3] He believed he had been called upon by the Lord to speak against the American separation between legalistic externals and the gospel of the soul as well as against materialism and selfishness, which involved slavery and bloodshed.[4] Cresson was committed to restoring the Holy Land and took a lively interest in the efforts of the Mormons, Isaac Leeser, and M. M. Noah.

President Tyler's Secretary of State, John C. Calhoun, commissioned Cresson as the first American consul to Jerusalem on 25 May 1844. When former Secretary of the Treasury Samuel D. Ingham claimed that Cresson was a religious maniac out to convert Jews and Muslims the commission was withdrawn, but Cresson was already on his way to London, dove and American flag in hand. There he wrote that the time of the restoration of the Jews to their Land was imminent. Soon they would receive the *shekhina* as children of the coming kingdom described by Isaiah.[*] Cresson listed contemporary signs that the day of preparation, the time for human efforts at restoration, had come:

1. Turkish power was declining.
2. God's word that the time to find favor in Zion predicted in *Psalms* 102 was being realized.[†] For example, Queen Victoria and Frederick William IV of Prussia had established an Anglican church on Mount Zion with the converted Jew Michael Solomon Alexander (1799-1845) as bishop.[5]
3. Moses Montefiore (1784-1885) was building a hospital and public school in Jerusalem in anticipation of the Jews' return.
4. Like Pharaoh, the emperor of Russia had banished 100,000 Jews from his dominions to the Promised Land.
5. The prophecy for the era of redemption in *Isaiah* 18 was being realized—the "wings" were north and south America; the "rivers of Ethiopia," looking out from Jerusalem, were the Mediterranean Sea and the Atlantic Ocean; the "vessels" were America's steamboats.[‡6]

Cresson also cited the signs listed by Louis Gaussen (1790-1863): until recently Jews had been rebuffed from the Land of their fathers—at one point, for example, the Muslims would not allow more than 300 in Jerusalem. Now with 10,000 in Jerusalem, they were on the verge of outnumbering the Muslims. Remarkably,

---

[*]*Isaiah* 49:22, supra. "And kings shall be thy nursing fathers, and their queens thy nursing mothers: they shall bow down to thee with their face toward the earth and lick up the dust of thy feet." *Isaiah* 49:23.

[†]"Thou shalt arise and have mercy upon Zion: for the time to favor her, yea, the set time, is come. For thy servants take pleasure in her stones, and favor the dust thereof." *Psalms* 102:13-14.

[‡]*Isaiah* 18:1-2, supra.

the Jews were using the ancient Hebrew language in conversation, a language not spoken in its purity since the Babylonian captivity.[7] Given these signs, Cresson anticipated the battle of Armageddon, the end of exile, pardoning of Israel's sins, preparation of the way of the Lord with "flaming chariots" (i.e., railroads and locomotives), and the revelation of God's *shekhina*.*

Cresson rejected the view, which he attributed to Gaussen, that Jews as a nation were to convert to Christianity by human effort, whether self-induced or evangelized, prior to their national restoration. That is, while restoration was man's doing (i.e., postmillennial), conversion to Christianity was God's (i.e., premillennial). As Paul was converted by the appearance of the "man-child," the Jews would be converted in a moment by the appearance of their messiah as the *shekhina*.† The people of Israel would be redeemed by an act of divine mercy, in the form of Christianity.‡ Cresson believed in the Zion of the Land of Israel only. He opposed those trying to build other Zions, as if to declare, "The Temple of the Lord we are!" When the set time to favor Zion came,

Woe, woe to that man that is found fighting against God, by supporting their different Zions, one at Rome [New York, Millerites?], another at Nauvoo [Illinois, Mormons], another at Sing Sing [New York, Millerites?], another at [Zion City,] Illinois, another at New Lebanon, [New York, Shakers], another our Zion or church, another in the heart, as all spiritualizers say. Woe! woe! be unto these when God is about to establish his Mount Zion at Jerusalem, and nowhere else. These will, like the Jews of old, not know the day of their visitation, and their house will be left unto them desolate.#

---

*"The chariots shall rage in the streets, they shall jostle one against another in the broad ways: they shall seem like torches, they shall run like the lightnings." *Nahum* 2:4. *Isaiah* 40:1-2, supra. "The voice of him that crieth in the wilderness, Prepare ye the way of the Lord, make straight in the desert a highway for our God." *Isaiah* 40:3. "The shield of his mighty men is made red, the valiant men are in scarlet: the chariots shall be with flaming torches in the day of his preparation, and the fir trees shall be terribly shaken." *Nahum* 2:3. "And the glory of the Lord shall be revealed, and all flesh shall see it together: for the mouth of the Lord has spoken it." *Isaiah* 40:5.

†"Before she travailed, she brought forth; before her pain came, she was delivered of a man-child." *Isaiah* 66:7.

‡"Even so have these also now not believed, that through your mercy they also may obtain mercy." *Romans* 11:31.

#See, for example, *Zephaniah* 1:13: "Therefore their goods shall become a booty, and their houses a desolation."

Such Zions were opposed to God. They shut out the coming dispensation of the *shekhina*, to and through the Jew, who, as Paul said, was the first recipient.*[8]

Cresson went to Jerusalem because he was convinced that the appearance of God's *shekhina* required the physical presence in the Holy Land of individuals such as he to participate in the restorative process.[9] His Christian messianism, however, disappeared once he was there: on 28 March 1848 he was circumcised and converted to Judaism, despite the objection of Sephardic Chief Rabbi Haim Abraham Gagin (1787-1848) of Jerusalem.[10] He returned to Philadelphia later that year to gather his family. His Episcopalian wife and a son tried to have him declared legally insane, but he was exonerated on the grounds that insanity was not demonstrable by religious opinion.[11]

In 1851, using the name Michael Boaz Israel and back in Palestine, Cresson called for human initiative by Jews to restore the Land of Israel in anticipation that God would "co-work" with His people, which included the return of the nine and a half tribes.[†] He called first of all for faith and trust in God—the same "that enabled Moses and all Israel to *lay hold* upon God's *invisible* arm, so as to enable them to come out of Egypt." With this faith, it was up to the Jew to act. Specifically, the "promise of restoration, union, mercy and compassion, depends only upon one thing to be done on Israel's part, and that is our most sincere repentance." Then God would perform His part. The "blessing and the curse" having taken place—Cresson did not specify—the path was clear for repentant return, whereupon God would participate in the restoration, Israel's enemies would be vanquished, and presumably the Jewish messianic age would begin.[‡12]

Cresson also called for unification. Throughout Israel's history, when there was division, Israel became weakened and vulnerable to enemies; when there was

---

*"For I am not ashamed of the gospel of Christ: for it is the power of God unto salvation to every one that believeth; to the Jew first, and also to the Greek." *Romans* 1:16. "But glory, honor, and peace to every man that worketh good, to the Jew first, and also to the gentile." *Romans* 2:10.

†"Return for Thy servants' sake, the tribes of thine inheritance." *Isaiah* 63:17. *Joshua* 14:2, supra.

‡"And it shall come to pass, when all these things are come upon thee, the blessing and the curse, which I have set before thee, and thou shalt call them to mind among all the nations, whither the Lord thy God hath driven thee. And shalt return unto the Lord thy God, and shalt obey his voice according to all that I command thee this day, thou and thy children, with all thine heart, and with all thy soul. Then the Lord thy God will turn thy captivity and have compassion upon thee, and will return and gather thee from all the nations, whither the Lord thy God hath scattered thee . . . And the Lord thy God will put all these curses upon thine enemies, and on them that hate thee, which persecuted thee." *Deuteronomy* 30:1-3, 7.

union, Israel became powerful and triumphant.* Moreover, the work toward social unity, rooted in faith, coincided with God's unity; those who attempted to divide the divine, everlasting union were inevitably divided themselves. Cresson viewed this unity in apocalyptic terms. Through it Israel remained upright during the onset of the four beasts of Daniel.† Gathering together prevented the onslaught of God's anger.‡

To effect the restoration, Cresson urged formation of the "Great American and Foreign Association for Colonizing and Promoting Welfare and Interest of Our the Jewish People." It would work to make America and Europe recognize the Hebrew people as a nation; to facilitate immigration by those who desired to be restored in the Land given by God to Abraham and his seed forever; to improve the moral and physical condition of Jews in Palestine; to educate and assist in the agricultural and rural sciences and work "to reduce those parts settled to cultivation"; to finance schools (infant, juvenile, adult) requiring Moses and the prophets as fundamental; and to gather information on the resources of the Holy Land and the moral and physical condition of its Jewish settlers.[13]

The Scottish cleric Horatius Bonar saw Cresson in 1856:

We set out for the house of a rather peculiar being, by name of Cresson, who was to introduce us to the rabbi. He is an American, and was once professedly a Christian. But he has renounced Christianity, embraced Judaism, parted with his American wife, and married a [Sephardic Jewess, Rahel Moleano, with whom he had two children]. He is, as might be expected, more Jewish than the Jews, and does all he can like Elymas of old to hinder the gospel, and thwart the missionaries.# We had hardly seated

---

*"And Jeroboam said in his heart, Now shall the kingdom return to the house of David. If this people go up to do sacrifice in the house of the Lord at Jerusalem, then shall the heart of this people turn again to their lord, even unto Rehoboam King of Judah, and they shall kill me, and go again to Rehoboam King of Judah. Whereupon the king took counsel, and made two calves of gold, and said unto them, It is too much for you to go up to Jerusalem long: Behold thy gods, O Israel, which brought thee up out of the land of Egypt." *I Kings* 12:26-28. "And Samuel spake unto all the house of Israel, saying, If ye do return unto the Lord with all your hearts, then put away the strange gods and Ashtaroth from among you, and prepare your hearts unto the Lord, and serve Him only: and he will deliver you out of the hand of the Philistines." *I Samuel* 7:3.

†"He shall also set his face to enter with the strength of his whole kingdom, and upright ones with him; thus shall he do." *Daniel* 11:17.

‡"Gather yourselves together, yea, gather together, O nation not desired. Before the decree bring forth, before the day pass as the chaff, before the fierce anger of the Lord come upon you, before the day of the Lord's anger come upon you." *Zephaniah* 2:1-2.

#"But Elymas the sorcerer (for so is his name by interpretation) withstood them, seeking to turn away the deputy from the faith." *Acts* 13:8.

ourselves in Cresson's house, when he began to praise the Jews in the most extravagant manner, giving us to know that with them were all religion, morality, and wisdom. I reminded him of the charges which their prophets bring against them. He kindled up, and affirmed that all these things were long past. I called his attention to the fact that many of these prophecies related to the latter day, and that they intimated that Israel would grow worse and worse, until "the redeemer came to Zion."* He got fiercer still and denied that there were any such prophecies. Several other things of similar bearing, and with similar explosions on his part, were spoken. At last he blazed up into utter fury and I thought he would have struck us, if he durst, in his zeal for Judaism. He rose, however, at length to fulfill his promise of conducting us to the rabbi's house.[14]

Albert Rhodes

Cresson was followed by Boston physician John Warren Gorham in 1857, appointed by President Franklin Pierce; William R. Page in 1860; Franklin Olcott in 1861; and Isaac von Etten (who was appointed but never arrived) in 1863.[15] Albert Rhodes served for two years (1863-1865) and published *Jerusalem As It Is* in 1865. Attentive to Jewish life in the Land, he envisioned a Holy Land in which the Jews would become Christians.

In describing the Jewish community of Jerusalem, Rhodes relates the following incident. On a Day of Atonement a Jewish goldsmith's shop was broken into and gold articles taken; the culprit was the son of the Jewish community president. Rhodes felt the theft reflected the general moral corruption of Jewish society in the Holy Land despite strict religious observances. Perhaps the worst aspect was that "this same man—the housebreaker, hypocrite, and blasphemer—was shortly afterward sent as a delegate to Europe to collect money for the poor! Of course he was armed with a circular from the community, addressed to all believers and certifying that this pious, honorable, learned rabbi had been selected from among others."

Rhodes reported that there were three thousand Ashkenazim in Jerusalem, divided into six groups:

1. The community of "Pharisees" (*Kollel Perushim*), followers of the Gaon of Vilna, led by Rabbi Zondel Salant (1786-1866) and Rabbi Samuel Salant (1816-1909). They were bigoted, contentious, and as obsessed with the outer form of the law as the Pharisees of Jesus' time. Natives

---

*"And the redeemer shall come to Zion, and unto them that turn from transgression in Jacob, saith the Lord." *Isaiah* 59:20.

of Russia, when ordered to return there to reregister as Russians they refused and placed themselves under Austrian or British protection.

2. The community of Volhynian Hasidim (*Kollel Volhyn*), numbering one thousand members and led by the Bak family (notably Israel Bak [1792-1875] and his son Nissan Bak [1815-1889]). They shared the religious view of the "Pharisees" but worshiped according to sephardic ritual. Their morals were higher than the "Pharisees'," and there was "a kind of idealism among them which tends to 'cabalism.'"

3. The Austrian Hasidim, who split off from the Volhynian over a money issue.

4. The community of Habad Hasidim (*Kollel Habad*), centered in Hebron with 50 or 60 members in Jerusalem. Their worship was similar to that of the "Pharisees'."

5. The Dutch-German community (*Kollel Anshe Ho'd*), numbering 70 or 80. In the course of time "orientalized" in their behavior, they shared religious views with the "Pharisees" and intermarried with them. In one incident a member died in Jerusalem and his effects were appropriated by the rabbis. His surviving brother in New York claimed a watch and chain prized as a family relic. A Prussian rabbi, one of the most respected members of the society, denied he had ever seen them, was imprisoned, and then suddenly recalled that he had them after all.

6. The Warsaw *Kollel*, numbering about 700.

The Sephardim numbered five thousand. Rhodes attributed the ease and dignity he found among them to eastern influence. They were cleaner than the Ashkenazim, who were dirty, fond of dispute, and—especially the "Pharisees"—overly proud of their Talmudic learning. The Ashkenazim looked ridiculous in their long locks and ugly hats, which they said were commanded by the Talmud. They knew little of the Bible itself. As a "race" the Sephardim were healthy looking, often handsome, while the Ashkenazim looked dwarfed, sickly, bilious, and often ophthalmic. The Ashkenazim were more corrupt than the Sephardim. Moses Montefiore (1784-1885) once came with a barrel of money to distribute among the poor. By mistake he gave away his own travel money and had to borrow to return home to England. The lender, who the day before had claimed to be among the neediest and received a silver dollar, demanded interest. The Ashkenazim also excommunicated Montefiore for allegedly entering the Mosque of Omar atop the Temple site. In essence, the "Pharisees" hadn't changed since the day they bore palm branches and shouted "Hosanna to the son of David: Blessed is He that cometh in the name of the Lord" (*Matthew* 21:9) and then were prepared to kill Him Whom they praised.[16]

The whole fundraising system (*haluka*) of the Jewish community, according to Rhodes, was corrupt.[17] When the rabbis wanted money they would sell an old Tora scroll or the right to beg abroad on behalf of Holy Land residents. The beggars usually kept most of what they collected. Meanwhile, the *kollel* presidents raised money from the countryside and distributed it capriciously in the cities. If anyone complained, they would retaliate by reducing the plaintiff's allocation. When the treasury was empty—and they could declare this at any time by saying that funds from abroad were delayed—they loaned their personal assets against interest. When the regular allocation arrived, they took it for themselves. The presidents' families were the aristocrats of Jerusalem:

> Their wives wear the best of silk gowns, and strings of gold coins about their heads and around their necks, and carry in their hands *massabeh* of fine amber. Their families are feared, courted, and flattered by the humble and pliant Jewish democracy. Occasionally, a poor Jew, driven to desperation by some act of fraud or despotism on the part of the president, covertly complains to his consul, who, of course, will not interfere.

Rhodes also commented on evangelical work among the Jews. The LJS Mission Hospital, under Dr. Theodore Chaplin, was exclusively for Jews.[18] Their lifestyle and ignorance of health laws, Rhodes claimed, often made them sick. They were treated extremely well at the hospital or, if they were too ill to be moved, at home by Chaplin. Sometimes their gratitude led to conversion:

> When the Jew is converted, a transformation takes place in his appearance. The filthy gown, slatternly shoes and furred caps are thrown aside, and the dangling frontlocks are shorn. From a thorough scouring, his complexion assumes a different hue. He is seen in clean linen, and a good plain suit of European clothes. He has a more civilized air, and partly loses his excessive Jewish humility, which made him cringe and bow before every passer-by. He walks erect, and in short, recovers his lost manhood.[19]

In 1872 Rhodes expressed his contempt for Arabs:

> Occasional opportunities are furnished in the consulate for the study of Arab nature, and it is not long before the national vices are discovered to be lying and cheating. They are inherent, and no missionary or court of justice will ever eradicate them. There is a defect in the moral nature of the Arab, and he is apparently unconscious of the turpitude involved in his acts; withal, such an agreeable liar and cheater, that one is disposed to regard him with indulgence, just as one pardons Falstaff's vices on account of his inimitable humor. The only way to get the truth out of the Arab is with a stick or kurbash, well laid on. A half dozen whacks generally fetch it, and this mercurial creature may yelp with pain at the time, but he is found fifteen minutes afterward in the best of humor.

Rhodes thought the Jew of Jerusalem shared Arab vices, but "in an abject, cringing manner, unrelieved by the latter's sprightliness and originality. Compared to him the Arab is cleanly." The Jerusalem Jew lived on charities from the rest of the Jewish world, wailing "O Lord, how long? Wilt Thou be angry with us forever?" He lived "in the blessed hope of dying in the Holy City and being buried in the Valley of Jehoshaphat." Rhodes summed up the Holy Land as "A country of idleness and ignorance: monks ignorant of the elementary principles of faith; Jews living three thousand years ago; natives with the minds of children; all sitting, eternally sitting, and none working."

Rhodes had his religious side. The night had a special effect on him, as it would on others, like Mark Twain.[20] In the silence atop Mount Zion the history of the Holy Land was like a palimpsest. Rhodes saw "the shining helmets and waving plumes of the valiant hosts who came to wrest the Holy Tomb from the Saracen—the glittering spears and battle-axes, the banners bearing the symbol of their cause, and their renowned leader Godfrey de Bouillon [1060-1100], who on the day and the hour of the passion stood victorious on the walls of Jerusalem." On the road of the Convent of the Cross Rhodes beheld the consecration of Solomon amidst the acclamations of the people (*I Kings* 1:40). southeast of Jerusalem, where the valleys of Hinnom and Jehoshaphat converged into the vale of Mar Saba, the dark shadows emitted the shriek of victims sacrificed by fire to Molech (*Jeremiah* 32:35). As his eye crossed the dome of the Mosque of Omar to rest on the Mount of Olives, encircled with moonbeams, his thought became

absorbed in Him Who made it live in history. At the base of that hill He often taught man the wisdom of life and death; around the southern shoulder of that Olivet it was His wont to journey out to Bethany, to the house of Mary and Martha; down that road He rode upon an ass in the midst of a multitude who bore palms in their hands and sang hosannas.[21]

Victor Beauboucher

Victor Beauboucher, a French-born Catholic who became a journalist in Belgium, came to America to fight for Abraham Lincoln against slavery.[22] His term as consul, from 1865 to 1870, coincided with the arrival of George W. J. Adams and his followers, and he supported their right to settle. On 24 November 1866 he wrote on their behalf to Secretary of State William H. Seward. They were committed to agriculture, and 40 of the 152 members had arrived with families; most were engaged in handicrafts or were carpenters, joiners, shoemakers, or tailors. He later changed his mind. On 9 July 1867 he even tried to secure a vessel to help 70 disenchanted members leave as soon as possible. He became concerned about Adams' alcoholism and obscenity and had him arrested for fraud, immorality and drunkenness. Soon after most of the colonists left aboard the *Quaker City*, he wrote Seward about how Adams had fanaticized them—they thought he was sent by God—and ignored Beauboucher's advice and that of his staff. Fortunately, they were on their way back to America. The colonists signed a petition supporting Beauboucher's request for his own transfer.[23]

In 1868 Beauboucher became involved in an LJS controversy with the Jewish community of Jerusalem. Two orphans, Sarah Steinberg and her brother, were admitted to the Rothschild Hospital. The brother died, and a custody battle over Sarah ensued between her sister, Deborah Golupsoff, converted by LJS missionaries in Jerusalem in 1858, and Rabbi Arye Marcus of the Grand Synagogue. Deborah, afraid that Marcus would marry Sarah to a Jew to prevent her conversion, appealed to Beauboucher. When the rabbi refused to surrender the girl, Beauboucher brought him by force to the Pasha's residence and, after a skirmish, had him imprisoned. The Jews of Jerusalem said their rabbi was beaten because he tried to rescue a Jew from the missionaries. The affair exploded into an international incident. The Board of Delegates of American Israelites in New York contacted the State Department. The Prussian Diet asked why an American consul was allowed to arrest Rabbi Marcus, a Prussian subject. Eventually the rabbi was freed and the girl went off to Alexandria. Beauboucher wrote Seward on 25 November 1868 about his being victimized—he was accused of trying to force Sarah's conversion and of wanting to elope with her. His positive record vis-à-vis Jews, he said, should have precluded any imputation of fanaticism, and his continued benevolence toward them demonstrated the "puerility" of the accusations.[24]

Frank S. de Hass

Beauboucher was succeeded by Richard Beardsley (1870-1873), a Freemason, and Frank S. de Hass (1874-1877). De Hass, who had a doctorate of divinity, conducted biblical archaeology and was a member of the American and English Palestine Exploration Societies and the American Geographical Society. As consul he demonstrated interest in the welfare of the Jews. On 18 May 1877 he advised the head of the Board of Delegates of American Israelites, Myer Samuel Isaacs (1841-1904), to write President Hayes to protect those Jews in Jerusalem who had been born in the United States or had lived there, surrendered their citizenship, and now found their situation precarious because of the Russian-Turkish war (1877-1878). He also transmitted a request to Hayes from Russian-born Ashkenazi Perushim and Habad Hasidim for American consular protection. He was dismissed amidst a scandal over payments for passports.[25]

In *Recent Travels and Explorations in Bible Lands* (1880), de Hass expressed dismay over what he found in the Land. Russian and Polish Jews were coming not to develop it but solely to be buried with their fathers:

What the future of Palestine is to be under the protectorate of England time alone can tell. How far the Sublime Porte [i.e., Ottoman government in Istanbul, or *Bab Ali*] will carry out the proposed reforms remains to be seen. We predict, however, an utter failure, as the great mass of the population are bigoted Mohammedans, who would rather die than submit to Christian rule.

As to the return of God's scattered Israel to the Promised Land, we must await further developments. There are now about thirty thousand Jews in all Palestine. They are mostly from Poland and Russia, and come here not to develop the country, but from religious motives, to mourn over the desolation of Zion, and to die, that their bodies may sleep with their fathers in holy ground. They are generally aged and poor, living on the alms of their people collected in Europe and America. It will require a different class of immigrants altogether to restore this cursed Land to what it once was.

Jerusalem was a disappointment, a mass of windowless stone houses, of narrow and gloomy streets without drainage, lamps or sidewalks. A Muslim crescent was elevated atop Mount Moriah, above the location of Solomon's Temple. The royal city of David, built atop Mount Zion, was mostly without walls and used as a cemetery.[*] Ophel, once Jerusalem's most magnificent section, was now "plowed like a field"—as the prophet Jeremiah had once predicted—and overrun by weeds and prickly pear.[†] The valley of the brook Kidron was dry and filled with stones up to 50 feet deep. The city within the walls was trodden down by gentiles, its courts filled with garbage, its squares deserted or surrendered to lepers and dogs.[‡]

But de Hass overcame his disappointment. He found Christ's Jerusalem buried 100 feet beneath the surface, Christianity's "city of the great King" under offal accumulated at the rate of one inch a year over 20 centuries:[#]

It was through these subterranean streets that the "man of sorrows" bore the weighty instrument of His torture and death to the scene of His crucifixion;

---

[*]See, for example, *II Samuel* 5:7: "Nevertheless David took the strong hold of Zion: the same is the city of David."

[†]See, for example, *II Chronicles* 27:3: "He built the high gate of the house of the Lord, and on the wall of Ophel he built much." "Zion shall be plowed like a field, and Jerusalem shall become heaps, and the mountain of the house as the high places of a forest." *Jeremiah* 26:18.

[‡]"But the court which is without the temple leave out, and measure it not: for it is given unto the gentiles: and the Holy City shall they tread under foot forty and two months." *Revelation* 11:2.

[#]"Jerusalem . . . is the city of the great king." *Matthew* 5:35.

and in the present ruined condition of the place we see the literal fulfillment of the prophecy He uttered in reference to this city, "There shall not be left one stone upon another, that shall not be thrown down" [Matthew 24:2].*

Beyond the ruin and desolation throughout the country, poverty and ignorance among the people, neglected and barren land, filthy and cheerless towns, de Hass perceived an ennobled Christian history. It all testified to the tragedy of Israel, to the prophecies about Jerusalem's being laid waste:† "Over this waste the Jews are constantly pouring their lamentations . . . on the eve of their Sabbath, hundreds of the children of Abraham may be seen kissing the cold stones [of the Western Wall], some praying or reading portions of Scripture, and others weeping as if their hearts would break over the desolation of Zion."

Once the Land became the scene of God's revelation to man it was no longer dismal. De Hass sensed a sacred mystery within it: "The whole country seems to breathe an inspiration, and to the devout mind is fragrant with the most sacred memories [and] can no more be exhausted than deity Himself. The more we read and know about Palestine the more interest it awakens." The chirping sparrow recalled the Savior's discourse on special providence.‡ The lepers, the fig tree, the shepherds, the women grinding at the mill, and the hyssop springing from the walls all impressed upon de Hass the truthfulness of the inspired record.# As to Jerusalem, God chose it for the habitation of His holiness: "So long as our race occupies the globe the name of Jerusalem will be sacred. It must always be regarded as the capital of Christendom, the great center of religious interest, and the most memorable spot on earth." He felt the glory of Jesus' presence pervading the entire Land, and the weary footprints of the "man of sorrows" deeply and permanently stamped upon its rocks.**

De Hass felt his dismay lift when he passed into the timeless drama of Christian Scripture. A violent gale broke out when he arrived at the port of Jaffa: "I thought of Jonah's adventure on this same coast, of Paul's shipwreck in this same sea, and of Andromeda chained to the rocks over which the waves

---

*"He is despised and rejected of men; a man of sorrows and acquainted with grief: and we hid as it were our faces from him; he was despised, and we esteemed him not." *Isaiah* 53:3.

†See, for example, *Jeremiah* 26:18, supra.

‡"But even the very hairs of your head are all numbered. Fear not therefore: ye are of more value than many sparrows." *Luke* 12:7.

#See, for example, *Luke* 17:35: "Two women shall be grinding together; the one shall be taken, and the other left." "And he spake of trees, from the cedar tree that is in Lebanon even unto the hyssop that springeth out of the wall." *I Kings* 4:33.

**Isaiah* 53:3, supra.

were now dashing, threatening us with the same fate." As he left the valley of the Dead Sea he reflected:

> Even passing travelers adopt the peculiar customs of Palestine and so fully do all these regions claim our veneration—by historical ruins and by traditional sites; by inspired records and by Mohammedan legends; and especially by an indescribable antique and oriental quality pervading every sight and sound and feeling—that, in spite of ourselves, we are transported to other days, and in fancy live again the lives of patriarchs and judges, of prophets and monarchy, of Christian disciples and knightly crusaders.[26]

Selah Merrill

De Hass was followed by Joseph Wilson (1877-1882) and Selah Merrill (1837-1910). Merrill was appointed three different times, coinciding with Republican administrations: 1882-85, 1891-93, 1898-1907. A graduate of New Haven Theological Seminary, he had been a Congregational minister and instructor in Hebrew at ATS. In addition to his years as consul, he spent two years (1875-1877) as explorer for the American Palestine Exploration Society. He published three books based on his experiences in the Land.[27]

Merrill looked down on the Muslims; he said his guide, Haj Ali, "prays often, and looks toward Mecca; but I wonder if he knows anything of God."[28] Father Andrew E. Breen of Rochester, New York, who visited the Holy Land in 1904, spoke of Merrill's opposition to the American Colony of Jerusalem, founded in 1881 by Chicago attorney Charles Spafford. Interested in Protestant missions, he was not positively disposed toward the colony, which considered missions effete.[29] The colony also had liberal ideas about sharing property and innovative concepts of marriage, and Merrill supposed it was a center of sin and corruption.[30]

After all was said and done, Merrill thought, Jews came to the Holy Land solely to rest and die.[31] In his 1891 *Consular Report* he contended that 150,000, the number given of Jews who had settled in the Land, was inflated. In fact, wealthy Jews who immigrated soon left because there was no chance for profit. Poor people did not come in the first place, because there were no opportunities for them. The recent upsurge of interest had to do with the rise of real estate values in reaction to talk about a railroad, but this was a matter of business. The only reason left was to be buried there—or because the Rothschilds paid the way. Jews born in Palestine or who had lived there for long periods were leaving for the United States to improve their situations. In general, and contrary to the visions of enthusiasts in England and America, Jews in the Holy Land did not find it a paradise. Given the business conditions and the climate, Merrill thought it would be calamitous if tens of thousands of Jews were to pour into the country. By contrast, the German Pietist Templars (founded in Württemberg in the mid-nineteenth century) succeeded in their settlements—outside Haifa (1869) and Jaffa (1869, 1872) and in Jerusalem (1878)—because they had deep religious motives.

Merrill spoke of a land boom in 1890 and the first half of 1891, when people thought the "redemption of Israel" was at hand and that Palestine was rapidly passing to the control of the Hebrew race. Much land changed ownership, with great profit to the seller. This was not because of new manufacturing, mines, fertile soil, reduction of taxes, or prediction of wealth but because a railroad was being built between Jaffa and Jerusalem and was scheduled for completion in summer 1892, because "friends" of the Jews were talking about how Palestine would soon be repeopled by them, and because interested parties in the Holy Land were circulating reports in Russian, English, and American newspapers about fortunes being made in land speculation. In fact, even if the railroad were completed, it probably would never pay for itself. The Blackstone Memorial of March 1891 exemplified all the extravagant talk. Those best acquainted with Eastern politics or the character and habits of the modern Jew did not sign it; its originators did not know the designs which Russia or France had for the Land, or that Turkey was not in the habit of giving away whole provinces for the asking. In any event the boom did not last. In summer 1891 the Turkish government ruled that no more Russian Jews could enter Palestine, and land prices fell.

Merrill spoke with many of the Jews who arrived in spring 1891 and then left. They freely acknowledged that they came not to buy land, settle, develop the resources, and thereby make the historic Land prosperous but simply to make money. Not even two percent of the seven million Jews in the world would be ready to settle. He also inquired of hundreds of well-to-do Jews in Europe and America and sensed no general desire to settle. That desire existed only among the poorer classes, and there only to a limited extent. Jews in the western world were comfortable and had no interest in leaving to face the hardships of colonizing. Moreover, Jews were not involved in ocean commerce, manufacturing, or tilling the soil. They were not producers of wealth in any important sense. As a race, they were not "seeking a country" and did not want land. They did best in commerce and industry in the cities and wanted to continue in that work. Even in Palestine this was so—more than half the Jews lived in Jerusalem, Haifa, and Jaffa. They were not interested in being located in the small colonies. Of the 439 families in the different colonies, 255 were subsidized monthly by the Rothschilds, and all enjoyed free rent, education, water, synagogue service, and medical care. The American West, by contrast, was settled not by subsidies but out of personal energy and will. In the city of Jerusalem itself the poorer classes were supported by *haluka* funds collected from around the country, a system that was demoralizing, killed individual independence, and encouraged pauperism. The Jewish agricultural colonies were failing not because of climate, soil, or government but because of peculiar traits of Jewish character (which he did not specify). "As this phase of the question is constantly overlooked by the friends of the Jews, I have thought best, since I have had unusual opportunities for many years of studying the matter, to give to it special prominence in this report."[32]

With regard to his own religious experience in the Land, Merrill wrote in 1898 that even the unemotional, critical Bible student in the west would be transformed in the city where David reigned, where Christ was crucified: "That heart must be dead that is not powerfully moved by the associations of this ancient city. These stirrings of the soul . . . constitute a rare phase of experience gained only by each individual for himself and which once gained, cannot be imparted to another." After passing Jaffa and the Plains of Sharon to climb the mountains of Judea, one arrived at that spot which "centers so much that is sacred to history, so large a part of all that is tender and spiritual in his own religious experience and hopes . . . Little does he realize that he is about to undergo, almost immediately, a sort of faith-trial . . . for the Jerusalem of today is far from being the Holy City of his religious dreams."[33]

Henry Gillman

Damascus-born Nageeb J. Arbeely, appointed by President Cleveland, served in 1885. He was succeeded by Henry Gillman (1833-1915) for the period between Merrill's first and second terms.[34] Gillman, who originally wanted to be a priest, worked as a Great Lakes surveyor and a librarian in Detroit. He wrote sociology, anthropology, ethnology, and poetry and is credited with publishing *Teaching of the Twelve Apostles* and *Epistles of Saint Clement*.[35] He served as consul 1886-1891 and wrote a novel drawn from his experience when he returned to America.[36]

Gillman dwelt on the less positive aspects of Jewish life, the sin of deicide and consequent degradation. He reported that thousands of aged Jews found their way to Jerusalem to die and be buried on the Mount of Olives. The desire to be buried there arose from the "curious superstition" that all Hebrews who were not would ultimately be dragged there for judgment from wherever they were interred. It was to avert this "hideous doom" that a little bag of earth from Jerusalem was placed beneath the head of the dead. He found Jewish dress ridiculous, especially the hats—from the turban and tarbush of the Oriental to the black plush hat of the Hebrew of Jerusalem to the uncouth cap trimmed with bristling fur of the Polish Jew:

Those bleary-eyed old fellows, tottering with age, with tangled gray or snow-white beards, and corkscrew ringlets on each side of the face, are a wonder among humanity. No other people are like them. They have an individuality of the most pronounced order, separating them from all other members of the human family.

Given the unique history of the Jews, Gillman continued, it could be expected that they would be such a "wonder." Never had any people possessed greater light and then sinned against it, never had any been so disgraced. They were delivered by God from Egypt and led by a pillar of cloud and fire through the Red Sea and wilderness into the Land of promise. The Almighty made a covenant with them, as He had done with no other people. He showed Himself in their holy place, presumably the Temple, in the mystical *shekhina*. Yet they were also, according to their own prophets, stiff-necked, rebellious and adulterous. While God loved them and showed loving-kindness, they murmured against Him, longed for the fleshpots of Egypt and set up the golden calf. They practiced the very idolatry they were sent to destroy; they defiled the holy place itself and turned their backs on the *shekhina*. They slew their own prophets (presumably including Jesus). Finally, as God had promised, He scattered them among all the nations of the earth.* Jerusalem was indeed desolate. The filth of the Jewish quarter was without equal; many of its houses were fit more for wild beasts than human beings. The architecture was deplorable—"dark, tunnel-like vistas, often clammy with fetid nastiness, and even in the daytime pervaded with semi-darkness. Out of these, again, on either side, stretch similar overarched passages full of dramatic possibilities and nocturnal dreariness. Even a tragic and sepulchral atmosphere is not wanting." The residents went about their petty business, which they magnified beyond proportion, with the "hovering keenness of vultures." Gillman recalled the body odor: "Sickening odors float out with an acrid, penetrating quality from those ancient looking gabardines, which are so stiff with greasy filth, it is impossible to imagine they could ever have been new and clean." He summed up his attitude toward Jerusalem's Jews thus: "Were it not for the distinct realism of certain features, these unmanlike men would seem to be phantoms of unwholesome creation, dark and vague apparitions from Gehenna." They had piercing eyes with an acquisitive gleam, beaklike noses curving over flabby, protruding lips, and shrill voices half-choked in discordant gutturalness. They accompanied their speech with uncouth gesticulations.[37]

Whatever his theological and personal feelings, however, Gillman successfully opposed Turkish attempts to expel American Jews from Palestine, and he facilitated the entry of Russian Jewish refugees.[38]

---

*"O Jerusalem, Jerusalem, thou that killest the prophets, and stonest them which are sent unto thee, how often would I have gathered thy children together, even as a hen gathereth her chickens under her wings, and ye would not! Behold, your house is left unto you desolate. For I say unto you, Ye shall not see me henceforth, till ye shall say, Blessed is he that cometh in the name of the Lord." *Matthew* 23:37-39.

Edwin S. Wallace

Edwin S. Wallace, who served 1893-1898, between Merrill's second and third terms, trained at the Presbyterian Princeton Theological Seminary and served as pastor in Aberdeen, south Dakota.[39] Like Merrill, Wallace opposed the American Colony.[40] He also had some negative reactions to Jerusalem's Jews. Since they prayed so much for "the peace of Jerusalem" he expected there would be peace among them.* To the contrary, they were quarrelsome, and they treated the Arabs greedily:

The same business traits which made the character of Shylock possible are manifest in many a modern Jew in the Holy City, and there are faces to be seen that no artist could improve upon were he seeking to illustrate Shakespeare's immortal type. Every lineament betokens the hard, grasping money getter, who forgets everything else in the absorbing desire to increase his stock of cash.

But Wallace was basically sympathetic and respectful. He described Samuel Salant—who became chief rabbi of the Jerusalem *Perushim* in 1878—as polite, admired, and using his power to win the affection of his disciples. While intolerant of those who would weaken Orthodoxy, he bore "no evidence of bigotry in his countenance." The practice of gathering at the "Wailing Place" touched Wallace deeply: "No one who has carefully watched this service at the Wall can doubt the religious sincerity of the majority who participate in it. They are as genuinely earnest and as truly devout as people can be . . . their earnestness in prayer and devotion to a seemingly hopeless task cannot fail to awaken in him a feeling of sympathy." Unlike Merrill, Wallace saw a real interest in having the Land settled. He believed that if immigration were unrestricted, the Jewish population of Jerusalem would double. Theologically speaking, he thought the Land and the Jewish people were waiting for one another, and that scriptural prophecy assured that Jews would soon restore the Land. Wallace facilitated the establishment of the Orthodox Talmudic study group, *Kollel Amerika Tiferet Yerushalayim.*[41] He was concerned that Jerusalem's Jewish population was declining and regretted that the Jews remained shopkeepers and artisans instead of tilling the soil, although he also believed that they could not succeed in agriculture. The Jerusalem newspaper *Havatselet* reported that when worshippers at the Wall were disturbed on 9 Av (30 July 1895) and sent fleeing by hooligans, Wallace protested, and the Turkish authorities guaranteed protection in the future.[42]

---

*"Pray for the peace of Jerusalem: they shall prosper that love thee." *Psalms* 122:6.

He observed that Christian missionaries failed in the attempt to lead Jerusalem Jews to the messiahship of Jesus: "The soil is a hard one to work. The Jerusalem Jew is so well satisfied with his present condition, religiously speaking, that he considers himself beyond improvement. [He] considers himself one of God's chosen race, considered by God to be infinitely superior to the most favored gentile." In April 1897, Wallace reported, the LJS established a new mission hospital, under Dr. Percy D'Erf-Wheeler, which treated Jews free of charge. The rabbis placed a ban (*herem*) on it, and Jews who went there for treatment were threatened with excommunication. One such woman died and was denied burial in a Jewish cemetery. The matter was considered by English consul John Dickson, who consulted with the pasha. But Samuel Salant prevailed, and she was buried outside the Jewish cemetery.[43]

Wallace supported Jewish nationalism. The numbers of Hebrews around the world were respectable, their wealth and abilities impressive, and the prospect of their fulfilling the destiny of the nation in the Land pleased him. But Israel needed a home to call her own, where Jews could work out their salvation instead of living in lands which were not their own even though they shed blood for them. The Land was wasting and the people ready to come, which they would do as soon as life and property were protected. The present (presumably Zionist) movements around the world indicated the Jews' commitment to prophecy; their eyes were turning toward the Land once theirs, and their hearts longed for the day when they could dwell securely in it. Wallace anticipated a time when Israel would "no more be termed forsaken," indeed believed that restoration was imminent.[*] Jerusalem would become the real center for the Jewish people. The prophecies were undeniable.[†]

Wallace excluded Muslims, who oppressed the Jews and left the Land in a deplorable condition, from Jerusalem's future. Mecca, after all, was their first holy city. Christians did have a place in the Land, and Wallace had a vision that Judaism and Christianity would ultimately be sublimated together into a new religion special to the Holy Land. It would be of the life of the spirit, "whose adherents shall be 'Israelites indeed.'"[‡] When Judaism reached the "spiritual" stage—which Christianity had already achieved—the wall between them would

---

[*]"And they shall call them, The holy people, The redeemed of the Lord: and thou shalt be called, Sought out, A city not forsaken." *Isaiah* 62:12.

[†]*Isaiah* 11:13, supra. *Jeremiah* 31:10, supra. "For I will take you from among the heathen, and gather you out of all countries, and will bring you into your own land." *Ezekiel* 36:24.

[‡]"Jesus saw Nathanael coming to Him, and saith of him, Behold an Israelite indeed, in whom there is no guile! Nathanael saith unto Him, Whence knowest thou me? Jesus answered and said unto him, Before that Philip called thee, when thou wast under the fig tree, I saw thee. Nathanael answered and saith unto him, Rabbi, thou art the son of God: thou are the King of Israel." *John* 1:47-49.

break down.* A union would be effected, and a religion would emerge closer to the "divine ideal" than any religion had ever been. In the end, Wallace's recognition of Judaism and Jewish nationalism was part of his vision of a dominant religion in the Land identifiable with Christianity.[44]

Observations

The nineteenth-century American consuls contributed to the shift of the Holy Land idea from America back to the Land of Israel, a shift inseparable from Christian triumphalism. Cresson was the exception. Initially committed to converting Jews to Christianity in a metahistorical context, once in the Land he converted to Judaism, risking family and fortune to contribute to the onset of the *shekhina*. Rhodes concerned himself with the bad traits of the Jews in the Land of Israel, evidence of their hopeless status in history, and wished they would become Christians for the sake of their own humanity. De Hass was disappointed with the realities of Jewish life in the Land, although he gave Jews humanitarian help. He found solace in the sacred Christian reality which enveloped that life—physically under the Land's surface; historically in the Christian view of history; geographically in the reverberations of Jesus' life throughout the country, especially in Jerusalem; and transtemporally in the eternity of Christian Scripture. Merrill did not think Jews were really interested in developing the Land—he thought them incapable of doing so through agriculture. Gillman, like de Hass, assisted Jews on a humanitarian level, but he focused on their bad traits, evidence of squandering their special blessings from God, sinning against Him and eventually killing Christ. Unlike Merrill, Wallace believed in Jewish Zionism, but he envisioned a "spiritual" religion which would ultimately envelop both Judaism and Christianity, a spirituality indistinguishable from Christianity.

---

*"But now in Christ Jesus ye who sometimes were far off are made nigh by the blood of Christ. For He is our peace, Who hath made both one, and hath broken down the middle wall of partition between us." *Ephesians* 2:13-14.

Notes

1. See Ruth Kark and Joseph Glass, "Biographies of the American Consuls in Jerusalem, 1844-1917," *Cathedra* (forthcoming, Hebrew).

2. Frank S. de Hass, *Recent Travels and Explorations in Bible Lands: Consisting of sketches written from personal observations. Giving results of recent researches in the East and the recovery of many places in sacred history long considered lost* (New York 1880):9.

3. On Cresson, see Frank Fox, "Quaker, Shaker, Rabbi: Warder Cresson. The Story of a Philadelphia Mystic," *Pennsylvania Magazine of History and Biography* 95 (April 1971):147-194; Abraham Karp, "Zionism of Warder Cresson," in Isidore Meyer, ed., *Early History of Zionism in America* (New York 1958):1-20; Aaron Zeitlin, "Warder Cresson, American Convert to Judaism: His Struggle and His Writing on Jewish Topics," *Hebrew Thought in America* (Tel Aviv 1974, Hebrew):3:182-192; Ruth Kark, "Millenarism and Agricultural Settlement in the Holy Land in the Nineteenth Century," *Journal of Historical Geography* 9 no. 1 (1983):47-62; Naomi Bar-Yosef, "Warder Cresson: Commitment to Judaism and the Holy Land" (Hebrew University of Jerusalem, [1985?]); Ya'akov Shavit, "'Land in the Deep Shadow of Wings' [*Isaiah* 18:1] and the Redemption of Israel: A Millenarian Document from Jerusalem, 1847," *Cathedra* 50 (December 1988, Hebrew):98-110.

4. Warder Cresson, *An Humble and Affectionate Address to the Select Members of the Abington Quarterly Meeting* (Philadelphia 1827); idem, *Babylon the Great Is Falling! The morning star or light from on high. Written in defense of the rights of the poor and oppressed* (Philadelphia 1830), both cited in Fox, "Quaker, Shaker, Rabbi."

5. Alexander, born Wolff in the Grand Duchy of Posen, was trained in rabbinical texts and served as teacher of Talmud and *shohet* (ritual slaughterer). Baptized in 1825 in Plymouth, England, he became a missionary for the LJS, 1827-1841. As the first Anglican bishop in Jerusalem in 1841 "his chief missionary care [was to] be directed to the conversion of the Jews, to their protection, and to their useful employment." William T. Gidney, "Statement of Proceedings Relating to the Establishment of the Bishopric," in *The History of the London Society for Promoting Christianity amongst the Jews* (London 1908):205-210. See Muriel Corey, *From Rabbi to Bishop: The Biography of the Right Reverend Michael Solomon Alexander* (London 1959).

6. Cresson communicated with Mordecai M. Noah about these ideas. See Fox, "Quaker, Shaker, Rabbi," 163n, and Shavit, "'Land in the Deep Shadow.'"

7. See Louis Gaussen, *Die Juden und die Hoffnung ihrer baldigen Wiederherstellung vermittelst des Evangeliums: Ein Vortrag, gehalten am 12 März 1843 im Museum zu Genf*, K. Mann, trans. (Karlsruhe 1843):24-32. On Gaussen, see Isaac C. Wellcome, *History of the Second Advent Message and Mission, Doctrine, and People* (Yarmouth, Me., 1874):533-534.

8. Cresson, *Jerusalem, the Center and Joy of the Whole Earth, and the Jew the Recipient of the Glory of God* (London 1844):1-11. Cresson reiterated his opposition to conversion prior to restoration after he converted to Judaism:
> It must be particularly remarked that God and all His prophets place the *repentance* of Israel *before* their *restoration*, and their *redemption* not until *afterwards*. Compare *Ezekiel* 36:24 with *Ezekiel* 36:25 and *Ezekiel* 28:25-26.
> This puts an *end forever* to the endeavors of *missionaries*, and apostates in Jerusalem and elsewhere, to *attempt* to *convert* Israel, or the *literal* Jew, *before* his restoration.

Warder Cresson, *The Great Restoration and Consolidation of Israel in Palestine: And the "masora" or Jewish counterfeit detector* (Philadelphia 1851):5n.

9. Cresson, *Jerusalem, the Center*, 125-126.

10. On Haim Abraham Gagin, see A. Elmaliah, *The First Ones to Zion* (Jerusalem 1970, Hebrew); Ben-Tsiyon Dinur, "From the Archives of Haham Bashi R. Haim Abraham Gagin," *Me'assef/Tsiyon* 1 (1926, Hebrew):84-121. Lipman attributed Cresson's conversion to his respect for starving Jews who refused to convert, his increasing awareness of contradiction in the New Testament, and loss of belief in the doctrine of the trinity. Vivian D. Lipman, *Americans and the Holy Land through British Eyes, 1820-1917: A Documentary History* (London 1989):90.

11. Cresson, *The Key of David: David the true messiah of the anointed of the God of Jacob. The two women who came to King Solomon were designed, in the greatest depth of wisdom, to represent the true and false churches and the living and dead child or messiah. Also reasons for becoming a Jew. With a revision of the late lawsuit for lunacy on that account together with an appendix* (Philadelphia 1852). See also idem, *Civil and Religious Liberty: A landmark in American growth to religious equality* ([1852?]), cited in Kark, "Millenarism and Agricultural Settlement," 52.

12. Cresson, *The Great Restoration*.

13. See Cresson, "Circular Letter for the Promotion of Agricultural Pursuits and also for the Establishment of a Soap House for the Destitute Jews in Jerusalem," *The Occident and American Jewish Advocate: A monthly periodical devoted to the diffusion of knowledge on Jewish literature and religion* (OAJA) 10 (February 1853):608-612; idem, "A Few Practical Observations Before Commencing Agriculture in the East," *OAJA* 12 (June-July 1855):133-137; Shavit, "'Land in the Deep Shadow.'"

14. Horatius Bonar, "A Fanatic," in *The Land of Promise: Notes of a spring journey from Beersheba to Sidon* (New York 1858):208-209.

15. Ron Bartour, "Episodes in the Relations of the American Consulate in Jerusalem with the Jewish Community in the 19th Century," *Cathedra* 5 (October 1977, Hebrew):109-143; idem, "Governmental Resources," in Moshe Davis, ed., *With Eyes toward Zion* (New York 1977):1:129-162.

16. Rhodes mistakenly translated "Perushim" ("separatists") as "Pharisees." On the subdivisions of the Jewish community, see Yehoshua Ben-Arieh, *Jerusalem in the 19th Century: The Old City* (Jerusalem 1984):280-296; Ben-Tsiyon Gat, *The Jewish Yishuv in Erets Israel in the Years 1840-1881* (Jerusalem 1973, Hebrew):112-125. On *Kollel Anshe Hod,* see Mordekhai Eliav, *Love of Zion and Men of Hod: German Jewry and the Settlement of Erets Israel in the 19th Century* (Tel Aviv 1970, Hebrew); Sherman Lieber, *Mystics and Missionaries: The Jews in Palestine, 1799-1840* (Salt Lake City, 1992):120-156. Rhodes apparently lifted most of his information about *kollels*, the goldsmith, Montefiore's barrel of money and the *haluka* system from Ludwig A. Frankl, *Nach Jerusalem!* vol. 2, *Palästina* (Leipzig 1858); idem, *The Jews in the East*, vol. 2 (London 1859), Rev. Patrick Beaton, trans. Cf. Jeff Halper, "Ludwig Frankl and the Laemel School," in *Between Redemption and Revival: The Jewish Yishuv of Jerusalem in the Nineteenth Century* (Boulder 1991):100-105.

17. On the *haluka* system, see Ben-Arieh, *Jerusalem: The Old City*, 321-325; idem, *Jerusalem in the 19th Century: The Emergence of the New City* (Jerusalem 1986):122-125, 391-392; Halper, *Between Redemption and Revival*, passim.

18. Chapin succeeded Dr. Edward MacGowan (d. 1860), who headed the hospital from the time it was founded in Jerusalem 12 December 1844 until his death in 1860. On the hospital, see Cresson, "A Review of the Jerusalem Mission for 1846," in *Key of David,* 281-287; Shaul Sapir, "Historical Sources Relating to the Anglican Missionary Societies Active in Jerusalem and Palestine toward the End of Ottoman Rule, 1800-1914," *Cathedra* 19 (April 1981, Hebrew):155-170; Arye Morgenstern, "The First Jewish Hospital in Jerusalem," *Cathedra* 33 (October 1989, Hebrew):107-124; Norbert Schwake, *Die Entwicklung des Krankhauswesens der Stadt Jerusalem vom Ende des 18. bis zum Beginn des 19. Jahrhundert*, 2 vols. (Herzogenrath 1983); Ben-Arieh, *Jerusalem: The Old City*, 255-256.

19. Albert Rhodes, *Jerusalem As It Is* (London 1865):359-367, 452-454.

20. At night Twain was able to separate himself from his daytime disappointments in the Land:

Night is the time to see Galilee. Genessaret under these lustrous stars, has nothing repulsive about it. Genessaret with the glittering reflection of the constellations flecking its surface, almost makes me regret that I ever saw the rude glare of the day upon it. Its history and its associations are its chiefest charm, in any eyes, and the spells they weave are feeble in the searching light of the sun. Then, we feel the fetters. Our thoughts wander constantly to the practical concerns of life, and refuse to dwell upon things that seem vague and unreal. But when the day is done, even the most unimpressible must yield to the dreamy influences of this tranquil starlight. The old traditions of the place steal upon his memory and haunt his reveries, and then his fancy clothes all sights and sounds with the supernatural. In the lapping of the waves upon the beach, he hears the dip of ghostly oars; in the secret noises of the night he hears spirit voices; in the soft sweep of the breeze, the rush of invisible wings. Phantom ships are on the sea, the dead of twenty centuries come forth from the tombs, and in the dirges of the night wind the songs of old forgotten ages find utterance again.

In the starlight, Galilee has no boundaries but the broad compass of the heavens, and is a theater meet for great events; meet for the birth of a religion able to save a world; and meet for the stately figure appointed to stand upon its stage and proclaim its high decrees. But in the sunlight, one says: Is it for the deeds which were done and the words which were spoken in this little acre of rocks and sand eighteen centuries gone, that the bells are ringing today in the remote islands of the sea and far and wide over continents that clasp the circumference of the huge globe?

One can comprehend it only when night has hidden all incongruities and created a theater proper for so grand a drama.

Mark Twain, *Innocents Abroad* (Hartford 1871):512-513.

21. Rhodes, "Our Consul at Jerusalem," *Galaxy: A magazine of entertainment reading* 14 no. 4 (October 1872):437-447.

22. Bernard Finkelstein served as Beauboucher's vice-consul. His sister Lydia Mamreoff von Finkelstein Mountford (1848-1917) lectured in America and became a Mormon in 1897 in Salt Lake City. See Lydia M. von Finkelstein Mountford, *Jesus Christ in His Homeland* (Cincinnati 1911); idem, *The Life Sketch of Lydia Mamreoff von Finkelstein (Madame Mountford)* (New York 1908); "The Jerusalem of Today: Madame Lydia von F. Mountford," *Relief Society Magazine* 8 (February 1921):71-77.

23. Reed Homes, *The Forerunners* (Independence, Mo., 1981):193-195, 234-235. See also Lester Vogel, "Zion as Place and Past, and American Myth: Ottoman Palestine in the American Mind Perceived through Protestant Consciousness and Experience" (diss., George Washington University, 1983):248-275. Also, *STHP* 4 no. 5 (Indian River, Me., 15 May 1867):50-51.

24. The incident is reported in Frank E. Manuel, *The Realities of American-Palestine Relations* (Washington, D.C., 1949):26-31. Haim Z. Sneersohn brought his dissatisfaction with Beauboucher to the attention of President Grant. On 19 January 1870, after Beauboucher was replaced by Beardsley, Sneersohn wrote the President: "In the appointment of a new U.S. Consul for Jerusalem I see the fulfillment of the promise thou gavest me that the government of the United States would do all in its power toward ameliorating the lot of my wretched brethren residing there." Haim Z. Sneersohn, *Palestine and Romania: A description of the Holy Land and the past and present state of Romania and the Romanian Jews* (New York 1872):85-89.

25. See Bartour, "Episodes"; Vogel, "Zion as Place and Past," 325-329.

26. De Hass, *Recent Travels,* 10-11, 117-118, 120, 124, 127-130, 135, 136, 312. The work went through many editions; the fifth, which added an appendix, was published as *Buried Cities Recovered; or, Explorations in Bible Lands. Giving the results of recent researches in the Orient, and recovery of many places in sacred and profane history long considered lost* (Philadelphia 1883).

27. Selah Merrill, *East of the Jordan: A record of travel and observation in the countries of Moab, Gilead, and Bashan during the years 1875-1877* (New York 1881); idem, *Ancient Jerusalem* (New York 1908); idem, *A New Comprehensive Dictionary of the Bible* (New York 1922).

28. Merrill, *East of the Jordan*, 133.

29. Andrew E. Breen, *A Diary of My Life in the Holy Land* (Rochester, N.Y., 1906):472.

30. Cf. Vogel, "Zion as Place and Past," 291-293. On the American Colony, see Bertha Spafford Vester, *Our Jerusalem: An American Family in the Holy City, 1881-1949* (Garden City, N.Y., 1950).

31. Merrill, *East of the Jordan*, 134.

32. Merrill, "Jews and Jewish Colonies in Palestine [Jerusalem 3 October 1891]," *U.S. Consular Relations* (Washington, D.C., 1949):68-75, 93-95.

33. Merrill, "'Within Thy Gates, O Jerusalem' [*Psalms* 122:2]," *The Biblical World* 12 no. 5 (November 1898):293-302. Dr. Burgheim may have been the pharmacist Melville Peter Bergheim (1815-1880), a convert from Judaism who worked at the LJS mission. See Schwake, *Die Entwicklung*, 119-120.

34. See Ron Bartour, "An American in Palestine," *Moznaim* 57 nos. 1 and 2 (June-July 1983, Hebrew):53-55.

35. Henry Gillman, *Marked for Life* (New York 1863). Gillman's religious inclination is apparent in this volume of verse. Examples of his other works are "The Mound-Builders and Platycnemism in Michigan," *Annual Report of the Board of Regents of the Smithsonian Institution* (Washington, D.C., 1874):364-390; "Certain Characteristics Pertaining to Ancient Man in Michigan," ibid., (1876):234-245; "The Ancient Men of the Great Lakes," *American Association for the Advancement of Science* (16 August 1875). After his consulship ended he published a series in 1893-1894 on the wildflowers and gardens of Jerusalem and Palestine; see *The National Encyclopedia of American Biography* 7 (New York 1897):359-360.

36. Gillman, *Hassan—A Fellah: A romance of Palestine* (Boston 1898).

37. Ibid.

38. See Manuel, *Realities*, 65-68, 91, 96.

39. See Robert T. Handy, ed., *The Holy Land in American Protestant Life* (New York 1981):154-163.

40. The British Consul John Dickson wrote on 14 November 1897,
   With regard to charges against Mr. Wallace, the United States Consul, the enclosed copies and extract of letters will show that they in reality have no grievance. They seem rather to have been animated by a spirit of retaliation in consequence of Mr. Wallace and his predecessor Dr. Merrill having endeavored to expose the "Community."
Lipman, *Americans and the Holy Land*, 152.

41. Simha Fishbane, "The Founding of Kollel Amerika Tiferet Yerushalayim," *American Jewish Historical Quarterly* 44 no. 2 (1974-1975):120-136.

42. Described by Moshe Davis, "American Christian Devotees in the Holy Land," *Christian-Jewish Relations* 20 no. 4 (1987):3-20, citing David M. Deinard, "Expressing Thanks," *Havatselet* (6 September 1895, Hebrew):405.

43. D'Erf-Wheeler succeeded Chaplin in 1886. See Schwake, *Die Entwicklung,* 163-188; Gidney, *History of the London Society,* 549-550; Ben-Arieh, *Jerusalem: The New City,* 323-324.

44. "For [Wallace], past and present, prophecy and reality were all part of an organic whole, leading to the new future. Wallace's narrative is inspired by Christian commitment, but his text is factual." Davis, "American Christian Devotees." See Edwin S. Wallace, "The Jews in Jerusalem," in *Jerusalem the Holy: A brief history of ancient Jerusalem; with an account of the modern city and its conditions political, religious, and social* (1898; reprint, New York 1977):289-310, 353-355; idem, "The Jews in Jerusalem," *Cosmospolitan: A monthly illustrated magazine* 26 (November 1898-April 1899):317-324.

Part Three

Religious Groups
of the Nineteenth Century

7 Christianity among Blacks:
The Spiritual Holy Land

Black Christians in the nineteenth century believed in a Zion that transcended both geographic America and geographic Palestine.[1] The slaves were unable to overcome their oppressive masters; reconciliation was impossible between reality and their sense of right and wrong. But God and the scriptural drama of liberation strengthened their belief that, in terms of moral rectitude, they had indeed mastered the slavemaster. The tie to the just God and His Zion provided a moral anchor and source of hope amid the dismay of the blacks' real world.[2]

Blacks participated in a Zion-centered scriptural drama of sin, divine judgment, love and deliverance that transcended their existential situation. History was lifted up into myth, and the myth invested American soil with fresh meaning.[3] Absalom Jones (1746-1818) and Richard Allen (1760-1831) founded the Free African Society in 1787, which would become the African Methodist Episcopal Church (AME) in 1816. On 1 January 1808 Jones delivered a sermon at the African Episcopal Church in Philadelphia, where he served as rector, in thanksgiving for the Congressional abolition of the African slave trade. He took *Exodus* 3:7-8 as his text.[*]

"Affliction," Jones explained, referred to the slaves' loss of liberty in Egypt. The children of Israel were slaves to the kings in Egypt. Brickmaking was hard work, the rays of the sun burned them, and their masters were stern and oppressive. Their food, mainly leeks and onions, was of bad quality and offered little nourishment. While these daytime sufferings were painful, those at night were worse, for then families cried over their baby sons who were dragged away and drowned to limit population and with it the danger of insurrection. God,

---

[*]"And the Lord said, I have surely seen the affliction of my people which are in Egypt, and have heard their cry by reason of their task-masters; for I know their sorrows; and I am come down to deliver them out of the hand of the Egyptians." *Exodus* 3:7-8.

however, did not forsake the people. He heard their complaint, their groans, and was so much moved that He came down from heaven in His own person to deliver them. Israel's ancient liberation had the same divine source as the contemporary liberation of American blacks.

Israel's liberation from bondage was not to be the only instance where God appeared on behalf of the oppressed nation, delivering the innocent who called upon His name. God was unchangeable in nature, the same "yesterday, and today, and forever."* God had, accordingly, visited with tender mercy the ancestral land of Africa. He saw that wars were fomented there among the African tribes to produce captives for the slave trade. He saw the ships from Europe and America freighted with "trinkets to be exchanged for the bodies and souls of men." He saw Africans thrown en masse into the holds of ships, some dying from lack of air, others drowning in the ocean attempting either to escape or commit suicide. God saw them sold like cattle at American seaports. He saw the pangs of shattered families, how the slaves were driven to labor and fainted in the fields under the burning sun, "with scarcely as much clothing upon them as modesty required." He saw them return to their huts in the evening to eat a few roots, cultivated on the very day which God ordained as a day of rest for man and beast. God saw their masters mistreating their immortal souls by preventing religious instruction. He saw the masters and mistresses, "educated in fashionable life, sometimes take the instruments of torture into their own hands and, deaf to the cries and shrieks of their agonizing slaves, exceed even their overseers in cruelty." God heard and saw all this and acted as He had in Egypt:

Inhuman wretches! Though you have been deaf to their cries and shrieks, they have been heard in heaven. The ears of Jehovah have been constantly open to them. He has heard the prayers that have ascended from the hearts of His people; And He has, as in the case of His ancient and chosen people the Jews, *come down to deliver* our suffering countrymen from the hands of their oppressors.† He *came down* into the United States when they declared in the *Constitution* which they framed in 1788, that the trade in our African fellowmen should cease in the year 1808. He *came down* into the British Parliament, when they passed a law to put an end to the same iniquitous trade in May 1807. He *came down* into the Congress of the United States, the last winter, when they passed a similar law, the operation of which commences on this happy day.[4]

---

*"Jesus Christ is the same yesterday, and today, and forever." *Hebrews* 13:8.

†"I have seen, I have seen the affliction of My people which is in Egypt, and I have heard their groaning, and am come down to deliver them. And now come, I will send thee into Egypt." *Acts* 7:34.

In 1862 Brother Thornton spoke to his fellow slaves in Fort Monroe, Virginia:

We have been in the furnace of affliction, and are still, but God only means to separate the dross, and get us so that like the pure metal we may reflect the image of our purifier, Who is sitting by to watch the process. I am assured that what God begins, He will bring to an end. We have need of faith, patience, and perseverance, to realize the desired result. There must be no looking back to Egypt. Israel passed forty years in the wilderness, because of her unbelief. What if we cannot see right off the green fields of Canaan, Moses could not. He could not even see how to cross the Red Sea. If we would have greater freedom of body, we must free ourselves from the shackles of sin, and especially the sin of unbelief. We must snap the chain of Satan, and educate ourselves and our children.[5]

Shortly after arriving in Alabama in 1865, Union Army Chaplain W. G. Kiphant wrote that black slaves considered Moses an ideal man—indeed, Christ was less a spiritual deliverer than a second Moses Who would lead them out of their own prison house of bondage.[6] In 1917 AME minister Reverend C. Ransom would speak of emancipation as a reflection of scriptural exodus. He believed that his people had passed from the "wilderness" and had begun their victorious march around the "Jericho walls" of American prejudice.[7]

Prayers and Spirituals

The mythic meaning of history was expressed in song and ritual. In antebellum prayer meetings slaves shuffled around in circles till they reached ecstasy in a ritual called the "shout." Transformed, they walked through the Red Sea, stood with Moses on Mount Pisgah to see the Promised Land, and marched with Joshua around the walls of Jericho.

In the slaves' spirituals biblical figures and events merged with contemporary contexts:

Oh! Fader Abraham [Lincoln]
Go down into Dixie's land
Tell Jeff Davis
To let my people go.
Down in de house of bondage
Dey have watch and waited long,
De oppressor's heel is heavy,
De oppressor's arm is strong.
Oh, Fader Abraham.

Or

> He delivered Daniel from de lion's den,
> Jonah from de belly ob de whale
> And de Hebrew children from de fiery furnace
> And why not every man?

Noah, Jacob, Moses, Joshua, Daniel and Mary were paradigms for passing the test of faith.

Individual repentance, conversion, and redemption were grafted onto scriptural dramas. The believer descended into the "lonesome valley of Jehoshaphat and crossed the Jordan to "Canaan's bright shore." From beginning to end the process was painful:

> De lightnin' and de flashin' . . .
> I can't stand the fire.*

It was long lasting:

> Rassal Jacob, rassal as you did in the days of old
> Gonna rassal all night till broad daylight
> And ask God to bless my soul.†

The very universe reverberated with the existential turmoil: "And de moon will turn to blood on dat day, O-yoy my soul!"‡ Throughout, Jesus stood by the believer: "Jesus set poor sinners free."#

> Jesus call you.
> Go in de wilderness
> To wait upon de Lord.**

---

*See, for example, *I Corinthians* 3:13: "Every man's work shall be made manifest: for the day shall declare it, because it shall be revealed by fire: and the fire shall try every man's work of what sort it is."

†"And Jacob was left alone; and there wrestled a man with him until the breaking of the day." *Genesis* 32:24.

‡"The sun shall be turned into darkness, and the moon into blood, before that great and notable day of the Lord come." *Acts* 2:20.

#"But if we walk in the light, as He is in the light, we have fellowship one with another, and the blood of Jesus Christ His Son cleanseth us from all sin." *I John* 1:7.

**"And He withdrew Himself into the wilderness, and prayed." *Luke* 5:16.

Or

> He have been wid us, Jesus,
> He still wid us, Jesus.
> He will be wid us, Jesus,
> Be wid us to the end.

Ultimately, salvation was inevitable:

> De rough, rocky road what Moses done travel,
> I's bound to carry my soul to de Lawd.

> All dem Mount Zion member,
> dey have many ups and downs
> But cross come or no come,
> for to hold out to the end.[8]

Ironically, the very Christianity of the master which suppressed the slaves' African religious background became the vocabulary of liberation. Indeed, spirituals became codes for escape. The slave sung about Pharaoh's—i.e., the master's—evil. "Steal away to Jesus" was a call to secret meetings. "O Canaan, sweet Canaan, I am bound for the land of Canaan" or "de Promised Land on de oder side of Jordan" meant the heavenlike north toward which the slave would escape across the Ohio River.[9]

Pilgrims

American black Christians who made pilgrimages to the Holy Land in the nineteenth century sought to come closer to the life and death of Jesus. They also sought confirmation of the scriptural myth of liberation, which validated the ideals of their people. When they returned home they shared their experiences and the confirmation of Scripture that they had witnessed with other blacks.

Blacks were less interested in geographical reality than the spiritual experience of scriptural myth evoked by it. For example, the editor of the *AME Church Review* averred in 1918 that the golden age of the fulfillment of prophecy was about to arrive. The Jews should not look for their chief joy in returning to Jerusalem, to build the foundations of a Jewish state where once the throne of David stood. They should find it rather in the homecoming of all exiles "to Him who opened in the house of King David a [baptismal] fountain for sin and uncleanness." Christians should return to Jerusalem less to cherish the places made sacred by Jesus than to honor Jesus by following His commandments and His will in terms of neighborliness, brotherhood, justice, righteousness and peace.[10]

David Dorr

David Dorr, a slave in New Orleans, was a quadroon whose father was white and slave mother half white and half black.[11] He traveled to the Holy Land in 1853 with Colonel Cornelius Fellowes (1802-1871), a prosperous white New Orleans businessman—who "treated me as his own son, and could look on me as free a man as walks the earth."[12] Starting in Liverpool in June 1851 they toured Europe, Asia, and Africa, returning from Le Havre in July 1853 for New York City aboard the *Sir John Franklin*. Dorr proceeded to New Orleans and visited Fellowes, who had promised to improve his situation. But Fellowes refused "on old bachelor principles," and Dorr went on to Ohio, where he could enjoy the "moral liberties of the legal freedom of England, France, and our New England states." When he published his book in Cleveland in 1858 he remarked that "if local law has power over man, instead of man's effects, I was legally a slave and would be today, like my mother, were I on Louisiana's soil instead of Ohio's."[13]

Dorr dedicated *A Colored Man Round the World: By a quadroon* to his slave mother—whether she was in heaven or in a "lesser world," free or enslaved, he knew not. He explained his title thus:

> The author of this book, though a quadroon, is pleased to announce himself the "colored man round the world." Not because he may look at a colored man's position as an honorable one at this age of the world, he is too smart for that, but because he has the satisfaction of looking with his own eyes and reason at the ruins of the ancestors of which he is the posterity. If the ruins of the author's ancestors were not a living language of their scientific majesty, this book could receive no such appellation with pride.

When Dorr spoke of ancestral sources of pride, he had in mind the Egyptian cities of Luxor and Karnack and the pyramids. He also thought of Moses, great because "learned in all the learning of the Egyptians and mighty in words and in deeds."* The Egyptians were black: "Well, who were the Egyptians? Ask Homer if their lips were not thick, their hair curly, their feet flat, and their skin black."[14] Dorr's travels to Europe, Asia and Africa, including the Holy Land, inspired him with hope that the American "federated government is destined to be the noblest fabric ever germinated in the brain of men or the tides of time." The American people, moreover, would be the Persians of the nineteenth century; as the Persians liberated Israel from exile in 538 B.C.E., so Americans would liberate the blacks. On the basis of what Dorr saw around the world, he believed

---

*"And Moses was learned in all the wisdom of the Egyptians, and was mighty in words and in deeds." *Acts* 7:22.

that because America had the power, her principle of the will of the whole people would become the world standard.

In Hebron Muslim boys and women threw stones at Dorr and Fellowes to keep them from going too near the sacred Muslim dead, Abraham and Sarah, in the Cave of Makhpela.[15] As the two approached Jerusalem, Dorr observed the Mosque of Omar's dome glittering in the sun. This Muslim holy place towered over all other buildings in the city that was once "the glory of the world" because of its godliness: "Yes, the mosque of the Turk looked down upon our glorious Sepulcher, as it were with contempt." At the Holy Sepulcher, Dorr was overwhelmed:

> I made my way straight to our humble edifice, and fell upon the marble slabs that once entombed the flesh and blood of the greatest man ever tabernacled in a body of flesh. In the middle of the Latin Church, which means the church we Christians of the world built over Calvary, is another small house like a large sepulcher . . . In this little house are the sides, bottoms, and cover of the tomb of our Savior, just as it was taken from the earth and placed on this stone floor, this little house and the large church were built around it . . . An English lady, who came in before me, was prostrated on the floor, kissing the tomb with great devotion. She was a lady of rank who had pilgrimed here, and now had given way to her devoted feelings toward the dull, cold marble that once, in the midst of thousands of enemies, our Savior had lain in, uncorrupted, though bleeding and mangled.

The monks at the church were strict in every way. One of their aides told Dorr that no animals were allowed in the area because "by their courting habits they might lead the mind of man from spiritual reflection to groveling desires." Dorr walked around the walls of the city in an hour and a quarter and then rode on a small Arab steed to Bethlehem. He and Fellowes passed the Tomb of Lazarus, an hour out of Jerusalem at Bethany, and proceeded to the Bethlehem convent which housed the manger and the altar built above it.

They went on to Jericho. When they came to a free-running spring their guide had the "impudence" to explain that the water ran freely because the jawbone with which Samson fought so bravely was buried there. The guide had another "absurd" story about Jeremiah's Cave, "but I was not inclined to believe anything I heard from the people about here, because I knew as much as they did about it. I came to Jerusalem with a submissive heart, but when I heard all the absurdities of these ignorant people, I was more inclined to ridicule right over these sacred dead bodies, and spots, than pay homage."[16] The travelers camped at Jericho, where for supper they had doves and quails they had killed. They bathed in the Jordan—Dorr did not mention baptism—"and tried some of its water with *eau de vie* [hard liquor] and found it in quality like the water of the Mississippi."[17] They also bathed in the Dead Sea. Dorr did not describe

Jericho because not even a temple was left there. He returned to Jerusalem for seventeen days and visited the Western Wall, Calvary, Mount Moriah and the Mount of Olives. He left the city with a wish never to return and proceeded to Galilee, Tabor, Nazareth, and Damascus. His recollections were those of a tourist:

> I saw the [Mediterranean] Sea, as no doubt it was when the whale vomited [Jonah]; I saw the little house where water was turned into wine. I saw Tabor, ascended and took my chances with the wild boar; I returned from Tabor to Nazareth, where I had left my baggage and provisions; [and ate] some camel's meat.

Dorr passed through Lebanon, then Acre—where he "looked at its strong walls, and heard its foolish citizens talk of the impossibility of any nation being strong enough to take it"—on his way to Jaffa. From there he took passage to Marseilles, France.[18]

Dorr was essentially a tourist, and he approached the Land as a sceptical sightseer: the only souvenir he took home was some cedar burrs from Lebanon. There were moments of religious experience (for example, at the Holy Sepulcher) and moments when present and past came together (as when he walked around Jerusalem and recalled how Titus took the city). He also asserted his Christian identity: he resented the Muslim architectural dominance of Jerusalem. But in the end he was ready to leave Jerusalem and never return. His visit to the Holy Land was submerged in his search for sources of black dignity and freedom on the one hand and his tourist interests on the other.[19]

Daniel P. Seaton

Daniel P. Seaton was born in 1835 in Reisterstown, Maryland, to William and Louisa Seaton, who were then free. He received his license "to exhort" from the Quarterly Conference of the Vine Street AME Church in Buffalo (1864) and graduated from the American University of Medicine in Philadelphia (1871). Seaton served as pastor in numerous churches, including Saint Stephen's in Wilmington, Delaware (1865-1867); Union Bethel (Metropolitan AME) in Washington, D.C. (1869-1871); and Bethel AME in Indianapolis (1874-1876). He also served at Lincoln AME Church (later renamed Seaton Memorial) in Lanham, Maryland. He traveled to the Holy Land in 1877 and possibly again in 1887-1888.[20] Levi J. Coppin (1898-1923) recalled the journey in 1888:

> When Dr. Seaton informed Dr. B. T. Tanner [1835-1923] of his purpose the editor stated in substance as follows: "Dr. D. P. Seaton has the push in him to do the work; and should he accomplish it he will be the first AME

preacher whose eyes ever rested upon the city that is declared to be 'beautiful for situation.'"* The doctor undertook the journey under very unfavorable circumstances, yet he pressed on until full arrangements were made for the tour. He purchased a ticket for a passage on board the steamer *City of Chester* for Liverpool, England; thence he went to London, Paris, Turin, and Genoa. From there he continued to Alexandria, Egypt, up to Cairo, to the Red Sea; from thence to Port Said, from which point he crossed over in a French steamer to Jaffa. There he began his Palestine tour, visiting all the cities, towns and places of Bible distinction between Jaffa and Jerusalem . . . Dr. Seaton has the distinction of being the first and only colored man who has visited the Holy Land as a tourist. He delivered several speeches in Europe, which were received with enthusiasm. At one time he addressed seven thousand people.[21]

In 1922 Charles S. Smith wrote that "Dr. Seaton's career in the ministry was long and eventful. The presumption is that he was the first colored American to visit the Holy Land."[22] Seaton's account of his travels were published by the AME Church.[23] Then living in Washington, D.C., he wrote:

The author has endeavored to present in this volume, an unbiased statement of men and things, as they appear now and were in ancient times. His object is to more fully impress men with the importance of accepting the word of God upon the plain basis on which it is founded, and permit the truth to have full force in the world. The author has repeatedly requested for years before making his last visit through Palestine, to give a book to the world; but feeling it necessary to make another trip there and spend more time in taking observations, he deferred it until the last visit was finished. Now that we have completed the long-desired task, we shall feel more than repaid for the time and sacrifice made, if this work will accomplish half the good intended. We have taken pains to select texts for some of the most important subjects, so that the Bible student may easily turn to them and become more familiar with the word of God.

Seaton took stereoptic pictures, which he showed when he lectured about his travels.[24] His book is primarily a biblical history in geographical context related by an observer rather than participant. For example, at the Sea of Galilee he found few "Old Testament associations" but many "references to it in the New Testament." He explained his orientation:

---

*"Beautiful for situation, the joy of the whole earth, is mount Zion, on the sides of the north, the city of the great king." *Psalms* 48:2.

The Land which discloses the greatest religious thought, and furnishes the clearest information of the mercy and benevolence of Jesus Christ is the "Land of promise" . . . Every one who visits that country may find something of profound interest to write, which will give the world more information on the facts contained in the Holy Scriptures. The Land of promise is the country in which the principal events revealed to man in the Bible were developed, and where the Lord Jesus spent most of His time teaching the way of salvation . . . The Land of promise is so replete with Bible history, no one who will take the time to visit it can fail to see and learn more of its connection with God's word in one day than he could in a whole year's study away from it . . . The history of the Bible was presented in an entirely different light, and so distinctly clear, previous knowledge of the country seemed as but a simple speculation.

He was particularly concerned with the Hamite—i.e., black—aspect of biblical history:

It has been our aim to accord to each race its proper place in history as nearly as possible; especially the Hamite, whom we have reasons to believe has been greatly slighted by many authors who have attempted to write his history as relates to Palestine.[25]

He averred that the Phoenicians were of Hamitic "stock or race," a powerful and energetic people, never expelled from their territory on the Syrian coast from Jeliel (Jablah?) on the north to Acre on the south.

There were moments, however, when Seaton became a participant and his experience was sublimated into scriptural eternity. When he first saw Jerusalem he entered into its sacred time:

When my eyes first beheld the Holy City I was most solemnly impressed; the sufferings of my Lord came vividly to my mind, and I exclaimed: "O Jerusalem, Jerusalem! thou hath stoned the prophets and killed them that my Lord hath sent you, how many times would He have gathered thy children together as a hen gathers her brood under her wings, but ye would not."* Indeed there was no day during my stay in the Holy City that I was not moved with awe while visiting the many places of sacred memory . . . When the gate of Jaffa is opened and the feet of the eager visitor stand on Mount Zion, his mind is immediately crowded with many events of its glorious past

---

*"O Jerusalem, Jerusalem, which killest the prophets, and stonest them that are sent unto thee. How often would I have gathered thy children together, as a hen doth gather her brood under her wings, and ye would not." *Luke* 13:34.

age. He rejoices that he is standing on the holy hill of Zion, the mount on which patriarchs and prophets have been known to walk, where the Lord Jesus once stood, and apostles preached repentance toward God and faith in Christ.

The view from the Mount of Olives was especially impressive:

When the visitor contemplates the historic associations connected with the sacred mount upon which he is walking . . . He remembers the same ground he is traveling over was once marked by the sacred feet of the Savior of the world and somewhere near here once stood a cluster of trees He frequented when burdened in spirit, heavily oppressed with the sin of the world, to commune with His father, and drop tears of sorrow.[26]

Seaton portrayed Jews in the Holy Land from a Christian triumphalist perspective. They came from Russia, Germany, Poland, Romania, Spain, India, Egypt, Africa and other countries, young and old. Their devotion at the Wailing Wall was a deep lamentation, based upon *Psalms* 79, on account of divine displeasure. The Jews prayed for God's favor, for Him to restore Jerusalem and all the country to them. Seaton considered it worth going through the sickening odor of the Jewish quarter to see "Jews of both sexes assemble along the stupendous walls of the time-stricken building each Friday afternoon, and weep aloud from three o'clock until five." Their mistaken faith had "launched them into a deep gulf of adversity." Their agonizing gestures and penetrating cries were almost bewildering. The grief would continue until the Jews accepted Christ:

This method of expressing their griefs because their sanctuary had become dishonored and desolate, in connection with their own destitute and humiliating condition, has been continued for many centuries, and doubtless will be perpetuated until they make a full and complete surrender of their cherished religion, and embrace the Lord Jesus Christ, which, to my mind, is only a comparatively short time.

Seaton pointed out that hundreds had already espoused the Christian faith—presumably through the efforts of the LJS—and worshipped Christ on the hill of Zion under the auspices of the Church of England. He considered Mount Calvary, where the Lord reconciled justice and made it possible for fallen man to be at peace with God, the most sacred of the holy places in Jerusalem. There Jesus died for the Jews' redemption, but they derived no faith from the crucifixion, the scene of which was but a few minutes' walk from the walls at which they wailed. They still despised the Savior of man, "even as did their fathers who slew Him." Seaton felt like telling them, "Turn and look to Calvary and accept the Christ whom your forefathers crucified and all these blessings you seek will be given you for His name's sake." He hoped that the LJS Christ Church on Mount Zion would grow in number and influence (his group's chief guide, a converted Jew, was an official minister of the church). Then, "instead of a promiscuous gathering of aimless people seen each Friday at the Haram [i.e., the Temple], they will be found in the house of the Lord, bowing before their redeemer." The Temple was destroyed because Christ was rejected:

> The Temple siege was a literal fulfillment of the prophecy concerning the destruction of Jerusalem, declaring it should be trenched about and the people should be compassed by their enemies.* It seems very strange they did not call to mind this doleful prediction, which had only been spoken about forty years prior. They had eyes but could not see, and hearts but did not understand, and their enmity was so strongly expressed against our Lord, they could not allow themselves to confide in Him, although everything He had said was glaringly manifested before them.† Their blindness and obstinacy led them to destruction.[27]

At Hebron, Seaton wrote,

> The descendants of those whose prominence and piety so greatly distinguished the city have lost their control of it and are now subordinate to the sons of Hagar [Muslims], who, with relentless ostracism, refuse them permission to look upon the site in which are deposited the dusty remains of their illustrious ancestor [Abraham]. These self-destroyed people, who in the morning of their glory boasted in the fact that Abraham was their father, may be seen every day standing by the wall enclosing the rocky chamber, of which his sepulcher is composed, and drop a tear, impress a kiss, and then mournfully return to their homes, having no real prospect of ever being permitted to gaze upon the sacred tomb, or even enter the gates of the Haram leading to it. They prayerfully wait for the time when those who oppose and cause many sorrows to depress them, will be compelled to surrender the Makhpela Cave to them without a struggle, and yet they have not learned to trust in Him whose arm alone can help them.[28]

---

*"For the days shall come upon thee, that thine enemies shall cast a trench about thee, and compass thee round, and keep thee in on every side." *Luke* 19:43.

†"And when Jesus knew it, He saith unto them, Why reason ye, because ye have no bread? perceive ye not yet, neither understand? have ye your heart yet hardened? Having eyes, see ye not? and having ears, hear ye not? and do ye not remember?" *Mark* 8:17-18.

But Seaton had hope for the Jews, for they would become Christians. After Rome conquered their city of Jerusalem and forbade them to return, those very Jews who for a long time were nursed with the milk of divine love and protected by an all-powerful hand became wanderers without a shepherd, and the hand which released them from bondage turned against them. But that condition would change:

> It was their own hand that destroyed them, and it is their hand that keeps their Land subordinate to foreign powers. But they have a hopeful future; the time is coming when they will fully accept Christ, whom their fathers nailed to the cross, and reverently come before Him in devout worship, return to their own Land, and pay Him their tribute on the very summit where the pathetic prayer was offered by the Lord Jesus in their behalf, while the arrows of death were piercing His soul, "Father, forgive them; for they know not what they do" [*Luke* 23:34].

At that point the Jews would return from Syria and Turkey, from Poland and Russia, from Germany and Holland, from China and Japan, from Australia and America, from all over Europe, from Africa and the ends of the earth. They would gather at the Wall to shout praise to the God of their fathers—whose son, rejected by them, made it possible for them to return. There would be a restoration—which is why Jews have been preserved as a distinct nation. Their blindness would be removed forever and they would receive the light of conversion. Those who returned from other lands would "have already acknowledged Christ before starting home; and those whom they greet on their arrival not be strangers to Him." Jesus would be "all in all."*

> What a glorious time, what a blessed period when the people, once dispersed and unsettled, shall again "sing the Lord's song" in their own Land.† Then will the returning hosts set up a standard on Mount Zion with the motto stamped thereon, "This God is our God forever and ever; and will be our guide even until death."[29]

Charles T. Walker

Charles T. Walker (1858-1921), pastor of Atlanta's Tabernacle Baptist Church, traveled to the Land of Israel in 1891.[30] He went as a Christian pilgrim to the Holy Sepulcher, to Calvary, and the Wailing Wall. He found himself shifting between past, present and future—he saw the prophecy of Jeremiah being

---

*"Which is His body, the fullness of Him that filleth all in all." *Ephesians* 1:23.

†"How shall we sing the Lord's song in a strange land?" *Psalms* 137:4.

fulfilled with the rebuilding of Jerusalem, starting with the tower of Hananeel.* Feeling that he represented his Atlanta congregation in the Holy Land, Walker kept his congregants in mind throughout. He wrote to the *Atlanta Sentinel* that he would wait to describe Jerusalem until he preached about Palestine in his church.[31] His observations of Jaffa were brought into scriptural context:

> We saw the spot where Jonah took ship to Tarshish, when commanded to go to Nineveh—it is now called Jonah's Bay. We saw the house where it is claimed Peter restored Dorcas to life; and on the seaside, where we landed, is the house of Simon the Tanner, where Peter was lodged when the angel appeared to Cornelius at Caesarea, and told him to send men to Jaffa for Peter, and that he would be found at Simon's house [*Acts* 9:43-10:6].†

Walker's group—he did not identify his companions—then visited the port of Jaffa, to which King Hiram rafted timbers from Lebanon for Solomon's Temple.‡ From Jaffa they went by carriage—the railroad would not be built for another year—to Jerusalem. The group passed the Plains of Sharon, where they observed the rose of Sharon blooming, and then Ramleh.# In ancient times, Walker pointed out, Ramleh had been the stopping place of caravans from Damascus to Egypt. They ascended Ramleh's great tower and were able to see as far as Gath, the home of Goliath. They walked over the field near Ashkelon where Samson set fire to the wheat by igniting the tails of foxes.** Walker mused, "The field is now entirely bare. I do not know whether it is because it has not sufficiently overcome the burning to be used or not." They passed through the Valley of Ajalon, where Joshua conquered the five Amonite kings and Joshua proclaimed, "Sun, stand thou still upon Gibeon; and thou, Moon, in the valley of Ajalon" (*Joshua* 10:12). They crossed the brook where David gathered stones to fight

---

*"Behold, the days come, saith the Lord, that the city shall be built to the Lord from the tower of Hananeel unto the gate of the corner." *Jeremiah* 31:38.

†"Now there was at Joppa a certain disciple named Tabitha, which by interpretation is called Dorcas: this woman was full of good works and almsdeeds which she did." *Acts* 9:36.

‡"My servants shall bring them down from Lebanon unto the sea: and I will convey them by sea in floats unto the place that thou shalt appoint me, and will cause them to be discharged there, and thou shalt receive them: and thou shalt accomplish my desire, in giving food for my household." *I Kings* 5:9.

#"I am the rose of Sharon, and the lily of the valleys. As the lily among thorns, so is my love among the daughters." *Song of Solomon* 2:1.

**"And when he had set the brands on fire, he let them go into the standing corn of the Philistines, and burnt up both the shocks, and also the standing corn, with the vineyards and olives." *Judges* 15:5.

Goliath.* They "picked up some as a memento, but I don't think that any of us got hold of the identical one that slayed the giant." Before Jerusalem they came to the highway on which the ark of God was borne in triumph to Mount Zion, and on which Titus led Roman soldiers to attack Jerusalem.

In Jerusalem they visited the ancient tower of Hananeel. Walker foresaw the fulfillment of Jeremiah's prophecy, for beginning with the restored tower the city of Jerusalem was indeed being rebuilt.† He understood the rest of the prophet's prediction (*Jeremiah* 31:39) to mean the overthrow of paganism, Islam, and Roman Catholicism in Jerusalem and the reestablishment of true Christianity in that sacred city where it was first preached. "It is coming, coming, coming! God hath said it. They have begun to build just where the prophet said they would."

The group proceeded to the Church of the Holy Sepulcher and viewed the Stone of Unction, where the Lord was laid for anointing when taken from the cross. In the center of the Church was the Tomb of Christ, over which a marble chapel 26 by 18 feet was built. The marble slab over the Tomb was worn and cracked, because nearly every visitor bowed down to kiss the spot where blessed Jesus lay. Walker described his own transformation:

> I knelt where He was placed after being crucified. I wept as I gazed on the empty tomb. Some visitors have disputed that this was not the real burial place, but I have not a doubt of its being the identical spot where my dear Lord lay, and a solemn feeling came over me which language can but very feebly express. It seemed to me I could hear the words of the angel to the women: "Why seek ye the living among the dead?"‡ "He is not here: for He is risen, as He said. Come, see the place where the Lord lay."# I wrote in my book, as I turned away, "Thank God He is a risen, exalted Savior. He lives no more to die."

north of the Sepulcher was an open court, where Jesus had said to Mary Magdalene, "Woman, why weepest thou? Whom seekest thou? She, supposing Him to be the gardener, saith unto Him, Sir, if thou hast borne Him hence, tell me where thou hast laid Him, and I will take Him away" (*John* 20:15).

---

*"And he took his staff in his hand, and chose him five smooth stones out of the brook, and put them in a shepherd's bag which he had, even in a scrip; and his sling was in his hand: and he drew near to the Philistine." *I Samuel* 17:40.

†*Jeremiah* 31:38, supra.

‡"And as they were afraid, and bowed down their faces to the earth, they said unto them, Why seek ye the living among the dead?" *Luke* 24:5.

#"He is not here: for He is risen, as He said. Come, see the place where the Lord lay." *Matthew* 28:6.

At Calvary they saw a rock which was said to have split during the crucifixion and the spot where Mary stood. Walker recalled the gospel of John and entered into the scriptural drama:*

> I imagined, as I stood on Calvary, that I could see my Savior ascend the hill on that Friday morning, bearing His cross. So we went to the street from where Simon took the cross all along Calvary. I followed His footsteps. The place where Simon picked up the cross is marked with a stone, and thousands of Jews bow there, and weep and pray.

Walker spoke of Calvary as the place where "my Savior fought Apollyon, attacked the old canon of Eden, put out the fire of Sinai and magnified God's transgressed law."

At the Temple Mount Walker bemoaned that the Temple which Christ said would be a house of prayer for all people had become a place of heathen worship—in the Mosque of Omar Muslims worshipped Mohammad, a dead man and a false prophet.† At the Wailing Wall the Jews gathered every Friday afternoon to read *Lamentations* and *Psalms* 79 in Hebrew, weeping and leaning against the Wall. They related their tragedies and sins, reciting the self-deprecating litany "For the palace that lies waste": because of the deserted palace, destroyed temple, broken walls, departed greatness, precious temple stones ground to powder, priests who went astray, kings who condemned God, "We sit alone and weep."‡ Walker felt compassion, but "Christ told them so. Here is prophecy fulfilled."[32]

Observations

In the American black Christian experience of the Holy Land during the nineteenth century, the social reality of suppression and the existential plight of sin and repentance were transformed and elevated into scriptural myth. Within that myth the black Christian found liberation and salvation. Through spirituals the singer became part of biblical suffering and redemption. Dorr—whose religious background is not known—visited the holy places with a tourist's frame of mind, reflecting at times on Christian experiences. He pointed to facts about

---

*"When Jesus therefore saw His mother, and the disciple standing by, whom He loved, He saith unto His mother, Woman, behold thy son! Then saith He to the disciple, Behold thy mother! And from that hour that disciple took her unto his own home." *John* 19:26-27.

†"And He taught, saying unto them, Is it not written, My house shall be called of all nations the house of prayer? but ye have made it a den of thieves." *Mark* 11:17.

‡Supra, Chapter 4.

biblical lands to assert his black identity and call for racial equality in America. Seaton tried to demonstrate a "Hamite"—i.e., black—tie to the Holy Land and spoke confidently about Christian triumphalism. Walker was an authentic pilgrim who found himself shifting between past, present, and future as he made his way through the Holy Land. He became caught up in the scriptural drama of redemption, which he was intent upon sharing with his black congregants in Atlanta.

For Dorr, the plight of black Christianity pervaded his interest in the Holy Land; ancient Scripture was a potential source for black cultural dignity and liberation. Seaton was interested in Hamitic origins, presumably to provide dignity to his people by demonstrating their link to Scripture. But he did not integrate this interest with his Christian triumphalism vis-à-vis Judaism. Walker, liked Seaton, felt the pitiable condition of Jews stemmed from their rejection of Christ. He wished to enliven his congregants' beliefs in the scriptural dimension to their lives but did not feel a need to demonstrate ties between blacks and the biblical period.[33]

Notes

1. See Erskine Clark, *Wrestlin' Jacob: A Portrait of Religion in the Old south* (Atlanta 1979); Donald G. Matthews, *Religion in the Old south* (Chicago 1977); Benjamin E. Mays, *The Negro's God as Reflected in His Literature* (New York 1938); Cain H. Felder, *Troubling Biblical Waters: Race, Class, and Family* (Maryknoll, N.Y., 1989); Eugene D. Genovese, *Roll, Jordan, Roll* (New York 1976); Dena J. Epstein, *Sinful Times and Spirituals: Black Folk Music to the Civil War* (Urbana, Ill., 1979).

2. Timothy L. Smith, "Slavery and Theology: The Emergence of Black Christian Consciousness in Nineteenth Century America," *Church History* 41 no. 4 (December 1972):497-512.

3. Lawrence Jones, "Afro-Americans and the Holy Land," in Moshe Davis, ed., *With Eyes toward Zion* (New York 1977):1:57-64.

4. Absalom Jones, *A Thanksgiving Sermon: Preached 1 January 1808 in Saint Thomas's, or the African Episcopal Church, Philadelphia. On account of the abolition of the African slave trade, on that day, by the Congress of the United States* (Philadelphia 1808), reprinted in Dorothy Porter, ed., *Early Negro Writing, 1760-1837* (Boston 1971):335-342.

5. *American Missionary* 6 no. 2 (February 1862):33, cited in Albert J. Raboteau, *Slave Religion: The Invisible Institution in the Antebellum south* (New York 1978):320.

6. W. G. Kiphant, letter of 9 May 1864, Decatur, Alabama American Missionary Association Archives, Amistad Research Center, Dillard University, New Orleans, cited in Albert Raboteau, "Black Americans," in Davis, *With Eyes toward Zion* (New York 1986):2:311-322.

7. "The Exodus," *AME Church Review* 33 no. 3 (January 1917):151, cited in Raboteau, "Black Americans." See Wilson J. Moses, *Black Messiahs and Uncle Toms: Social and Literary Manipulations of a Religious Myth* (University Park, Pa., 1982):112.

8. Lawrence W. Levine, *Black Culture and Black Consciousness: Afro-American Folk Thought from Slavery to Freedom* (New York 1977):3-80; idem, "Slave Songs and Slave Consciousness: An Exploration in Neglected Sources," in *Anonymous Americans: Explorations in Nineteenth Century Social History*, Tamara K. Hareven, ed. (Englewood Cliffs, N.J., 1971):99-130. Cf. Raboteau, *Slave Religion*, 243-266.

9. Lawrence Jones, "Afro-Americans and the Holy Land."

10. *AME Church Review* 34 no. 3 (January 1918):179-180, cited in Raboteau, "Black Americans."

11. Dorr's knowledge of western literature indicated the education of a "Free Man of Color," but he was not legally free. He was ever mindful of his fellow slaves back home. In England he heard a group of journalists from England, France, and America discussing the weak points of American policy:

> One held that if the Negroes of the southern states were fit for freedom, it would be an easy matter for four million . . . slaves to raise the standard of liberty and maintain it against 250,000 slaveholders. The other gentleman held that it was very true, but they needed some white man, well posted in the south, with courage enough to plot the entree. He continued, at great length, to show the feasibility under a French plotter. He closed with his expression, "One intelligent Frenchman like [the socialist leader Alexandre] Ledru-Rollin [1807-1874] could do the whole thing before it could be known." I came to the conclusion that they were not so careful in the expression of their views as I thought they ought to be. I was quite sure that they would not be allowed to use such treasonable language at Orleans or Charleston, as that they had just indulged in.

David F. Dorr, *A Colored Man Round the World: By a quadroon* (Cleveland 1858):16-17. On 28 July 1851 in Saint James's Park in London he observed:

> I was, indeed, ashamed to see the piles of India rubber shoes, coats and pants, and clocks that stood out in *bas* relief in that part of the [Crystal] Palace appropriate to the American arts and sciences—pegged shoes and boots were without number. Martingales and side saddles, horse shoes, ploughs, threshing machines, irrigators, and all the most worthless trash to be found in the States. I saw everything that was a prevailing disgrace to our country except slaves [pp. 19-20].

Of Cornelius Fellowes he remarked,

> He is so proud, or haughty, or perhaps I had better say, naturally aristocratic, that he can descend from his sphere to vulgar without knowing it and joke, laugh, and even offer some of his drink, but if you forget yourself, he will recollect himself. He can treat a free colored man as polite as he can a poor white one, and a class that are below them must be in his estimation what they are [p. 62].

I was unable to identify Dorr further. The Louisiana Division of the New Orleans Public Library could find nothing about him. See Herman C. Woessner, "New Orleans 1840-1860: A Study in Urban Slavery" (thesis, Louisiana State University, 1967); Donald E.

Everett, "Free Persons of Color in New Orleans, 1803-1865" (diss., Tulane University, 1952).

12. There is a description of Cornelius Fellowes in the New Orleans Public Library:
This gentleman is esteemed senior of the widely known and much respected firm of Fellowes and Co., one of the oldest, most stable and extensive houses in New Orleans. It is probable that the consignments of this house, embracing as they do a very wide range of the products of the great Mississippi valley, exceed largely those of any other house in the city, and perhaps in the country. There is probably no other similar firm in the United States that possesses at the present moment a higher standing or is in the enjoyment of a more general and favorable reputation both in this country and in Europe, than this house.

Through all the commercial reverses and disasters which for many years past have affected the mercantile world, it has passed and in every instance come out unsullied. The house of Fellowes and Co. is beyond doubt unsurpassed by any other in this city in point of stability and in the extent to which it enjoys the public confidence. Mr. Fellowes, its head, is a gentleman of excellent business capacity, of great enterprise and energy of character, and is universally esteemed for his strict integrity and great private worth.
Cited in Madeleine McClenney, "David Dorr: An African American Pilgrim in the Holy Land" (thesis, America-Holy Land Project, Hebrew University, 1991). The *New Orleans Annual and Commercial Register for 1846* (New Orleans 1846), 246, lists "Fellowes, Johnson and Co. commission merchants. 91 Camp St. Fellowes, Cornelius, above firm." An obituary for Fellowes appeared in the New Orleans *Daily Picayune* (10 December 1871):4.

13. Dorr, *A Colored Man*, 12. "But as Mr. Fellowes never cares much for looks or position, and as he is an old bachelor and never had a house, and a slave holder is his equal, he hesitates not to go to the ladies' ordinary and order his seat at table, and call on the rustic gentleman and family to dine with him, where they drink such wine as they would most likely take at home for stump water and cider." Dorr, *A Colored Man*, 64.

14. I was unable to find such a description of Egyptians in Homer. See Henry Dunbar, *A Complete Concordance to the Odyssey and Hymns of Homer: To which is added a concordance to the parallel passages in the Iliad, Odyssey, and Hymns* (Oxford 1880). Cf. Frank M. Snowden, *Blacks in Antiquity: Ethiopians in the Greek-Roman Experience* (Cambridge, Mass., 1970).

15. Seaton had a similar experience:
The ancient mosque, formerly known as the Cave of Makhpela at Hebron, is called Abraham's Mosque. It is strictly guarded by the Mohammedans, in whose absolute charge it is, as well as the whole city. The great mosque is built over the entire space occupied by the cave, and closes it in from the gaze of the outside world. The Arabs can be seen about this sacred resting-place of the immortal Abraham, and others of his family, by the hundreds from day to day, fully prepared for any emergency. Such is the love and veneration for his tomb, they are willing to lay down their existence, that it may be protected against the encroachments of those whom they regard as unbelievers.

Daniel P. Seaton, *The Land of Promise; or, The Bible Land and its revelation* (Philadelphia 1895):155.

16. The Cave of Jeremiah, near the Damascus gate, was believed to be the place where Jeremiah wrote his *Lamentations*. Fisk and King offered this description on 5 May 1824:
> It was one of the rudest and grandest caves we ever saw. It is about forty paces long, the roof supported by two huge pillars. It is evidently a natural cave, though it has been altered by art. The interior is damp, and through some parts of the vaulted roof, water is continually oozing. The interior forms a kind of semicircle. The entrance is nearly as wide as the cave itself, and over it the rock rises forty or fifty feet perpendicularly. Just as you enter the cave there is a cleft in the rock on the left hand, called the bed of Jeremiah, where it is supposed he used to sleep. Whether it be fact or fiction, the thought of Jeremiah writing his *Lamentations* in this place is certainly sublime.

[Pliny Fisk and Jonas King], "American Board of Foreign Missions: Palestine mission. Journal of Messrs. Fisk and King at Jerusalem," *MH* 20 no. 3 (March 1824):69.

17. Seaton said later that after Easter hundreds of pilgrims rushed to the Jordan and plunged fully clothed into the sacred stream for a new baptism at the spot opposite Gilgal where, it was generally believed, Jesus was baptized by John. *Land of Promise*, 212-213.

18. Dorr, *A Colored Man,* Preface, 11-12, 183-192.

19. There is no indication of what Dorr thought of Jews in relation to the Land. In Rome he had this brief encounter with a Jew:
> One day when it was very warm, I went down to the Tiber to waste a little time reflectively, where the golden candlestick that was brought from Jerusalem fell off the bridge and never afterwards was found. Whilst I laid there on its banks listening to its almost inaudible murmur, a Jew came and stretched himself close to my feet. I asked him if he recollected who it was that Plutarch says was condemned to the hideous punishment of being nailed up in a barrel with serpents and thrown in the Tiber to float on the sea. He had never heard of such a thing. I then asked him if he was aware that the golden candlestick out of the Temple of Solomon lay at the bottom of that muddy stream. He said yes, and added that the Pope had been offered millions of piastres by the Jews to let them turn the current of the Tiber twenty miles above Rome, that they might recover all the lost and hidden treasure of nearly three thousand years standing, but the Pope had refused because he was too superstitious to allow the Tiber's current to be changed.

A Colored Man, 99-100.

20. See Charles S. Smith, *A History of the AME Church* (Philadelphia 1922); Alexander W. Wayman, *Cyclopaedia of African Methodism* (Baltimore 1882); idem, *My Recollections of AME Ministers* (Philadelphia 1881); R. R. Wright, ed., *The Encyclopaedia of the AME Church*, 2nd ed. (Philadelphia 1947); [Levi J. Coppin and Benjamin T. Tanner], "Rev. Daniel P. Seaton, M.D.," *AME Church Review Quarterly* 5 no. 2/18 (Philadelphia October 1888):131-132. Some *AME Church Review* editions were not numbered, and in some cases the numbers are unavailable (indicated by a question mark).

21. Coppin and Tanner, "Seaton." Cf. Rodney Sadler, "Parallel Pilgrimages: A Study of a Pilgrim, Daniel A. Seaton, and a Comparison of Pilgrimage Experiences" (thesis, America-Holy Land Project, Hebrew University, 1990).

22. Smith, *History of the AME Church*, 83.

23. Seaton, *Land of Promise,* iv. The working title of the book was "The Bible Land and Its Developments." *Christian Recorder: Official organ of the AME Church* 43 no. 7 (13 June 1895):2.

24. "Dr. D. P. Seaton will deliver a lecture in Zion Mission, Philadelphia, 5 December 1889, on his travels in the Holy Land. Stereopticon views will be given of important men, places, and things," *Christian Recorder* 27 no. 48/673 (28 November 1889):1.

25. See also Seaton, *Land of Promise*, 11, 237, 348. Cf. A. J. Kershaw, "The Hamitic Influences upon the Past, the Present and the Future Ages of the World"; *AME Church Review* no. ? (1888):229-234; [Levi J. Coppin and Benjamin T. Tanner], "The Hamitic Origin of the Negro: Reply to notes on *Genesis* 6:10 as published in *Sunday School Journal*," *AME Church Review* 4 no. ? (September 1887?):550-557.

26. Seaton, *Land of Promise,* iii, 62-63, 103.

27. Ibid, 69-74, 95-97, 133.

28. Ibid., 161.

29. Ibid., 72-74, 95-100, 141-143.

30. Silas X. Floyd, *Life of Charles T. Walker, D.D.* (Nashville 1902).

31. Charles T. Walker, *A Colored Man Abroad: What he saw and heard in the Holy Land and Europe* (Augusta, Ga., 1892):66.

32. Ibid., 68-69, 80-84.

33. In the first decades of the twentieth century the number of black Christian pilgrims increased: W. L. Jones, *The Travel in Egypt and Scenes of Jerusalem* (Atlanta 1908); James E. Willis (a Baptist pastor in Washington, D.C.), *My Experiences in the Holy Land: My First Two Days in the Holy Land. Donkey Ride Outside the Gates of Jerusalem. Two Days' Excursion from Jerusalem to Jericho, the Dead Sea, and the Jordan* (Washington, D.C., 1914); William S. Brooks (an AME pastor in Chicago), *Footprints of a Black Man: The Holy Land* (St. Louis 1915); Alexander Walters (pastor of the Mother Zion Church in New York City), *My Life and Work* (New York 1917):74-81; Garfield T. Harwood (pastor of the Oneness Pentecostal Church in Indianapolis), *A Trip to the Holy Land* (Indianapolis 1927); Caroline Bagley, *My Trip through Egypt and the Holy Land* (New York 1928). See David Klatzker, "American Christian Travelers to the Holy Land, 1821-1939" (diss., Temple University, 1983), and Albert Raboteau, "Black Americans."

8 Protestant Literalists:
Jewish Return and Christian Kingdom

The Protestant denominations of America that stressed the literal meaning of Scripture were dedicated to the revival of the Land of Scripture in the Christian millennium. They differed on how Jews would and should prepare for and participate in the coming apocalypse.[1]

Millerites

For the Millerites—followers of William Miller (1782-1844) of Vermont, a literalist intrigued with the apocalyptic sections of the Bible, especially *Daniel*—involvement with the Land of Israel entailed excluding Jews.[2] In 1822 Miller spoke of the restoration of the Land, but only for Christians. At the end of Christ's millennium, he believed, the dead would be resurrected, the world would convert to Christ, and the earth would be regenerated.* Restoration would be limited to those who were of Christ, "the putting on of Christ constituting them Abraham's seed, and heirs according to the promise."[3]

On 31 March 1840 Miller wrote to Joshua V. Himes (1805-1895), the man most responsible for transforming Miller's ideas into a movement, about his objection to a Jewish restoration. Some of the "brothers"—he named David Campbell and Universalist clergymen Thomas Whitemore and Otis A. Skinner—had defied Peter's admonition about God's accepting only the righteous with their "vain supposition" that the Jews must return.† No, the Jews first had

---

*"But the rest of the dead lived not again until the thousand years were finished." *Revelation* 20:5.

†"Then Peter opened his mouth, and said, Of a truth I perceive that God is no respecter of persons: But in every nation he that feareth Him, and worketh righteousness, is accepted with him." *Acts* 10:34-35.

to be respected by God and truly become His covenant people in order to be gathered in by Him.* Then they would no longer be Jews but grafted in among the gentiles who believed in Christ.† Had the Apostle Paul been alive he would have felt accursed had the brothers told him that God would not cast away His ancient people, that Jewish Israel would be saved, and he would have addressed the consequences to Jewish activities.‡ Had the Apostle James been alive the brothers would have attempted to divert him from the "twelve tribes scattered abroad" and faith of Christ, directing him to tell Jews how to remain steadfast as Jews so that in the end they would be gathered in as Jews.# In Miller's view, to say that the Jews in the flesh would be saved in the end perverted God into a blanket "respecter of persons" irrespective of righteousness.**

Moreover, if the Jews were to be gathered into their own Land and never "pulled up" again, what of Paul's view that in Christ not circumcision but becoming a new creature was decisive?†† How could Christ explain His statement that there would be one fold and one shepherd if Jews remained a

---

*See, for example, *Isaiah* 44:7: "And who, as I, shall call, and shall declare it, and set it in order for Me, since I appointed the ancient people? and the things that are coming, and shall come, let them shew unto them." "And they shall bring all your brethren for an offering unto the Lord out of all nations upon horses, and in chariots, and in litters, and upon mules, and upon swift beasts, to my holy mountain Jerusalem, saith the Lord, as the children of Israel bring an offering in a clean vessel into the house of the Lord." *Isaiah* 66:20.

†"For there is no difference between the Jew and the Greek: for the same Lord over all is rich unto all that call upon Him." *Romans* 10:12.

‡"For I could wish that myself were accursed from Christ for my brethren, my kinsmen according to the flesh." *Romans* 9:3. "Tribulation and anguish, upon every soul of man that doeth evil, of the Jew first, and also the gentile. But glory, honour, and peace, to every man that worketh good, to the Jew first, and also to the gentile." *Romans* 2:9-10.

#"James, a servant of God and of the Lord Jesus Christ, to the twelve tribes which are scattered abroad, greeting." *James* 1:1.

**"To them who by patient continuance in well doing seek for glory and honor and immortality, eternal life: . . . For there is no respect of persons with God . . . For he is not a Jew, which is one outwardly; neither is that circumcision, which is outward in the flesh: But he is a Jew, which is one inwardly; and circumcision is that of the heart, in the spirit, and not in the letter; whose praise is not of men, but of God." *Romans* 2:7, 11, 28, 29.

††"And I will plant them upon their Land, and they shall no more be pulled up out of their Land, which I have given them, saith the Lord thy God." *Amos* 9:15. "For in Christ Jesus neither circumcision availeth anything, nor uncircumcision, but a new creature." *Galatians* 6:15.

separate people?* When would the "partition wall" be broken down by Christ?† If the church, which is Christ's body, is the fullness of Him, how could the Jew, as Jew, be part thereof?‡ How could the old Jerusalem be part of the new? Those Hebrew scriptural passages which spoke of the Jews' return to their own Land referred to the first exile and return from Babylon. Statements that Jews should "never be pulled up" alluded to the new covenant, which was Christian and spiritual.# When Isaiah spoke of gathering the remnant of His people, he meant the new covenant, as did Jeremiah when he spoke of Jews being gathered out of Babylon, and Ezekiel when he spoke of dwelling in the Land forever.**4

Henry D. Ward (1797-1884), an Episcopal clergyman of New York who joined Miller in 1838, wrote in 18 December 1841:

> Israel, the seed of the house of Jacob, are themselves in the Bible but a shadow of the heavenly family in Christ, as their tabernacle, their Temple, their ritual, their Jerusalem, their Canaan, their Joshua and David, were shadows of the heavenly patterns. And as the shadow is lost in the manifesting of the substance, so does the Jew vanish in the manifestation of the sons of God, and the Jew's Zion in the manifestation of the new Jerusalem, and his Canaan in the world to come, and his restoration vanishes in the resurrection from the dead . . . If the carnal Jews must have a

---

*"And other sheep I have, which are not of this fold: them also I must bring, and they shall hear my voice; and there shall be one fold, and one shepherd." *John* 10:16.

†*Ephesians* 2:14, supra.

‡"And hath put all things under His feet, and gave Him to be the head over all things to the church, Which is His body, the fulness of Him that filleth all in all." *Ephesians* 1:22-23.

#*Amos* 9:15, supra.

**"And in that day there shall be a root of Jesse, which shall stand for an ensign of the people; to it shall the gentiles seek: and his rest shall be glorious. And it shall come to pass in that day, that the Lord shall set His hand again the second time to recover the remnant of His people, which shall be left, from Assyria, and from Egypt, and from Pathros, and from Cush, and from Elam, and from Shinar, and from Hamath, and from the islands of the sea." *Isaiah* 11:10-11 and 11:12, supra. "Behold, I will gather them out of all countries, whither I have driven them in Mine anger, and in My fury, and in great wrath; and I will bring them again unto this place, and I will cause them to dwell safely. And they shall be My people and I will be their God . . . And I will make an everlasting covenant with them, that I will not turn away from them, to do them good; but I will put My fear in their hearts, that they shall not depart from Me." *Jeremiah* 32:37-38, 40. Thus saith the Lord God, Behold, I will take the children of Israel from among the heathen, whither they be gone, and will gather them on every side, and bring them into their own land . . . Moreover I will make a covenant of peace with them; it shall be an everlasting covenant with them: and I will place them, and multiply them, and will set My sanctuary in the midst of them for evermore." *Ezekiel* 37:21, 26.

restoration in order to fulfill the Scripture, it is apparent that the restoration of which the prophets delight to speak embraces all the chosen and faithful in Christ; and any peculiar promise to the carnal Jews, compared to the literal promise of the resurrection, is no better than a pine torch compared to the sun: suitable for a type, and withal a most useful and necessary thing to guide the traveler in a land of darkness: but when the sun is once risen, the pine torch is no longer of use; it is a troublesome encumbrance, and every wise traveler will dispense with it.[5]

In 1842 Henry Jones (1804-1880), who served as a Congregational minister in New York, wrote that the unbelieving Jew would not be involved in the return or restoration of Israel to her own Land. The restored Israel would be composed of God's true saints, the "Israel only by faith in Jesus Christ." Her return and restoration belonged to the "mighty *events* of Christ's second coming *itself*, and *not* as a lingering work done by mortals in the flesh, as only a preparation for it." Jones considered theories about the return of the unbelieving Jew prior to Christ's coming as an "imaginary mighty block before the chariot wheels of the Almighty." In fact, there would be no such obstruction in the way of Christ's lightninglike arrival from heaven to save His people and destroy His unbelieving enemies, both Jew and gentile. Jones was enthusiastic about converting Jews so they could return:

> We are most heartily united with [LJS] in our desires and labors for the conversion of the unbelieving Jews, as a preparation for their *glorious* return to a "*heavenly Jerusalem*," with all others of the redeemed, at the anticipated now speedy coming of our Lord in glory, to receive to Himself all that are His, both Jews and gentiles, without distinction, at the making up of His jewels.*

Jones addressed recent excitement among Jews about the imminent appearance of the messiah and the return of "natural" Jews. When he inquired among New York Jews, he was told, "What should we want to go there for? We have here all the privileges we can ask—here is a good place for our business, but not there. If we wished to go, we could have gone before now; we have means sufficient to procure a conveyance, and purchase the country if we wanted it." The "learned priests" of the Jews (rabbis) told him that the expected messiah would not move them to Palestine as a worldly country but rather destroy the enemy and gather the saints in a "heavenly Jerusalem" forever.

---

* "But ye are come unto Mount Sion, and unto the city of the living God, the heavenly Jerusalem, and to an innumerable company of angels." *Hebrews* 12:22.

Jones also referred to statements by London's chief rabbi Solomon Hirschell (1762-1842), which he received through Rabbi Samuel Myer Isaacs (1804-1878) of New York. Since 1807 Hirschell had objected to LJS work in restoring Jews to the Land. He denied that Jews were looking expectantly for the messiah to come and rule over them. Hirschell considered contemporary Jewish messianic expectations no different from any before and rejected the notion attributed to him of "a day of special intercession for the return of the messiah recently appointed." Yom Kippur had not been "recently appointed," and the Jew did not believe in the "*return* of the messiah." Finally, Jones cited testimonies given to him by rabbis Isaacs and Jacques J. Lyons (1814-1877), the latter also from New York:

With regard to their return to Jerusalem or "Judah," they understand all the prophecies to foretell it, though they profess not to see any more signs of the event now near than there have heretofore been since their dispersion. They have no anticipation or desires of going to inhabit that country at present, or under existing circumstances, and would by no means consent to go as a people, even if the whole country were given them with the city and Temple at Jerusalem already built, unless the eastern powers would become pledged to protect them as citizens and as Jews, not being able to protect themselves. When their messiah shall come, and they as a people shall return, they expect him to come not as a mortal man, but with great power and glory, as Daniel and the prophets have described it—to destroy all his and their enemies, in the end of all worldly things—to dwell with them, and they with him, in a glorious state forever, and ever; when their Land, being created anew, will flow and with the milk and honey of spiritual and everlasting enjoyments—then with angels in a heavenly state.[6]

The 1842 Millerite conference in Boston held that the New Testament did not intimate that Jews were to be restored to "old Jerusalem." Indeed, "the notion of the return of carnal Jews to Palestine either before or after the second advent is a snare by which many will be lost forever."[7] In January 1844 Isaac P. Labagh (1804-1879) of New York enunciated the Millerite position:

We discover it to be the purpose of the God of Abraham, of Isaac and of Jacob, to remember once more His ancient people the Jews, who at the second coming of Christ, shall be delivered out of the hands of their enemies of the gentile nations (heathen and Christian) by the exercise of His almighty and miraculous power; and shall be restored to their own Land, converted, and become the center of unity of the visible church of Christ; the *chief* of the nations of the earth, during the millennial reign of universal righteousness and peace . . . The Jews, being restored and converted to the faith of Christ, shall be formed into a state, and become the *chief of the kingdoms of the earth*, and have judges and counsellors over them as formerly. The Lord shall be their *king*, who shall also be acknowledged as king over all the earth.[8]

The theme of the 1842 Millerite Conference was reiterated in the 2 April 1845 conference resolution, labelling as subversive the doctrine of the restoration of natural Jews as a nation, before or after Christ's second advent, as inheritors of the Land. The doctrine raised up the wall of partition between Jew and gentile which Christ had broken down.[*] It contradicted New Testament declarations which neutralized differences between Jew and Greek, which defined the inheritance of the world in terms of righteousness of faith and not law, and which made all, including Abraham's seed, one in Christ.[†] The concept of Jewish restoration was a "Judaizing doctrine" which claimed that the children of the flesh, not the children of spirit, were the seed, that the distinction still prevailed between Jew and gentile.[‡] The conference considered it fundamental to the gospel to protest such teachings as a "gross absurdity." Those who believed in Christ and called upon the Lord's name would be saved, others would be damned.[9]

Clorinda S. Minor

Clorinda S. Minor was raised as a member of the "Congregational Church of a Puritan ancestry." Committed to the literal meaning of the Bible, she was dismayed at the discrepancy between contemporary forms of religion and scriptural expressions of divine power. Turning inward, she struggled "with fasting and tears for a greater nearness to the life of Christ." In 1842 she committed herself to Miller's gospel of the kingdom of God and the premillennial advent of Jesus in 1843.[10] During 1844 she objected to the return of "natural" Jews:

Many who make great professions of godliness, have not faith in His promises, and deny the evidence of His coming, or openly maintain that their Lord delays, and "begin to eat and drink with the drunken" [*Matthew* 24:49],

---

[*]*Ephesians* 2:14, supra.

[†]*Romans* 10:12, supra. "For the promise, that he should be the heir of the world, was not to Abraham, or to his seed, through the law, but through the righteousness of faith." *Romans* 4:13. "There is neither Jew nor Greek, there is neither bond nor free, there is neither male nor female: for ye are all one in Christ Jesus. And if ye be Christ's, then are ye Abraham's seed, and heirs according to the promise." *Galatians* 3:28-29.

[‡]See, for example, *Romans* 3:1, 9: "What advantage then hath the Jew? Or what profit is there of circumcision? . . . What then? Are we better than they? No, in no wise. For we have before proved both Jews and gentiles, that they are all under sin."

and to despitefully entreat those who are waiting for Him. These fearful symptoms of a professed church demonstrate the last lukewarm stage of nominal Christianity. The expectation of the world's conversion, the return of the carnal Jews, and other modern traditions, like fatal opiates, effectually seal the vision to the threatening omens of coming crisis.[11]

Again:

We perceive that they who have faith in Christ are children of the promise and heirs with faithful Abraham. We expect therefore that all this true Israel will be restored to the Promised Land, the new Jerusalem, and the new earth. Everyone who believes in his heart, and confesses with his mouth, the Lord Jesus, shall be saved. But he that denies that Jesus Christ is come in the flesh, is anti-Christ, and we cannot, therefore, believe that the carnal seed of Abraham have any right to the promise, unless they repent and believe in Christ. We therefore look for no return of the carnal Jews, previous to the coming of the Lord of the vineyard; when we believe that He will let it out to other husbandmen.[*12]

When the expected kingdom did not appear in 1843, Minor committed herself to a new date, 22 October 1844. As 1843 came to an end she spoke of the "advent children" remaining unified in their commitment "to send the glad news in His coming on every wind" until "He appear to reign Whose right it is." Indeed, the next exclamation to be heard would be "Hallelujah!" for God would soon reign.[13] She urged others not to despair or grow weary, for once man did God's will He would come quickly.[14] When she was asked three months later, "What will you do if it don't come?" she responded:

We have no sympathy with the motives of expediency which prompt this question. We are striving to know what we shall do when it does come, and are engaged in a great work, and are unwilling to come down to discuss the vague dreams of unbelief. Sufficient unto the day is the evil thereof, and we can therefore take no sceptical thought for tomorrow . . . His will is our will and we know that it will assuredly be done, on earth, even as it is in heaven. When we professed this faith we counted the cost in the fear of God, and our expression was only the sign of the substance and evidence within, which works by love, and we are persuaded that neither death or life, nor angels, nor principalities, nor powers, nor thing to come, nor height, nor depth, nor

---

*"They say unto him, He will miserably destroy those wicked men, will let out his vineyard unto other husbandmen, which shall render him the fruits in their seasons." *Matthew* 21:41.

any other creatures shall be able to separate us from the love of God, which is in Christ Jesus, and in the previous hope of His immediate appearing.[15]

In May 1844 she admonished her fellow believers to be ready:

> If when the Lord once descended on Mount Sinai to give laws to the people, they were commanded to wash themselves with water, to cleanse and sanctify themselves lest His anger should break out upon them: how much more when He is coming to make His dwelling among men, should we sanctify ourselves and "keep ourselves in the love of God," and seek His cleansing blood, and the immersion of the Holy Ghost, for he that hath not His spirit, is none of His.* Who shall stand when He appeareth, or who shall abide the day which shall try as by fire, every man's work of what sort it is?† Let us be diligent; let us not sleep, lest when He comes, our raiment should be found stained with the shades of worldliness and sin. But let us *realize* the peaceful and glorious position of *waiting for Jesus.*[16]

On 6 June 1844, in anticipation of the coming apocalypse, Minor feared for the disbelievers:

> In these last moments, when the glimmerings of the true and the eternal already illuminate our path, when the hearts of many have been opened to understand the Scriptures—when the confirming records of the ages that sleep in death have fulfilled each inevitable promise down to the momentous crisis of the coming of the son of man, how fearful is such scepticism! How fatal such unbelief! For soon the avenging wrath of Jehovah will sweep as the whirlwind, and cleanse with fire a sin-polluted earth, and the succeeding glory unfold to us the Eden-loveliness of a redeemed creation.[17]

On 13 June 1844 she said, "The last signs are thickening, and a sin darkened world is hasting like the resistless circles of the maelstrom to its final consummation," and urged others to awaken from sadness, put on garments of righteousness, look upward, and ready their hearts to meet Him at the first sound of His footsteps.[18] On 26 September 1844 (5604 on the Jewish calendar) she declared "The six thousandth year closing, and the great and final jubilee approaches. The

---

*"Keep yourselves in the love of God." *Jude* 21. "And the blood of Jesus Christ His son cleanseth us from all sin." *I John* 1:7. "Now if any man have not the spirit of Christ, he is none of His." *Romans* 8:9.

†"But who may abide the day of his coming? and who shall stand when he appeareth? for he is like a refiner's fire." *Malachi* 3:2. "Every man's work shall be made manifest: for the day shall declare it, because it shall be revealed by fire; and the fire shall try every man's work of what sort it is." *I Corinthians* 3:13.

feast of ingathering and the day of redemption is just upon us." The world would soon be in crisis, "and nothing but faith in God, and the power of His indwelling spirit will be able to stand the fire of its decision."[19] On 12 October 1844, "the hour hasteth greatly."[20]

The date of 22 October 1844 passed without Christ's arrival, and Minor renewed her hopes once again.[21] On 28 February 1845 she wrote:

> For a few months past, we have heard so much about "indefinite time," "delusion," etc., our Lord's coming upon His waiting people "as a thief," that our hearts have been made very sad, and the faith of many has been overthrown. But now the dark trial is nearly over, and we again . . . see the standard of *truth* upraised, in the early dawn . . . We are crying continually, "Come Lord Jesus, and come quickly," and have *set our faces*, as did Daniel, to give Him no rest until He make Jerusalem a praise in the earth* . . . This spring we expect that Jesus *will come*, and set the remaining captives *free.*[22]

On 15 April 1845 she anticipated Christ's arrival during Passover in poetry:

> Undaunted yet, without the camp,
> Christ's bleeding steps pursue,
> And cherish well thy priceless lamp
> And gird thyself anew . . .
> Though long our pleadings He hath borne
> The avenging hour is near;
> And He is faithful who hath sworn
> To come, to save, to hear.[23]

When Christ did not arrive with Passover (22-30 April), Minor reflected that 1843 was the liberation, when God took the adventist children out of "Egypt." The children, however, were still drawn to Egyptian culture and idolatry. They were not aware of the purification required to stand before Christ, or the need to pass through a wilderness before arriving in Canaan. Christ's failure to appear during Passover was a further testing in the wilderness. Now it was 5 May 1845, and the wilderness period was ending. In fulfillment of His promise to Abraham, God was leading a tried people into the kingdom. For Minor, the God-Israel drama was resolved in identity with Christ: "As we pass from one crucible to another, we feel that the world and its claims are receding, and our sympathies and nature are more and more united to Christ, and swallowed up in the love of

---

*"And I set my face unto the Lord God, to seek by prayer and expectations, with fasting, and sackcloth, and ashes." *Daniel* 9:3.

God." She expected Christ's arrival and the new Christian Jerusalem momentarily: "Brother, look up, the morning surely breaks upon us, and though weeping and wailing and stripes have been ours through the long watches of the night, yet now, joy, joy, is gleaming in the opening day." Her commitment was so powerful as to separate her from the world of time and space, whence Christ would deliver her: "Being thus separated from the world, thus spoiled for earth, thus groaning for full redemption, and made *one* with Christ, He will immediately appear for our deliverance. Not for *our sake*, but for His sake, for His word's sake, *He will come*."[24]

On 17 June 1845 Minor observed a great increase in love. She believed it was a manifestation of God, indeed the mustard seed and leaven of the kingdom of heaven.* She spoke of the coming realm of spirit:

> We are spoiled for earth, and have no sympathy with its blood-stained shadow . . . Heaven and earth shall pass away, but His words shall every one be *fulfilled* . . . Although this narrow path, between the fire and water, may be crucifying to the flesh, and exterminating to all the dross of common life, listen to the sweet words, "What I do thou knowest not now, but thou shalt know hereafter" [*John* 13:7].

As "willing clay" Minor awaited being fashioned anew by God's hand, in the purity and power of Eden's life.[25] On 10 July 1845 she continued to expect God's "tried, afflicted, and despised remnant" to be delivered at any hour.[26] On 22 November 1845 she remained firm in her conviction: "There is therefore no retreat for me. The work of visitation, judgement, and restoration has commenced, and will surely and immediately bring the perfect manifestation of the sons of God."[27] In January 1846 she prayed that Satan's last desperate efforts not break the ranks of those who were still waiting "in the narrow passage of deliverance." She remained resolute: "With my face set as a *flint*, for victory, my eye fixed upon the promise of *Jehovah*, and my soul resting in His present salvation, as I run, I send my salutation to every saint in Christ Jesus."[†28]

At some point during the next two years something made Minor change her position: a "day of preparation" had to take place in which "many shall be purified and made white and tried" before Christ would appear.‡ In this view,

---

*"The kindgom of heaven is like to a grain of mustard seed . . . The kingdom of heaven is like unto leaven." *Matthew* 13:31, 33.

†"For the Lord God will help me; therefore shall I not be confounded: therefore have I set my face like a flint, and I know that I shall not be ashamed." *Isaiah* 50-7.

‡See, for example, *Luke* 23:54: "And that day was the preparation, and the sabbath drew on." "Many shall be purified, and made white, and tried; but the wicked shall do wickedly." *Daniel* 12:10.

the world had to change in order for Christ to come. But no real signs of preparatory purification manifested; Minor could not discover "where the ark of His testimony was resting, and where was the moving and hiding of His power." She feared that His glory was departing, and her anxiety made her physically ill. During her confinement she was inspired by a passage from *Chronicles* to write this poem:

In the hold, long oppressed by earth's wearisome strife,
My soul is athirst for the waters of life—
And longs for the well-spring at Bethlehem's gate,*
Where its fount gushes freely, this thirst to abate.
Oh! who will break *through*, in the strength of the Lord,
And at once overcome—by His spirit and word—
The uncircumcised host, that opposeth His reign,
And bid the sweet waters of life *flow* again?
Oh! who will "go up" and the Land now possess,†
In the name of the highest His Sabbaths redress—
Till the praise of that *name* in loud chorus shall rise,
From mountain and valley, from ocean and skies?
Oh! who shall *between* the bright cherubim pass,
And restore the *lost* garden of beauty at *last*;
Who shall give to its long desert bowers their bloom,
And say to the saved, and the ransomed *return*?
For *one* we have waited, for *one* we have sought—
While lords and gods *many*, great wonders have wrought;
But none has brought forth—the *salvation*, the *love*,
And we *wait* yet *another*, to come from above.
His name must be *Jesus*!—no other we know,
Who can bid the wide stream of *redemption to flow*;
Who can *break* through the host, the inheritance bless,
And *restore* the lost children of *Eden* to rest.

That is, the day of preparation would have to begin in the Land. The waters of Christ awaited someone to break through to them, someone to go to the Land to welcome Him. By the strength of Christ, Minor resolved to go there to release these waters, whereupon Christ would bring redemption.

---

*"And David was then in the hold, and the Philistines' garrison was then at Bethlehem. And David longed, and said, Oh that one would give me drink of the water of the well of Bethlehem, that is at the gate!" *I Chronicles* 11:16-17.

†"And Caleb stilled the people before Moses, and said, Let us go up at once, and possess it; for we are well able to overcome it." *Numbers* 13:30.

Material obstacles to the journey defied her inspiration, but in the belief that God was calling her, totally reliant upon Him, Minor began preparations. Four days before the planned departure she received half her needs from an unexpected source, and one half hour before departure two "dear friends" provided the rest: the temporal aligned itself with Minor's myth and divine direction. Convinced that the assistance was a manifestation of divine will, she went from Philadelphia to New York and departed for the Holy Land in early May 1849.[29]

Minor's experience in the Holy Land was filled with Christ. On 24 September 1849 in Hebron she envisioned the time when He would "set His hand to recover Israel." She saw God visiting the gentiles to "take our people for His name," after which He would "return and build again the tabernacle of David" for mankind to seek the Lord."[*30] On 7 October 1849, while attending *Simhat Tora* celebrations in Jerusalem, she noted that everyone tried to touch the Tora "cylinders" and then kiss their hands as the Tora procession passed by, that most women were pushed back and aged grandmothers "insolently repelled" by lads of ten years, and that one young mother with a male infant in her arms did get through so her child could touch the "beautiful tinkling pageant." Minor's mind remained with Christ:

> I cannot easily express the tender emotions of sorrow and reverence that oppressed me, while witnessing the ceremonies of this feast, which are here celebrated by the remnant of Jehovah's ancient and chosen people, on this ruined altar in *the place of the name of the Lord of hosts.*[†] To see them through so many weary centuries still clinging to these types of unfulfilled promises, and still engraving them upon the hearts of their infant sons, despite their low estate and long activity. This practice, of so early engaging their children in the active service of the sanctuary, is a pleasing contrast to the distance prescribed for the young, by some of the gentile sects. We understand by this how the children were in the Temple, ready to be witnesses for Jesus, by "crying Hosanna!" etc.[‡] I pointed an aged man, who was conversing with me, to the embroidered crown of gold above the law,

---

[*]"Simeon hath declared how God at the first did visit the gentiles, to take out of them a people for his name. And to this agree the words of the prophets; as it is written, After this I will return, and will build again the tabernacle of David, which is fallen down; and I will build again the ruins thereof, and I will set it up: That the residue of man might seek after the Lord and all the gentiles, upon whom my name is called, saith the Lord, who doeth all these things." *Acts* 15:14-17

[†]"A nation meted out and trodden under foot, whose land the rivers have spoiled, to the place of the name of the Lord of hosts, the mount Zion." *Isaiah* 18:7.

[‡]"People took branches of palm trees, and went forth to meet Him, and cried, Hosanna: Blessed is the king of Israel that cometh in the name of the Lord." *John* 12:12-13.

and signified to him that Messiah's *reign* was near, with which he was much pleased; and another said, "This is the *father religion!"* But while the multitude shouted so loud, that we could not hear each other, I also praised *my* Redeemer, "The king of the Jews."*[31]

In late spring 1850 Minor returned to America to raise funds for the Agricultural Manual Labor School in Palestine. According to Jane Marsh Parker (1836-1913), she was successful. The remnant of William Miller's followers "took up the Palestine mission with enthusiasm . . . How plain it was that the Land of promise must first be made habitable before it might become the very center of the earth, drawing all men into it." Presbyterians and Seventh-day Baptists "pretty well appropriated" the "mission" as "the only plausible plan" to help Jews in the Holy Land. *The Presbyterian* (Philadelphia) raised a considerable sum for the school.[32]

Minor left Philadelphia for the Holy Land on 3 November 1851 with her son Charles and seven followers; they were committed to permanent renewal of the Land through agricultural restoration, to replacing the "thorn" with the "fig-tree."† Minor considered Jewish involvement in farming to be bound up with conversion to Christianity. For example, in 1850 she wrote of Meshullam (b. 1800), son of a devout London Jew, influenced by Joseph Wolff, and converted on Malta by Samuel Gobat (1799-1879) of LJS. Meshullum developed a farm in Artas, south of Bethlehem:

We have been constrained by the love of Christ to give this relation of what we have seen and heard, being fully convinced that the Lord has been in a peculiar manner sustaining this true Israelite. He is the first Christian Hebrew who has succeeded in cultivating the soil of his fathers since the dispersion. Through his *sustainment* and blessing we believe that God had a design of opening an humble way of escape and salvation to "*a remnant*" of His ancient people.‡ This cannot be effected by direct preaching or other spiritual efforts; but if Meshullam had means supplied to extend his farming operations, he would gladly offer his starving brethren employment, and hundreds would gladly offer to labor with him at two and a half piasters per day (the same as five and a half pence, or eleven cents) which would bring

---

*"And when they had platted a crown of thorns, they put it upon His head, and a reed in His right hand: and they bowed the knee before Him, and mocked Him, saying, Hail, king of the Jews!" *Matthew* 27:29.

†"Ye shall know them by their fruits. Do men gather grapes of thorns, or figs of thistles?" *Matthew* 7:16.

‡See, for example, *Ezekiel* 14:22: "Yet, behold, therein shall be left a remnant that shall be brought forth."

them under the influence of his Christ-like love and example. It would make them independent of the charity fund of the rabbis, to which they are now in bondage, and which is scarcely sufficient to sustain life in the coarsest and most frugal manner. Those who are already inquiring, and half convinced of the truth, among the pious poor, would have a refuge, and be placed in a position where they might afterwards be reached and won by the love of Christ.

It must be distinctly understood that Meshullam makes no appeal for himself, and will receive nothing; for the Lord has so prospered him in his recent course, that he is helping others. But he is willing, *without reward,* to apply any assistance that the friends of Christ may send to relieve and win his poor brethren to the truth, and preparation of "a remnant," to meet the Lord at His coming.[33]

Minor began working with Meshullam at Artas in late fall 1851. On 27 July 1852, in response to a letter from her American "brethren and sisters in Christ," she described Jews visiting Artas from Jerusalem and appealing to remain: "It would break your heart to see the quivering lip, and look of despair, and sometimes tears, when from such companies dear brother M[eshullam] can only select one or two to remain with us, and sends the rest to the city." Some said that Meshullam's cultivation of the land was a sign, "that if they would leave off their evil and idle ways and cultivate this land, and earn their honest bread, their messiah would soon come." Jews also wanted to join Artas because the Sabbath was observed there. One group of 63 Jews, represented by a rabbi, entreated Minor's group to teach them to till the soil. They also asked for support in soliciting American funds to lease land in the area. Minor turned to English Consul James Finn (1806-1872) for assistance. Finn formed a committee, including Edward MacGowan of the LJS hospital and James T. Barclay of ACMS, to oversee fundraising. Meshullam balked, whereupon Finn requested all leasing and building at Artas be done with his consent. Minor was despairing over these "rich and determined enemies" when a package arrived at the end of the Sabbath with funds from the "brethren and sisters in Christ," sent through the Jerusalem banking agent Dr. Burgheim, a "converted Israelite."

Minor also reported an appeal by "principal rabbis" to Moses Montefiore for funds to support agriculture (they had been encouraged by Meshullam's success with the land) and that a "converted Jew and his wife" near Jaffa sought the Artas group's advice. Another 20 Jews, mostly rabbis' sons, wanted to study agriculture at Artas so they could work for Rothschild. "If we had many thousands, we could use it in the most judicious way for opening the door for Christian influence among their whole nation in Palestine! O, where are the lovers of Israel now?"[34]

Sometime in the next few months Minor's group broke with Meshullam and left. Barclay and other missionaries housed them until the winter of 1853, when they transferred to the Jaffa area. On 4 April 1854 she responded to Isaac Leeser (1806-1868), leader of Historical Judaism, concerning Christian missionaries in Palestine, stating that neither she nor her followers were missionaries or sponsored by missionaries. Ten years earlier, she said, a study of Hebrew Scripture had convinced her that "the appointed time of the gentiles' treading down the sanctuary and host of Israel, spoken of in *Daniel* 8:13-14, was accomplished—that the times of the gentiles were expiring and the set time to favor Zion had come."* She had observed the division between Jews and gentiles, the alienation of most from "the holy teachings of the Law and the gospel," and read of God's promises to gather, restore, and purify Israel, and to bless all nations in Abraham's seed. God would do that work (*Ezekiel* 34 and 36); she had lost confidence in the ability of Jew or gentile to accomplish it. God would produce food in the Land for His people, He would gather them and reverse their departure from His will, the desolate Land would become like the Garden of Eden.†

Minor believed that Christ the Messiah would come soon to "purify the sons of Levi, and purge them as gold and silver, that they may offer unto the Lord an offering in righteousness" (*Malachi* 3:3). She wished to cooperate with God in the "outward preparatory work to open the way for Israel's return, when God Himself would manifest His glory and accomplish their salvation in His own way." Accordingly, "in the two years of intimate labor and converse with Israelites" she and her followers did not make even a "first direct effort to proselyte or change their faith." The end of history was near, and it was under God's aegis. Her role within the eschatological drama was solely to restore the Land so the people of Israel, and through them the gentiles, could return under God's direction. Within the Land she aimed "to emancipate from worse than American slavery the half-covered, starving, imprisoned, spirit-crushed Hebrew captives of Palestine." Minor's creed read: "We do believe that Jesus Christ is the Redeemer that shall come to Zion, and that David will truly be raised up and

---

*"Then I heard one saint speaking, and another saint said unto that certain saint which spake, How long shall be the vision concerning the daily sacrifice, and the transgression of desolation, to give both the sanctuary and the host to be trodden under foot? And he said unto me, Unto two thousand and three hundred days: then shall the sanctuary be cleansed." *Daniel* 8:13-14.

†"But ye, O mountains of Israel, ye shall shoot forth your branches, and yield your fruit to my people of Israel; for they are at hand to come. For, behold, I am for you, and I will turn unto you, and ye shall be tilled and sown: And I will multiply men upon you, all the house of Israel, even all of it: and the cities shall be inhabited, and the wastes shall be builded . . . Then will I sprinkle clean water upon you, and ye shall be clean: from all your filthiness, and from all your idols, will I cleanse you." *Ezekiel* 36:8-10, 25. "And they shall say, This Land that was desolate is become like the garden of Eden; and the waste and desolate and ruined cities are become fenced, and are inhabited." *Ezekiel* 36:35.

be a prince over his people forever." Until that happened she would "labor in patient love and zeal in this good work of preparation, and wait until God will restore the one pure language and demonstrate His truth."[35]

Beneath the ambiguity, Minor's message was this: she did not consider hers missionary work because Jewish Israel did not have to undergo conversion in the usual sense. Israel's true, inner identity was already Christian. This inner truth became explicit in the process of return to the Land and would culminate in outer identity with Christianity upon Christ's arrival. Minor had resolved the original conflict she experienced between inner scriptural truth and outer reality by believing in William Miller's apocalypse. When the end did not come, instead of surrendering hope she further invested herself in the millennium. As the investment increased, the natural world became ever darker. Her hope reached the point, that unless Christ arrived immediately she would be left with nothing in this world. When Miller's universe collapsed, leaving her to the emptiness of the world, she became physically ill. Her health returned after the concept of the day of preparation resolved her spiritual crisis. She threw herself into effectuating that day through restoring the Land to prepare for Christ's arrival. Within this existential and cosmic religious drama, Minor viewed Judaism as the outer covering to the inner, Christian identity of Israel. The inner and outer identities would be resolved by Christ Himself.

Minor established Mount Hope Colony near Jaffa in 1855 and died of dysentery on 6 November 1855. Charles Minor assumed leadership, with the support of Seventh-day Baptist missionaries Charles and Martha Saunders, agricultural missionary Walter Dickson (1799-1860), from Groton, Massachusetts, and his Prussian sons-in-law, Frederick and John Steinbeck.[36]

Contemporary Responses to Minor

What reaction did Minor elicit among her contemporaries? The Millerites were divided. In March 1851 John B. Cook considered *Meshullam!* a uniquely interesting work.[37] Meshullam's report that recent rains were removing the barrenness of the Land*—which Cook took as fact—demonstrated "an outer position of the divine hand in fulfillment of His promised mercy to His people."[38] Cook believed that God's hand was in the Artas work, and to him it held "a higher interest than any other labor now opened before the eye of faith."[39] He observed that Meshullam's work began in the wake of the 1843-1844 period of the expected second advent, and it fulfilled prophecies about

---

*"Then will I remember My covenant with Jacob, and also My covenant with Isaac, and also My covenant with Abraham will I remember; and I will remember the Land." *Leviticus* 26:42. "That I will give you the rain of your Land in his due season, the first rain and the latter rain." *Deuteronomy* 11:14.

restoring the Land.* Minor's mission was "extraordinary and originating in a special providence."[40] In early November 1851 Cook supported her "missionary labor" for redemption. He saw "a multitude of promises and prophecies that seem now not to concentrate, as a focal point, on 'Zion' and 'the Land.'"[41]

Other Millerites opposed Artas. *AHBA* editor Joseph Marsh (d. 1863) did so on theological grounds. The conclusion that it was time to join Minor, to cultivate the soil and prepare a people to receive the Lord, was no more than an "inference" from Scripture. The time for the Messiah had, in fact, not yet come. Warfare in Jerusalem had not ended; it was trodden down by gentiles.† Turks dominated Palestine, a mosque occupied the sacred place of the Temple. Zion was still "plowed as a field," David's tabernacle was yet in ruin, Jerusalem "in heaps."‡ "The time has not yet come to say unto Jerusalem that her sin is pardoned and her warfare ended."#[42] Since Scripture did not support a move to Jerusalem, he had no "faith in it," and "whatever is not of faith is sin." His disposition remained purely premillennial: "Let the dear saints abide in the truth in these days of deception; and patiently wait to be escorted by angels, under Christ our leader, by the way of the heavens to Jerusalem."[43] Marsh also questioned Minor's credibility. Her descriptions of Palestine were not based in fact, and "a faith founded on romance is sure ultimately to punish its deluded victims."[44]

Millerite Owen S. L. Crozier (1820-1913) observed that in 1823 missionary Jonas King had described the revival of the Land. As the facts were clarified, "the more is the subject divested of the air of mystery and special providence which Mrs. Minor has thrown around it."[45] He questioned the reliability of her inspiration to go to Jerusalem since she was also inspired to encamp outside Philadelphia and await the Lord to "translate" her and her followers in fall 1844. "She professes to have acted entirely by the guidance of the Holy Spirit in answer to prayer, for several years; yet few have committed more glaring errors than she." Crozier offered evidence from James T. Barclay and a "distinguished Christian minister" in America—presumably the historical geographer Edward Robinson (1784-1863), professor of biblical literature at Union Theological Semi-

---

Ezekiel 36:8-10, supra.

†"But when ye shall hear of wars and commotions, be not terrified: for these things must first come to pass; but the end is not by and by . . . And Jerusalem shall be trodden down of the gentiles, until the times of the gentiles be fulfilled." *Luke* 21:9, 24.

‡"Zion shall be plowed like a field, and Jerusalem shall become heaps." *Jeremiah* 26:18.

#"Speak ye comfortably to Jerusalem, and cry unto her, that her warfare is accomplished, that her iniquity is pardoned: for she hath received of the Lord's hand double for all her sins." *Isaiah* 40:2.

nary—calling into question descriptions by Minor of how rain was restoring the soil.[46]

Robinson visited Artas on 7 May 1852 and found the colonists dissatisfied and ready to leave as soon as they could. "The idea of speedily converting the Jews, living as strangers in Palestine, into an agricultural people, was altogether visionary."[47] Herman Melville visited what was left of the colony in 1857 and described Minor a "woman of fanatic energy and spirit." He thought she was the first to train Jews for agriculture and understood that she had been successful in raising money for her project when she returned to America in 1850. But he considered the undertaking a failure: "They had troubles. Not a single Jew was converted either to Christianity or to agriculture. The young ladies sickened and went home. A month afterward, Mrs. Minor died."[48]

Isaac Leeser dismissed millennialist thinking in 1843, remarking that readers of *The Occident* would have no immediate interest in the pamphlet he received, *Prophecy Interpreted, Literally or Spiritually; or, The Millenarist and Millenarian views of Scripture interpretation.*[49] In March 1845 he rejected Mordecai M. Noah's overtures to Christian conversion societies intent on restoring the Land: missionaries were "dangerous enemies . . . Conversion of the Jews means destruction of the Jews." Missionaries were out to "destroy the Jews by picking up a Jew at a time." Admitting them into Palestine was "fraught with the greatest evil to our future infant state."[50] But when it came to Minor's group, Leeser thought differently. He separated missionary from agricultural activity:

> If those missionaries can do the good they propose, to improve the temporal condition of the people, we, for our part, will not lay the smallest hindrance in their way, as far as this attempt goes. We shall be happy indeed to see, instead of ten, hundreds of sturdy American farmers, mechanics, and machinists go out, to teach the children of Judah how to labor, and how to live by their own exertions.

He cited a proposal by Charles Minor to restore fertility to the Land and independence to the Jews by using some of the funds raised for the poor.[51] Clorinda S. Minor's ambiguous views, stated 4 April 1854, on agricultural restoration and conversion apparently did not change Leeser's attitude, for when she died he wrote:

> She was a true friend of Israel, notwithstanding the conviction that conversion is the best method of making us Jews happy. By her practical labors in horticulture, feeble and lone woman as she was, she has proved that Palestine may be made to bloom under the hand of the husbandman, if proper pains are only bestowed; and when the Land of Israel again smiles with plenty and glows in beauty let the name of her benefactress, Mrs. Minor, be remembered with a blessing. And may He who receives alike the devotion of those

who call on His name, and those who know Him not, give her everlasting rest in His presence among the righteous of His people; because she faithfully endeavored to fulfill her duty, and to glorify, as far as she could, Him who is father of all.[52]

A similar reaction to her death appeared in *The Presbyterian:*

Who will venture to say that her mission has been in vain? . . . Something has been accomplished for suffering humanity, and we earnestly wish that a colony of intelligent Christian agriculturists of our own church would now undertake the good work which it has been proved is entirely practicable.[53]

Minor had anticipated Christ's advent to initiate the millennium, resolving for herself the disjunction between Scripture and religious life in America. When the second coming did not occur in October 1843 as the Millerites said it would, she renewed her hopes at least through early 1846. Eventually she came to the view that Christ would return only after the world was prepared for Him, and that the key to the preparation was direct involvement in the Holy Land. Practical conditions fell into line with her calling; she journeyed there and experienced a Land trembling with Christian expectation. Agriculture became the direct means of preparing the Land for Christ; it also provided a vehicle for Jews to come to Christ, itself a factor in the preparation. Cultivation of the Land would rehabilitate the Jew in such a way that he could turn to Christ; it would allow Christ to enter Jewish life without theological confrontation.

As a colonist Minor reversed the positions she had held as a Millerite. Instead of waiting until Christ changed the world, she would help prepare the world for Him to come. Instead of keeping carnal Jews from Palestine, she would involve them in its restoration, thereby transforming them into the true Israel of Christ. Instead of the spiritual, transcendental experience of Christ of the apocalypse, she labored in time and space, in the earth of Israel. For Melville and Robinson, Minor's work in agriculture and conversion failed together. Leeser divided her agricultural work from her Christian postmillennial myth, praising the former.

The Millerite doctrine that the Jews would not return was retained by another successor to Millerism, Ellen G. White, founder of the Seventh-day Adventists.[54] In 1911 she wrote about her vision of a heavenly millennium centered in Jerusalem. At the end of the epoch Jesus would return to the earth with His righteous followers, and they would battle the forces of Satan. Ultimately the entire earth would be cleansed and become an eternal paradise. The small remnant of Jews who converted would enter the center at Jerusalem.* The Jews who had lost connection with God by murdering Christ would be excluded from Jerusalem and destroyed:

> Then shall they that obey not the gospel be destroyed with the brightness of His coming.† Like Israel of old, the wicked destroy themselves; they fall by their iniquity. By a life of sin they have placed themselves so out of harmony with God, their natures have become to debased with evil, that the manifestation of His glory is to them a consuming fire.[55]

William E. Blackstone

William E. Blackstone (1841-1935) believed that in the seventh dispensation of history Christ would reappear to reign for eternity.[56] The church, the heavenly people, would rise from earth to meet Christ as His bride, and the earth would experience three and a half years of tribulations for Israel.‡ One hundred and forty-four thousand Jews would survive to convert to Christianity and live in the restored Holy Land.[57]

In his famous *Jesus Is Coming* (1889), Blackstone gathered scriptural evidence to support the restoration of Israelites to Palestine and rebuilding Jerusalem. He distinguished two stages of return. The first, for Jews only, had already taken place. The Jews had returned to the Land from exile in Babylon and then blindly and with hardened hearts rejected and killed Jesus. That restoration was temporary, and the Jews were driven out. The second return, yet to come, would be permanent. In it, all twelve tribes would flow into the Land. Because their sins were "mountain high," because they bore the guilt for Christ's innocent and precious blood, Jews would suffer through an awful time of trouble. God (Christ) would appear with His saints, the Christian church, and they would execute judgement amidst a flaming fire.# The Jews would repent for their act

---

*"The remnant shall return, even the remnant of Jacob, unto the mighty God." *Isaiah 10:21.*

†"And then shall that wicked be revealed, whom the Lord shall consume with the spirit of His mouth, and shall destroy with the brightness of His coming." *II Thessalonians 2:8.*

‡See, for example, *Daniel* 12:11: "And from the time that the daily sacrifice shall be taken away, and the abomination that maketh desolate set up, there shall be a thousand two hundred and ninety days." "Then we which are alive and remain shall be caught together with them in the clouds, to meet the Lord in the air." *I Thessalonians* 4:17.

#See, for example, *Revelation* 20:9: "And they went up on the breadth of the earth, and compassed the camp of the saints about, and the beloved city: and the fire came down from God out of heaven, and devoured them." "In flaming fire taking vengeance on them that know not God, and that obey not the gospel of our Lord Jesus

of murder; they would become clean of heart and accept Christ as king while the church remained in rapture in the distance. Then the millennium would take place.[58]

Blackstone visited Palestine in 1889, and the experience moved him to work for restoration. Upon his return he organized the "first conference between Christians and Jews in Chicago," which he called The "Conference on the Past, Present, and Future of Israel" (1890). It resolved that President Harrison should confer with European leaders and the Turkish sultan to consider an international meeting on "the condition of the Jews in modern nations and the possibility of opening a way for their restoration to Palestine."[59] In March 1891, following Russian pogroms against Jews, Blackstone petitioned Harrison on behalf of 413 Christians and Jews for the return of the Jews to the Land. A number of rabbis—including Emil Hirsch (1852-1923) of Chicago and Solomon Schindler (1842-1915) of Boston, both of the Reform movement—opposed the petition, suspecting a hidden plan to convert Jews.[60] Reform Rabbi Bernhard Felsenthal (1822-1908) signed the petition but regretted doing so when he realized in fall 1891 that he was deceived regarding the missionary intent of the effort.

In October 1891 Blackstone observed that while Reform Jews did not wish to return, the Orthodox who comprised at least "19:20" of Jewry "consistently hold to the value of their ancestral inheritance and an unfailing desire and expectation to possess" the Land. He rejected the Christian objection that the Jews' rebellion against God annulled their claim to the Land: Jews "have recognized their sins and the fact that they have caused calamitous punishment." He pointed out that they had legal right to the Land because they neither abandoned it voluntarily nor relinquished their original claim. The Land had room for an additional three million Jews without violating native (Arab) rights. Moreover, Scripture indicated wider boundaries to the Land, if demographically necessary. In principle, the Land—which to Blackstone's mind was without a people—should be brought together with the people without a land. As it was, Jews had no refuge; the doors of the nations were closed to them. Blackstone expected America, which had the money and political power, to help; he felt that Christians all over, whose inheritance was rooted in the holy word, were obligated to send the "life boat."[61] He planned another conference of Jews and Christians for December 1892, but it did not materialize. Orthodox Rabbi Abraham J. G. Lesser (1834-1925) of Chicago, another signer of the 1891 petition, prepared a paper for the conference entitled "The Future of Israel."[62]

In an 1898 address to student missionaries, Blackstone connected the themes of Land and the people of Israel. Jews, he said, were inseparable from their God-given Land. God selected the Land, and he did so because it was the earth's

---

Christ." *II Thessalonians* 1:8.

natural geographic center and therefore the best location for a world capital.* Its variegated climate and scenery made it a microcosm, appropriate for a supernatural book intended for worldwide circulation; its soil was so fertile that every single jubilee (fiftieth) year it produced enough for three years. The Land was, indeed, glorious and good.† God cared for it; it was the home of God's prophets and the place where God revealed Himself.‡

For their part, the people of Israel were chosen, holy and special.# Universal history was disposed of in the first eleven chapters of *Genesis*, while all the rest of Hebrew Scripture dealt solely with Israel. Over 38 centuries ago God had told Abraham He would make him "a great nation."** Indeed, God's people were already hoary with age when Rome was born. They had seen Babylon, Egypt, and Greece rise and pass away. Western nations were ephemeral by comparison. Israel had greater riches than any other nation.†† Her political structure constituted the best basis for substantial government. The indestructibility of Israel evidenced the truth of God's word and argued indisputably for biblical inspiration.‡‡ Since Oliver Cromwell (1599-1658) had begun the process of emancipation, the Jews "have shown their traditional ability, with a free chance, to outstrip all competitors," e.g., Benedict Spinoza (1632-1677), father of rationalism; Felix Mendelssohn (1809-1847), prince of musicians; church historian August Neander (1789-1850); the Rothschilds, the

---

*"In the day that I lifted up mine hand unto them, to bring them forth of the land of Egypt into a land that I had espied for them, flowing with milk and honey, which is the glory of all lands." *Ezekiel* 20:6.

†"But he that cometh against him shall do according to his own will, and none shall stand before him: and he shall stand in the glorious Land, which by his hand shall be consumed." *Daniel* 11:16. "And they spake unto all the company of the children of Israel, saying, The Land, which we passed through to search it, is an exceeding good land." *Numbers* 14:7.

‡"A Land which the Lord thy God careth for: the eyes of the Lord thy God are always upon it, from the beginning of the year even unto the end of the year." *Deuteronomy* 11:12.

#See, for example, *Deuteronomy* 14:2: "For thou art an holy people unto the Lord thy God, and the Lord hath chosen thee to be a peculiar people unto Himself, above all the nations that are upon the earth."

**"And I will make of thee a great nation, and I will bless thee, and make thy name great; and thou shalt be a blessing." *Genesis* 12:5.

††"And the king made silver to be in Jerusalem as stones, and cedars made he to be as the sycomore trees that are in the vale, for abundance." *I Kings* 10:27.

‡‡"Ye are My witnesses, saith the Lord, and My servant whom I have chosen: that ye may know and believe Me, and understand that I am He: before Me there was no God formed, neither shall there be after Me." *Isaiah* 43:10. "For I am with thee, saith the Lord, to save thee: though I make a full end of all nations whither I have scattered thee, yet will I not make a full end of thee." *Jeremiah* 30:11.

world's bankers; Karl Marx (1818-1883), leader of socialism; and Adolf Cremieux (1796-1880), statesman. Most of all, Israel's religion was preeminent. Its divine "oracles" revealed truth, forecast the future, taught morality.* Though Christians despised the Jews, Christians still received God's word through them. Indeed, Christianity's consolation and hope for happiness beyond the grave came through God's revelation to Jews.† For Blackstone, the special Land of God and the special people of God were appropriate to one another. Indeed, God gave it to Abraham's descendants; Israel's deed to the Land (Hebrew Scripture) was recorded in every language.‡

Given the grand harmony between special Land and special people, Blackstone objected to the attitude of Reform Judaism. The prominence and prosperity brought on by the Emancipation, he explained, had caused an increasing number of Jews to give up the ancestral hopes of messianic coming and restoration to Palestine. They have "accepted as their Palestine the countries granting them such liberty, as their Messiah the liberal spirit of the nineteenth century. Intoxicated with position, money, and power, they call themselves 'Reformed' and have settled down to stay in these various adopted countries." Blackstone believed that God would put a harsh stop to this.# The Orthodox Jew, however, properly looked upon the Land as his rightful heritage.** He prayed daily to be restored to the Land to rebuild the Temple; on Passover he said pathetically, "At present we celebrate it here, but the next year, hopefully, in the Land of Israel."††

---

*"What advantage then hath the Jew? or what profit is there of circumcision? Much every way: chiefly, because that unto them were committed the oracles of God." *Romans* 3:1-2.

†"Ye worship ye know not what: we know what we worship: for salvation is of the Jews." *John* 4:22.

‡See, for example, *Genesis* 13:15: "For all the land which thou seest, to thee I will give it, and to thy seed forever." "Yet He promised that He would give it to him [Abraham] for a possession, and to his seed after him, when as yet he had no child." *Acts* 7:5

#"And that which cometh into your mind shall not be at all, that ye say, we will be as the heathen, as the families of the countries, to serve wood and stone. As I live, saith the Lord God, surely with a mighty hand, and with a stretched out arm, and with fury poured out, will I rule over you." *Ezekiel* 20:32-33.

**"Thine eyes shall see the king in his beauty: they shall behold the land that is very far off." *Isaiah* 33:17.

††"This is the bread of our affliction which our ancestors ate in the land of Egypt. Let all who are in need come and celebrate Passover. This year we are here. Next year, in the Land of Israel! This year we are slaves. Next year, free men!" "Maggid," *Passover Haggada.*

Blackstone was pleased that the events of history were aligning themselves with the grand harmony. He reiterated his October 1891 theme: after "eighteen centuries of dispersion, behold an astonishing anomaly on earth—a Land without a people and a people without a Land." After seventeen centuries (since Bar Kokhba) Jews were making their first effort to regain their home. More Jews were in the Land now than in the days of Zerubabel (*Ezra* 2); there were Zionist societies throughout Europe, and a Zionist Congress had been held in Basel in 1897. The return would revivify the mission of Israel amidst the forces of assimilation. Restoration meant both continuity of the people and prevention of persecution. It meant that the people were "again stirred up as an eagle stirrith up her nest."* Blackstone felt "the powers of Europe ought to give them their Land and let them go home if they wish to, just as they have done for the Romanians, Serbians, Bulgarians and Greeks."

What of Jewish-Christian relations? Blackstone blamed Israel's suffering mainly on Israel herself. She became haughty in her prosperity, fell into the sins of idolatry and unbelief, and was punished: her cities were besieged to the point that her people ate the flesh of their own children, Jerusalem was destroyed amidst woe and carnage, the people were evacuated twice from their Land, "millions" were scattered with the four winds of the earth, persecution had been relentless.†

Christianity was also responsible for Israel's pain: the crusades and massacres led by King Richard I (1189-1199), the horror of Spanish expulsion (1492), the sanctification by Pope Alexander VI (1492-1503) of the Spanish crown for its monstrous cruelty. The church had forgotten about Paul's love for Israel and "turned the cruel hand of persecution upon poor, blind Israel for fifteen centuries."‡ The Protestants were also guilty, notably for antisemitism in Luther's homeland and "even in our boasted United States." Suffering aside, Blackstone wanted all Jews to convert to Christianity. He was pleased to report that since the LJS had begun to preach the simple gospel to the Jews in 1809, over 100,00 had converted, and some, such as Joseph Rabinowitsch (1837-1899) of Kishinev and Paul Lichtenstein of Germany, even became missionaries.[63] In the United States, where antisemitic hatred continued, many missions were established, notably in New York.[64] Ordinarily a missionary should be a

---

*"He found him in a desert land, and in the waste howling wilderness; He led him about, He instructed him, He kept him as the apple of His eye. As an eagle stirreth up her nest, fluttereth over her young, spreadeth abroad her wings, taketh them, beareth them on her wings." *Deuteronomy* 32:10-11.

†"And I will cause them to eat the flesh of their sons and the flesh of their daughters." *Jeremiah* 19:9.

‡"For I could wish that myself were accursed from Christ for my brethren, my kinsmen according to the flesh." *Romans* 9:3

thorough Bible student able to show how the New Testament fulfilled the Old, but "so great is the stir among the 'dry bones' of Israel now, and so earnest is the spirit of inquiry, that many Jews can be reached by those less skilled in the word, if they will only go to them in love and kindly present to them the New Testament and other literature to show that Jesus is indeed their messiah."[65]

In *Satan, His Kingdom, and Its Overthrow* (1900) Blackstone attacked the secular Zionist movement in the name of Christ. It was "Satan's counterfeit" and would evoke God's fierce anger.* A "prominent Zionist Jew" even told Blackstone, "Ours is not a religious movement. We accept men who are agnostics, sceptics, or who have no religion at all, if they are only in sympathy with our national movement." The leaders were "for the most part Reformed Jews who have thrown away all the messianic hopes of their ancestors." With the help of sceptics and infidels, they sought to gather themselves in the Land solely through human effort. This was the Antichrist's covenant with Israel, a covenant with death, one which would not stand.† It would "turn upon Israel such persecutions as they have never known before." This was the time of trouble, but Christian Israel would be spared and gathered back to her Land forever.‡[66]

In 1916 Blackstone sent a second memorial—the first was not successful—to President Wilson. The signers included businessman John R. Wanamaker (1838-1922) and Reform Rabbi Judah L. Magnes (1877-1948).[67] Then, at a January 1918 Zionist meeting in Los Angeles, Blackstone proclaimed, "I am and for over thirty years have been an ardent advocate of Zionism. This is because I believe that true Zionism is founded on the plan, purpose, and faith of the everlasting and omnipotent God, as prophetically recorded in His holy word, the Bible."[68]

Blackstone was a Dispensationalist who identified the return of the Jews with suffering, repentance, and conversion associated with the second advent of Christ,

---

*"Gather yourselves together, yea, gather together, O nation not desired; Before the decree bring forth, before the day pass as the chaff, before the fierce anger of the Lord come upon you, before the day of the Lord's anger come upon you." *Zephaniah* 2:1-2.

†"O Lord, righteousness belongeth unto Thee, but unto us confusion of faces, as at this day; to the men of Judah, and to the inhabitants of Jerusalem, and unto all Israel, that are near, and that are far off, through all the countries whither Thou hast driven them, because of their trespass that they have trespassed against Thee." *Daniel* 9:7. "And your covenant with death shall be disannulled, and your agreement with hell shall not stand; when the overflowing scourge shall pass through, then ye shall be trodden down by it." *Isaiah* 28:18.

‡"Alas! for that day is great, so that none is like it: it is even the time of Jacob's trouble; but he shall be saved out of it." *Jeremiah* 30:7. "For then shall be great tribulation, such as was not since the beginning of the world to this time, no, nor ever shall be." *Matthew* 24:21. "For I will take you from among the heathen, and gather you out of all countries, and will bring you unto your own Land." *Ezekiel* 36:24.

and so he labored to fulfill the precondition for the apocalypse, the return of the Jews. The Jews had to either convert and then return or return and transform themselves into the true (Christian) Israel once in the Land. Blackstone had contempt for Reformers, for they did not want to return; he threatened secular nationalists with a destruction appropriate to the Antichrist. He admired the Orthodox for their belief in the Jerusalem-centered messianic age. That is, he wished the Jews to be theologically suited to the apocalyptic conversion he anticipated. In laboring for the ingathering of the Jews, Blackstone argued legally, historically, and in terms of human compassion. Human history was to be transformed according to the truths of *Revelation*, so he expected Jews to convert or be destroyed. Indeed, the "dry bones" of Jewry were stirring and about to live again in Christ.

Observations

In 1874 an eminent historian of the "second advent message" categorized the beliefs concerning the return of Jews to Palestine:

1. Jews would return first and then be converted to Christ along with the gentiles. The millennium and the judgement would follow.*
2. The advent of Christ would be tied to the return of the Jews.
   a. Jewish return would be prior to and a sign of His advent.
   b. Jewish return would be immediately after His advent.
3. Only the true Israel would return, namely Christians of all ages including those of Jewish and gentile origin.[69]

The Millerites, Adventists, and Dispensationalists were all committed to restoring the Land while differing on the Jewish role. The Millerites and Ellen White believed (3), and Minor believed (1) and (2a), specifically that Jews should bring themselves to Christ through agriculture and help prepare the Land for His advent. Blackstone believed (1) and (2a) as well, but in much more radical fashion. All saw their efforts as human counterparts to mythic dramas based upon the Christian Bible.

The Millerites adamantly denied Jews a role in the restoration as Jews. To do otherwise would destroy the messages of Christ Himself and His apostle Paul. Only the righteous were to be part of the Jerusalem-centered kingdom of the

---

*See, for example, *Revelation* 20:6-7, 10, 12: "Blessed and holy is he that hath part in the first resurrection: on such the second death hath no power, but they shall be priests of God and of Christ, and shall reign with him a thousand years. And when the thousand years are expired, Satan shall be loosed out of his prison . . . And the devil that deceived them was cast into the lake of fire and brimstone . . . And the dead were judged out of those things which were written in the books, according to their works."

second advent, and Jews "in the flesh" did not belong to that category. After a series of disappointments regarding Christ's predicted return, Minor struck out independently to stress the preparation for His advent, eventually going to Palestine. She found in Scripture her calling to go to the Land to precipitate the second advent; presence there would accelerate purification and eventually coincide with Christ's actual coming. Minor chose agriculture as the avenue for Jews to prepare themselves. She refuted "the common idea of the indolence of the Jews" and instead associated farming with positioning the Jew for Christ's love; economic independence from outside charity *haluka* was implicitly linked to theological independence from Judaism.[70] Minor was a passive missionary. She expected the process of conversion to happen naturally in working the Land and culminate with the arrival of Christ, when Israel would reach her higher truth and be sublimated into the word of the Redeemer.

Blackstone was a "Zionist" who admired Orthodox commitment to Zion. But this was part of his Dispensationalist scheme, according to which Jews would return to the Land so that Christ could come and administer apocalyptic conversion through fire. Blackstone attacked secular Zionism for not being religious and Reform Judaism for not being Zionist: his Dispensationalist expectations required an authentic, religiously based return prior to the apocalypse of *Revelation*. That is, Blackstone's intense Zionism and his justification for Jewish return and restoration were all part of his intense expectation of Christian apocalypse. While Minor employed agriculture to preserve Israel and prepare her for the advent of Christ, into which Jewish Israel would be sublimated, Blackstone used politics, both Jewish and American, to bring Jews into Jerusalem for their ultimate exclusion from the Christian millennium.

Notes

1. I have opted for the term "literalist" over "fundamentalist" because of the ambiguity of the latter. See, for example, *The Fundamentals: A Testimony to the Truth*, 12 vols. (Chicago 1910); and "The Conference on Fundamentals," *Watchman Examiner: A National Baptist Paper* 8 no. 28 (1 July 1920):838-840.

2. See Francis D. Nichol, *The Midnight Cry: A Defense of William Miller and the Millerites* (Takoma Park, Md., 1944); Julia Neuffer, *The Gathering of Israel: A Historical Study of Early Writings* (Washington D.C., n.d.):74-76 (on Ellen G. White); *The Disappointed: Millerism and Millenarianism in the Nineteenth Century*, Ronald L. Numbers and Jonathan M. Butler, eds. (Bloomington 1987); Yonah Malachy, "Seventh-day Adventists and Zionism," *Herzl Yearbook* 6: *Essays in Zionist History and Thought* (New York 1965):265-301; and David A. Rausch, "American Christian Groups: Their Relation to Jerusalem, pre-Civil War to 1918" (America-Holy Land Project, Hebrew University, 1990).

3. William Miller, "Compendium of Faith, 1822," in *William Miller's Apology and Defense* (Boston 1845), cited in Sylvester Bliss, ed., *Memoirs of William Miller; Generally known as a lecturer on the prophecies and the second coming of Christ* (Boston, 1853):73-74.

4. Miller, "On the Return of the Jews," in *Views of Prophecies and Prophetic Chronology: Selected from manuscripts of William Miller. With a memo of his life by Joshua V. Himes* (Boston 1881):225-231. On the role of Ethan Smith in this controversy, see Isaac C. Wellcome, *History of the Second Advent Message and Mission, Doctrine, and People* (Yarmouth, Me., 1874):163-169.

5. Henry D. Ward, "The Hope of Israel; or, The restoration of Israel identified with the resurrection of the dead," *Methodist Quarterly Review* (April 1842):192-220. See also idem, "The Hope of Israel; or, The restoration of Israel identified with the resurrection of the dead. Concluded," *Midnight Cry!* (*MC*) 4 nos. 1 and 2 (13 April 1843):1-5; and idem, *Israel and the Holy Land: The promised Land. In which an attempt is made to show that the Old and New Testament accord in their testimony to Christ and His celestial kingdom and in their testimony to His people Israel and also to the promised Holy Land* (Boston 1843). The text contains "Theological arguments against the doctrine of the return to Palestine of the literal Jews, and evidence in behalf of the view that the true Israel include all who are Christ's." Nichol, *Midnight Cry*, 536. On Ward, see LeRoy E. Froom, *The Prophetic Faith of Our Fathers: The Historical Development of Prophetic Interpretation* (Washington, D.C., 1946-1954):4:569-576.

6. Solomon Hirschell, "Letter to Henry Jones, 2 October 1840." *Liverpool Standard* (17 and 22 October 1839); Henry Jones, "Dissertation on the Restoration of Israel," in *American Views of Christ's Second Advent: Consisting mostly of lectures delivered before late general conventions in the cities of Boston, Lowell, and New York. Vindicating the Lord's personal and glorious appearing on earth, to judge the world "at hand." Without fixing the time, with a previous millennium, or return of the Jews to Palestine* (New York 1842):1-24. On Jones, see Froom, *Prophetic Faith*, 576-581.

7. [Joshua V. Himes and Josiah Litch], *The Signs of the Times: Devoted to the exposition of the prophecies relating to the second coming of Christ* (1 June 1842):69, cited in Yona Malachy, *American Fundamentalism and Israel: The Relationship of Fundamentalist Churches to Zionism and the State of Israel* (Jerusalem 1978):24

8. [Isaac P. Labagh], "The Restoration of the Jews to Their Own Land," *American Millenarian and Prophetic Review* 2 no. 8 (1 January 1844):121-124. Cf. idem, "Restoration of the Jews," in *Twelve Lectures on the Great Events of Unfulfilled Prophecy: Which still await their accomplishment and are approaching their fulfillment* (New York 1859):24-40. On Labagh's relationship to the Millerites, see Froom, *Prophetic Faith*, 327-329.

9. Wellcome, *History of the Second Advent*, 422. Other statements against Jewish return included Josiah Litch, *Judaism Overthrown; or, The kingdom restored to the true Israel. With the Scripture evidence of the epoch of the kingdom in 1843* (Boston 1843); idem, "When Did the Mosaic Age End?" in *Christ Yet to Come: A review of Dr. I. P.*

Warren's Parousia of Christ (Boston 1880):126-129; George Storrs, "The Return of the Jews," *MC* 4 nos. 5 and 6 (4 May 1843):8-11; idem, "The Restoration of the Kingdom of Israel," *MC* 4 no. 25 (10 August 1843):194-196; idem, "The Jews: the literal descendants of Abraham ever a people to be returned to the Land of Palestine?" *The Western Midnight Cry!!!* 2 no. 13 (4 March 1844):97-99; and L.C. Collins, "The Doom of Israel," *Advent Herald* 13 no. 5/305 (10 March 1847):38-39.

10. Miller chose the year 1843 in 1818:
> Reckoning all these prophetic periods from the several dates assigned by the best chronologers for the events from which they should evidently be reckoned, they would all be terminate together, about A.D. 1843. I was thus brought, in 1818, at the close of my two years study of Scriptures, to the solemn conclusion that in about twenty-five years from that time all the affairs of our present state would be wound up.

Bliss, *Memoirs of Miller,* 76. O.S. [Otis A. Skinner?], "End of the World, Voice of Warning; The wheat and the tares shall grow together until the harvest. The harvest is the end of the world," *Voice of Warning* 1 no. 1 (1 October 1842):11, calculated the date as follows:
> I begin, I say, at the crucifixion, and reckon back 70 weeks, in which there are just 490 days, and what do I find? I find the identical thing which the angel told Daniel should form the *starting point* of the vision, viz., the decree of Artaxerxes to restore and to build Jerusalem. Here, then, is the *sealing event* of Daniel's vision, fulfilled according to the chronology of the Bible, in just 490 years, reckoning a year a day. From this, I think, we are fully authorized to reckon the whole vision by the same rule; and therefore, just as surely as that Christ was crucified 490 years from the going forth of the commandment to build Jerusalem, just so surely will the *whole vision* be fulfilled in 2300 years from the same period. Those 2300 years will expire *next year*, 1843!

In 1842 Clorinda S. Minor described the transformation of the earth into the kingdom of heaven in *The New Earth: A poem* (Philadelphia 1842).

11. Minor, "Life from the Dead, No. 2," *MC* 6 no. 12/117 (4 April 1844):300.

12. "Fundamental Principles: The return of the Jews," *The Advent Message to the Daughters of Zion* 1 no. 1 (May 1844):23.

13. Idem, "The Advent Principle," *MC* 5 no. 25/105 (18 January 1844):204.

14. Idem, "Do We Realize It?," *MC* 6 no. 23/107 (1 February 1844):220.

15. Idem, "What Will You Do If It Don't Come?" *MC* 6 nos. 9 and 10/115 (21 March 1844):283.

16. Idem, "Waiting for Jesus," *MC* 6 no. 19/124 (23 May 1844):358.

17. Idem, "The Testimony of the Prophets Concerning the New Earth," *MC* 6 no. 21/126 (6 June 1844):373-374.

18. Idem, "Who Is on the Lord's Side?" *MC* 6 no. 22/127 (13 June 1844):37-?.

19. Idem, "Are We Ready?" *MC* 7 no. 12/143 (26 September 1844):93.

20. Idem, "Morrisville Camp Meeting," *MC* 7 no. 16/147 (12 October 1844):61.

21. George Gregg reported about the encampment, which failed at the end of October 1844:

> Sister C. S. Minor and myself took the lead in the matter. I should think that the whole number that went out, including children, to be 150. We encamped in the field of one of our brethren, on the Darby Road, about four miles from Market Street Bridge. We had two large tents and being quite near the house of our brother, and also within a short distance of several country stores, we obtained all the necessaries we wanted. The next morning (Tuesday) my faith in the pretended vision of Dr. C. R. Gorgas entirely failed, and at ten minutes after three I laid myself on the floor in the house, and slept soundly till five.

MC (31 October 1844):141, cited in Nichol, *Midnight Cry*, 322. See Leon Festinger, Henry W. Riecken, and Stanley Schachter, *When Prophecy Fails* (Minneapolis 1956):12-23.

22. Minor, "Letter from Sister Minor: Philadelphia 28 February 1845," *The Day Star (DS)* 5 no. 4 (11 March 1845):14.

23. Idem, "To Those Who Remain," *DS* 5 nos. 9 and 10 (15 April 1845):38.

24. On the unfulfilled expectation for Passover 1845, see idem, "From the *Hope of Israel*: Letter from Sister Minor . . . Retrospect of the 7th Month," *DS* 5 nos. 9 and 10 (15 April 1845):35-36; idem, "Letter from Sister Minor: Pine Cottage near Philadelphia 5 May 1845," *DS* 6 no. 1 (20 May 1845):6.

25. Idem, "Letter from Sister Minor: Jubilee year, 3d. month 12th day . . . Philadelphia 17 June 1845," *DS* 6 no. 8 (1 July 1845):30.

26. Idem, "Letter from Sister Minor: Of the mission and personality of the comforter . . . Philadelphia 20 July 1845," *DS* 6 no. 12 (29 July 1845):1.

27. Idem, "Letter from Sister Minor: Philadelphia 6 November 1845," *DS* 8 nos. 7 and 8 (22 November 1845):30-31.

28. Idem, "To the Remnant: 'Little children—love one another' . . . Philadelphia 16 January 1946," *DS* 9 nos. 7 and 8 (24 January 1946):34.

29. Minor and Charles Minor, *Meshullam! or Tidings from Jerusalem. From the journal of a believer recently returned from the Holy Land* (Philadelphia 1850):3-9; Joseph Marsh, "Case of Sr. C. S. Minor," *Advent Harbinger and Bible Advocate (AHBA)* 3 no. 20/410 (1 November 1851):156; Jane Marsh Parker, "A Fanatic and Her Mission: A story historical," *Churchman: An illustrated weekly news-magazine* 74 nos. 15-18/2699-2702 (10-31 October 1896):448-449, 484-486, 524-526, 568. Parker said she had inherited the Minor correspondence twenty years earlier from a person who was preparing to write a work entitled "Clorinda S. Minor: Martyr and Prophet of These Last Days." About Minor's decision to go to the Holy Land, she wrote:

Clearly and unmistakably it was revealed to her as she read her well-worn Bible that she, Clorinda S. Minor, was called to the Lord. As the anti-type [i.e., modern version] of Esther of old, she must go before the king. She must go to the literal Mount Zion. She must drink of the well in Bethlehem and satisfy her strange thirst. There only would her path be made plain before her; there she would see the king in His beauty. It was here to make ready the Land of Israel for the king's return.

30. Minor and Minor, *Meshullam,* 46-53.

31. Ibid., 63-64.

32. Parker, "A Fanatic." Minor's report to the Presbyterians was published in August 1854. M[inor], "Letter from Palestine. Correspondence of *The Presbyterian.* Origin of the agricultural mission. Discouragements at the outset. Objections because of the idleness of the people and sterility of the experiment. Readiness of the people. Articles of food and number of crops raised. Importance of extending these operations. Exaggerated reports as to disturbances in the country. Call for help. Hebrew Biarra [i.e., grove], 3 miles north of Jaffa. 1 July 1854," *The Presbyterian* 24 no. 33/1226 (19 August 1854):129. On Presbyterian support, see also "Affairs in Palestine," *The Presbyterian* 25 no. 47/1292 (24 November 855):186:

> When this humble and unpretending [agricultural mission on the plains of Sharon near Jaffa] was commenced, it had very few friends, and was generally regarded as an indiscreet, if not fanatical enterprise. It commended itself to our affection because it was poor, and involved a principle which we thought deserved a trial. Palestine was lying waste; that once rich and fertile land, which God Himself selected as a fitting residence for His chosen people, was without tillage or fruitage; why might not the time be come for reclaiming it, and why might not its starving and oppressed inhabitants be stimulated to derive their sustenance from its soil? Surely a few thousand dollars might be adventured on an experiment so practical and benevolent. We commended it to our readers. Many of them responded, and if any success has attended the measure, much of it is to be attributed to their collective donations.

33. Minor and Minor, *Meshullam,* 91-92. Minor detailed the involvement of Moses Montefiore and Lady Montefiore in "Letter From Palestine. From our correspondence in Palestine: Jews cutting wheat. Manner of threshing. Variety of fruits. The late Mr. Touro of New Orleans. Interesting efforts of Sir Moses Montefiore. His hospitals and schools. Purchase of the present American settlement. Arrangements for a new one. Hebrew Biarra, north of Jaffa. Near the sea. 1 September 1855," *The Presbyterian* 25 no. 47/1292 (24 November 1855):184.

34. T.B.S., "'C. S. M., Artas 27 July 1852: Dear Brethren and Sisters in Christ.' Agricultural Mission in Palestine," *AHBA* 4 no. 19/461 (23 October 1852):149-150. See James Finn, *A View from Jerusalem, 1849-1858: The Consular Diary of James and Elizabeth Anne Finn,* Arnold Blumberg, ed. (Rutherford, N.J., 1980); and Joseph March, "Palestine—The Petition," *AHBA* 4 no. 24/466 (27 November 1852):189.

35. See Isaac Leeser, "Palestine III," *The Occident and American Jewish Advocate: A monthly periodical devoted to the diffusion of knowledge on Jewish literature and religion (OAJA)* 11 no. 11/131 (February 1854):541-542; Minor, "Letter from Palestine: Plains of Sharon, three miles north of Jaffa 4 April 1854," *OAJA* 12 no. 4 (July 1854):200-206.

36. Parker, "A Fanatic"; Kark, "Millenarism and Agricultural Settlement"; Vivian D. Lipman, *Americans and the Holy Land through British Eyes, 1820-1917: A Documentary History* (London 1989):119-138.

37. J. B. C[ook], "Meshullam!, or, Tidings from Jerusalem. From the journal of a believer recently returned from the Holy Land," *AHBA* n.s. 2 no. 37/375 (1 March 1851):293. Cf. Cook, *A Solemn Appeal to Ministers and Churches: Especially to those of the Baptist denominations relative to the speedy coming of Christ* (Boston 1843). On Cook, see Froom, *Prophetic Faith,* 666-669.

38. C[ook], "'The Land'—Meshullam," *AHBA* n.s. 2 no. 39/377 (15 March 1851):307.

39. Idem, "Meshullam," *AHBA* n.s. 3 no. 10/400 (23 August 1851):77.

40. Idem, "A Plain Question, Kindly Put to the Stewards of the Lord," *AHBA* n.s. 3 no. 11/401 (30 August 1851):85.

41. Idem, "Pilgrims to Zion," *AHBA* n.s. 3 no. 37/427 (28 February 1852):291.

42. [Joseph Marsh], "What Is Duty?" *AHBA* n.s. 2 no. 50/388 (31 May 1851):396. Cf. idem, *The Bible Doctrine; or, The gospel faith concerning the gathering of Israel—the millennium—personal coming of Christ* (Rochester, N.Y., 1849). On Marsh, see Froom, *Prophetic Faith,* 703-705.

43. [Marsh], "Jerusalem," *AHBA* n.s. 3 no. 13/403 (13 September 1851):101-102; idem, "Case of Sr. C.S. Minor," *AHBA* n.s. 3 no. 20/410 (1 November 1851):156.

44. Idem, "Palestine."

45. The passage by Jonas King appeared in *Western Record* (6 January 1824), cited in [Owen R. L.] C[rozier], "Jerusalem Thirty Years Ago," *AHBA* n.s. 4 no. 23/465 (20 November 1852):180:

> The prophecy of Ezekiel, with regard to this people, is literally fulfilled. "It shall be the basest among the nations" [Ezekiel 29:15]. I feel as though misery lives here incarnate. The Turks walk about in pride, while the people groan under the deepest oppression. The country is fertile and beautiful, and might be one of the happiest places in the world; but the people live in poverty, and are clothed in rags. They are ignorant and degraded and vicious. I thought I had seen something of vice in America, and in France, but those countries, I had almost said, are pure compared with this. Every sin enumerated by St. Paul, in the first chapter of his *Epistle to the Romans* (1:26-31), is literally committed here without a blush, and without any apparent remorse. O, how important to bring among them the pure principles of the Gospel. But whoever comes here to labor as a missionary must not be afraid to die; or at least, he must have that submission that will enable him to drink a bitter cup, and say "not my will, but thine, be done [*Luke* 22:42]."

46. Crozier cited a letter of 13 July 1852 from Barclay in Jerusalem about Meshullam which said nothing about a recent rain ending the soil's sterility. He mentioned Barclay's hope that the Jews of Jerusalem "may soon embrace Christianity, if brought under Mr. Meshullam's influence." Robinson wrote Crozier on 3 December 1852 that in his recent visit to Jerusalem he was in daily intercourse with all members of the LJS mission, including Edward MacGowan and Mr. E. S. Calman, the lay missionary at the hospital. The fact that the *Sabbath Record*, the "chief medium" for publishing Artas reports, now stood "aloof" from it was further evidence that the Artas reports about the rains were not credible. Crozier, "The Palestine Movement," *AHBA* n.s. 4 no. 26/468 (11 December 1852):204-206. Cf. T.B.S., "C. S. M., Artas 27 July 1852." On Crozier, see Froom, *Prophetic Faith*, 890-893.

47. Edward Robinson, *Later Biblical Researches in Palestine and in the Adjacent Regions: A journal of travels in the year 1852* (Boston 1856):274. In his letter of 3 December 1852 to Crozier, Robinson stated:

> I saw Mr. Meshullam for half an hour at Artas, where he has some fifteen or twenty acres under cultivation. He was also just sowing some cotton seed on a small field at another village. Mr. Meshullam is a convert from Judaism; he formerly kept a hotel in Jerusalem; but left it for his present undertaking. I know not what his motives may be; but I never heard of any other than his own private advantage.

Crozier, "The Palestine Movement: Reply [to Robinson's letter of] 3 December 1852," *AHBA* n.s. 4 no. 26/468 (11 December 1852):204-206.

48. Herman Melville, *Journal of a Visit to Europe and the Levant, 11 October 1856-6 May 1857*, Howard C. Horsford, ed. (Princeton 1955):156-157.

49. Leeser, "New Items," *OAJA* 1 no. 3 (June 1843):154. *Prophecy Interpreted* is listed in none of the following: Froom, Bibliography, in *Prophetic Faith;* Nichol, *Midnight Cry;* Cyrus Adler, *Catalogue of the Leeser Library* (Philadelphia 1883); or Vern Carner, Sakae Kubo, and Curt Rice, "Bibliographical Essay," in Edwin S. Gausted, ed., *The Rise of Adventism: Religion and Society in Mid-Ninteenth-Century America* (New York 1974):207-317.

50. Leeser, "Literary Notices: Discourse on the Restoration of the Jews Delivered at the Tabernacle, N.Y., 28 October and 2 December 1844. By M. M. Noah (New York 1845)," *OAJA* 2 (March 1845):600-606. See Mordecai M. Noah, Preface, in *Discourse on the Restoration of the Jews* (New York 1845):iii-viii.

51. Leeser, "Palestine," *OAJA* 11 nos. 9-11/129-131 (December 1853-February 1854):429-434, 477-487, 541-552.

52. Leeser, "New Items: Death of Mrs. Clorinda S. Minor," *OAJA* 13 no. 12/156 (March 1856):603. See Minor, "Letter from Palestine . . . 4 April 1854," *OAJA*.

53. *The Presbyterian,* cited in Parker.

54. Ellen G. White recalled Minor as follows:
> There was a Mrs. Minor who had been to Jerusalem. When she returned [1850-1851] she advocated some of these sentimental, spiritualistic sophistries. She invited me to visit her and relate what the Lord had shown me. Brother Nichols took my sister and self to her home in Roxbury [Mass], where we found a company of about twenty assembled. Among them were brethren and sisters whom I loved and highly esteemed. They had believed the testimonies that I had borne to the people. But they had been led astray by spiritualistic ideas which were nothing less than a love-sick sentimentalism.

White to Dr. J. H. Kellogg and associates, 26 November 1903, White Estate, Washington D.C.

55. Idem, "Salvation to the Jews," in *The Acts of the Apostles in the Proclamation of the Gospel of Jesus Christ* (Mountain View, Calif., 1911):372-381. idem, "Destruction of Jerusalem," in *The Great Controversy Between Christ and Satan: The Conflicts of the Ages in the Christian Dispensation* (Mountain View, Calif., 1911):17-38; and idem, *Spiritual Gifts: My Christian experience, views and labors in connection with the rise and progress of the third angel's message* (Battle Creek, Mich., 1860):72-74.

56. On Blackstone, see David Brodeur, "Christians in the Zionist Camp: Blackstone and Hechler," *Faith and Thought* 100 no. 3 (1972/73):271-29. Anita L. Lebeson, "Zionism Comes to Chicago," in Isidore S. Meyer, ed., *Early History of Zionism in America*, (New York 1958):155-190; Moshe Davis, "American Christian Devotees in the Holy Land," *Christian-Jewish Relations* 20 no. 4 (1987); Carl F. Ehle, "Prolegomena to Christian Zionism in America: The Views of Increase Mather and William E. Blackstone Concerning the Doctrine of the Restoration of Israel" (diss., New York University, 1977); and Ya'akov Ariel, "An American Initiative for the Establishment of a Jewish State: William E. Blackstone and the Petition of 1891," *Cathedra* 49 (September 1988, Hebrew):87-102.

57. William E. Blackstone, *Jesus is Coming* (1889; reprint, Chicago 1908):75-82, 162-176. The six earlier periods were: (1) Innocence—from creation through Adam's fall, (2) Conscience—from the fall until Noah, (3) Government—from Noah through Abraham, (4) Promise—from Abraham through Moses, (5) Law—from Moses through Jesus, and (6) Grace—from crucifixion through the Second Coming. See Daniel P. Fuller, *Gospel and Law: Contrast or Continuum? The Hermeneutics of Dispensationalism and Covenant Theology* (Grand Rapids, Mich., 1980); and Ernest R. Sandeen, *The Rocks of Fundamentalism: British and American Millenarianism, 1800-1930* (Chicago 1970). Cf. Warder Cresson *Jerusalem, the Center of the Whole Earth, and the Jew the Recipient of the Glory of God* (London 1844).

58. Blackstone, *Jesus Is Coming*. According to Rausch, "American Christian Groups," *Jesus Is Coming* was formed from two tracts Blackstone wrote upon the encouragement of premillennialist leaders. By 1927 843,000 copies had been printed in 36 different languages. It was translated by J.I.L. into Hebrew as *Hofa'at Ha'mashiah Ha'shnia* (Chicago 1925).

59. Brodeur, "Christians in the Zionist Camp."

60. On Emil Hirsch, see Marver Bernstein, "The Blackstone Memorial," *Midstream* 14 no. 2 (June 1961):76-89.

61. Blackstone, "May the United States Intercede for the Jews?" *Our Day* 8 no. 46 (October 1891). Cf. Theodor Herzl, *Der Judenstaat* (Leipzig 1896).

62. On Lesser and Felsenthal, see Brodeur, "Christians in the Zionist Camp"; on Lesser, see also Chapter 10. Blackstone's papers are held by the Moody Bible Institute and the American Messianic Fellowship in Chicago, and the paper which Lesser prepared may be among them.

63. See Joseph Rabinowitsch, *Neue Dokumente der suedrussischen Christentums-bewegung: Selbstbiographie und Predigten von Joseph Rabinowitsch* (Leipzig 1887). "Paul Lichtenstein is a descendent in the sixth generation of one Aaron, a Christian Israelite, the son of a rabbi, who was baptized at Hamburg about 200 years previously." William T. Gidney, *The History of the London Society for Promoting Christianity amongst the Jews* (London 1908):307.

64. See Jonathan Sarna, "American Christian Opposition to Missions to the Jews: 1816-1900," *Journal of Ecumenical Studies* 23 no. 2 (Spring 1986):225-238.

65. Blackstone, "The Land and the People," in *The Student Missionary Appeal: Addresses at the Third International Convention of the Student Volunteer Movement for Foreign Missions. Held at Cleveland, Ohio, 23-27 February 1898* (New York 1898):407-412.

66. B[lackstone], *Satan: His Kingdom and Its Overthrow* (Chicago 1900):41-42.

67. On Wilson, see Reuben Fink, *The American War Congress and Zionism: Statements by Members of the American War Congress on the Jewish National Movement* (New York 1919). Idem, *America and Palestine* (New York 1944). Lewis R. Wanamaker sponsored the trip to the Holy Land of black Christian painter Henry O. Tanner (1858-1939), the son of Benjamin T. Tanner. Benjamin Ivry, "The Holy Land in American Black Art" (Yale University 1981). On Benjamin T. Tanner, see Chapter 7.

68. Cited in Lebeson, "Zionism Comes to Chicago."

69. Wellcome, *History of the Second Advent*, 162.

70. Minor and Minor, *Meshullam*, 91.

9 Mormons: Dialectical Holy Lands

Mormons believe that Lehi, a descendant of the biblical Joseph, brought his family from Jerusalem, via Arabia and the Indian Ocean, to America in 590 B.C.E.[1] The family divided into two peoples: the white-skinned and civilized Nephites, descended from Lehi's son Nephi, and the dark-skinned and savage Lamanites, from his son Laman. Most Nephites were destroyed by the Lamanites toward the end of the fourth century near Hill Cumorah, in what is now northeastern New York State. Before he was slain, the Nephite prophet Mormon handed the sacred writings of the Nephites to his son Moroni. In 1827 the resurrected Moroni provided them to Joseph Smith (1805-1844). Smith set them down in the Book of Mormon and founded the Church of Jesus Christ of Latter-day Saints (LDS). He endeavored "to combine a restoration of primitive Christianity as it had been lived in the time of the apostles with modern revelation from on high. The new religious group claimed nothing less than a reopening of the heavens and a resumption of divine revelation through the agency of its founder."[2] The Mormons believed both in restoring ancient Jerusalem in the Land of Israel and in establishing Zion in the western United States.

The American Zion

According to Mormon belief, some six weeks after His resurrection Christ made a series of visitations to the Nephites in America.[3] Those Nephites who through baptism accepted Christ's gospel, as manifested in Mormon scripture, would be numbered among the covenant people and share in the new Jerusalem to be established on the American continent.[4] In 1831 Smith identified Jackson

County, Missouri, as the city of Zion consecrated for the ultimate gathering of the saints.*

In May 1838 Smith found the ruins of what he believed was a Nephite altar on an elevation above a fertile valley in Davis County, Missouri. He was informed in a vision that the valley was the location of the beginning and end of history. He was told to call it "Adam-ondi-Ahman," indicating the place where Adam would visit his people and where the Ancient of Days would sit, as foretold by Daniel.[†5] On 24 October 1838 "Zion's poetess" Eliza Snow (1804-1887), plural wife of Joseph Smith (and later Brigham Young), brought Adam, the Messiah, and Zion-as-America together mythically at Adam-ondi-Ahman. There, she said, God spoke directly to Adam and through him to all the righteous of history. After buying the land, however, the saints were driven out to the north. There they expected Christ the Messiah. They prepared for Zion and gathered the "camp of God" toward its consecrated territory. They thought that Zion's towers would glow there in splendor, that the metropolis of the earth would in time stand there. Snow awaited an apocalyptic scourge in America followed by the building of the city of Zion as "the pride of nations and the pilgrim's home." After that, Zion-as-America and Zion-as-Land-of-Israel would be physically joined: "Judah's mountains of the Land of Israel shall become a plain and the two continents unite again." Then the tribes of Israel—except those which had become Mormon—would dwell in Zion at Jerusalem.[‡6]

Benjamin Winchester (b. 1817), editor of the LDS *Gospel Reflector*, identified the millennium with Zion-as-America in 1841. The "upper city" which David acquired from the Jebusites and Jerusalem of the Land of Israel were not exclusive: Isaiah's Zion at Jerusalem implied a Zion not at Jerusalem.[#] There was another Jerusalem, one built in another land for deliverance in the last days.

---

*"Hearken, O ye elders of my church, saith the Lord your God, who have assembled yourselves together, according to my commandments, in this land, which is the land of Missouri, which is the land which I have appointed and consecrated for the gathering of the saints . . . And also that you might be honored in laying the foundation, and in bearing record of the land upon which the Zion of God shall stand." *Doctrine and Covenants* 57:1-2, 58:7.

†"Adam-ondi-Ahman because, said he [the Lord], it is the place where Adam shall come to visit his people, or the Ancient of Days shall sit, as spoken of by Daniel the prophet." *Doctrine and Covenants* 116. See also, *Revelation* 3:14: "These things saith the Amen, the faithful and true witness, the beginning of the creation of God." "Until the ancient of days came, and judgement was given to the saints of the most High; and the time came that the saints possessed the kingdom." *Daniel* 7:22.

‡"For the people shall dwell in Zion at Jerusalem." *Isaiah* 30:19.

#"But ye are come unto Mount sion, and unto the city of the living God, the heavenly Jerusalem, and to an innumerable company of angels." *Hebrews* 12:22. "Nevertheless David took the stronghold of Zion: the same is the city of David." 2 *Samuel* 5:7.

Located in America, this was the Zion of the millennium where saints would gather, the refuge from God's apocalyptic wrath against the nations of the world. Isaiah indicated this location when he spoke of Mount Zion in the land beyond the rivers of Ethiopia, of Zion as a "wilderness," Jerusalem as a desolation.* David referred to his other Jerusalem when he spoke of Mount Zion "on the sides of the north" as the city to be established forever and of Zion "in the fields of the wood."†

Winchester believed that the Lord would establish the gathering place in America "near the center of the north division of the continent." At the end of history America and the Land of Israel would both be central places of gathering and deliverance but part of a larger unity. At the beginning of history waters and lands had separate places, and in the days of Peleg the earth was divided.‡ According to Isaiah, once Zion was built in the west on the American continent it would be reunited with the eastern Zion.# The House of Joseph (Mormons) in America and the House of Israel (Jews) in Canaan would come under one government, one code of law, and one king.** However, the city of David and "Zion at Jerusalem" would be "an auxiliary and not the principal"; America-as-Zion would be more central than Zion-as-Land-of-Israel.††7

---

*Isaiah 18:1, supra. "In that time shall the present be brought unto the Lord of hosts of a people scattered and peeled, and from a people terrible from their beginning hitherto; a nation meted out and trodden under foot, whose land the rivers have spoiled, to the place of the name of the Lord of hosts, the Mount Zion." *Isaiah* 18:7. "Thy holy cities are a wilderness, Zion is a wilderness, Jerusalem a desolation." *Isaiah* 64:10.

†"Beautiful for situation, the joy of the whole earth, is Mount Zion, on the sides of the north, the city of the great king . . . As we have heard, so have we seen in the city of the Lord of hosts, in the city of our God: God will establish it forever. Selah." *Psalms* 48:2, 8. "I will not give sleep to mine eyes, or slumber to mine eyelids, Until I find out a place for the Lord, an habitation for the mighty God of Jacob. Lo, we heard of it at Efratah: we found it in the fields of the wood . . . For the Lord hath chosen Zion; he hath desired it for his habitation." *Psalms* 132:4-6, 13.

‡"And God said, Let the waters under the heaven be gathered together unto one place, and let the dry land appear: and it was so." *Genesis* 1:9; 10:25, supra.

#"Thou shalt no more be termed forsaken; neither shall thy land any more be termed Desolate: but thou shalt be called Hefzibah, and thy land Beulah: for the Lord delighteth in thee, and thy land shall be married." *Isaiah* 62:4.

**"And I will make them one nation in the land upon the mountains of Israel; and one king shall be king to them all: and they shall be no more two nations, neither shall they be divided into two kingdoms any more at all." *Ezekiel* 37:22.

††"For Zion's sake will I not hold my peace, and for Jerusalem's sake I will not rest, until the righteousness thereof go forth as brightness, and the salvation thereof as a lamp that burneth." *Isaiah* 62:1.

In April 1844 Smith proclaimed "the whole America Zion itself from north to south."[*8] The tenth of his Articles of Faith of the Church of Jesus Christ of LDS declares, "We believe in the literal gathering of Israel and in the restoration of the Ten Tribes, converted to the Christian-Mormon gospel; that Zion be built upon this continent."[9] In the last days a "new Jerusalem" or "Zion" would be built in America, the land superior to all others, for the Mormon remnant of the seed of Joseph.[†] Smith predicted that not many years would pass before the United States became a scene of unparalleled bloodshed, pestilence, hail, famine, and earthquakes. The wicked would be swept from the land, while those who complied with the new covenant would gather in Zion in the state of Missouri.[10]

Like the Puritans, the Mormons reinforced and implemented their belief in Zion-America with the language of Hebrew Scripture. Smith studied Hebrew in Kirtland, Ohio, in the winter of 1836 under Joshua Seixas, the son of Gershom M. Seixas of Congregation Shearit Israel. Other leaders—Oliver Cowdery (1806-1850); Sidney Rigdon (1793-1876); Orson Pratt (1811-1881); Orson Hyde (1805-1878); and Lorenzo Snow (1814-1901), who was brought to Oberlin College by his sister Eliza Snow to study Hebrew under Seixas—also studied the language. The Mormons made Hebrew words and names part of American geography. For example, the name of Nauvoo, Illinois, settled by Mormons in 1839, came from the Hebrew *naveh*, meaning "beautiful" (*Isaiah* 52:7), Utah Lake was known as the Sea of Galilee, Salt Lake was regarded as the Dead Sea, and the two were connected by the Jordon River. Two Mormon settlements were named Ephraim and Menassas, for the tribes from which Lehi's family was descended, and the Colorado River was called Bashan.[11]

---

[*]"And behold, this people will I establish in this land, unto the fulfilling of the covenant which I made with your father Jacob; and it shall be a New Jerusalem. And the powers of heaven shall be in the midst of this people: yea, even I will be in the midst of you." *III Nephi* 20:22.

[†]"But, said he [Lehi], notwithstanding our afflictions, we have obtained a land of promise, a land which is choice above all other lands; a land which the Lord God hath covenanted with me should be a land for the inheritance of my seed." *II Nephi* 1:5. "Behold, Ether saw the days of Christ, and he spake concerning a New Jerusalem upon this land." *Ether* 13:4. "And that a new Jerusalem should be built up upon this land, unto the remnant of the seed of Joseph, for which things there has been a type. For as Joseph brought his father down into the land of Egypt, even so he died there; wherefore, the Lord brought a remnant of the seed of Joseph out of the Land of Jerusalem, that he might be merciful unto the seed of Joseph that they should perish not . . . Wherefore, the remnant of the house of Joseph shall be built upon this land; and it shall be a land of their inheritance; and they shall build up a holy city unto the Lord, like unto the Jerusalem of old." *Ether* 13:6-8.

Restoration of the Land of Israel

Smith received a revelation from Moroni on 3 November 1831 at Hiram, Ohio, that the people of Judah (Jews) should flee unto Jerusalem.* On 16 December 1833 at Kirtland, Ohio, the Lord revealed to him that Zion would "not be moved out of her place" even though her children were scattered. Those Jews who survived and were "pure at heart" would return to their inheritance to build up the "waste places of Zion" in fulfillment of the words of the prophets.† On 27 March 1836 Smith offered a prayer at the dedication of Kirtland Temple about God's real love for "the children of Jacob," and he asked God to have mercy, to redeem Jerusalem immediately and return the children of Judah to the Land which He gave to their father Abraham. Smith prayed that those of Jacob's remnants who were cursed and smitten because of their transgression (Judah and Benjamin) be converted from their savage condition to the fullness of the everlasting (Mormon) gospel and that the other scattered remnants of Israel (Ten Tribes excluding Mormon descendants) come to a knowledge of the gospel truth and be redeemed from oppression.‡ Nephi spoke of the father's covenant with the Jews, of His gathering them together in His own "due time" and giving them the Land

---

*"And let them who be of Judah flee unto Jerusalem, unto the mountains of the Lord's house." *Doctrine and Covenants* 133:13.

†"Zion shall not be moved out of her place, notwithstanding her children are scattered. They that remain, and are pure in heart, shall return, and come to their inheritances, they and their children, with songs of everlasting joy, to build up the waste places of Zion—And all these things, that the prophets might be fulfilled. And, behold, there is none other place appointed than that which I have appointed; neither shall there be any other place appointed them that which I have appointed, for the work of the gathering of my saints." *Doctrine and Covenants* 101:16-20.

‡"And verily, I [Jesus] say unto you again that the other tribes hath the Father separated from them; and it is because of their iniquity that they know not of them." *III Nephi* 15:20. "And then shall the work of the Father commence at that day, even when this gospel shall be preached among the remnant of this people. Verily I say unto you, at that day shall the work of the Father commence among all the dispersed of my people, yea, even the Tribes which have been lost, which the Father hath led away out of Jerusalem." *III Nephi* 21:26. "But thou knowest that thou hast a great love for the children of Jacob, who have been scattered upon the mountains for a long time, in a cloudy and dark day. We therefore ask thee to have mercy upon the children of Jacob, that Jerusalem from this hour may be redeemed. And the yoke of bondage may begin to be broken off from the House of David; and the Children of Judah may begin to return to the lands which thou didst give to Abraham, their father. And cause that the remnants of Jacob, who have been cursed and smitten because of their transgression, be converted from their wild and savage condition to the fullness of the everlasting gospel; that they may lay down their weapons of bloodshed, and cease their rebellions. And may all the scattered remnants of Israel, who have been driven to the ends of the earth, come to a knowledge of the truth, believe in the Messiah, and be redeemed from oppression, and rejoice before thee." *Doctrine and Covenants* 109:61-67.

promised to their fathers forever.[*] The return would involve overcoming the original rejection of Christ. The Jews of Jerusalem once stiffened their necks against God, crucifying Jesus, and as a result suffered destruction, famine, pestilence, bloodshed and dispersion. When they believed that God was Christ, the patriarchal covenant to restore the Jews to their Land would be fulfilled, and the gentiles would serve by bringing them back.[†]

In April 1840 Smith's associate Oliver Cowdery wrote about the restoration as communicated by Moroni to Smith. It was evident "that the Lord has decreed to bring forth the fullness of the gospel in the last days, previous to gathering Jacob, as a preparatory work." God will bring Israel (other than the Mormons), driven and scattered, from the ends of the earth. They will come together, "weeping and with supplications,"[‡] led by God while seeking Him, saying, "Arise, and let us go up to Zion, unto the holy Mount of the Lord our God, for He will teach us of His ways, and instruct us to walk in His paths."[#] To clear the path to Zion, God will destroy the "Egyptian sea," create a dry passageway,

---

[*]*III Nephi* 21:26, supra. "And I will remember the covenant which I have made with my people; and I have covenanted with them that I would gather them together in mine own due time, that I would give unto them again the land of their fathers for their inheritance, which is the land of Jerusalem, which is the promised land to them forever, saith the father." *III Nephi* 20:29. "And verily I say unto you, I give unto you a sign, that ye may know the time when these things shall be about to take place—that I shall gather in, from their long dispersion, my people, O house of Israel, and shall establish again among them My Zion." *III Nephi* 21:1.

[†]"But because of priestcrafts and iniquities, they at Jerusalem will stiffen their necks against him, that he be crucified. Wherefore, because of their iniquities, destructions, famines, pestilences and bloodshed shall come upon them; and they who shall not be destroyed shall be scattered among all the nations. But behold, thus saith the Lord God: When the day cometh that they shall believe in me, that I am Christ, then have I covenanted with their fathers that they shall be restored in the flesh, upon the earth, unto the lands of their inheritance. And it shall come to pass that they shall be gathered in from their long dispersion, from the isles of the sea, and from the fours parts of the earth; and the nations of the Gentiles shall be great in the eyes of me, saith God, in carrying them forth to the lands of their inheritance." *II Nephi* 10:5-8. See also *Pearl of Great Price, Moses* 7:61-62: "And the day shall come that the earth shall rest, but before that day the heavens shall be darkened, and a veil of darkness shall cover the earth; and the heavens shall shake, and also the earth; and great tribulations shall be among the children of men, but my people will I preserve. And righteousness will I send down out of heaven; and truth will I send forth out of the earth, to bear testimony of mine Only Begotten." "And it came to pass that I, Nephi, spake much unto them concerning these things; yea, I spake unto them concerning the restoration of the Jews in the latter days." *I Nephi* 15:19-20.

[‡]*Jeremiah* 31:9, supra.

[#]*Jeremiah* 31:6, supra.

and make a highway out of Assyria.* Every corner of the earth will be visited by God to gather all of (Jewish) Israel; He will have friendly hunters bring glad tidings calling for their return.† Cowdery concluded that although the House of Israel once forsook the Lord for false gods, this time they will "know the voice of the shepherd," for the day of His power will soon come, and His people will "be willing to hearken to His counsel." Indeed, "they are already beginning to be stirred up in their hearts to search for these things, and are daily reading the ancient prophets, and are marking the times and seasons of their fulfillment. Thus God is preparing the way for their return."[12]

In 1843 Smith specified that the return of Judah (Jews) and the restoration of the Land had to take place before the son of man appeared: "Judah must return. Jerusalem must be rebuilt. And the Temple. And the water come out from under the Temple.‡ And the waters of the Dead Sea be healed. It will take some time to rebuild the walls of the city of the Temple. And all this must be done before the son of man will make His appearance."[13]

Smith's successors continued his theology of the Land. In 1845 Brigham Young's Council of Twelve proclaimed that Jews were commanded in the name of the Messiah to prepare to return to Jerusalem and establish a political government.[14] In 1879 Elder Wilford Woodruff (1807-1898), who would later become LDS president, stated that wealthy Jews would soon be called upon to purchase land in and around Jerusalem and rebuild the city and the Temple with God's help.[15] In 1899 Joseph M. Tanner, president of Brigham Young College, predicted that within a few years the hills of the Land of Israel would be covered with forests and the valleys nourished by gushing rivers, and that within two decades five or six million Jews would settle there.[16]

Thus the Zion of history for the Mormons was tied to the ancient Land of the Hebrews on one side of the globe and rooted in Hebraic origins on the other, while Zion of the *eschaton* was for Jewish Israel-become-Mormon. According to Mormon belief, at the end of history the two centers of religion will unite and

---

*"And the Lord shall utterly destroy the tongue of the Egyptian sea; and with His mighty wind shall He shake his hand over the river, and shall smite it in the seven streams, and make men go over dryshod. And there shall be an highway for the remnant of his people, which shall be left, from Assyria; like as it was to Israel in the day that he came out of the land of Egypt." *Isaiah* 11:15-16.

†"Behold, I will send for many fishers, saith the Lord, and they shall fish them; and after will I send for many hunters, and they shall hunt them from every mountain, and from every hill, and out of the holes of the rocks." *Jeremiah* 16:16.

‡"Afterward he brought me again unto the door of the house; and, behold, waters issued out from under the threshold of the house eastward: for the forefront of the house stood toward the east, and the waters came down from under from the right side of the house, at the south side of the altar." *Ezekiel* 47:1.

restore the original formation of the earth. The American continent and the Land of Israel will move together and form one government. The principal center will be America, it will be the thesis into which the antithesis of the Land of Israel will synthesize. The Mormons believed in Zion-in-America, made possible by Christ's visit and effected by the Book of Mormon. Here eschatology involved an apocalypse, to be followed by the gathering of the saints in Adam-ondi-Ahman' and the establishment of new Jerusalem there. As for Zion in the Land of Israel, the scattered Jewish descendants of the tribes of Israel will hear the gospel and return to the Land. Collectively Israel will atone for the crucifixion by accepting Christ as portrayed in the Book of Mormon. The Land, notably Jerusalem, will return to its original glory and, once restored, join the American-centered world-Zion physically, politically and spiritually. The founders of the Mormon religion expected restoration immediately.

Ritual Travel and Apocalyptic Myth

Orson Hyde

In 1834 Smith assigned Orson Hyde prophetic status, predicting that in due time he would go to Jerusalem, the Land of his fathers, and be a watchman unto the House of Israel.[17] By Hyde's hands, the Most High would do a great work, preparing the way and facilitating the gathering of the people of Israel.[18] For the Nauvoo church conference of April 1840, Hyde's activity was part of a mythic apocalyptic drama. Jews were scattered among the gentiles as a sign of the ultimate bloody overthrow of earthly governments by the "potency of His almighty arm" and of the second coming of the Messiah. This overthrow was imminent: "signs of the times" and "declarations contained in the oracles of God" were also indications that Jews would soon begin to return to the Holy Land.* To help Mormons prepare for the impending apocalypse and save mankind from the "abomination that maketh desolate," the church was sending Hyde and John E. Page (1799-1867) to London, Amsterdam, Constantinople and Jerusalem to elicit Jewish knowledge—Jews presumably had some inner understanding—about the coming events.†[19] On 14 May 1840 Smith wrote Hyde and Page that as the Lord's spirit was with those who sought the "outcasts of Israel" (Judah and Benjamin) and the "dispersed of Judah" (Ten Lost Tribes), so the God of the fathers of Israel would care for Hyde and Page as instruments

---

*"O ye hypocrites, ye can discern the face of the sky; but can ye not discern the signs of the times?" *Matthew* 16:3.

†"And from the time that the daily sacrifice shall be taken away, and the abomination that maketh desolate set up, there shall be a thousand two hundred and ninety days." *Daniel* 12:11.

of His precious promises to the children of Abraham."[20] Page did not proceed as planned. Instead, Hyde was joined in New York by George Adams—who would form his own colony in 1866—and the two sailed on 13 February 1841 for England. Adams decided to remain in England to aid Brigham Young (1801-1877) and other members of the Quorum of Twelve Apostles in missionary work.[21]

In London Hyde tried to see Solomon Hirschell, but "Providence laid an embargo" on a personal interview because Hirschell had broken a leg. Hyde wrote instead, informing Hirschell of the apocalypse. He explained that the writings of the Jewish prophets had won his affections and that the "scattered and oppressed condition" of the Jews evoked his sympathy. Quoting Hosea's declaration that God would consider those outside of Israel to be His people, he hoped Hirschell would not be prejudiced against him for being unable "by an existing document or record, to identify himself with" the Jewish nation and would listen to his concerns.[†]

Nine years earlier, Hyde explained, Joseph Smith, "in whose bosom the Almighty had deposited many secrets," gave him a "divine appointment" to go to Jerusalem. One night in early March 1840—a month before the Nauvoo conference—he had a six-hour vision.[‡] London, Amsterdam, Constantinople, and Jerusalem appeared to him. The spirit of the Lord told him that the children of Abraham in those cities would be gathered by Him to the Land He gave to their fathers. Hyde was instructed to tell them to "set up the standard toward Zion," for God was about to bring "great destruction," and to share Isaiah's words of comfort following God's punishment.[#] He was also to call upon the gentiles to help, in God's name. Hyde then explained that in ancient days the Jews had a kingdom, a Land flowing with milk and honey, and Jehovah's strong arm taught surrounding nations to pay them homage. "Their banner floated on every breeze; under its shade the sons and daughters of Israel reposed in perfect safety; and the golden letters of light and knowledge were inscribed on its fold." Now there was no kingdom, no standard, no security, no tribute. Jerusalem had

---

*See *III Nephi* 15:20, supra.

[†]"And I will sow her unto Me in the earth; and I will have mercy upon her that had not obtained mercy; and I will say to them which were not My people, Thou art My people, and they shall say, Thou art My God." *Hosea* 2:23.

[‡]"And it shall come to pass afterward, that I will pour out My spirit upon all flesh; and your sons and your daughters shall prophesy, your old men shall dream dreams, your young men shall see visions." *Joel* 2:28.

[#]"Blow ye the trumpet in the land: cry, gather together, and say, Assemble yourselves, and let us go into the defenced cities. Set up the standard toward Zion: retire, stay not: for I will bring evil from the north, and a great destruction." *Jeremiah* 4:5-7. *Isaiah* 40:2, supra.

fallen dramatically since the days of David and Solomon.[*] Israel's scepter had departed.[†] Instead of the light and knowledge which once elevated them above other nations, most Jews now wanted, above all, to accumulate "sordid gain by buying and selling the stale refuse with which their fathers would never have defiled their hands." Why had such a radical change occurred? Because God was just, and His punishment was proportionate to the crime, as stipulated by Mosaic law. The Jews were first exiled into Babylon for idolatry and shedding innocent blood. Then, in 70 C.E., the Romans invaded the heart of Jerusalem, burned the Temple, killed inhabitants, and dispersed the remnant to the four ends of the earth for the crime of deicide:

> The fiery storm that burst upon your nation at that time and the traces of blood which they have, ever since, left behind them in their flight and dispersion, together with the recent cursed cruelties inflicted upon them in Damascus and Rhodes, but too plainly declare that the strong imprecation which they uttered on a certain occasion has been fulfilled upon them to the letter: "Let His blood be on us and on our children."[‡] If condemning and crucifying Jesus of Nazareth was not the cause of this great evil; what was the cause of it?

Hyde told Hirschell all this, he said, out of love toward the Jewish nation, and "a heart grateful to the Almighty that the time has arrived when the day star of your freedom already begins to dispel the dark and gloomy clouds which have separated you from the favor of your God." The light of God was rising upon the Jewish people.[#] Hyde took to poetry:

> The morning breaks, the shadows flee,
> Lo! Zion's standard is unfurled;[**]
> The dawning of a brighter day
> Majestic rises on the world.
> The gentile fullness now comes in,[††]
> And Israel's blessings are at hand;

---

[*]"The beauty of Israel is slain upon thy high places: how are the mighty fallen!" *II Samuel* 1:19.

[†]*Genesis* 49:10, supra.

[‡]"Then answered all the people, and said, His blood be on us, and on our children." *Matthew* 27:25.

[#]"Arise, shine; for thy light is come, and the glory of the Lord is risen upon thee." *Isaiah* 60:11.

[**]*Jeremiah*, 4:6, supra.

[††]*Romans* 11:25, supra.

Lo! Judah's remnant cleansed from sin
Shall in their promised Canaan stand.

Hyde proclaimed directly to the "children of the covenant . . . Repent of all
your backslidings and begin, as in the days of old, to turn to the Lord your
God.* Arise! Arise! and go out from among the gentiles; for destruction is
coming from the north to lay their cities waste.[†] Jerusalem is thy home. There
the God of Abraham will deliver thee."[‡] The "bending heavens" would soon
reveal the Messiah in Jerusalem in clouds of light and glory, and He would
execute vengeance upon Israel's enemies and lead world Jewry and the Ten Lost
Tribes to conquest. In a subsequent letter to Hirschell, Hyde added an
afterthought: "Now if you have any counsel concerning the gathering, in addition
to that already given, I shall be happy to receive it, and execute as far as
opportunity offers."[22]

On 20 June 1841 Hyde left for Holland where, as he wrote Smith on 17 July
1841, he called upon the "Hebrew rabbi" (Chief Rabbi Emanuel Y. Loewenstam,
1807-1845?) in Rotterdam. Despite the language barrier, Hyde was able to elicit
the rabbi's views on apocalyptic matters:

1. Did the rabbi expect his messiah to come directly from heaven or be
   born of a woman on earth? He expected the latter, that the woman
   would be of the "seed and lineage of David."[#]
2. When would the event happen? Jews had been looking for a long time
   and were "now living in constant expectation of his coming."
3. Did the rabbi believe in the restitution of his nation to the Land of his
   fathers, called the "Land of *promises*?"[**] He hoped so, and added that
   many Jews would return to Jerusalem, rebuild it, rear a Temple in God's
   name and restore ancient worship. Jerusalem would be the capital of the
   Jewish nation, the center of the union, the ensign of its national

---

*"Return, ye backsliding children, and I will heal your backslidings. Behold, we
come unto thee, for Thou art the Lord our God." *Jeremiah* 3:22.

[†]"Egypt is like a very fair heifer, but destruction cometh; it cometh out of the north."
Jeremiah 46:20.

[‡]"And it shall come to pass, that whosoever shall call on the name of the Lord shall
be delivered: for in Mount Zion and in Jerusalem shall be deliverance, as the Lord hath
said, in the remnant whom the Lord shall call." *Joel* 2:32.

[#]"The city of David, which is called Bethlehem; (because He was of the house and
lineage of David)." *Luke* 2:4.

[**]See, for example, *Deuteronomy* 19:8: "And if the Lord thy God enlarge thy coast,
as He hath sworn unto thy fathers, and give thee all the Land which He promised to give
unto thy fathers."

existence. Not all Jews would go, nor was the Land large enough for all, but Jews were in fact gathering there.

After a week Hyde left for Amsterdam, where he called on the "president rabbi" (Tsevi-Hirsch Lehren 1784-1853).[23] He was not at home, so Hyde left a large number of "addresses" for him and his followers. He went on to Arnheim am Rhine, Frankfurt am Main, and Bavaria, where he received financial help for his journey from the local rabbis.[24]

Hyde arrived in the Holy Land in early October 1841. Immediately he felt drawn from time into eternity. At the port of Jaffa he saw a glittering sword held by a perfect hand in the night sky. Two women grinding wheat reminded him of the prediction about the death of one and the survival of the other at the second coming.* Hyde was conscious of much intermingling between the present and the transtemporal realm: "Is it a reality, that I am gazing upon this scene of wonders? Or am I carried away in the forceful reveries of a night vision? Is that city which I now look down upon really Jerusalem, whose sins and iniquities swelled the Savior's heart with grief, and drew so many tears from his pitying eye? . . . Oh yes!"[25] In the Holy Land Hyde became immersed in sacred history, whose apocalyptic dimensions he had felt chosen to proclaim to Jews in Europe.

On Sunday, 14 October 1841, Hyde ascended the Mount of Olives and piled stones to witness his presence. He prayed in the manner of a traditional Jew but interjected a petition to God to create a Jewish state in the name of Jesus. He began by recalling his March 1840 vision, how under God's "outstretched arm" he arrived at "this place to dedicate and consecrate this Land unto Thee, for the gathering together of Judah's scattered remnants, [according] to the predictions of the holy prophets—for the building up of Jerusalem again after it has been trodden down by the gentiles so long, and for rearing a Temple in honor of Thy name." He reiterated God's covenant with Abraham—renewed with Isaac and confirmed with Jacob—and God's covenantal oath to give them the Land for an everlasting inheritance. But the people were scattered and the Land became barren "since it drank from murderous hands the blood of Him who never sinned." He asked God to bring life to the Land again, "in the name of Thy well-beloved son, Jesus Christ," and to conquer the unbelief of His people: "take from them their stony heart, and give them a heart of flesh; and may the sun of Thy favor dispel the cold mists of darkness which have beclouded their atmosphere. Incline them to gather in upon this Land according to Thy word." Hyde petitioned God to inspire the powers of the earth to recognize that it was His "good pleasure to restore the kingdom unto Israel—raise up Jerusalem as its

---

*"Two women shall be grinding at the mill; The one shall be taken, and the other left." *Matthew* 24:41.

capital, and constitute her people a distinct nation and government, with David Thy servant, even a descendent from the loins of ancient David, to be their king." He asked God to find favor in those nations which helped in the restoration, "in the name of Jesus to remember Zion . . . She has been grievously afflicted and smitten."[26] Thus Hyde recalled the themes of Israel's ingathering, Jewish sin, and Christ-centered restoration that he had enunciated in Europe and prayed about in the sacred space of the Mount of Olives. In the Holy Land, where sacred history and the present intermingled, Hyde's March 1840 vision found its temporal context.

Hyde endeavored to advance Judaism's passage into Christianity—a theological necessity—through missionary work in the Land. Writing from Trieste on 1 January 1842, he said that he failed to have ABCFM missionaries Charles S. Sherman and George B. Whiting and a Mr. Gager introduce him to Jerusalem's Jews.[27] He did initiate a meeting with the "very respectable" German Jew Mr. Simons, who had recently converted to the Church of England, and the convert Bishop Michael Solomon Alexander of LJS. Simons and Alexander questioned Hyde's claim that God had sent him—a query, Hyde speculated, that would not have been posed to a member of ABCFM or LJS. While his hosts were committed to prepare for the millennium, they were not receptive to the prophetic (i.e., Mormon) content of Hyde's revelation. He nonetheless called upon them to repent, reverse their ways, become baptized as Mormons to remove their sins, receive the Holy Ghost, and enter into the new covenant. If they did not he knew that God would turn His wrath upon them.* Hyed explained that as the Jewish nation had been broken down by political power, so it would be restored politically. England would lead the way; already there was "increasing anxiety in Europe for the restoration of that people" from the pale of religious communities to the courts of kings. Special ambassadors and consuls were appointed, e.g., the Austrian consul in Beirut, who protected the growing number of Austrian Jews moving to Syria and Palestine. The rigorous policies in Europe toward Jews were being softened out of friendship and humaneness, the centuries of suffering having touched the gentile power centers. "May the God of their fathers, Abraham, Isaac, and Jacob fan the flame of celestial breezes, until Israel's banner, sanctified by a Savior's blood, shall float on the walls of old Jerusalem, and the mountains and valleys of Judea reverberate with their songs of praise and thanksgiving to the Lamb that was slain." That is, the political restoration of Israel already underway would ultimately hinge on Israel and the crucifixion; Christ's blood would sanctify Israel, while Israel would praise the Christ she once condemned.[28]

---

*"Then shall He speak unto them in His wrath, and vex them in His sore displeasure." *Psalms* 2:5.

Hyde spent the spring and summer of 1842 in Regensburg completing an explication of Mormon church history which he had started in summer 1841. He had it translated into German by one of the people he was teaching English in anticipation of a Mormon mission to Germany. In it he speaks of the refuge being prepared for the imminent second coming of Christ:

> Zion's banner is being unfurled, and invites believers in that area of heaven to come and rest under its shadow. Jerusalem will arise, because a word of grace was spoken to it—albeit not for the sake of those who oppressed the Jews because they were Jews, and removed their privileges.

There was personal theological reason for Hyde's affection for Jews:

> I am not a Jew, also not the son of a Jew. But I am a friend of the Jews, because the well-being of the Christian religion caused their affliction. Were Christ not crucified, and His blood not poured, He could not have redeemed mankind. Someone had to kill Him, for that is why Christ indeed came into this world—but whoever killed Him had to endure all kinds of beatings and pains. The Jews stepped forward and caused His death—and since then they have been placed under the whip; so that the well-being of the nations would come about. How ungrateful must a Christian therefore be, who despises a Jew! The good attributes of a people can best be calculated according to the amount of suffering and deprivation they have undergone in order to do good to someone else. What greater good could the nations encounter, than for the light of Christianity to spread over them? Truly, no greater! And who among us has suffered the most to bring about such blessings for the world? The Jews, and they suffer for that even until today. It appears that they were virtually left to a blind fate to do as they did. And the future will show whether or not, after everything, they have been the greatest benefactors of the world, and whether it belonged to the eternal plans of the invisible God to have these great events happen.[29]

Hyde found the *telos* of Israel in Christ, and so Israel was to be glorified, punished, and ultimately transformed into the Mormon religion. Hyde apparently considered himself a type of Christian Elijah, appointed to carry out the divine mission of preparing the ingathering of Israel, a prelude to the imminent transformation of the universe. Toward this end he was assigned to solicit Jewish knowledge about the apocalypse; he warned Israel to repent of her sins, notably crucifixion; he prepared her for the destruction of her enemies and admonished her to commence the ingathering. He sought to convert Jews, out of love and concern; deicide was a sacrificial act on their part for the sake of Christ's role in the world, but it was also a sin punishable by God.

Once in the Holy Land, experiencing the entry of the sacred into time and space, Hyde prayed to God to effect the ingathering in Christ's name. Having spoken to his fellow man in Europe, in the Holy Land he turned first to God, ever acting within the mythic drama of impending apocalypse. As to man, ABCFM and LJS would not provide him access to Jews, so he tried to bring Jews converted to Christianity into the Mormon religion. Hyde was an emissary from Zion-as-America who believed he was acting out, and thereby reinforcing, the mythic end to history according to Mormonism. In his clarifications, prayers and missionary work he was attempting to hasten the millennium. Then the Jewish Zion-as-Land-of-Israel would be fulfilled within the universal Mormon Zion, centered in America.

Having advanced the salvational history of Israel and her Land, Hyde stopped off in Liverpool on his way home to recruit more Mormons for Zion-as-America. He returned to Nauvoo, Illinois, in December 1842.

George Washington Joshua Adams

George Washington Joshua Adams (1811-1880) was officially a Mormon from 1840 through 1845.[30] He joined the church after listening to Heber C. Kimball (1801-1868), future first counselor to President Brigham Young.[31] He became well-known as a Mormon preacher and was appointed "Apostle to the Gentiles."[32] In July 1842 Adams rejected the Millerite view that the Land would be restored but without Jews, believing that Jews as Jews would be gathered home from their long dispersion to rebuild Jerusalem.[33] Then Christ would come and they would convert to Mormonism.[34] In February 1843 he stated that "the Jews and all the House of Israel" would soon be gathered from their dispersion and "become the nation in the Land upon the mountains of Israel, never more to be divided or overcome." Once in the Land, the Jews would all be brought to the knowledge of God and become a holy (Mormon) nation. Adams believed that the advent of the Messiah was "near at hand," that God had established the LDS church and "set the truth in order among them as a commencement of this great restoration."[35]

In April 1845 Brigham Young "disfellowshipped" Adams for "the most disgraceful and diabolical conduct . . . under the sacred garb of religion." In 1846 he was taken into the Strangite branch of the Church of Jesus Christ of LDS, founded by James J. Strang (1813-1856).[36] He founded his own Church of the Messiah in Maine on 1 January 1861 to succeed to the Mormon church,

That we may the more fully confess the Lord Jesus, the anointed one, before men and angels; and, that we may openly confess ourselves pilgrims and strangers on earth, seeking a city out of sight, a city that hath foundations whose maker and builder is the living God.

> We do therefore most solemnly covenant and agree to form ourselves into a church of the ever living, and only true God; to be called the *Church of the Messiah*; to be governed by the commandments, precepts, and teachings of the Lord Jesus, the Messiah, and His apostles, and to contend earnestly for the faith once delivered to the saints, and to seek after and embrace all truth past, all truth present, and all truth to come.[37]

In October 1862, speaking for the Church of the Messiah, Adams attacked attempts to convert Jews prior to restoration. With all the commotion and money put into the effort in the last 50 years, especially by the LJS, the Jews still remained "incorrigible, impenitent, hard-hearted, and unconverted to the corrupt and spurious christianity [*sic*] of the present age." The Jews would be converted only by the Messiah and as a nation. When Christ first appeared to the Jews they were "in a state of apostasy from the faith of their fathers" and split into sects, and so they rejected Him. They "have been blind ever since, and they will be blind until He makes them willing in the day of His power." Adams stressed that the Jews would never be converted in dispersion; they first had to return to the Land of their fathers. All this was "the eternal and unchangeable decree and word of God."[38]

In February 1864 Adams wrote that the ingathering was already underway. Jews were coming to the Land from all over, except from America where they would not leave the flesh-pots. They were settling not only in the cities but in the countryside and villages, where they could purchase land. They were not coming to die and avoid "rolling underground" toward the Holy Land during the resurrection but to live on the soil of their fathers. Jews were being aroused from "the deep lethargy which lay heavily upon them like a nightmare for many centuries." They were beginning to believe that Christ would soon appear to rule over them. He would restore Israel to more than her ancient glory (i.e., as Church of Messiah-Mormon-Christians) and restore the fertility of the Land itself. The sense of the *eschaton* was confirmed for Adams, as it had been for the Meshullam-Minor group, by the fact that over the last five years "the early rain and the latter came down from heaven as regularly as in the days of David and Solomon . . . everything grew and blossomed, almost visibly to the beholder." Adams sensed "the signs of the times, when He will favor again Zion, and gather again the remnants of Israel and Judah, and be their God."[39]

From July through September 1865 Adams went on an exploratory mission to the Land of Israel. In his *Sword of Truth and Harbinger of Peace* he describes lush citrus groves, fertile land, and the great opportunities for shoemakers, cabinetmakers, and boatbuilders. On 22 August 1865 he ascended the Mount of Olives and, echoing Orson Hyde's prayer 25 years earlier, proclaimed God's majesty over history, the God "who raised Messiah from the dead, and gave unto

Him the key of David."* He implored God to have mercy upon the Land, remove its curse, and restore it to His people Israel. He asked for God's mercy upon His covenant people, who suffered so much, and that God turn nations to favor Israel and the restoration of Zion. He reminded God of His oath about the Land to Abraham, Isaac, Jacob, and David, and asked Him to destroy the nations and churches which oppressed Israel.[†40] Unlike Hyde, however, Adams did not pray for a Mormon-cum-Christian culmination to Israel in preparation for Christ. Hyde considered conversion to Mormonism coincident with return. Adams believed that Jewish return, under human or divine auspices, would precede the conversion of Israel under Christ upon His advent.

Adams returned to America in fall 1865 as the self-appointed first president of the Palestine Emigration Association. Secretary of State Seward helped to secure Turkish authorization for a colony near Jaffa. In February 1866 Adams spoke of the proposed emigration to Palestine in apocalyptic terms: history had reached the point of the "dispensation of the fulness of times," or the fullness of "the times of the gentiles," when there would be "restitution" and "the gathering together of the people of God" as foretold by prophets, apostles and Jesus Christ.[‡] The prophecies were fulfilled. Jerusalem was trodden under foot, Jews wandered, God let the Land lie waste and withheld the latter rain and heavenly dews.[#] The time had come for Israel to gather from dispersion back to her Jerusalem home.

The Church of the Messiah felt separated by "our Lord" from the sinful confusion of the age and called from Babylon (America) to do pioneer work in bringing history to fulfillment by going to the Land. It was to help fulfill the testimony of the prophets, to prepare the Lamb's wife, Jerusalem, for the

---

*"And the key of the house of David will I lay upon his shoulder; so he shall open and none shall shut; and he shall shut, and none shall open." *Isaiah* 22:22.

†"For the nation and kingdom that will not serve thee shall perish; yea, those nations shall be utterly wasted." *Isaiah* 60:12.

‡"That in the dispensation of the fulness of times He might gather together in one all things in Christ, both which are in heaven, and which are on earth." *Ephesians* 1:10. "The time is fulfilled, and the kingdom of God is at hand." *Mark* 1:15. *Luke* 21:24, supra. "Whom the heaven must receive until the times of restitution of all things, which God hath spoken by the mouth of all His holy prophets since the world began." *Acts* 3:21.

#"Be patient therefore, brethren, unto the coming of the Lord. Behold, the husbandman waiteth for the precious fruit of the earth, and hath long patience for it, until he receive the early and latter rain." *James* 5:7. "And the heavens shall give their dew; and I will cause the remnant of this people to possess all these things." *Zechariah* 8:12.

bridegroom.* The church was not to missionize in the Land: "We are going there to become practical benefactors of the Land and people; to take the lead in developing its great resources. We are not going there as religious, proselytizing bigots . . . We shall treat the seed of Abraham as our true brothers, whether they believe our faith or not." The church would teach the natives about agriculture, not "rail at them about their religious faith." It would, however, serve as an example; it would "show many an eye, and many a hand, by gentleness from error won, raised in pure devotion to the true, and only God." Soon, presumably, Christ would come, and with Him there would be conversion.[41]

Adams and 156 followers sailed in August 1866 aboard the *Nellie Chapin* to prepare the Land for the Jewish ingathering and return of the Messiah.[42] They reached Jaffa 22 September 1866 and set up camp on a beach surrounded by a graveyard for cholera victims, a garbage dump for butchers' offal, and dirty Arab villages. Nine followers, including six children, died within the first month, before the encampment was moved to a better location nearby. Adams remained undaunted, convinced that Palestine would "soon shake herself from the dust of the ages, and arise in glory and grandeur as in the days of old."[43] But in the next few months crop failures and Adams' alcoholism and curious behavior—he once tried to arouse a corpse—brought the group to despair.[44] The American State Department provided funds for 42 of the group to board the *Quaker City* in September 1867 and return home. Several ended up together in the Jonesport-Indian River area in Maine. Of those who remained in the Land, Rolla Floyd became a reputable tour guide and Herbert F. Clark (b. 1856) became Vice Consul in Jerusalem.[45]

Adams' work evoked varied responses. Some commended his religious intensity, others ridiculed it, and the Mormons remained coldly indifferent. On 26 September 1866 British Vice Consul H. A. Kayat wrote from Jaffa that the group was motivated by a desire to live and die in the Holy Land during the expected era of great change, when Jews would gather around the world and Christ's advent would occur. According to what he heard from the colonists, they did not come as missionaries. Kayat believed that some members were "part of the tribe of Ephraim" and that Adams himself was "of Jewish descent."[46] In 1874 George A. Smith, leader of the 1872 Mormon pilgrimage which had met Adams in November 1872 in London, made this comment:

---

*"And there came unto me one of the seven angels which had the seven vials full of the seven last plagues, and talked with me, saying, Come hither, I will show thee the bride, the Lamb's wife." *Revelation* 21:9. "And at midnight there was a cry made, Behold, the bridegroom cometh; go ye out to meet Him." *Matthew* 25:6.

In the vicinity of this city [Jaffa] is a colony of about six hundred Germans under the presidency of D. V. Christopher Hoffman, who consider themselves the spiritual temple of Christ . . . We also saw a number of persons who were connected with the scheme of one George J. Adams, and who, after its failure, where left in that country, one of whom, Mr. Floyd, is now a dragoman. They built some houses, but they have been purchased by this German colony.[47]

In 1880, standing on the balcony of a Jaffa hotel built by the Adams group, Thomas de Witt Talmage recalled that the wood was "brought to Jaffa in pieces from the state of Maine by some fanatics who here expected to see Christ reappear in Palestine."[48]   In 1900 James E. Hanauer (b. 1850) transmitted particulars furnished by Herbert F. Clark's mother and sister: Adams had claimed that God called him to preach the Christian gospel and begin a colony to show Jews it was time to return and build the country, to cover it with "unwalled villages." Despite terrible sickness and other difficulties, the colony was built and the colonists continued to believe that God's hand had led them to the Land. As they believed would happen, the Jews began to build unwalled villages in all directions. But the difficulties became too much, and when the German Templars arrived the "Adamites" sold their property to them and returned to America. Their sad story, Hanauer observed, deterred others about to go to Palestine.[49]

As a Mormon Adams rejected both the Millerite exclusion of Jews from the restored Land and Hyde's view of coincident return and conversion, preferring the idea that Jews would return first and convert later.   His Church of the Messiah retained the Mormons' interest in the Land and the ingathering of Israel but disapproved of attempts to convert Jews.   Adams wanted Jews to initiate humanly what was set by God and return, remaining Jews until the entire nation of Israel would be converted under Christ's direction from above.   By settling the Land Adams was expressing and reinforcing the imminent apocalypse. Specifically, he would help Jews restore the Land, participating in the pre-messianic phenomenon of the great fertility of the Land.   And he would provide Israel with exemplars of Christ-committed individuals. Adams attempted to move ahead of history, to establish a community of priests in the Land of Israel.   Like mainstream Mormons, Adams believed Jews were reprobate for killing Christ and that their return would ultimately involve a response to the sin.   Unlike the Mormons, he left their conversion in God's hands.   Nor did he see the Jewish-Christian restoration as part of the larger America-centered Zion but as the end of history and beginning of the Jerusalem-centered millennium.

1873 Pilgrimage

In 1872 the Mormon church authorized a pilgrimage under George A. Smith (1817-1875), the official church historian who succeeded Heber C. Kimball as counselor to President Brigham Young in 1868. The group included Lorenzo Snow (1814-1901), Eliza R. Snow, missionary Paul A. Schettler (1827-1884), lawyer and *Deseret News* editor Albert Carrington (1813-1889), banker Feramorz Little (1820-1886) and his daughter Clara S., Thomas W. Jennings, and Idaho Bishop George Dunford (1822-1891).[50] On 15 October 1872 Brigham Young spelled out the mission to Smith:

> When you go to the Land of Palestine, we wish you to dedicate and consecrate that Land to the Lord, that it may be blessed with fruitfulness, preparatory to the return of the Jews in fulfillment of prophecy, and the accomplishment of the purposes of our heavenly father.[51]

Before leaving America the group paid a visit to President Ulysses S. Grant—who himself would travel to the Holy Land in 1878—so their journey would begin with an expression of respect for their chief magistrate.[52] They left New York aboard the *Minnesota* on 6 November 1872. In London on 24 November, Schettler reported, "George J. Adams, of former notoriety, came on the stand to see President George A. Smith and gave us an invitation to call on him, in order to give us some useful information in regard to the Holy Land, where he has resided," There is no indication the invitation was accepted.[53]

Once they arrived in the Land, the pilgrims experienced its holiness in various ways. Lorenzo Snow felt the presence of Abraham, the kings of ancient Israel, the prophets, Jesus and the apostles:

> We felt that we were passing over the Land once occupied by the children of Abraham, the plains once trod by kings of Israel with their marshalled hosts, the Land of the apostles and the prophets. We were in Palestine! The Holy Land! The consciousness of the fact was inspiring . . . Yes, there is Jerusalem! Where Jesus lived and was crucified. Where He cried, "It is finished" and bowed His head and died.*[54]

At Galilee Lorenzo Snow said he heard the same sounds of the lapping of the water, the same smell from the fisheries that Jesus did. He could imagine terror

---

*"When Jesus therefore had received the vinegar, He said, It is finished: and He bowed His head, and gave up the ghost." *John* 19:30.

seizing the Savior's disciples when their boat was struck by a sudden storm.* In Jerusalem Lorenzo and Eliza Snow explained that although there were doubts about some locations, e.g., of the Stone of Unction, they felt satisfied that the areas were authentic; most importantly, they knew they really were standing where ancient Jerusalem once was, where Jesus was crucified for the redemption of man, resurrected, and ascended where "at no very distant day" He would descend. On their 2 March 1873 ascent of the sacred Mount of Olives they realized they were at the very place frequented by the Prince of life. They camped at the summit, where Carrington recited an opening prayer and "testimonies" were offered. Smith dedicated the entire Land for the ingathering of the Jews and thanked God for "the fullness of the gospel and for the blessings bestowed on the LDS."

Smith saw Scripture through the Land, and after returning to Salt Lake City he recalled his thoughts at the banks of the Jordan on the Savior's baptism, how Elijah smote the waters with his mantle, and how he and Elisha crossed over dryshod, as did Joshua. At the house in Jaffa purported to be that of Simon the Tanner, Smith realized he was in the neighborhood where the Lord revealed to Peter that it was proper for him to preach and whence Peter departed to visit Cornelius and administer the gospel to those not of Israel's seed. But Smith was not so overcome by the Land of sacred Scripture as to avoid pointing out that the Jordan River in Utah was larger, and that Mormon abilities with irrigation could make a unique contribution to the Land:

> I was often asked if we were going to settle in Palestine. I replied that we were not but I could take a thousand "Mormons," go up the Jordan, put in a dam to take out the water, and irrigate several thousand acres. But there is little, however, at present inviting about the country, but it would no doubt be productive if irrigated. The valleys near the source of the Jordan would be much the best for cultivation, and the climate would be more agreeable.

For Smith the restoration was Christ centered. On 4 March 1873 Avraham Ashkenazi (1811-1880),[55] Sefardic chief rabbi, along with three Jewish elders visited Smith's tent in the Hinnom Valley. A San Francisco rabbi (Aaron J. Messing 1843-1916?) had introduced Smith and Ashkenazi, and Ashkenazi had shown him the home for widows and orphans he was building. During the visit Ashkenazi said that Jewish life in the Land was improving. Jews could buy land; he himself had received a land title enabling him to build a home. They also discussed eschatological matters. Ashkenazi said that although he could not locate the descendants of the Ten Tribes, he knew they were alive and would return to

---

*"But as they sailed He fell asleep: and there came down a storm of wind on the lake: and they were filled with water, and were in jeopardy." *Luke* 8:23.

the Land. God would ultimately bless Israel, and the waters of Jerusalem would be as abundant as Ezekiel said (*Ezekiel* 47).

After Ashkenazi and the elders left, Smith observed that "there is no infidel on the face of the earth who can disbelieve the mission of the Savior more than they do." Echoing Hyde, Smith explained that God's glory was once in the Land; "irrigation and industry and the blessing of the Lord prevailed." But that ended, and Rome captured Jerusalem. Defeat was in part due to the rival Jewish parties: "An old proverb says that whom the gods would destroy they first make mad. It was so with these Jews." Another cause was deicide: "They had slain the Savior, they had violated the commands of God, and they had brought upon their heads the curses pronounced upon them in the 27th chapter of *Deuteronomy* and in a great many other places." Recovery and restoration hinged upon the Mormon message. When he spoke at the New Tabernacle in Salt Lake City on 22 June 1873, Smith recalled the group's prayer on Mount Zion:

> When on the Mount of Olives, with our faces bowed toward Jerusalem, we lifted our prayers to God that He would preserve you and confound your enemies. We felt in our hearts that Zion was onward and upward, and that no power could stay in her progress; that the day was not far distant when Israel would gather, and those lands would begin to teem with a people who would worship God and keep His commandments, that plenty and the blessings of eternity would be poured out bounteously upon that desert land, and that all the prophecies concerning the restoration of the House of Israel would be fulfilled. God has commenced His work by revealing the everlasting gospel to the LDS, and may we all be faithful and fulfill our part is my prayer in the name of Jesus.[56]

Eliza Snow expressed her immersion in the Land's eternity and sanctity through poetry. At the Sea of Galilee she

> Thought of the present—the past: it seemed
> That the silent Sea with instruction teemed;
> For often, indeed, the heart can hear
> What never, in sound, has approached the ear.
> Full oft has silence been richly fraught
> With treasures of wisdom and stores of thought,
> With sacred, heavenly whisperings, too,
> That are sweeter than roses, and honey dew.
> There's a depth in the soul, that's beyond the reach
> Of all earthly sound—of all human speech.
> A fiber too sacred and pure, to chime
> With the cold, dull music of earth and time.
> 'Tis the heart's receptacle, naught can supply

But the streams that flow from the fount on high
An instinct divine, of immortal worth,
An inherited gift, through primeval birth.

Jesus was fully present. As dawn broke Snow "walked on the bank of this self-same Sea, / Where once our Redeemer was wont to be." Past and present blended in Scripture: "And here, while admiring this scriptural Sea, / The bold vista of time brought the past up to me." She thought of Jesus, Who endured the world's hatred, in Whom the omnipotent was revealed, through Whom the wide breach of law was healed, and Who led the way through death into day.[57]

Like Hyde and Smith, Snow found the history of Israel turning upon Christ. She was reluctant to leave Jerusalem, the city of "sacredly interesting histories of the past and of bright prophetic anticipation for the future." She felt God's curse on the Land and the people.[58] Once Jerusalem had been blessed with sacred fame, God's glory shone in the Temple built according to His directions, He was with the city and made His presence known through prophets. All the Land of Israel was favored, its mountains lush and its hillsides filled with wine and oil. Now Jerusalem was degraded, divested of heavenly rites, estranged from wisdom, its glory departed. It had withdrawn from God and been forsaken by Him, its walls surrounded by beggars, its streets filthy, its pools pestilent sewers. There was no longer a Temple designed by God, no prophet inspired to reveal His mind. Under the Turkish iron yoke the Muslim crescent replaced the biblical "royal banner."* Jerusalem was crucified, blood upon its brow, a "sable wreath" on its head. This radical decline was traceable to the crucifixion:

The curse of God thy changes wrought,
Through crimes the Jews have done,
When they His counsels set at nought,
And crucified His Son.
Since then has retribution's hand
Put forth its fearful skill
Upon thy structure and thy Land,
A destiny to fill.

The seed of Israel, under God's "peculiar care," was judged and scattered.[†] But that was not the end; the terrible decline could be reversed. Indeed, God

---

*See for example, *Isaiah* 13:2: "Lift ye up a banner upon the high mountain, exalt the voice unto them."

†"And the Lord has chosen thee to be a peculiar people unto Himself." *Deuteronomy* 14:2.

would fulfill His purpose concerning Palestine, His covenant with Abraham. Jerusalem would be redeemed:

> Thy walls shall be of previous stones —
> Thy gates of richest pearl;
> And on thy towering battlements,
> Shall sacred banners furl.
> The seed of Jacob there shall dwell
> In bold security;
> More than the former glory shall
> Thy latter glory be."[59]

For the pilgrims of 1873 the experience in the Land was a holy one. They were committed to the restoration of the Land and the ingathering of the Jews in terms of three points of theological history:

1. In ancient times the Land was glorious and filled with God.
2. The Jews sinned by killing Christ.
3. Not only the people but the Land, Jerusalem in particular, suffered the consequences; sin affected human as well as geographical reality.

Jerusalem would be restored to its original glory, but the sin that separated Israel—and through her mankind—from Jerusalem had to be overcome. The Mormon church made this possible, espousing conversion and restoration together.

Observations

The dialectical Zion of the Mormons, with its synthesis in America, was expressed, effectuated, and reinforced through Zion-as-Land-of-Israel activity. Orson Hyde traveled in Europe to stimulate the repentance and return of the Jews and prayed to God in Jerusalem to accelerate the onset of Christ-centered eschatology. George Adams set out to precipitate a Jerusalem-centered apocalypse by building the Land. The pilgrims of 1873 experienced the sacred Land and enunciated triumphalist Mormon theology. Overall, Mormon involvement with the Land had negative implications for Jews and Judaism. It developed in terms of the end of sinful Judaism and envisioned bringing about Christ's kingdom—as sublimated into the spiritual realm revealed to Joseph Smith.

Notes

1. Truman G. Madsen, *The Mormon Attitude toward Zionism* (Haifa 1981); William D. Davies, "Israel, the Mormons, and the Land," in Truman G. Madsen, ed., *Reflections on Mormonism: Judaeo-Christian Parallels* (Provo, Utah, 1978); Eldin Ricks, "Zionism and the Mormon Church," *Herzl Yearbook 5: Essays in Zionist History and Thought. Studies in the History of Zionism in America, 1894-1919* (New York 1963):147-174; Steven Epperson, *Mormons and Jews: Early Mormon Theologies of Israel* (Salt Lake City 1993).

2. Thomas F. O'Dea, "Who Are the Mormons?" in *The Mormons* (Chicago 1957):2.

3. See Karen Lynn, "The Mormon Zion and the Jewish Golden Land," *Modern Jewish Studies* 5 no. 4 (Fall 1984): 107-115; Joseph F. Smith, "The New Jerusalem or City Zion," *Church History and Modern Revelation* (Salt Lake City 1953):1:410-416.

4. James E. Talmage, *Jesus the Christ: A Study of the Messiah and His Mission according to Holy Scripture both Ancient and Modern* (Salt Lake City 1915):734.

5. Joseph Smith, *History of the Church of Jesus Christ of LDS*, 4th ed., Brigham H. Roberts, ed. (Salt Lake City 1964):3:388.

6. The relationships among Lehi's family, the American Indians, the Jewish crucifiers of Christ (see III *Nephi* 10:5-8 and 15:20), and the ancient tribes of Israel remain unclear to me. Eliza Snow, "The Gathering of the Saints and the Commencement of the City of Adam-ondi-Ahman," in *Poems: Religious, historical, political* (Liverpool 1856):1:7-14. On Snow's messianic expectations for America, see also "The Temple of God" and "A Word to the Saints Who Are Gathering," ibid., 91-94, 234-235.

7. [Benjamin Winchester], "The Location of Zion or the New Jerusalem," *The Gospel Reflector: In which the doctrine of the Church of Jesus Christ of LDS is set forth* 1 no. 7 (1 April 1841):213-217. See also idem, *"The Lord's Ensign and the Restoration of the House of Israel,"* ibid., 178-191; idem, "Evidence to Sustain the Divine Authenticity of the Book of Mormon," in *A History of the Priesthood: From the beginning of the world to the present time. Written in defense of the doctrine and position of the Church of Jesus Christ of LDS. And also a brief treatise upon the fundamental sentiments, particularly those which distinguish the above society from others now extant* (Philadelphia 1843):129-168.

8. [Joseph F. Smith, ed.], *Teachings of the Prophet Joseph Smith* (Salt Lake City 1938):362.

9. See Talmage, *A Study of the Articles of Faith* (Salt Lake City 1960):258-260, 350.

10. Joseph Smith, *Documentary History of the Church*:1:312-316, cited in Joseph F. Smith, *Teachings of the Prophet Joseph Smith* (Salt Lake City 1938):17-18.

11. See Joseph Smith III and Herman C. Smith, *A History of the LDS* (Lamoni, Iowa, 1901):391-396; Leroi C. Snow, "Who Was Professor Joshua Seixas?" *Improvement Era* 39 no. 2 (February 1936):67-71; Louis C. Zucker, "Joseph Smith as a Student of Hebrew," *Dialogue: A Journal of Mormon Thought* 3 no. 2 (Summer 1968):41-55; Lottie Davis, "Old Names, New Names," *Land of the Bible Newsletter* 1 no. 5 (May 1959):1, and 1 no. 7 (August-September 1959):1-2.

12. Oliver Cowdery, "A Remarkable Vision . . . Extract from *The LDS Messenger and Advocate (LDSMA)* (February 1835)," *LDS Millennial Star (LDSMS)* 1 no. (June 1840):42-44. Further installments from *LDSMA* (from April, July, and October 1835, pp. 109, 156, and 195) appeared in *LDSMS* 1 nos. 5, 6, and 7 (September-November 1840):105-109, 150-154, and 174-178.

13. Smith, *Teachings*, 26.

14. Ricks, "Zionism and the Mormon Church," 159.

15. Le Grand Richards, *Israel, Do You Know?* (Salt Lake City 1956):234-235.

16. Joseph M. Tanner, "The Zionist Movement," *Improvement Era* 3 no. 1 (November 1899):1-8.

17. See [Orson Hyde], *A Voice from Jerusalem; or, A sketch of the travels and ministry of Elder Orson Hyde, missionary of the Church of Jesus Christ of LDS, to Germany, Constantinople, and Jerusalem. Containing a description of Mount Zion, the Pool of Siloam, and other ancient places, and some account of the manners and customs of the East as illustrative of Scripture texts, with a sketch of several interviews and conversations with Jews, missionaries, etc., with a variety of information of the present state of that and other countries with regard to coming events and the restoration of Israel* (Boston 1842). See Aharon Jaffe, "The Contribution to Settlement and to the Development of Erets Israel on the Part of Four Protestant Denominations During the Nineteenth and Twentieth Centuries," (thesis, Hebrew University of Jerusalem, 1986, Hebrew); Howard H. Barron, *Orson Hyde* (Bountiful, Utah, 1977); Marvin S. Hill, "An Historical Study of the Life of Orson Hyde, Early Mormon Missionary and Apostle, 1805-1852" (thesis, Brigham Young University, 1955); Reed M. Holmes, *The Forerunners* (Independence, Mo., 1981):36-40.

18. Barron, *Orson Hyde*, 109.

19. [William E. Berrett and Alma P. Burton, eds.], "Orson Hyde's Credentials as a Missionary to Palestine," *Readings in LDS Church History* (Salt Lake City 1953):1:393-394.

20. Smith, *Teachings*, 163.

21. See George J. Adams, "Sectarian Folly and Wicked Made Manifest, northampton 22 June 1841," *LDSMS* 2 no. 3 (July 1841):33-37; idem, "Correspondence: Liverpool 14 December 1841 [to Elder Parley P. Pratt]," *LDSMS* 2 no. 8 (December 1841):141-143; idem, "Bedford, 5 October 1841, Beloved Brother [Parley P. Pratt]," *LDSMS* 2 no.

8 (December 1841):143-144; and idem, "Letter from Elder George J. Adams, New York 21 April 1842," *Times and Seasons (TS)* 3 no. 16/52 (15 June 1842):826-827.

22. Hyde, "Letter to Joseph Smith: Manchester 17 April 1841," *TS* 2 no. 18/30 (15 July 1841):482-483; idem, "Letter From Elder O. Hyde: London 15 June 1841," *TS* 2 no. 23/35 (1 October 1841):551-554; idem, "Rev. Dr. Solomon Hirschell, President Rabbi of the Hebrew Society in England," ibid., 554-555. How Hirschell would have responded may be surmised from his reaction to Joseph Wolff's request for an interview:

Dr. Hirschell acknowledges the receipt of Mr. Wolff's letter, but feels it is inconsistent with his official situation, as it is incongruous with his personal feelings, that he should admit Mr. Wolff to be capable of reporting any conversation between them on his return to Palestine.

Dr. H. has, however, no objection to receive any observation Mr. W. may think for to communicate to him in writing.

C. Duschinsky, "The Rabbinate of the Great Synagogue, London, 1756-1842 II," *Jewish Quarterly Review* n.s. 10 no. 4 (April 1920):503. Earlier, on 24 April 1822, Menahem Mendel ben Barukh Bendet of Shklov gave Wolff several letters to forward to Hirschell. [Joseph Wolff], "Extracts from the Journal of Mr. Wolff: Jerusalem 12 March 1822," *Jewish Expositor and Friend of Israel: Containing monthly communications respecting the Jews and the proceedings of the LJS (JEFI)* 7 (October 1822):417-427.

23. Tsevi-Hirsch Lehren was a founder of the Pekidim and Amarkalim society for helping Jews in the Holy Land. On Lehren (and his relationship to Hirschell) see Arye Morgenstern, "The Correspondence of Pekidim and Amarkalim as a Source for History of Erets Israel," *Cathedra* 27 (March 1983, Hebrew): 85-108. Myrtle S. Hyde wrote me, 13 October 1991, that the Amsterdam personality may have been one of two *dayanim*, J. S. Hirsch or Abraham Suzin.

24. Hyde, "Letter to Joseph Smith: Ratisbon on the Danube 17 July 1841," *TS* no. 24/36 (15 October 1841):570-573. I have been unable to identify the addresses that Hyde left in Amsterdam or the local rabbis in Bavaria.

25. Barron, *Orson Hyde*, 128.

26. Barron, *Orson Hyde*, 316-320.

27. On Whiting, see *Report of the ABCFM: Presented at the thirty-third annual meeting. Held in the city of Norwich, Connecticut, 13, 14, 15, and 16 September 1842* (Boston 1842):117. Gager (b. 1814), a "licentiate" of the Presbyterian or Congregational Church, left Jerusalem with Hyde and died in Cairo. [Hyde], *Voice from Jerusalem, 28.*

28. [Hyde], *Voice from Jerusalem,* 14-15.

29. [Hyde], "Letter from Elder O. Hyde [to Joseph Smith]: London 15 June 1841," *TS* 2 no. 23/35 (1 October 1841):551-552; Orson Hyde, *Ein Ruf aus der Wüste, eine Stimme aus dem Schoose der Erden: Kürzer Überblick des Ursprungs und der Lehre der Kirche Jesus Christ of LDS in Amerika, gekannt von Manchen unter der Benennung "Die Mormonen"* (Frankfurt 1842):106-107; idem, "News from the Old World: A Call from the Wilderness: A Voice out of the earth, a short review of the origin and teaching of

the Church of Jesus Christ of LDS in America, known by many by the name of Mormons, by Orson Hyde, Elder of said Church . . . Preface . . . Frankfurt am Main August 1842. Translated [into German] by Alexander Neibauer, a German Jew," *TS* 3 no. 24/60 (15 October 1842):949-951.

According to Joseph Wolff, Hyde's father, whose name was Heidelmann, was a German Jew who emigrated to England in the early part of the nineteenth century and became an Anglican. Heidelmann was to join the English mission in Jerusalem but instead married a Scottish woman, moved to Boston, and changed his name to Hyde. Joseph Wolff, *Travels and Adventures* (London 1860):2:537-570, cited in Jaffe, "The Contribution to Settlement."

30. Peter Amann, "Prophet in Zion: The Saga of George J. Adams," *New England Quarterly* 37 no. 4 (1 December 1964):477-500; E. Cecil McGavin, "Apostate Factions: Following the Martyrdom of Joseph Smith," *Improvement Era* 47 no. 8 (August 1944):498, 510; Reed M. Holmes, "G. J. Adams and the Forerunners," *Maine Historical Society Quarterly* 21 no. 1 (Summer 1981):19-52; Harold Davis, "The Jaffa Colonists from Downeast," *American Quarterly* 3 (1951): 344-356; George W. Chamberlain, "A New England Crusade," *New England Magazine* 36 no. 2 (April 1907):195-207. Adams changed his middle name from "James" to "Washington Joshua" after arriving in Palestine. Cf. Vivian D. Lipman, *Americans and the Holy Land through British Eyes, 1820-1917: A Documentary History* (London 1989).

31. Adams described his rapid conversion:
I am about 30 years of age, have been 13 years a Methodist, heard the first sermon by a Latter-Day Saint in February 1840 by Elder H. C. Kimball, and believed the gospel as soon as I heard it, and have never doubted it since. I was baptized eight days after I heard the first sermon, and called to be an Elder in eight days after I was baptized, called by the spirit of prophecy, by Elder Kimball, and ordained by Elder P. P. Pratt just previous to the time they sailed for England.
[George J. Adams], "Brother [Ebenezer] Robinson and [Don Carlos] Smith: New York 7 October 1840," *TS* 2 no. 2/14 (15 November 1840):220-221.

32. In October 1841, now separated from Hyde, Adams spoke in Liverpool:
I opened the discussion by showing that the Bible did not contain all the word of God, but that it spoke of many books written by the prophets which, if they had been in the Bible, would be Bible just as much as any of the books already contained in it.

I then set forth that the *Book of Mormon* was the book spoken of by *Isaiah* ch. 29, and also that it was the record of Joseph in the hands of Ephraim, to be brought forth in the last days, just previous to the gathering of Israel, and this in fulfillment of *Ezekiel* ch. 27 and many other plain prophetic declarations.

When my opponent arose he seemed astonished that I should prove the *Book of Mormon* true by the Bible.
Adams, "Correspondence, Liverpool 14 December 1841." See also idem, *A Few Plain Facts Showing the Folly, Wickedness, and Imposition of the Rev. Timothy R. Mathews: Also a short sketch of the rise, faith, and doctrine of the Church of Jesus Christ of LDS* (Bedford, England, 1841); "LDS or Mormons," *TS* 3 no. 17/53 (1 July 1842):835-836;

Adams, "What Do the Mormons Believe? A short sketch of the rise, progress, and faith of the LDS or Mormons," *Daily Bee* 2 no. 7 (27 February 1843), reprinted as *A Lecture on the Authenticity and Scriptural Character of the Book of Mormon: Delivered at the town hall, Charleston, Mass., on Sunday evening 4 February and Wednesday evening 7 February* (Boston 1844); idem, *A Lecture on the Doctrine of Baptism for the Dead: And preaching to spirits in prison. As originally delivered in the City of New York on 7 January 1844* (New York 1844); idem, *A Letter to his Excellency John Tyler, President of the United States: Touching the signs of the times, and the political destiny of the world* (New York 1844).

33. On Adams and Millerites see Adams, "Defamation of Character, "*Sword of Truth and Harbinger of Peace (STHP)* 1 no. 9 (1 June 1863):7. *STHP* was first published in south Lebanon, Me.; during 1864 it was moved to Indian River, Me.

34. "LDS or Mormons," *TS* 3 no. 17/53 (1 July 1842):835-836.

35. Adams, "What Do the Mormons Believe?"

36. Brigham Young, "Notices to the Churches Abroad," *TS* 6 no. 7/115 (15 April 1865):878. See George Adams, *A True History of the Rise of the Church of Jesus Christ of LDS—of the Restoration of the Holy Priesthood: And of the late discovery of Ancient American records collected from the most authentic sources ever published to the world, which unfold the history of this continent from the earliest ages, after the flood, to the beginning of the fifth century of the Christian era: With a sketch of the faith and doctrine of the Church of Jesus Christ of LDS. Also a brief outline of their persecution, and martyrdom of their prophet, Joseph Smith, and the appointment of his successor James J. Strang* (Baltimore [1846?]).

37. "The Church of the Messiah: Its history and rise - taken from the *Book of Remembrance* or *Record* of said Church. Chapter 1, "*STHP* 1 no. 2 (15 October 1862): 7. Successive chapters appeared in *STHP* 1 no. 3 (15 November 1862):7; no. 4 (1 January 1863):7; no. 5 (1 February 1863):7; no. 6 (1 March 1863):7; no. 7 (1 April 1863):3; no. 9 (1 June 1863):3; no. 10 (1 July 1863):7; 2 no. 10 (1 September 1864):7; 3 no. 2 (15 February 1865):5; and no. 4 (15 April 1865):7. Adams placed mainline Mormons in the same questionable light as other churches: "We shall seek for truth and contend for it, whether in the Catholic church, the Swedenborgian church, the Spiritual church, the Advent church, the Mormon church, or any of the long array of Protestant churches; we shall oppose error, false doctrine, tyranny, and priestcraft, wherever and whenever we encounter it." "Truth Endureth Forever. Prospectus of *STHP*," *STHP* 1 no. 1 (15 September 1862):7. Adams considered himself a Mormon until the end of his life. In 1860 his faith was a "[theological] Mormonism with the [cultural] Mormonism excised." In 1878 he made "overtures for admission into the Reorganized Church." Dale L. Morgan, "A Bibliography of the Church of Jesus Christ of LDS [Strangite]," *The Western Humanities Review* 5 no. 1 (Winter 1950-1951):43-126; idem, *A Bibliography of the Churches of the Dispersion* (n.p. 1953):177-178.

38. Adams, "The Jews, Jerusalem, and the Holy Land: The conversion of the Jews," *STHP* 1 no. 2 (15 October 1862):5. There was considerable discussion about Jews in *STHP*; for example, [Adams], "Literature of Jews"; idem, "Israel," *STHP* 1 no. 8 (1 May 1863):8; idem, *"The Wealth of the Jews,"* *STHP* 1 no. 4 (1 January 1863):6; L., "The Jewish Race," *STHP* 2 no. 2 (1 December 1863):3; Noel, "Claims of the Jews," *STHP* 3 no. 3 (15 March 1865):3.

39. Adams, "The Jews, Jerusalem, and the Holy Land - Jerusalem," *STHP* 2 no. 4 (15 February 1864):8.

40. Idem, *"Jerusalem and the Holy Land: Editorial journeying,"* *STHP* 3 no. 9 (1 November 1865):4-6.

41. Idem, "Palestine and the Emigration Thereunto," *STHP* 3 no. 11 (1 February 1866):5. See also idem, "A Poem: On the restoration of the Jews and the millennium. Written over twenty-five years ago," *STHP* 1 no. 1 (15 September 1862):8; *STHP* 1 no. 2 (15 October 1862):8; "Lecture: On the restoration of the Jews to the Land of Palestine, and their past, present and future destiny," *STHP* 1 no. 4 (1 January 1863):1-3, 6; successive lectures appeared in *STHP*, 1 no. 5 (1 February 1863):1-3; no. 6 (1 March 1863):1-3, 6; no. 7 (1 April 1863):1-2; no. 8; no. 9 (1 June 1863):1-3; and 4 no. 4 (15 September 1866):25-27; "Zion," *STHP* 2 no. 12 (1 December 1864):7; "Palestine As It Was and As It Is . . . Palestine as it becomes . . . Palestine as it will be in the Restoration," *STHP* 3 no. 12 (1 April 1866):1-2; "The Restoration of Israel: Association for Promoting Jewish Settlement in Palestine. Address to the public (by the Jews)," *STHP* 4 no. (15 May 1866):8; "Palestine - Once More . . . Palestine and the emigration thereunto . . . Our object in going to Palestine. . . . Our new home in Palestine," *STHP* 3 no. 12 (1 April 1866):18-19; [Adams], "Lecture: Israel and Jerusalem. An abridged extract from 'Briefs on Prophetic Themes,'" *STHP* 4 no. 6 (15 June 1867):1-2.

42. The passengers of the *Nellie Chapin* were listed in *STHP* 4 no. 5 (15 November 1866):38-39. Cf. Holmes, *Forerunners,* 165-170.

43. Cited in Holmes, *Forerunners,* 188-189.

44. On arousing corpses see Adams, "Spiritualism in All Ages," *STHP* 2 no. 4 (15 February 1864):2-3, who cites the views of Elias Boudinot.

45. See Robert Morris, John Sheville, Rolla Floyd, and Samuel Hallock, *Bible Witnesses from Bible Land: Verified in the researchers of the explorers and correspondents of the America-Holy Land exploration* (New York 1874); Rolla Floyd, *Letters from Palestine,* 1858-1912, H. P. Parsons, ed. (Dexter, Me., 1981).

46. Lipman, *Americans and the Holy Land,* 141.

47. George A. Smith, "Remarks by President George A. Smith, Delivered in the New Tabernacle, Salt Lake City, Sunday Afternoon, 22 June 1873: An account of his journey to Palestine," *Journal of Discourses by President Brigham Young and His Counselors, the Twelve Apostles, and Others* (Liverpool 1874):87-102.

48. Thomas de Witt Talmage, *Talmage on Palestine: A series of sermons* (Springfield, Ohio, 1890):20-21. Cf. idem, *The Utah Abomination: All sorts of cruelty, treachery, and murder, practices under a cloak of religion . . . A few facts with regard to the Utah "LDS." A sermon preached by the late Rev. T. de Witt Talmage, D. D., in the Tabernacle, Brooklyn, U.S., on 26 September 1880* (Brooklyn, N. Y., 1880).

49. James E. Hanauer, "Notes on the History of Modern Colonization in Palestine," *Palestine Exploration Fund Quarterly Statement* (London 1900):124-142.

50. See Edward W. Tullidge, *The Women of Mormondom* (New York 1877):481-486.

51. [George A. Smith, Lorenzo Snow, Paul A. Schettler, and Eliza R. Snow], *Correspondence of Palestine Tourists: Comprising a series of letters . . . Mostly written while traveling in Europe, Asia, and Africa, in the years of 1872 and 1873* (Salt Lake City 1875):1-2.
    Eliza Snow said Joseph Smith himself predicted her pilgrimage:
    Some years before the death of the prophet, Joseph Smith, long before the thought had entered the mind of Pres. Young to propose a visit to the "Holy Land," the prophet said to me, "You will yet visit Jerusalem." I recorded the saying in my *Journal* at the time, but had not reviewed it for many years, and the, for me, strange prediction had entirely gone from my memory—even when invited to join the tourist party, although the anticipation of standing on the sacredly celebrated Mount of Olives inspired me with a feeling no language can describe; Joseph Smith's prediction did not occur to me until within a very few days of the time set for starting, when a friend brought it to my recollection, and then by reference to the long neglected *Journal*, the proof was before us. While on the tour, the knowledge of that prediction inspired me with strength and fortitude.
    Eliza R. Snow "Sketch of My Life," Bancroft Libraries, University of California. I am indebted to Maureen U. Beecher for providing this citation.

52. See W. H. Hick, *General Grant's Tour Around the World: With a sketch of his life* (Chicago 1879):115-121; Haim Z. Sneersohn, "Rabbi Sneersohn and President Grant," in *Palestine and Romania: A description of the Holy Land and the past and present state of Romania and the Romanian Jews* (New York 1872):86-89. See Israel Klausner, *Rabbi Haim Z. Sneersohn* (Jerusalem 1943, Hebrew); Norton B. Stern and William M. Kramer, "Pre-Israeli Diplomat on an American Mission, 1869-1870," *Western States Jewish Historical Quarterly* 8 (1970):232-242. In November 1870 Brigham Young wrote Sneersohn about coming to Salt Lake City to speak in the Tabernacle. Sneersohn, *Palestine and Romania*, xv-xvi.

53. [George A. Smith et al.], *Correspondence*, 30-31.

54. Ibid, 203-205.

55. Avraham Ashkenazi wrote a commentary on the response of Rashba's student Avraham Tazarat, *Laws and Judgements*, 3 vols. (Jerusalem 1970, Hebrew) and for *Ha'levanon* and *Havatselet*. Cf. Cyrus Adler, *Memorandum on the Western Wall: Submitted to the special mission of the League of Nations on behalf of the Rabbinate, the*

Jewish Agency for Palestine, the Jewish community of Palestine, and the Central Agudat Israel of Palestine (Jerusalem 1930):53-57.

56. George A. Smith, "Remarks . . . 22 June 1873"

57. Eliza R. Snow, "At the Sea of Galilee," in *Poems: Religious, historical, and political* (Salt Lake City 1877):2:113-114.

58. [George A. Smith et al.], *Correspondence, 3.*

59. Snow, "Apostrophe to Jerusalem," in *Poems,* 210-213. The theme that Jerusalem's glory had departed was echoed by Mormon pilgrim Lydia Dunford Alder (b. 1846) when she poeticized about her 1905 Holy Land pilgrimage. She spoke about the beauty of ancient Jerusalem, with its inspiring Temple, where God's face could be seen in the Holy of Holies. But the people of Israel had sinned, and now they cried at "the senseless stones" of the Wall, worn smooth by their kisses and years. Alder begged God to forgive the Jews, who had suffered enough for their sins. "Heed Him [Jesus] / Who pleads, 'Forgive,'" she prayed. She expected that the Temple would stand again as earlier; that all Israel would confess that Jesus was Christ, Redeemer, God eternal; that Christ would be praised within the Temple: "Worthy the Lamb, He lives again who once was slain." Lydia D. Alder, *The Holy Land* (Salt Lake City 1912):250-251.

10 Judaism: American Impact and Internal Divisions

The views of the Holy Land within nineteenth-century Judaism were varied, differing not only among the Reform, Historical-Conservative, and Orthodox movements but within each of them as well.

Reform: Zion in America

Most Reform thinkers integrated Zion with America.[1] In 1825 Isaac Harby (1788-1828), a Reform pioneer in Charleston, south Carolina, identified America with the scriptural Land of promise:

> With what indescribable sensations must these pilgrims of the world have hailed the dawn of freedom as it illumined the western horizon! Here they have found a refuge and a home . . . Where is he that does not feel a glow of honest exultation, when he hears himself called an American . . . that does not offer praise and thanksgiving to providence, for the contrast of what man *is* in these United States, and what he *is* under almost every government. Thus appreciating, thus enjoying the natural and political blessings of our country, we are willing to repose in the belief that America truly is the Land of promise spoken of in our ancient scriptures; that this is the region to which the children of Israel, if they are wise, will hasten to come.

Moreover, the present Land of Israel was not physically viable:

> As regards the limits and resources of Palestine (however it may offend the pride of the ignorant), it is too true that the soil is poor and that the only navigable river throughout all Judea is the Jordan. From Dan to Beersheba, the proverbial limits of this small and renowned country are only 160 miles. Its breadth, if I extend it half that distance, I may extend too far. Of this

contracted space . . . the *Dead Sea*, that monument of wonder, occupies a considerable portion, and spreads desolation around. At present, the few scattered Arabs, the few Israelitish families, and the lazy population in this district, which belongs to the Ottoman empire, have barely the means of feeding themselves or their cattle, and numbers insufficient to resist aggression.

Within the limits of history, Harby was content with America. Israel's life beyond America should be left to the coming of the messiah:

> But, be the Promised Land what it may—whether new Jerusalem mean old Judea renovated and blessed by the munificence of heaven; or whether, with Chrysostom we take it to signify the city of God, happiness hereafter—yet we are contented, while we remain on earth in this temporal state, to live in America; to share the blessings of liberty; to partake of and to add to her political happiness, her power, and her glory; to educate our children liberally; to make them useful and enlightened and honest citizens; to look upon our countrymen as brethren of the same happy family worshipping the same God of the universe, though perhaps differing in focus and opinions. We are contented thus to act, and we hope and trust we act rightly and virtuously—until the annunciation of the *messiah* shall reunite us into one nation, offering with all mankind, in the name of the universal father, our common sacrifice on one common altar. Whether that annunciation be made this hour, or thousands of ages hence, let us, in the name of that *being*, who out of the depths heard the voice of His people, and brought them into salvation—that being who created all men for happiness and light and truth—let us, in His name, live in friendship with each other, and in charity with all mankind.[2]

In 1841, at the laying of the cornerstone of Bet Elohim Congregation, Charleston, the *hazan*, Gustavus Poznanski (1805-1879), dwelt on the civil and religious privileges enjoyed by the "House of Israel" in America, adding that

> This synagogue is our Temple, this city our Jerusalem, *this* happy land our Palestine, and as our fathers defended with their lives *that* Temple, *that* city, and *that* Land, so will their sons defend *this* Temple, *this* city, and *this* land, until the last drop of our blood shall be shed on the shrine of our religion and our country.[3]

At their conferences in Philadelphia (1869), Pittsburgh (1885), and Richmond (1886), Reform rabbis rejected the idea of return to and restoration of the Land of Israel. Isaac M. Wise (1819-1900) attacked the notion as "Zionmania." In the spirit of historical progress, Wise believed, American Jews should transcend primitive, national and soil-bound values and become universal. He predicted that by 1900 Tora principles would be implemented in America, which for him was the new messianic Zion. Wise also attacked those who lived in America while praying for Zion in the Land of Israel, accusing them of dual loyalties: it was unconscionable to pray for the messianic end to affliction while living in luxury. At most the Land of Israel could serve as a temporary refuge for Eastern European Jews where they could rehabilitate themselves through agriculture.[4]

David Einhorn wrote in his *Olat Tamid* (1856) prayerbook, "the one Temple in Jerusalem sank into the dust in order that countless temples might arise to know God all over the globe." America was Canaan, the Promised Land where Tora principles would be fulfilled, Washington, D.C., his new Jerusalem, the Capitol building his new Temple sanctuary. Even though he was repelled by American materialism and slavery, having earlier messianized Europe in his program of historically progressive Judaism, Einhorn was impelled to carry the messiah to America after Europe failed him.[5]

As mentioned above, Emil Hirsch opposed Blackstone's plans for restoration. Hirsch suspected missionary motives, and he was also convinced that modern Jews did not want restoration; for American Jews, America was Palestine. After the Blackstone Memorial episode Hirsch told Thomas de Witt Talmage that he thought "any Jew who has prospered in America would be a most foolish man if he were to remove to Palestine for any other than sentimental reasons."[6] Solomon Schindler, who also opposed Blackstone, thought that refuge in the Land was solely for Russian Jews, and the type of government they were liable to establish would probably evoke universal scorn. Schindler was afraid that if a Jewish commonwealth were established America would pressure Jews to go there. He wanted Jews to enter the spirit of whatever land they found themselves in.[7]

While Leo M. Franklin, future president of the Central Conference of American Rabbis (CCAR), was a student at Hebrew Union College (HUC) he rejected, in the name of open and progressive world culture and civilization, any territorially defined seclusion in Palestine. Savages might boast about pure race, but civilized human beings—especially Americans—took pride when a culture contained a mixture of races. It was madness to think of having a "national hermitage." Had the Jews never left Palestine they would have ended up in an "unmarked hermit's grave." They certainly would never have taught the world ethics, righteousness, and brotherhood. Franklin also considered the hope that territorial seclusion would end antisemitism erroneous. He wished that Jews everywhere, including those in the lands of persecution, would someday proclaim that "to be a Jew is an honor and a glory, to be a Jew in America is the noblest blessing of God."[8]

Hyman Enelow rejected the turn to Zion in the Land of Israel as violating the the universality of Jewish life. Identifying Zion with the particular Land of Israel was an anachronism involving the ancient practice where each deity had its special territory. In this case Jerusalem was Yahweh's territory. For the ancient

Jewish mind, God's presence was affirmed in terms of territorial annexation. Thus, by establishing Canaan as Yahweh's primordial home, the ancient Hebrews redeemed their obligation to God for the Egyptian liberation by establishing Him territorially. The Land/God identification had been expounded upon by prophets, Sages, and eschatologists to the point that it became a duty to live in Canaan and a beatitude to die there. For his part, Enelow subscribed to the view that the *shekhina* wandered and that Jewish life was universal, a view which spoke to the vitality of religion. The particularism of Zion, by contrast, was an archaic theological aberrancy, an "effete Jewish theology."

Specifically, the essence of Zionism was an ancient world phenomenon. As William R. Smith (1846-1894) put it, "In antique religion, gods as well as men have a physical environment, on and through which they act, and by which their activity is conditioned."[9] In ancient times gods had, so to speak, their "executive mansions." As long as the God of Israel was similar to other gods in terms of character, prestige, and power, He too was confined to this sort of limited sphere. Thus, Israel's conquest of Canaan meant subjugating local Baals and erecting the house of Yahweh planned by David—the true father of religious and political Zionism.[*] For the prophets, Yahweh was exclusive, and Zion and Jerusalem were inviolable. They had a nationalistic idea of God, and Yahweh had a particular residence. For example, Jerusalem might not have been conquered had Yahweh not left it right before the calamity, and Jerusalem would be rehabilitated once He returned.[†10] In Babylon, where the Israelites were without Yahweh, they could not sing His songs and became so despondent that they spoke of being in a valley of dry bones (Ezekiel 37).[‡] David regarded his expulsion from Judea as an enjoinder to worship strange gods.[#] As Ernest Renan (1823-1892) observed, the occupancy of Canaan brought on a religious retrogression because it banished the pure theistic universalism of the primitive Jewish mind and put in its place a cramped, nationalistic, localized concept.[11]

---

[*]"Go and tell My servant David, Thus saith the Lord, Shalt thou build Me an house for Me to dwell in? Whereas I have not dwelt in any house since the time that I brought up the children of Israel out of Egypt, even to this day, but have walked in a tent and in a tabernacle." *II Samuel* 7:5-6.

[†]"And, behold, the glory of the God of Israel came from the way of the East . . . And the glory of the Lord came into the house by the way of the gate whose prospect is toward the East." *Ezekiel* 43:1, 4.

[‡]*Psalms* 137:4, supra.

[#]"Now therefore, I pray thee, let my lord the king hear the words of His servant. If the Lord have stirred thee up against me, let Him accept an offering: But if they be the children of men, cursed by they before the Lord. For they have driven me out this day from abiding in the inheritance of the Lord, saying, Go, serve other gods." *I Samuel* 26:19.

Despite the physical conquests, Enelow continued, the religious inviolability of Jerusalem remained. It was still Yahweh's dwelling place, the only place where righteousness could be realized.* Once Jerusalem had been sanctified, it alone was fit for divine worship.† Jerusalem was to be Yahweh's eternal residence, forever sanctified as "Rest."‡ Even after its destruction, commitment to Yahweh's actual, physical dwelling place in Jerusalem was so strong that His return to His residence became a daily aspiration of the Jews. For example, soon after the Temple was destroyed in 70 C.E. the prayer "And to Jerusalem, the city, return in mercy and dwell therein as Thou hast spoken" was incorporated into the daily Eighteen Benedictions.[12] Eventually the inviolable sanctity of Jerusalem expanded to all of Palestine; it became a duty to live in the Holy Land. Indeed, it was better to live in the Land of Israel, even in a city where most residents were gentiles, than outside the Land in a city where all were Jewish (*Tosefta Avoda Zara* 4:3). Outside the Land of Canaan it was as if the people had no God.# To live outside the Land meant to be without God, to live in the Land meant to have a God.** Anyone who left Palestine voluntarily in peacetime was considered a willful idolater, whereas dwelling in the Holy Land was

---

*See, for example, *Psalms* 75:10: "All the horns of the wicked also will I cut off: but the horns of the righteous shall be exalted." "For there [Jerusalem] are set thrones of judgment, the thrones of the house of David. Pray for the peace of Jerusalem. They shall prosper that love thee." *Psalms* 122:5-6.

†"After the sanctification of Jerusalem it is not permissible [to set up high places elsewhere]." *Mishna Megilla* 1:11.

‡"'Rest'—'For ye are not as yet come to the *rest* and to the inheritance, which the Lord your God giveth to you' [*Deuteronomy* 12:9]—refers to Jerusalem. 'For the Lord hath chosen Zion; he hath desired it for his habitation. This is my rest forever: here will I dwell; For I have desired it' [*Psalms* 132:13-14]." Piska *66, Sifre* to *Deuteronomy*.

#"'I am the Lord your God, which brought you forth out of the land of Egypt, to give you the Land of Canaan, and to be your God' [*Leviticus* 25:38]. [That is] as long as you are in the Land of Canaan, behold I am God to you. When you are not in the Land of Canaan, so to speak I am not God to you." *Tosefta Avoda Zara* 4:4.

**"Our Rabbis taught, One should always live in the Land of Israel, even in a town most of whose inhabitants are idolaters, but let no one live outside the Land, even in a town most of whose inhabitants are Israelites; for whoever lives in the Land of Israel is like as if he has a God. But whoever lives outside the Land is like as if he has no God. For it is said in Scripture, 'To give you the Land of Canaan, and to be your God' [*Leviticus* 25:38]." *Ketubot* 110b.

equivalent to fulfilling all religious commands (Piska 80, *Sifre* to *Deuteronomy*). To be buried in the Land was like being buried beneath the altar of the Temple.*

The dogma of God's preference for Palestine reached into eschatology. The Sages accepted the prophetic vision of Zion as the scene of redemption.† As to how people from the world over could be accommodated in Jerusalem, Rabbi Levi explained that Jerusalem was destined to become as large as the entire Land of Israel, and the Land of Israel to become as large as the whole world (*Midrash Pesikta Rabbati* 2a). Residence in the Land guaranteed a place in the world to come.‡ The Land, and Jerusalem in particular, meant life.#

Enelow chose for himself the tradition where the *shekhina* was also outside Palestine. The God-in-Jerusalem principle of primitive theology survived unconsciously among some Jews, especially Kabbalists. But the religious mind of Israel generally deviated from it, and Jerusalem lost its monopoly on divine presence and on mediating between the Jew and God.** The *shekhina* wandered with Israel "from Babylon to Persia, from Persia to Greece, from Greece to Rome" (*Midrash Psalms* 120:5). During the Talmudic period God's presence was freed from the cincture of Zionism. The Tora, not Palestine, became the chief bond of union between the people and God. Wherever the knowledge and morality of Judaism were cultivated, there was the new Palestine. Thus Rabbi Judah says, "to live in Babylon was like living in the Land of Israel; for it is said in Scripture, 'Ho Zion, escape, thou that dwellest with the daughter of Babylon' [*Zechariah* 2:7]." Accordingly he says in Samuel's name, "As one was forbidden to emigrate from the Land of Israel to Babylon, so one was not allowed to leave Babylon for any other country" (*Ketubot* 111a). The consequent development of new centers for study and the spread of Judaism, Enelow concluded, signified the

---

*"Rabbi Anan said, Whoever is buried in the Land of Israel is deemed as if buried under the altar; since in respect of the latter it is written in Scripture, 'An altar of earth shalt thou make unto Me' [*Exodus* 20:21], and in respect of the former it is written in Scripture, 'And His Land doth make expiation for His people' [*Deuteronomy* 32:43]." *Ketubot* 111a.

†"And it shall come to pass, that from one new moon to another, and from one sabbath to another, shall all flesh come to worship before Me saith the Lord." *Isaiah* 66:23.

‡"'And spirit to them that walk therein' [*Isaiah* 42:5], said Rabbi Jeremiah bar Abba in the name of Rabbi Yohanan, that whoever walks four cubits in the Land of Israel is assured of a place in the world to come." *Ketubot* 111a.

#"The Land of Israel is designated living, as it is stated, 'And I will set glory in the land of the living' [*Ezekiel* 26:20]. Jerusalem is described by the expression *living*, as it is stated 'Even every one that is written among the living in Jerusalem' [*Isaiah* 4:3]." *Abot de Rabbi Nathan* 34:11.

**"Come and see how dear Israel is to God; to what place soever Israel has been exiled, the *shekhina* has been exiled with Israel." Piska 74, *Sifre* to *Numbers*.

practical decay of Zionism as a religious dogma, though it may have lived on in theory as an archaic theological aberrancy.[13]   Opposed to Zion in the Land of Israel, Enelow was left to focus any Zionist dreams he may have had on a life of sharing God's *shekhina* in America.

Reform and Zion-as-Land-of-Israel

Bernhard Felsenthal (1822-1908) drew Zion-in-the-Land-of-Israel into the present; he was convinced that by the turn of the century every Jew would be a Zionist. He identified ethnic nationality as Judaism's unifying factor and the basis of Jewish religion. The Jews had been scattered for most of their history but were united by national affinity. Religion contributed to the unity of the people in exile but only because there already was a national strength: "First the Jewish nation and then, as one of the characteristics of this nation, the Jewish religion." Thus the institutions, rituals, festivals, and ceremonies which made up much of the religion were drawn from the national being of the people. A political center would assure and enhance the national identity by preventing assimilation and stopping antisemitism. It would strengthen that affinity which Jews felt for each other as part of a nation, which drew them closer to one another and alleviated suffering. In addition it would have positive ramifications for the rest of man by evoking the sympathy of the world's nations for the persecuted and by allowing Jews to contribute to the "Grand Temple of Humanity."

If the "Zionistic" movement failed, on the other hand, the existence of the Jewish nation as separate and distinct could no longer be assumed. Felsenthal thought that a speedy extinction could be realistically expected, that the "disappearance of Israel from the world will become a sad fact." Assimilation and antisemitism were the major threats. The assimilation preached by anti-Zionists led to amalgamation, absorption, and ultimately the total annihilation of Israel. To be sure, some people honestly thought that "mankind would best be served by Israel committing a national suicide," but millions differed—most of whom had suffered because they were Jews. The contemporary plight of the Jews was incomparably tragic.   The most effective way to alleviate the degradations, expulsions, and deprivations was Jewish colonization of Palestine. Antisemitism would not cease until Israel had her national home.

When it came to the state he envisioned, Felsenthal spoke in romantic and idealistic generalities. It would be a model of justice, love, incorruptibility, peace, truth, freedom for the expression of all honest convictions and tolerance for doctrinal commitments. The state would have neither legal nor ecclesiastical power over Jews in the diaspora. The relationship would rather be one in which the state awakened a stronger and deeper attachment to the religion of Judaism and a shift from vulgar materialism to idealism. Felsenthal believed that the Land itself could become as agriculturally productive, populous and flourishing as during the time of Josephus (b. 38 C.E.). He thought that by 1907 there could be 50,000 Jews flourishing there, and he referred to a report by the U.S. consul in Jerusalem (presumably Edwin S. Wallace) to this effect.[14] Once a large majority of the inhabitants were Jewish, self-government would be justified, just as it had been with Greeks and Bulgarians. Felsenthal wanted a Jewish republic governed according to the principles of Jeffersonian democracy, not a Mosaic theocracy or government by Talmudic law. Each citizen would have the constitutional right to serve God according to the dictates of his conscience without fear of molestation—to be Orthodox or "progressive" Jew, Christian or Muslim. Each religion would possess its holy places; e.g., the Muslims would have the Mosque of Omar and the Cave of Makhpela, and the Christians would have the Holy Sepulcher.[15]

After the 1897 Basel Zionist congress, William Fineshriber (1878-1968) echoed the view that Jewish religion required Jewish nationalism and added that the distinctiveness of the Jewish race made nationalism natural. Caspar Levias (1860-1934) attacked the 1898 CCAR declaration in Cincinnati that a Jewish state was contrary to Israel's mission.[16]

Historical School: Zionism Both Present and Future

In the 1830s Isaac Leeser expressed confidence in the ultimate restoration of the Land and the ingathering of captives, but Israel had to resign herself to waiting until God would arrange it. Leeser thought that Mordecai M. Noah's drive for restoration would fail because God did not ordain it and that even though the Land was inhabited by alien religions and thieves while diaspora Jews were deprived of legal autonomy and enticed away from Judaism, Israel still had to wait for God to send the messiah and end the dispersion. What should Jews do in the meantime? Pray to God, repent for the sins of the people, do good deeds, and unify.[17]

In the late 1840s Leeser began changing his position concerning divine control. He urged his readers not to wait for God: divine initiative might not occur for another millennium. Meanwhile, there was the Damascus blood libel (1840), the Mortara kidnapping (1858), and General Grant's expulsion of Jews from the Tennessee military district (1862). Leeser now spoke about rebuilding Palestine within the framework of nature, even without revelation. He expected America, given her freedom, culture, and material well-being, to foster both Judaism and the restoration of the Jewish state.[18] He proposed agricultural and welfare programs and encouraged those in the Land to build libraries and hospitals. He hoped that diaspora Jews who could work—not just those ready to die—would go to the Land. By 1864 he sensed that restoration was actually underway and that very soon Palestine would be a Land for the Jews.[19]

Toward the end of the century a number of Zionist spokesmen emerged from within Historical-Conservative Judaism, and with a variety of positions.

Benjamin Szold (1829-1902) wrote in his *Avodat Israel* prayerbook that God consecrated whichever place He sent Israel to—but Szold also helped establish the Zionist Association of Baltimore.[20] Henry Pereira Mendes spoke of realizing Zion in the Land of Israel as a paradigm for justice, prayer, and education, making it a source for universal "spiritual" revival. When he reported on the 1897 Zionist congress in Basel, he pointed out that hopes for Palestine were distinct from other national hopes because they had no hint of "appeal to sword, to vomiting death-tubes, or to any of war's cursed furies." For him the Zionism of Basel was unlike the early nationalism of Bar Kokhba or the messianic movements of David Reuveni (d. 1538?), Solomon Molkho (1500-1532) and Shabbetai Tsevi (1626-1676). Basel did not advocate taking up weapons, either out of despair or irrational folly. Its program was based upon "a holy love of peace, a consciousness that time's wheel would bring the laggard justice to the side of the Jew." The congress sounded the "deathless nation's" call to the world to realize the biblical ideals of applied justice, quicken religious sentiment, and enhance the brotherhood of man and the fatherhood of God. Mendes also put his own thoughts into verse and, as if to emphasize the harmony between America and Israel, set it to the tune of "My Country, 'Tis of Thee":

> God, we implore of Thee
> And Zion misery,
>   Send her thine aid!
> Send Thou her sons to heal
> Wounds which the years reveal,
> Woes which at last in weal
>   For aye shall fade!

> God, loving, tender, good!
> As if in widowhood
>   She weeps for Thee!
> Be once more reconciled,
> As father pities child,
> Pity her grief so wild—
>   She weeps for Thee!

> Now bid her weep no more,
> Do Thou her sons restore—
>   Love-gift from Thee!
> Make those who still would stay
> In other lands obey
> Thy holy law, that they
>   World-priests may be!

For some by Thy command
Must live in ev'ry land
  To make Thee known!
Priests to the world are we,
This is our destiny,
For all shall bend the knee
  To Thee alone![21]

In 1899 Mendes's answer to whether a Jewish state should be established was an emphatic "Yes!" He sharpened his spiritual description of Zion: "This is what I understand by a Jewish state. A spiritual center, whence spirituality shall radiate to the end of the world." An American stood for material aspirations, a Jew for spiritual ones. The Jewish state was not necessary solely for national purposes, such as protection of citizenship rights; loyal citizenship by Jews had already brought protection in the gentile nations. Rather, the state would fulfill spiritual purposes, and so it was essential for the existence of society overall, for human liberty and the progress of humanity. The "temporal" concerns of Jews within and without the Land's borders should be secondary. For example, while Mendes did not object to the state's serving as refuge for oppressed Jews, for it to serve solely as such would belittle it. Although the Land's geography and resources could be great financial investments, this was the least worthy reason for a state. Instead, Mendes thought that from the state's "temple or college or university will proceed the highest expressions of thought for human guidance" and help in improving society and fostering liberty and human progress in all lands. As to Jews in particular, the state would exercise no temporal power over the diaspora nor claim the citizenship of diaspora Jews. It would claim spiritual loyalty, similar to Rome vis-à-vis world Catholics but without Rome's claim of temporal power. The Bible limited such powers to the area "from the White or Snow Mountain, usually called Lebanon, on the north, to the desert on the south, from the Mediterranean and river of Egypt on the West, to the Euphrates on the East."* Jews outside would remain loyal to the country of residence and serve it faithfully. They would look to Palestine for spiritual guidance, for example, in changing Jewish laws. Mendes foresaw a religious council, responsive to contemporary religious thought but faithful to Tora, which would serve as a supreme court for world Jewry. It would do such things as resolve disputes between Orthodoxy and Reform and provide a common standard for Judaism throughout the world. Above all, a spiritual force would flow from Palestine to

---

*"Will a man leave the snow of Lebanon which cometh from the rock of the field? or shall the cold flowing waters that come from another place be forsaken?" *Jeremiah* 18:14. "In the same day the Lord made a covenant with Abram, saying, Unto thy seed have I given this Land, from the river of Egypt unto the great river, the river Euphrates." *Genesis* 16:18.

quicken Jewish religious sentiment. It would inspire Jews to be "priests" who taught the pure, moral, ideal life for society, business, and politics by personal example.[22]

Mendes reiterated these ideas through the period of the Balfour Declaration (2 November 1917). Then he said the world university in the Land of Israel would have the "best brains of the world"; the state would be the world's religious and spiritual center. Palestine regained—must be made to mean "God first, the Jews second."[23]

Orthodox Messianism

Abraham J. G. Lesser held the traditional view of Zion, that it would be brought into reality by God alone.[24] Trained at the Mir Yeshiva and under Isaac Elhanan Spektor (1817-1896) in Kovno, Lesser served as rabbi in Eastern Europe and came to Chicago in 1880 to lead the Bet Hamidrash Hagadol U'bene Ya'akov Synagogue. In 1898 he moved to Cincinnati's Bet Tefilla Congregation. When William E. Blackstone attended Lesser's Passover Seder on 4 April 1890 he asked Lesser, upon Felsenthal's suggestion, to provide classical Jewish sources to support the 5 March 1891 petition to President Harrison. Lesser agreed lest Jewish loyalty to America become a matter for suspicion. But because the text Lesser produced, *In the Last Days* (1897), did not demonstrate that "the time of mercy" had arrived, Blackstone decided against publishing it. Lesser published it himself, afraid that someone might get hold of it, change it, and have it printed. He also did not want to give the impression that American Jews had any secrets to keep from their fellow citizens.

In the book Lesser warns against fraudulent messiahs and speaks of the end of exile as being in the distant future. For the time being Jews should be loyal citizens of America. Since redemption is far off, there is no conflict between being a loyal Jew in America and a Jew who hopes for messianic redemption—no more than there is between living a full life and hoping for a good afterlife at the same time. The prophet Jeremiah, for example, spoke of patriotism in the land of exile along with future restoration of the Land of Israel.* In Lesser's view it is up to God to initiate redemption; He will disclose Israel's righteousness and the truth of His law to the world. He will have world leaders arrange the ingathering, even have the nations of the world ask for Israel's forgiveness for persecut-

---

*"And seek the peace of the city whither I have caused you to be carried away captives, and pray unto the Lord for it: for in the peace thereof shall ye have peace." *Jeremiah* 29:7.

ing her.* Indeed, they will return Israel to her Land in chariots bedecked with robes of gold and purple, as Israel once brought the meal and firstfruit offerings into the Temple with song, timbrel, and harp.[†25]

Orthodox Zionism

On the other side, there were Zionist Orthodox Jews who spoke of initiating an immediate return. In *The Question of the Jews* (1893) Ralph B. Raphael (b. 1856), who arrived in America in 1871 and became the patriarch of Pittsburgh Zionists, criticized Orthodox Jews for studying *Zeraim* about the Land's agriculture while the Land itself was being used by strangers. He thought it foolish of Reformers to expect Christians to forget that Judaism testified against Christianity and to embrace Israel. The *maskilim* (proponents of enlightenment) were rushing into non-Jewish culture while antisemites like Adolf Stoecker (1835-1909) and August Rohling (1839-1931) were waiting there to assault them. Raphael was concerned that, because of their sedentary lifestyles, American Jews were letting themselves go physically. He believed that while American antisemitism might be in remission, it was bound to return; the only sensible path was settlement in the Land of Israel. By working the Land Jews could restore nature to its rightful role in Jewish life. With settlement the holy life spelled out in the Talmud could be implemented. Jews would finally be rescued from the gentiles and even have a foundation upon which to wreak vengeance against them. Jews could join the human family, which would share religious principles and respect theological differences.

Raphael had specific plans. A vanguard of pioneers would establish a republican government, a "Sanhedrin," a president and an army under Turkish authority. He wanted immigration to begin immediately and envisioned two million settlers by the early 1940s. At some point, agricultural development and massive settlement would constitute justification for a sovereign state. *Teshuva* (religious return) and redemption would follow and "set the cornerstone to rebuild the destroyed wall" of the Temple. The prelude to the messianic kingdom would include revived Talmudic holiness, reconciliation with nature, and justice vis-à-vis the gentile world.[26]

---

*"Thus saith the Lord God, Behold I will lift up Mine hand to the gentiles, and set up My standard to the people: and they shall bring thy sons in their arms, and thy daughters shall be carried upon their shoulders. And kings shall be thy nursing fathers, and their queens thy nursing mothers: they shall bow down to thee with their face toward the earth, and lick up the dust of thy feet: and thou shalt know that I am the Lord: for they shall not be ashamed that wait for Me." *Isaiah* 49:22-23.

†*Exodus* 28:6, supra. "Let them praise his name in the dance: let them sing praises unto him with the timbrel and harp." *Psalms* 149:3.

Simon I. ("Rashi") Finkelstein, born in Slobodka, came to America in 1886 and served as rabbi and *av bet din* (religious court head) in Baltimore (1886-1890), Cincinnati (1890-1896), Syracuse (1896-1902), and Brooklyn (1902-1947).[27] In *Harvest of Grapes* (1899)—endorsed by his mentor, Isaac Elhanan Spektor—Finkelstein explained that life in and of Tora was available naturally in the Land of Israel while religious Jewish life in exile would only get worse.[28] Exilic life would become so overwhelmed by outside influences that Jews would no longer even recognize the dangers to their Tora identity. Involvement in diaspora, with its material benefits, was incompatible with Tora. Finkelstein observed that Jews who were oppressed, hungry, and disgraced—i.e., alienated in exile—remained strong in their faith and holiness; those who took advantage of their freedom and equality and succumbed to material and societal values had their faith and holiness weaken. He advocated immediate *aliya*. Theoretically, Jews could wait passively until their rulers allowed them to return to their Land—Finkelstein presumed that all Jews ultimately would want or be forced to return—but by then authentic Jewish identity would be irretrievably lost while the Land would be taken over by other nations.

He cited a story about Rabbi Yehoshua bar Hananiah (*Baba Batra* 73a). Rabbi Yehoshua came upon a child at a crossroad and asked him the way to the city. The child said he could take a short path which would turn out to be long (a shortcut with terrible obstacles) or the long way which would turn out to be short (a long road easily traveled). The rabbi took the short path, but when he reached the city's outskirts he was blocked by a thick garden. Similarly, Finkelstein explained, the people of Israel were at a crossroads vis-à-vis their Land. Taking the shortcut that would turn out to be long, contemporary Israel sat quietly and took refuge under the shadow of the nations. Jews were good citizens and beloved. They hoped that love would move the nations to let Israel return to the Land of her fathers. This hope was empty, however, and the shortcut was deceptive. Instead, Israel was now actually moving further and further from her inevitable, central religious identity and restoration. He offered the precedent of Balak, king of Moab, who seduced Israel into becoming one with the nation of Moab by having its women attract the men of Israel (*Numbers* 22-24). There were short-term satisfactions, but involvement with Moab meant distancing from Judaism. That is, sooner or later Israel had to go to her Land, and it would be better that she went sooner. There was also the precedent of the Egyptian exodus: the people of Israel did not go through Philistine territory, even though that was the quickest way, because they might have become embroiled in war and considered returning to Egypt.* The shortest path would have led Israel astray, away from her destined goal. The point was clear: if Israel became attached to the nations of the world and avoided emigrating to the Land of her fathers, the wait for her Tora/Land identity—both desirable and inevitable—would be longer. Involvement with other nations would only delay the achievement of her goals. Instead of being co-opted by the outside world, Israel should renounce material wealth. Finkelstein wanted Jews to gather together, gird themselves with their weapon of war (Tora), and aim for the Land. At first the path would be longer and more difficult. But once initial difficulties were overcome Israel could easily reach the goal. As in the days of Cyrus of Persia some wealthy Jews did not return when they had the opportunity, so Jews at the end of the nineteenth century were being misdirected. However, if the people were united around their own religious center they could be turned.

In a related story, Rabbi bar bar Hanna tells about a group of people who happened upon a flock of geese (*Baba Batra* 73a). Some were so fat their feathers fell out and they could not fly. They mistakenly thought they had a place in the world to come. As explained by Rabbi Eleazar, the "fatness" within Israel was sinful; it meant intensified suffering and would delay the coming of the messiah.† For Finkelstein these "fat geese" were exilic Jews obsessed with the abundance in diaspora lands, with salary, status and career. These things did nothing to prevent the inevitable pain of diaspora; if anything they intensified the pain and delayed relief. Like the geese who could no longer fly, Finkelstein seemed to say, these Jews moved neither toward their inner Judaism nor to the Land.

In another story (*Baba Batra* 73a), Rabbi bar bar Hanna says he was traveling in the desert and met an Arab merchant. The merchant was able to tell where water could be found, near or far, just by smelling the sand. Similarly, the water of Tora could be near or far. Rabbi Yehoshua ben Levi explained that Tora became distant when people spent their time gathering wealth and had no time or energy left for study; Aaron and Moses, who were of Tora, did not pursue worldly pleasures.‡ Ultimately Tora was only in the Land of Israel, not

---

*"And it came to pass, when Pharaoh had let the people go, that God led them not through the way of the land of the Philistines, although that was near; for God said, Lest peradventure the people repent when they see war, and they return to Egypt." *Exodus* 13:17.

†See, for example, *Deuteronomy* 32:15: "But Jeshurun waxed fat, and kicked: thou art waxen fat, thou art grown thick, thou art covered with fatness; then he forsook God which made him, and lightly esteemed the Rock of his salvation."

‡"Thou didst blow with thy wind, the sea covered them; they sank as lead in the mighty waters." *Exodus* 15:10.

outside. In the Land of Israel the people were of Tora.* Although the glory of God filled the whole world, God's face was never hidden in the Land. When Jews lived in the Land of Israel their souls felt the presence of God. Outside the Land, although God was present, people were confused by temporal satisfactions, and God was not apparent to them. Rabbi Hiyya bar Gamada kissed the sand of the Land of Tora (*Ketubot* 12a) because it was a source of Tora, its atmosphere promoted Tora. In the lands of the gentiles there were too many obstacles, and they turned the heart from God.[29]

In 1947 Finkelstein spelled out his Zionism as follows:

The rebuilding of Palestine is of course a central motif in the Jewish prayerbook. The hope of our fathers, like our own, is that in the fullness of time, God will in His mercy bring about the resettlement of large numbers of the people of Israel in Palestine, imbue them with a renewed faith in Him, so that their community may again be a "kingdom of priests and a holy nation."[†] Ever since my youth I have myself been identified with the movement to restore Jews to Palestine, and I have spoken as energetically as I could on behalf of the efforts for this cause. I find the contemporary attitude of the world toward the problem of Erets Israel baffling and confusing; but I cannot doubt that in the course of time, perhaps even in our generation, the hope of centuries will be fulfilled, and there will be an effective Jewish settlement in Palestine.[30]

He did, however, set aside the earlier mutual exclusivity between Tora life in the Land of Israel and non-Tora life outside. He was overwhelmed by America's liberty and equality and found biblical meaning in them:

I feel that I am thoroughly American, loving my country with a passion possible only for one who has known autocracy. My heart swells with gratitude at the words, "I am an American." Among the many benefits which kind Providence has showered on me, none, it seems to me, outweighs that which guided me to the shores of this blessed land. I know of no merit on my part which can have justified this remarkable grace to me, denied to so many of my kindred; it was like God's gift to man generally, an undeserved expression of love. Nothing that I can do in the thankfulness and sense of obligation which comes over me, when I consider that He has redeemed me from the dungeon of Tsarism into which I was born and in which I was reared, and brought me to these shores.

Ketubot 110b, supra.
[†]"And ye shall be unto Me a kingdom of priests, and an holy nation." *Exodus* 19:6.

I love America, not primarily for its plenty, its high standard of living, its magnificent resources and power. The vast material improvement in my life which America has meant is secondary to the joy I derive from the spirit of the land . . . The feelings that overwhelmed me when I was admitted to American citizenship, when I first voted for an American president, when I watched my eldest child being registered in a public school, are ineffable. It was the breaking of a dawn after a long dark night. America represents for me a closer fulfillment of the biblical doctrine of human equality and the commandment to love one's neighbor as oneself than I had expected to see on earth, short of the coming of the messiah himself.[31]

Observations

Nineteenth-century Judaism divided into various positions vis-à-vis the Holy Land. The Reformers split into two wings. Those who identified Zion with America ranged from the view equating America with ancient Palestine (Poznanski), to the view that history moved ahead and America represented the latest and best expression of the components of Zion (Einhorn), to the view that Zion in the Land of Israel was a regression to primitive beliefs (Enelow). Those who identified Zion with the Land of Israel took either the mediated position, that life in America was appropriate for the present and that return to the Land was for the messianic future (Harby), or identified Judaism with an ethnic center which required an immediate political context to survive (Felsenthal). Historical-Conservative thinkers ranged from the view that historical conditions demanded human initiative in what was ultimately a divinely arranged drama of return (Leeser) to the view that there must be a homeland for Jewry now, one which was spiritual rather than political and part of worldwide spiritual Judaism (Mendes). Within Orthodoxy, Lesser took the mediated position, that Americans were to be loyal citizens without compromising their hopes for a messianic future; Raphael had an immediate plan for building a Jewish homeland; and Finkelstein believed that Tora life was incompatible with materialism and ultimately possible only in the Land, although later in life he was content to live in America and enjoy her sociopolitical and spiritual benefits.

In all, with the notable exception of Raphael, American Jewish thinkers of the nineteenth century confirmed the positive experience of America but differed in the degree of their confirmation. Several Reformers (Einhorn, Wise, Franklin, Enelow) wanted America and rejected the Land of Israel; Historical-Conservative and Orthodox thinkers combined America and the Land and resolved the relationship through time. They differed on man's role vis-à-vis God, with Leeser passing from a heteronomous position where God controlled all to a heteronomous-autonomous position, Lesser opting for a God-given drama, and Finkelstein supporting human efforts within a divine context. The Jewish thinkers did not take hard "party" lines. There was more in common between Harby and Lesser than between Enelow and Felsenthal; more between Raphael and Leeser than the realist Leeser and the spiritual Mendes. That is, the American experience became the crucial index for their deliberations.

Notes

1. See Arthur J. Lelyveld, "The Conference View of the Position of the Jew in the Modern World," in Bertram W. Korn, ed., *Retrospect and Prospect* (New York 1965):129-180; David Polish, *Renew Our Days: The Zionist Issue in Reform Judaism* (Jerusalem 1976); Alfred Gottschalk, "Israel and Reform Judaism," *Forum* 36 (Fall/Winter 1979):143-160; Evyatar Friesel, *The Zionist Movement in the United States, 1897-1914* (Tel Aviv 1970, Hebrew); Herschel Levin, "The Other Side of the Coin," *Herzl Yearbook 5: Essays in Zionist History and Thought. Studies in the History of Zionism in America, 1894-1919* (1963):11-31, 33-56; Naomi W. Cohen, *American Jews and the Zionist Idea* (New York 1975); Michael Meyer, "American Reform Judaism and Zionism: Early Efforts at Ideological Rapprochement," *Studies in Zionism 7* (Spring 1983):49-64.

2. Isaac Harby, *Discourse: Before the Reformed Society of Israelites for Promoting True Principles of Judaism According to Its Purity and Spirit. Delivered by appointment, in Charleston, S. C., on 21 November, 1825* ([Charleston? 1825?]):82-87.

3. "The Rebuilding of the Temple," *Charleston Courier* 39 no. 11, 731 (20 March 1841):2. Leeser commented that Poznanski "evidently denied the coming of the messiah, and the restoration of the Temple and the ancient worship." Isaac Leeser, "True and False Worship," *OAJA* 9 no 4 (July 1851):207-221.

4. Sidney Akselrad, "Leeser and Wise on the Messiah and Mission of Israel," (thesis, Hebrew Union College, 1947); Isaac M. Wise, trans., "Ninth of Av: Elegy of Rabbi Judah Halevi," *Minhag Amerika: The daily prayers I. Revised and complied by the Committee of the Cleveland Conference* (Cincinnati 1857):103-105.

5. Akselrad, "Leeser and Wise"; Gershon Greenberg, "The Messianic Foundation of American Jewish Thought: David Einhorn and Samuel Hirsch," *Proceedings of the Sixth World Congress of Jewish Studies 2* (Jerusalem 1975):215-226; Ralph D. Mecklenburger, "The Theologies of I. M. Wise and Kaufmann Kohler" (thesis, HUC, 1972); Richard Levy, "Messianism in Reform Judaism during the Nineteenth and Twentieth Centuries" (thesis, HUC, 1960).

6. Anita L. Lebeson, "Zionism Comes to Chicago," in Isidore S. Meyer, ed., *Early History of Zionism in America,* (New York 1958):155-190.

7. Marnin Feinstein, "The Blackstone Memorial," *Midstream* 10 no. 2 (June 1961):76-89.

8. Leo Franklin, "A Danger and a Duty Suggested by the Zionist Agitation," *HUC Journal* 2 nos. 5 and 6 (March 1898):143-147.

9. William R. Smith, *Lectures on the Religion of the Semites* (London 1894):91ff.

10. Enelow cited *Ezekiel* 10 and 11, but I did not find the evidence.

11. Ernest Renan, *Histoire du Peuple d'Israel* (Paris 1893-1895):1:110-173ff.

12. See Leopold Zunz, *Die göttesdienstliche Vorträge der Juden, historisch entwickelt*, 2nd ed. (Frankfurt am Main 1892):380-381.

13. Hyman Enelow, "Zionism as a Theologic Dogma," *HUC Journal* 5 nos. 5 and 6 (1901):108-117, passim.

14. The correspondence and reports of U.S. consular agents in Jerusalem covering Wallace's tenure are held by the U.S. National Archives and Records Service, Washington, D.C., under "Records of the Foreign Service Posts of the Department of State, RG 84—Jerusalem, 1856-1906."

15. Bernhard Felsenthal, "An Open Letter on Zionism" (1897), "As to a Jewish State" (1899), "Jew as Politician" (1899), "Jewish *Weltanschauung*" (1902), "Israel's Mission and Kindred Conceptions" (1902), all in Emma Felsenthal, *Bernhard Felsenthal: Teacher in Israel* (New York 1924):256-264; Michael A. Meyer, "American Reform Judaism."

16. Gottschalk, "Israel and Reform Judaism."

17. Leeser, *The Jews and the Mosaic Law* (Philadelphia 1834):156; idem, "The Messiah," in *Discourses, Argumentative and Devotional, on the Subject of the Jewish Religion: Delivered at the Synagogue Mikve Israel in Philadelphia in the years 5590-5597* (Philadelphia 1837):2: discourse 49 no. 6; Maxine Seller, "Isaac Leeser's Views on the Restoration of a Jewish Palestine," *American Jewish Historical Quarterly (AJHQ)* 58 no. 1 (September 1968):118-135; Akselrad, "Leeser and Wise"; Moshe Davis, "A Highway of Nations: A Chapter in 19th Century America-Erets Israel Activities," in Daniel J. Silver, ed., *In the Time of Harvest: Essays in Honor of Abba Hillel Silver on the Occasion of His 70th Birthday* (New York 1963):136-145.

18. Seller, "Isaac Leeser's Views"; Moses Mendelssohn, *Jerusalem: A treatise on religious power and Judaism,* Isaac Leeser, trans. (Philadelphia 1852):xviii.

19. *OAJA* 22 (April 1864):13, cited in Davis, "A Highway of Nations."

20. See Davis, *Judaism of America in Its Development* (New York 1950-1951, Hebrew):309.

21. H. Pereira Mendes, "The Zionist Conference at Basle," *North American Review* 167 no. 504 (November 1898):625-628.

22. Mendes, "Should a Jewish State be Established?" *American Hebrew* 64 (13 January 1899):392.

23. Mendes, "A Habitation for God's Holiness," *Menorah Journal* 4 (1918):152-153.

24. See Hyman Grinstein, "Orthodox Judaism and Early Zionism in America," in Meyer, *Early History of Zionism*; Simha Fishbane, "The Founding of Kollel Amerika Tiferet Yerushalayim," *AJHQ* 64 no. 2 (December 1974):120-136; Joel S. Geffen, "Whether to Palestine or to America in the Pages of the Russian Hebrew Press *Ha'melitz*

and *Ha'yom* (1880-1890)," *AJHQ* 59 no. 2 (December 1969):179-220; Judah H. Isaacs, "Rabbi Abraham J. G. Lesser," in Leo Jung, ed., *Guardians of Our Heritage* (Jerusalem 1968, Hebrew):73-80.

25. Abraham J. G. Lesser, *In the Last Days/Be'Aharit Ha'yamim: A dialogue between father and son, concerning the hope of Israel*, Herman Eliassof, trans. (Chicago 1897).

26. Ralph B. Raphael, *The Question of the Jews* (New York 1893, Hebrew):7-8, 28-44, 78, 104-105.

27. Simon I. Finkelstein, *The Beginning of My Harvest* (Berlin 1889, Hebrew): v-viii. Finkelstein's son Louis was Chancellor of the Jewish Theological Seminary of America (1940-1972). See Louis Finkelstein, ed., "Simon I. Finkelstein," in *American Spiritual Autobiographies: Fifteen Self-Portraits* (New York 1948):243-260. Louis described his father as "one of the first Zionists in America." Introduction to Louis Finkelstein, ed., *Order of Prayer: With the interpretation "Conversations of Yitshak" and Various Essays in Halakha and Aggada* [by Simon I. Finkelstein] (Jerusalem 1968, Hebrew):7-16.

28. Spektor himself spoke of liberating the Jew's better self from the bondage of *galut* through Tora and reconstruction of the Land of Israel, and of mutual exclusivity between material fascinations and the heavenly ties of the Jewish soul. See Nahum Sokolow, *Hibbat Tsiyon/The Love for Zion* (Jerusalem 1935, Hebrew):227.

29. Simon I. Finkelstein, *Harvest of Grapes* (Chicago 1899), Hebrew):21-24.

30. Louis Finkelstein, ed., "Simon I. Finkelstein."

31. Ibid.

Part Four

The Twentieth Century

11 Protestant Liberalism: Universal Ideals

American Protestant liberals' involvement with the Holy Land has been motivated by commitment to the American ideals of democracy and equality and by the prophetic ideals of peace and righteousness. The three men portrayed here had different concepts of how to implement that commitment. In 1918 Adolf A. Berle, Sr., thought in terms of an ideal world center. In 1927 Harry Emerson Fosdick conditioned support for a Jewish homeland on toning down Jewish nationalism and recognizing Arab rights. In 1942 Reinhold Niebuhr spoke of a Jewish national homeland as a moral necessity.

Adolf A. Berle, Sr.

Adolf A. Berle, Sr., served as Congregational pastor in Boston and Professor of Applied Christianity at the Crane School of Religion, Tufts University. He was married to a former missionary to the Sioux Indians, Lina Wright.[1] In *The World Significance of a Jewish State* he suggested that since Christianity had failed to prevent World War I or to ease its aftereffects it should open itself to the role Jews might play in improving the world. The religious rehabilitation and the unification of the Jews would serve humanity, and the best instrument to do that was a Jewish state. Thus, the racial and national interests of the Jews were world interests.

How could a revived Israel in a Jewish state improve the world? Berle had in mind a social commonwealth that would bring about the resurgence of Hebrew language and literature and enable the reenactment of ancient Hebrew law and national structure. The commonwealth would inspire Jews around the world to a new solidarity, a new religiosity, and stimulate them to restore the "ideals" of Israel. Upon the establishment of a Jewish state, the Jews would be "able to display, in their greatest beauty and radiance, those national traditions and idealisms which have made the politics of the Hebrew prophets an integral part of the Christian religion." There would be positive ramifications for Jewish-

Christian relations. Once a state existed the Jew would assume a prophetlike image in the gentile mind, antagonisms and prejudices toward Jews would be eliminated, and the absurdity of revering scriptural heroes while persecuting their descendants would be exposed and eliminated.

Berle further predicted that a Jewish state would be a positive moral force in the world. The current world condition lacked the moral cohesion needed to prevent ruthless slaughter or stop nations from organizing themselves to kill and destroy. Judaism had always been the crucible of moral order, the barometer of civilization, and so a Jewish state would provide a paradigm for moral development everywhere. The Jewish state's legal, ethical, social, sanitary, and dietary forms could serve as working laboratories for universal regeneration. Religious ideas from around the world could be clarified and enhanced by the traditional rationalism and mental sanity of the Jew, which would now be concentrated in a political entity. Indeed, a state would allow the world to be instructed in the religion of Israel. Once that happened the religion of the entire world could be positively modified.

Berle thought it was even possible for a new race of prophets, like Amos and Hosea, to arise in Palestine. They would lead the world to the heights of thought and action, toward world unity. Isaiah's prophecy was now a practical political possibility.*[2]

Harry Emerson Fosdick

The eminent New York Baptist minister Harry Emerson Fosdick toured the Land of Israel in 1920 and wrote about his experiences in *A Pilgrimage to Palestine* (1927). He used Scripture as his guide; the Land and text illuminated one another. But like his nineteenth-century Protestant predecessors, he experienced disjunctions between the biblical images he had cultivated and reality. The Jordan River turned out to be a muddy stream. The Land of so much biblical drama, which since childhood Fosdick had imagined very large, turned out to be about the size of Connecticut. The holy places did not appear as he imagined because they were abused—for example, by the construction of churches atop the Mount of Olives, and by sectarian conflicts and pretentious ceremonies at the Holy Sepulcher.

Fosdick had several impressions of the Zionist movement. Theodor Herzl (1860-1904) conceived of Zionism as "the movement of a people without a land

---

*"And the gentiles shall come to thy light, and kings to the brightness of thy rising," *Isaiah* 60:3. "For brass I will bring gold, and for iron I will bring silver, and for wood brass, and for stones iron: I will also make thy officers peace, and thine exacters righteousness. Violence shall no more be heard in thy Land, wasting nor destruction within thy borders. But thou shalt call thy walls salvation, and thy gates praise." *Isaiah* 60:17-18.

to a land without a people" was mistaken.[3] In fact, there were over half a million Muslim Arabs in Palestine, and they were understandably enraged that there could be a national home for the Jewish people in their country. Fosdick objected to the exclusiveness of the Zionists: "Zionism is explicitly not a religion but a racial movement. Jews of all shades of faith and of no faith at all are equally included in it. They are bound together, not by common religion, but by common racial tradition." He thought it "mad" on the part of Jews to think that Palestine would be Jewish just as America was American and England English. This exclusivistic attitude, which would alienate the Arabs, would have long-term negative effects. Fosdick opposed the growth of Jewish influence if it meant the degradation of Arabs or even a failure to promote Arab advancement.

Fosdick could empathize with the Arabs. They had already been betrayed by the Allies. They had won the war against Turkey for the Allies but were not granted autonomy in return as promised. By letting Jews into the Land Britain knowingly divided the people into two mutually suspicious groups. It did so maliciously, as a way to work one against the other—the interracial issue was itself loaded with dynamite—and thereby retain power. Moreover, the Arab could no more be expected to understand the notion that Jews had a right to the Land because of earlier occupancy than the American could be expected to understand an Indian claim to New York City. Further, the Arab feared the potential cultural imperialism of a Jewish homeland—the new economy, agricultural system, types of human relationships, and so forth. He feared, for example, that Solomon's Temple would be rebuilt, replacing the Mosque of Omar.

As for the Jews themselves, Fosdick was concerned about potential internal problems. Despite their racial, linguistic, and nationalistic ties, Jewish groups had grave disagreements with one another over religion, politics, economics, and customs. He supported the Zionist effort to rejuvenate the Land, but he wanted Zionism to renounce its ambitions for "political dominance" and its "chauvinistic nationalism." Fosdick thought the idea of finding refuge for millions of persecuted Jews in this "poor land" an "absurd pretense"; at most, a few thousand could be absorbed annually. Jews had already won and lost the Land before; he hoped that if they regained the Land they would continue to reside in it in a way that would benefit mankind.[4]

The year *A Pilgrimage to Palestine* was published Fosdick had an opportunity to speak less publicly to the students and faculty at Union Theological Seminary, a neighbor to his Riverside Church. According to one reporter Fosdick warned that unless Zionist leaders turned from their extreme nationalism, Zionism would be headed for supreme tragedy, one of the sorriest tragedies of all Jewish history. They were overlooking the fact that while Zionism was an idealistic movement as far as Jews were concerned, for Arabs it was a predatory one. They were also ignoring the likelihood that if Arab and Jew competed with each another the Arab would lose out to Jewish confidence and aggressiveness, becoming angry, resentful, and ready for violence. Zionism as defined by its current leaders was essentially nationalism, and nationalism per se was demonstrably a "false God which we have been worshiping, and magnifying past all reason." Fosdick would support a "modified form of Zionism only." Not a Zionism where, in the words of the English Zionist Israel Zangwill (1864-1926), the Arab would "trek along" but one of educational and cultural revival, as espoused by people like American Rabbi Judah Magnes (1877-1948), then chancellor of the Hebrew University of Jerusalem.[5]

Reinhold Niebuhr

Theologian Reinhold Niebuhr, professor at Union Theological Seminary, was the primary spokesman for the American Christian Palestine Committee (ACPC).[6] The ACPC resulted from the 1943 merger of the American Palestine Committee (formed in 1932) and the Christian Council of Palestine (founded in 1942). It viewed the Land of Israel as a potential outpost of freedom and social justice in the postwar era. It spoke directly to the evils perpetrated against the Jews and attributed them ultimately to national homelessness. ACPC advocated free immigration, unlimited colonization by Jews, and the development of a Jewish majority in Palestine empowered to establish a democratic government.[7]

As portrayed by Niebuhr's student Franklin Littell, Niebuhr's Zionism was unlike standard Christian Zionism. In the latter, Jewish return to the Land was but the central plank in the program of Christian eschatology. Niebuhr was concerned with the Jewish people themselves and committed to the belief that Jews had a right to their own self-definition. Moreover, given the fact that Christianity had not responded adequately to the plight of the Jews even under the Nazis, the Jews had to look to themselves for their survival.[8]

In 1942 Niebuhr criticized the liberal mentality, among non-Jews and Jews alike, for failing to acknowledge that ideals such as tolerance and goodwill did not deal with the realities of ethnic group diversity. Democracy had a tendency to promote "false universalism—which is actually a form of nationalizing Jews which devours them in a way not unrelated to Nazi tribal primitivism." Accordingly, beyond overthrowing the Nazis, Jewish survival required a defense against these identity-destroying ideals. The defense could be realized if the Jews had their own Land, where their unique identity could be preserved. As Louis Brandeis had observed in 1916, "Whole peoples have an individuality no less marked than that of a single person."[9] Niebuhr thought Zionists properly addressed the reality of historical peculiarities and correctly opposed flights into universals.[10]

In "Jews after the War" Niebuhr explained that the defeat of the Axis powers by itself would not solve the problem of the Jews; overthrow of the Nazis would be no more than the negative condition for the solution. Millions of Jews had been completely disinherited from their European homes, and after the war impoverished Europe would not find it easy to reabsorb them. Moreover, "a spiritually corrupted Europe will not purge itself quickly of the virus of race bigotry with which the Nazis have infected its culture." Indeed, the situation of Jews in Europe had been intolerable in Poland and the Balkans long before Hitler.

The problem of Jews in the postwar world was a compelling one for Christianity, not only because their suffering made a claim upon compassion but because contemporary civilization itself had a stake in how it reacted when one people became victim to attempted extermination. Niebuhr attributed the liberal world's early failure to aid the Jews to the a-ethnic credo inherent in the democratic mentality. to becoming inured to the depths of the ethnic group identity. Americans lost themselves in an abstract concept of tolerance, a universalism that defied the facts. As a result, Americans were unable to comprehend the violence that ethnic nationalism was capable of. Instead, they were satisfied to speak of a melting pot that transcended ethnic and racial distinctions, a view that was, ironically, a new form of American nationalism and cultural imperialism in which the minority suffered a painless death through assimilation. He asked, "Does the liberal-democratic world fully understand that it is implicitly making collective extinction the price of its provisional tolerance?"

Niebuhr wanted it to be clear that Jews constituted a particular nationality by reason of their ethnic core. Although their blood was mixed, they had maintained a center of racial integrity through the ages. They also had their own religious and cultural basis. Jews were "more than a race by reason of the admixture of culture and less than a nation by reason of the absence of a state." Their nationality was unique because Jews were scattered among the nations. Niebuhr thought that many Jews themselves had to learn to appreciate this. They served neither democracy nor Israel by denying their ethnic foundation, or by the self-delusion that they could dispel all prejudice by proving that they were a purely cultural or religious community. Civilization should not encourage simple homogeneity—"for if this is allowed complete expression it results in Nazi tribal primitivism"—but instead guarantee cultural pluralism. Perhaps Jews had a right to assimilate, or even to disappear without a trace. But pluralism cum tolerance is what enhanced civilization.

Beyond all this, Niebuhr averred, the Jews possessed a survival impulse as an ethnic group. No matter the ideological denials by modern liberals of this aspect of human existence, historical evidence demonstrated the reality of collective, group impulses, including that of the Jewish people. The Jewish impulse to survive was evidenced by the very fact of survival despite historical adversity and dispersion. According to the assimilationist, Jewish historical survival was determined by the feudal world's hostility on the one hand and the toughness of the Jewish Orthodox religious faith on the other; the liberal era dissipated both these causes. The existence of Nazism on one side and a Zionism that transcended Orthodoxy in expressing the national will on the other made this thinking irrelevant.

Zionists understood that the price of survival—either by absorption into Western culture or by maintaining racial integrity among the various nations—was too high. The Zionists' urge for survival as an ethnic group led them to work for a place where the Jews were not merely "tolerated," "understood," or "appreciated"—or the opposite. They wanted a place where they could preserve their own unique identity without asking permission. Niebuhr supported this approach. It was the logical outcome of the ethnic factuality of the Jews, and the sensible resistance to false or premature universalism or unconscious ethnic imperialism.[11]

As the Jewish state was being established, Niebuhr turned his attention to the Arabs. Since they were expected to surrender sovereignty over enough territory to allow the Jewish state sufficient integrity, political independence, and economic wherewithal, they should be provided the means—some sort of consolidation or federation—for a higher unity and independence.[12] Later, as western nations supported the state's development, Niebuhr traced their actions to a need to absolve their consciences for their involvement—presumably due to their blindness to racial realities—with the evil of Nazism.[13]

Observations

Protestant liberals distinguished themselves within American Christianity by not invoking the Christian-Jewish dilemma. Their concern was with the people of Israel, American principles, and Arabs. Berle looked to the Land for the revival of world morality under Jewish leadership. Fosdick, a Christian pilgrim, supported Jewish life in the Land but only to the extent it did not threaten Arabs. Niebuhr was committed to the Land as the means of Jewish ethnic survival. The themes of democracy, freedom, pluralism, and social morality pervaded their thinking. Liberals spoke of the present world in idealistic terms rather than of history as the way to Christian fulfillment. Instead of a narrow line of development in which Christianity or Judaism, but not both, would occupy center stage, their world was of the broad present, in which American principles—or Christianity sublimated into American principles—allowed Judaism and Christianity to co-exist.

Notes

1. See C. P. Snow, cited in Thomas W. Evans, *The School in the Home: A Primer for Parents of Preschool Children Based on the Works of Dr. A. A. Berle, Sr.* (New York 1973):vii. Cf. Adolf A. Berle, Sr., *The School in the Home: Talks with Parents and Teachers on Intensive Child Training* (New York 1912); idem, *The Education of a Minister* (Andover, Mass., 1907).

2. Adolf A. Berle, Sr., *The World Significance of a Jewish State* (New York 1918). See also idem, *Christianity and the Social Rage* (New York 1914); idem, *Democracy, Imperialism, and Christianity* (Boston 1901); David Schwartz, "A Christian Zionist," *Congress Weekly* 11 no. 20 (26 May 1944):8-9.

3. Davis suggests that Herzl took the phrase from Blackstone. Moshe Davis, "American Christian Devotees in the Holy Land," *Christian-Jewish Relations* 20 no. 4 (1987):3-20. It is notable that for his part, Herzl supported Christian Zionists at the Basle Congress: "The same people who reproach us that Zionism creates new barriers between mankind, find fault with us for aspiring to the friendship of Christian Zionists. But for us it is not only a mere question of opportunism when we press the hand so cordially stretched forth to us. It testifies above all that Zionism possesses a power for reconciliation." Cited by H. Pereira Mendes, "The Zionist Conference at Basle," *north American Review* 167 no. 504 (November 1898):626.

4. Harry Emerson Fosdick, "Palestine Tomorrow," *A Pilgrimage to Palestine* (New York 1927).

5. "Fosdick Sees Ruin Ahead for Zionism," *New York Times* (25 May 1927):8.

6. See Emil L. Fackenheim, "Judaism, Christianity, and Reinhold Niebuhr: A Reply to Levi Olan," *Judaism* 5 no 1 (Fall 1956):316-324; Abraham Heschel, "A Hebrew Evaluation of Reinhold Niebuhr," Charles W. Kegley and Robert M. Bretall, eds., *Reinhold Niebuhr: His Religious, Political, and Social Thought* (New York 1956):391-410; Egal Feldman, "Reinhold Niebuhr and the Jews," *Jewish Social Studies* 46 no. 3-4 (1984):293-302; Daniel F. Rice, "Reinhold Niebuhr and Judaism," *Journal of the American Academy of Religion* 45 no. 1 supplement (March 1977):101-146; Carl H. Voss and David A. Rausch, "American Christians and Israel, 1948-1988," *American Jewish Archives* 40 no. 1 (April 1988):52-54.

7. Voss, "The American Christian Palestine Committee," *Herzl Yearbook 8: Essays in American Zionism, 1917-1948* (New York 1978):242-261.

8. Franklin Littell, "Reinhold Niebuhr and the Jewish People," International Niebuhr Symposium, King's College, London, 20 September 1984.

9. Louis Brandeis, "The Jewish Problem—How to Solve It," *Jewish Frontier* 8 no. 10 (August 1918):195-203.

10. Reinhold Niebuhr, "Jews after the War," *The Nation* (21 and 28 February 1942):214-216, 253-255.

11. Ibid. Felix Frankfurter said of the essay, "I know nothing in print that faces the Jewish problem more trenchantly and more candidly." Cited in Franklin Littell, "Reinhold Niebuhr, the Church Struggle, and the Holocaust," Sixteenth Annual Scholars' Conference on the Church Struggle and the Holocaust (Evanston, Ill., 9 March 1986). See Daniel F. Rice, "Felix Frankfurter and Reinhold Niebuhr, 1940-1964," *Journal of Law and Religion* 1 no. 2 (1983):325-426.

12. Niebuhr, "The Jewish State and the Arab World," cited in Voss, "American Christian Palestine Committee," 247-248.

13. Niebuhr, "The Relations of Christians and Jews in Western Civilization," in *Pious and Secular America* (New York 1958):110.

12 Catholicism: Holy Land of Christ's Crucifixion

Romanticism

American Catholics have been attached to the Holy Land in a romantic way in the sense that the Land meant the scene of ancient Scripture, which needed to be preserved.[1] Central to this romanticism was the tie to holy places. For example, Philadelphia pilgrim William H. Bergan—a graduate of Villanova—wrote in 1874:

> It is useless to attempt to describe the feelings of my heart when in the presence of these sacred and dear localities, especially the Holy Sepulcher and the place of the crucifixion. It is impossible to enter the Tomb without a feeling of holy awe and reverence. What passed within my heart while I was present in them, God only knows . . . Who can imagine a higher and holier enthusiasm?[2]

As armed conflict threatened the Holy Land, the Franciscan editor wrote in *The Crusader's Almanac (CA)* of October 1917:

> What a terrifying thought for all who love the Holy Land! What horror it brings to the soul to think of the desecration and destruction of those places most dear and most sacred to the heart of every Christian!
> With deep concern we are asking which of these two events [military victory or defeat] is it to be, and in our anguish our hearts go out to the memorable, time-honored, hallowed sanctuaries sanctified by the earthly presence, the life, suffering, death, and resurrection of our Lord and savior Jesus Christ. During seven centuries the humble followers of Saint Francis of Assisi have stood watch beside these shrines. To preserve them to Christianity they have borne every form of suffering, persecution, imprisonment, and death.[3]

The romanticism revived the memory that Jews were responsible for killing Christ and remained culpable. Eugene Vetromile (1819-1881), a missionary to Indians in Maine who went to the Holy Land in 1870, considered the Jews of Jerusalem pathetic and attributed their plight to rejection of Christ. Every Friday, he observed, masses of Jewish men, women, and children gathered at the "Wailing Place" and shed tears of grief on the Wall's stones, smoothed over the years by kisses and tears.[4] Gray-headed men cried like children over the loss of the Temple. They looked ridiculous as they inserted their praying lips between the stones, into apertures caused by eroding mortar, or when they found a larger hole and blew their prayer inside to the remains of the Temple. "Poor creatures, deceived by diabolic fraud, and hardened in their hearts!" he thought.[*] They were not allowed to enter the Church of the Holy Sepulcher because they had committed deicide, knowing that if they tried, Christians from every sect would join the Turkish guards to throw them out. The Turks detested them for crucifying a just man, a holy prophet, and the Christians detested them for crucifying the son of God, the promised Messiah, the Savior of the world. For Vetromile, Jews continued to bear the curse they brought upon themselves nineteen centuries ago when Jesus was crucified.[†5]

Bergan described his participation in the procession along the stations of the Via Dolorosa on Good Friday night:

> On Mount Calvary the ceremony of nailing our Savior to the cross took place; with the bleeding figure upon it, they placed the cross in the hole, in the rock where eighteen centuries ago Christ was crucified. It was a scene that the most credulous could not behold unmoved. One could almost imagine that he heard the unbelieving Jews breaking the stillness with jibes and sneers, crying out: "If He be the King of Israel, let Him come down from the cross!" [*Matthew* 27:42]. After the body had remained some time suspended, two monks, probably personating Joseph of Arimathea and Nicodemus, approached the foot of the cross, took the crown of thorns from the head, then drew the long spikes from the hands and feet. Could anything be more affecting than this bloody drama?

Deicide had brought a universal curse upon the Jews that prevailed through the present. In Philadelphia, New York, Germany, France, Italy, and Turkey Bergan saw that Jews had become, as foretold, "a separate and peculiar people; and everywhere, under all poverty and oppression, waiting for and anxiously

---

[*]"For we are made partakers of Christ, if we hold the beginning of our confidence steadfast unto the end; While it is said, To day if ye will hear His voice, harden not your hearts, as in the provocation." *Hebrews* 3:14-15.

[†]*Matthew* 27:25, supra.

expecting the coming of a messiah, to call together their scattered tribes."
Jerusalem offered an intense expression of the dismal fate. From a distance,
Bergan wrote, Jerusalem fulfilled his "brightest daydream." But the vision was
dissipated when he entered the city:

> You look about and wonder, is this reality or is it a dream? Can this be
> Jerusalem, the Holy City, the Zion of the living God? . . . Alas! Why such
> a change? Wherever the eye rests, you are reminded of the lamentation of
> the prophet—"all her friends have dealt treacherously with her, they are
> become her enemies" [*Lamentations* 1:2]. The desolation foretold centuries
> ago has been fearfully accomplished—all "glory is departed" [*I Samuel* 4:12,
> 22].

The Holy Land bore "the marks of a Land cursed by the Almighty for having
rejected the promised Messiah, of having drawn down upon itself and its people
the blood which they shed of the son of God made man."[6] When Charles C.
Svendsen reported in April 1898 about his recent visit, he remarked that the one
place the Jews wanted to possess, Jerusalem, was "beyond the reach of their gold.
The self-invoked judgement seems to hover above them still."[7]

The romanticism involved resistance to doubts raised by archaeologists about
holy places. Bergan acknowledged that there were many contested points. For
example, the Greeks said that the angel Gabriel appeared to the Blessed Virgin
at the fountain over which they had erected their church, while Roman Catholics
said the angel appeared in her own house:

> One or the other tradition must be false. But what need the pilgrim care?
> He may not stand on the exact place where this or that happened. A few
> paces do not signify when he has the assurance that this is Nazareth, the city
> of Joseph and Mary, where our Redeemer condescended to live as one of us
> from infancy to manhood, and where the reconciliation of man with God had
> its beginning.[8]

John T. Durward (1847-1919) of Baraboo, Wisconsin, was interested in what
science had to say, but strong traditions were more likely to be correct than the
latest reasons provided by the "foreign mind." Ultimately, veneration was rooted
in the heart; the spot was holy because of the pilgrim's inner relationship to the
sacred event. "How forcibly stirred is the human soul by the spots where the
traces remain of those we love and admire," said Cicero. The physical also had
value; as long as Christians were not spirits without body, to worship Christ "in
truth" was to worship Him in accordance with human nature.[9] Andrew E. Breen
(1863-1938), Professor of Sacred Scripture at Saint Bernard's Seminary in
Rochester, New York, visited the Land as an undergraduate in 1890 and again
in 1904-1905 as a scholar at the Dominican École Biblique in Jerusalem. He

objected to the dominance of modern biblical criticism at the École; the Holy Sepulcher, for example, had been the center of Christian devotion for centuries, and its centrality would not be changed even if archaeologists did prove the location incorrect.[10]

Another expression of romanticism was the blending of the present into scriptural reality. When he left Nazareth, Bergan naturally felt reluctant to bid farewell to the "fields and paths trodden by His blessed feet." The surrounding mountains and valleys were surely those which Christ "knew and loved." Near Jezreel, "each summit has its sacred associations." As he wandered through the holy places of Jerusalem, "all worldly thoughts with their combinations for the moment cease, and as if touched by some talismanic power, a tender chord or spiritual life within rekindles the embers of a buried past, and brings vividly before the imagination the happier and prouder days of the time of Solomon." In the Holy City the "slumbering soul awakens from its profoundest depths, and bears testimony to a mystic sublimity which overshadows the peace—vitality is gone—but its halo of glory can never be extinguished." Every place in the Land had its history, the brain was "intoxicated, as it were, with the knowledge of so many miracles, with the thought that Christ was here in person."[11]

Franciscans

Franciscans have been tied to the Holy Land since Pope Clement VI entrusted the order with the care of sanctuaries there in 1342.[12] American Franciscans have had a special connection. Charles A. Vissani (1831-1896), the first head of the Franciscan Commissariat of the Holy Land in New York (1880-1889) and Washington, D.C., believed that Columbus originally intended to recover the holy shrines in Jerusalem.[13] Columbus stopped in America, on his way to the Indies, to gather troops and funds for his Holy Land campaign.[14] The editor of *The Crusaders' Almanac (CA)* observed in 1893 that Franciscan father Juan Péres arranged Columbus's audience with Queen Isabella of Spain and that several Franciscan missionaries participated in Columbus's second voyage.[15] As an American and Franciscan, he said, "It is astonishing how intimately the discovery of America is connected with the Franciscan Order."[16] *CA* included the tradition that Christ on the cross looked to the west, where religious freedom would help the church develop.[17]

Pilgrimage reinforced the special tie. For American Franciscans, pilgrimage was a journey to the scenes of the Savior's earthly home, loved by Him because His Father chose it for His Son's abode. As the *CA* editor explained in 1893, Catholics loved the Land even more than Jews did because it was the scene of the redemption, paid for with Christ's blood. Every inch of Jerusalem's soil was sanctified by Jesus and His blessed mother and evoked thoughts of the mysteries of Christ's life, suffering and death.[18] The Franciscans also had a "minor" pilgrimage to Washington, D.C., where Godfrey Schilling, second head of the

Commissariat, had holy sites of the Land replicated at the Franciscan monastery.[19]

Franciscans led the first group of American Catholics to the Holy Land in 1889. On 5 February 1888 Vissani announced the coming pilgrimage in *The Pilgrim in Palestine and Messenger of Saint Francis*:

> Ever since the sacred lips of our crucified Savior uttered His last words on the cross, Mount Calvary has become the center of religious thought and devotion. It is there that Jesus, offering Himself as a holocaust in atonement for the sins of men, reinstated them in their birth-rights to the kingdom of His Father and raised them to glorious immortality.
>
> How many are the sad but encouraging recollections that surround this sacred spot! Here in fancy we see our dear Savior led to the place of execution; here we behold Christ nailed to the cross, His feet that had trodden the land of Judea doing good to all, and His hand, many a time stretched out to bless His people, cruelly transfixed by nails. We witness the raising of the cross, and with Mary we feel a pang of piercing pain penetrate our sympathetical heart at the diabolical shout of triumph that goes up from the multitude. Oh, what a sad scene. Who can think of it without grief? No wonder Saint Paul exhorted the faithful to have the memorable place always fresh in their minds; that the crucifixion formed the principal subject of his discourses; and that for more than eighteen centuries Mount Calvary has become the most famous spot of pilgrimage where thousands of longing, penitent souls gather every year to worship God near the tomb of the dear master and sacred person of the blessed trinity.
>
> It is an ancient custom, this of visiting holy places. And dear mother church is pleased with it. She encourages it and showers her gifts on those who thus show their love to her divine spouse. Mary began it; the apostle continued it; and those having but a touch of love for Him practiced it to this day in spirit or in reality. The Crusades were nothing but great fighting pilgrimages. They do immense good. They soften the soul, expel malice, selfishness, ingratitude, and more closely unite man to his God and his Savior.
>
> All countries have at some time sent detachments to the Tomb of the blessed Redeemer. The United States remain still behind. It is true many from our beloved country, though singly and scarcely noticed, have visited the holy places. They have invariably returned with changed mind, changed at least in their feelings toward the Holy Land. If they felt indifferent toward Palestine before, they think differently now. There must be a great power for good in such a visit to Jerusalem, unexperienced by those who have not been there, or have not the childlike sympathy for the Savior's kind heart that Christians should have.[20]

The journey was reported by participants James Pfeiffer of Enochsburg, Indiana, and John T. Durward and by leader Vissani.[21] The pilgrims convened 20 February 1889 at the Female Orphan Asylum in New York. Everyone received a silver medal showing on one side the crucifixion with Saint Mary and Saint John standing by while Mary Magdalene kissed the Savior's feet. Around the scene is the legend, "First American Pilgrimage to Palestine." The other side depicted the sacred hearts of Jesus and Mary with the pilgrim's name around them. The group also received a banner to be placed in the Church of the Holy Sepulcher. On one side the resurrected Jesus was painted on white damask with the inscription "And His Sepulcher shall be glorious."* On the other appeared an eagle soaring aloft with the American flag. The eagle carried a war emblem with one foot and an olive branch with the other. Both sides were embroidered with costly silk and golden thread. A gold-fringed canopy above the flag bore the legend "First American Pilgrimage to Palestine 1889." Later that day the Bishop of Newark, W. M. Wigger (1841-1901), one of the pilgrims, offered a mass at Saint Patrick's Cathedral in New York. Archbishop Michael A. Corrigan (1839-1902) of New York spoke about Columbus's hope to find means to restore the sacred shrines to Christian hands: "And now . . . after nearly four hundred years, you go forth, the first pilgrims to the Holy Land from the country discovered by Columbus." On 21 February they departed aboard the *Wieland* for Cherbourg.

On 18 March 1889 the group was in Rome. Pope Leo XIII met first with pilgrims Bishop Joseph Rademacher (1840-1900) of Nashville, Msgr. Robert Seton (1839-1927) of Jersey City, and Vissani. They presented him with a statement explaining that his apostolic letter *De Eleemosynis pro Locis Sanctis Colligendis (Concerning Philanthropic Collections for the Holy Places)* of December 1887, which drew attention "to the places crimsoned with the precious blood of our divine savior," evoked devotion to the places among American Catholics and inspired the pilgrimage: "The love that fills our hearts toward the divine Savior has impelled us to undertake such a long journey, that we may be privileged to visit and venerate the sacred tomb which received His sacred body."[22] The pope then met with the whole group of 101, remarking that they were more fortunate than he because he had had a lifelong desire to visit Palestine but never got the opportunity to go. He hoped that other pilgrimages would follow and that in the course of time American Catholics would leave some "memorial" in the Land, as their brethren from other countries had done. Concerning the banner, the Holy Father observed, "Yes, the eagle is truly emblematic of the strength and ambition of your country, whose prosperity and glory we would wish to continue to increase." He granted absolute dispensation

---

*"And in that day there shall be a root of Jesse, which shall stand for an ensign of the people; to it shall the gentiles seek: and his rest shall be glorious." *Isaiah* 11:10.

to the pilgrims from fasting and abstinence even though they were traveling during Lent.

On Palm Sunday 7 April 1889 the pilgrims began a two-week stay in Jerusalem. That morning Consul Gilman accompanied them to the Church of the Holy Sepulcher, and they had an audience with the Latin Patriarch of Jerusalem from 1872 to 1889, Msgr. Vincenzo Bracco.[23] Each pilgrim received a palm, and they all marched in procession around the Holy Sepulcher between two files of armed soldiers. Durward composed a sonnet about the event, depicting the holiness of the moment, the commotion—and the exclusion of the Jew:

> The Muslim guards the Savior's gracious tomb;
> The Latin purchases the right to kiss—
> In transports higher than a lover's bliss—
> Prostrate, that hill from out whose rocky womb
> True life arose; and every dusky race,
> Greek, Copt, Armenian, Negro, fights for room
> To hang a lamp, or kneel in holiest place.
> The Jew would come, but dare not, to deface:
> Thus do the world's religions strive in blood
> This Sepulcher to hold, and striving prove—
> None struggling long for an uncertain good—
> The authenticity of all we love.
> Sceptic and scoffer learn from what ye see:
> Then kneel; these wranglings are our warranty.[24]

On the afternoon of Holy Thursday, 11 April 1889, Msgr. Bracco washed the feet of three priests on the pilgrimage. On the evening of Holy Thursday the pilgrims walked the five stations of the Via Dolorosa within the Church of the Holy Sepulcher. At each one Franciscan priests offered sermons. At Calvary Saint John's account of the passion was sung (*John* 19). Vissani later related that when the passage "and inclining His head, here He gave up the ghost" was recited, "many a tear rolled down the cheeks of those who could realize that they were on the very spot where Jesus, nineteen centuries ago, gave up His life for the redemption of mankind."*[25] Pfeiffer reported the following ceremony:

> On the spot where the crucifixion took place [Station 12] a subdeacon held a cross, on which was fixed a corpus. At the Thirteenth Station, where Christ is taken from the cross, a deacon took a pair of tongs with which he extracted the nails from the hands, after which the arms hung down naturally; after loosening the feet he took the corpus down, laid it in a fine linen cloth,

---

John 19:30, supra.

carried down from Calvary by four subdeacons wearing very precious black dalmatics; and coming to the Stone of Unction they laid the corpus thereon. The Franciscan Guardian embalmed it, as the body of Christ was embalmed according to the Jewish custom and carried it into the Holy Sepulcher Chapel [Station 14] to represent burial. I never before saw such a touching and beautiful ceremony. The whole service lasted three hours. The church was crowded, there being almost twenty thousand strangers in Jerusalem during Holy Week.[26]

Several pilgrims kept an overnight vigil in a church at the Tomb. On Good Friday, 12 April, they walked the nine stations of the Via Dolorosa outside the church. Seton recalled:

I entered the Church of the Holy Sepulcher with the Patriarch and his suite for the morning services, which began at 5:30. In the afternoon, beginning at 1 o'clock, I made the Stations of the Cross along the traditional Via Dolorosa, from the Ecce Homo arch to the Holy Sepulcher Chapel in the church. They were very devoutly conducted by a French Franciscan Father. The faithful who followed were about three hundred and the procession lasted two hours and a half.[27]

The pilgrims visited the Wailing Wall where, Pfeiffer said, the misery expressed by the Jews confirmed the curse that they brought down upon themselves by killing Christ. He recorded the "For the palace that lies waste" litany and the "We beseech Thee to have pity on Zion" prayer.*[28] The refrains, Pfeiffer said, verified Jeremiah's words to the stubborn people, that because of the multitude of their sins God punished them, and their sorrow was incurable.† Pfeiffer was saddened that Jews, "dispersed and wandering all over the world, come to Jerusalem to live and die, when it was their forefathers who were guilty of the fearful crime of killing their God, and who uttered this prophetic cry: 'Let His blood be upon us!'"‡ The unhappy nation offered permanent, terrible proof

---

*"For the palace that lies waste," supra, Chapter 4. "*Rabbi:* We beseech Thee to have pity on Zion. *People:* Reassemble the children of Jerusalem. *R:* Hasten, hasten, O savior of Zion. *P:* Speak in favor of Jerusalem. *R:* That beauty and majesty may surround Zion. *P:* Turn with clemency toward Jerusalem. *R:* That the royal power may soon be re-established in Zion. *P:* Comfort those who weep over Jerusalem. *R:* That peace and happiness may enter Zion. *P:* And the rod of Thy power be raised over Jerusalem."

†"Why criest thou for thine affliction? thy sorrow is incurable for the multitude of thine iniquity: because thy sins were increased, I have done these things unto thee." *Jeremiah* 30:15

‡*Matthew* 27:25, supra.

of the oracles of prophets and evangelists. It was "heartrending to see them weep in the Land where they crucified Him Who came to deliver them . . . Thus they have wept since the coming of Christ, and thus they will weep every Friday as long as this world will exist. The Messiah has come, and as man He will come no more. They expect the Messiah to come today or tomorrow and rebuild their Temple."[29] Seton returned by himself in the evening, "and standing off not to intrude—listened to the pathetic wailing of the Jews along a wall where once the Temple rose."[30]

The American Franciscans carried out the pope's wish for further pilgrimages to the Holy Land, both directly and indirectly.[31] In 1893 they called for a peaceful, spiritual crusade to protect and secure the holy places. This was a financial crusade: by donating money to protect the holy places the crusaders would participate in the masses being said in the Holy Land. If the contributors were sinners they would receive divine grace and their relatives' suffering would be alleviated. If they already had grace they would receive merit toward salvation. They would also receive a plenary indulgence at the hour of death if they also received the sacraments or invoked Jesus' name orally or mentally. A partial indulgence for seven years was granted if the crusader recited the Our Father, Hail Mary, and Gloria five times each with devotion and contrition to honor the Lord's five wounds. The spiritual crusader also received a medal of five crosses, the largest of which symbolized the wound to His sacred heart and the others affliction to His heart, soul, intelligence, and five bodily senses. Two of the small crosses represented the two thieves, and two represented the executioners and cruel spectators.* The four together represented the diffusion of the gospel to the four parts of the world.† The smaller crosses surrounding the larger signified that all Christians had to gather around and cling to the Savior. Anyone who wore the medal would receive a plenary indulgence after monthly confession and communion at all principal Christian feasts—assuming that mass was heard at least once a week, an act of charity was performed, or the needs of the Church were devoutly prayed for. It was also recommended to apply the medal to the body and recite five Our Fathers, Hail Marys, and Glorias to alleviate sickness. This united one's suffering with the Lord's when He offered His precious blood to the eternal Father for the relief of their infirmities.[32]

Godfrey Schilling, the first American citizen to live in the Church of the Holy Sepulcher, spoke of the authenticity of the official holy places, "proven by an uninterrupted chain of witnesses which has never lost a link from the death of

---

*"And with Him they crucify two thieves; the one on His right hand, the other on His left." *Mark* 15:27.

†"And He said unto them, Go ye into all the world, and preach the gospel to every creature." *Mark* 16:15.

Christ to Hadrian, from Hadrian to Saint Helena, from Saint Helena to the Crusaders, and from their day until the present time." Those who believed that other spots were authentic were "modest enough to suppose that the Christians and scientists of 1,800 years ago were all blind and misguided until these new theorists appeared."[33]

John T. Durward

For Durward, who participated in the 1889 Franciscan pilgrimage and made a trip on his own in 1910, the Land was imbued with Christ. As a Catholic he accepted Scripture totally; to doubt it was to cut himself off from the Church.[34] The Land blended with Scripture, it proved "luminously" that the supernatural events surrounding Christ were true. The Land was Christ's earthly abode and field of action and as such "historically and morally an epitome of the world's life, a microcosm of human biography." As Scripture was not ancient history for Durward but present fact, he wanted the ancient Land of Scripture preserved in the present. He was gratified that the Arab inhabitants preserved the Land's antiquity, not only physically but culturally in terms of habits, thinking, and language; he found much of Abraham in the Bedouin.[35]

In *Sonnets of the Holy Land* Durward explains that his pilgrimage helped him understand biblical descriptions of flora, such as Jotham's words atop Mount Gerizim about fig and olive trees and vines.* When he passed an Arab hut and smelled the lentil pottage he half condoned Esau's actions.† The customs and thought habits of the people of the Land, the seasons and characteristics of mountain and plain all illustrated the Scripture narrative. The true guidebook to carry through the Land was the Bible."[36] The pilgrimage to Palestine ran "parallel to our life of pilgrimage." Christ's life included the lives of all the saints—He was more a prophet than Isaiah, more an apostle than Peter, more a martyr than James, more a virgin than Mary, more a confessor than St. Meinrad of Einsiedeln. Similarly, the pilgrimage to the Holy Land included all others—the tomb of St. James at Compostela, Spain; Rome; and the house of the Blessed Virgin in Loreto, Italy.[37]

---

*"And when they told it to Jotham, he went and stood in the top of mount Gerizim, and lifted up his voice, and cried, and said unto them, Hearken unto me, ye men of Shechem, that God may hearken unto you. The trees went forth on a time to anoint a king over them; and they said unto the olive tree, Reign thou over us. But the olive tree said unto them, Should I leave my fatness, wherewith by me they honor God and man, and go to be promoted over the trees? And the trees said to the fig tree, Come thou and reign over us. But the fig tree said unto them, Should I forsake my sweetness, and my good fruit, and go to be promoted over the trees?" *Judges* 9:7-11.

†"Then Jacob gave Esau bread and pottage of lentils; and he did eat and drink, and rose up, and went his way: thus Esau despised his birthright." *Genesis* 25:34.

In *Holy Land and Holy Writ* Durward writes that the Holy Land should be visited with Bible in hand, "soul alive," and seen for what it offered on its own terms rather than compared to one's hometown. "It is thought's university for us, as it is indeed the stage over which we may see pass the history of time, yea—and of eternity—at least those revelations that bind us to eternity." The Land was a palimpsest, a page with Canaanite, Israelite, Babylonian, Egyptian, Roman, Turkish, Christian, and modern texts atop one another. "Every city of Palestine is a . . . book written and rewritten with the former words more or less scraped away from the page to receive the later message." Both temporal history and eternal revelations were included. Durward envisioned Adam and Eve, Cain and the patriarchs. He saw the prophets stretch their long, lean arms out in benediction, making kings tremble. He envisioned multitudes coming up from the south with 40 years of desert dust upon them. He heard the 300 warriors crying out about the sword of the Lord and Gideon.* Durward saw David with his sling and pebble, Samson with the ass's jawbone, and their routed opponents. He envisioned the sad procession of exiles moving northward into Babylon, where they wept over muted harp strings. He saw a few old men returning later to the Land only to lament that the new Temple was not equal to the old. He saw Rome coming to conquer and drenching its talons in the heart blood of martyrs while Christ led a spiritual processing out of Judea, the Turks entering, and then crusading knights with red crosses on their breasts replacing the cross above the Holy Sepulcher.[38] Eventually he arrived at the present: "Now we stand here with the jargon of the Arab in our ears and the unspeakable Turk holding the key of our shrines."

Durward was cognizant of the disjunction between expectation and reality. Instead of the ox and ass at Bethlehem, pilgrims would find an altar glittering with lamps; instead of the "stone rolled back" from the hillside Sepulcher they would find a vast basilica over the Tomb and Golgotha together.[†39] Disappointment was inevitable, for from infancy Catholics pictured the places not as they are but as they were when the beloved events originally occurred, and so the heart could never be satisfied in the Holy Land. The rude tools scattered around Joseph's workshop were nowhere to be seen, nor the unfinished plow beam shaped by the child Jesus. Now crowded markets stood around the Temple sanctuary door where the Lord, in wrath, scourged the buyers and sellers. Calvary was not a lone hill outside the city walls, with three crosses standing against a gray sky. The world changed, there were catastrophes in the Land, and churches were built over the holy spots in an attempt to preserve them.

---

*"When I blow with a trumpet, I and all that are with me, then blow ye the trumpets also on every side of all the camp, and say, The sword of the Lord, and of Gideon." *Judges* 7:18.

†"And they found the stone rolled away from the sepulchre." *Luke* 24:2.

Durward could overcome the disjunction. The mountains of Judea and blue waters of Galilee remained unchanged. The "same bending hills [Christ's] eyes rested on, and the same azure waters His feet pressed" were still there. At Bethlehem his thoughts flew "back to the beginning of things, and this Bethlehem-ite, in his jacket of sheepskin with the wool outside and his spade in his hand, is Adam going to his sweaty labor in garments God-made." Was the old man with flowing beard, followed by a boy, Abraham taking Isaac to Mount Moriah, there "to offer his son—hardest obedience ever asked of man?" He perceived the birth that identified a new calendar, the babe in the straw that made Christmas the feast of children. He heard the only songs of angels ever heard by mortals and the homage of the shepherds. In the city of David Durward pictured the boy with his sling and stones, the king with his harp, the penitent writing psalms. "We could go on endlessly, connecting event upon event with each locality; but this is enough to show what I mean. In every place many different histories come before one, and the imaginative man is almost dazzled."[40] The disjunction was even a source for inspiration. At Bethany on 14 April 1889 Durward wrote this:

Once flowers bloomed around this threshold lowly,
Trodden so oft by Him whose ways were peace;
Those feet most beautiful on mountain holy
Making all growth of noxious herbage cease,
Made, too, of rarest blossoms sweet increase;
Now poison weeds usurp the favored room;
Fragrance gives place to stench; brightness to gloom.
The wheat is dead, the cockle triumphs solely
So virtues spring where'er His feet are pressed;
So vices thrive where Jesus' steps ne'er come;
John glows to love upon the savior's breast,
But fades all truth where wisdom's voice is dumb.
That careless life is but of weeds possessed
By sacrifice and sacrament unblessed.[41]

What place did Israel have in Durward's Catholic experience of the Land? She was the "morning gleam" by the "noontide fire." On 8 April 1889 at the site of the Temple he wrote:

Shekhina's awe and tabernacle's glory
And Temple's stones and sacrificial pyre
That made this spot adored in Bible story,
Did they in ignominious end expire?
Say rather that the lower by the higher
Light was eclipsed, as stars by sunlight's beam;
Or, still more truly, as that noontide fire

Continues, not destroys, the morning gleam.
The real presence in our churches resting
For incompleteness of the past atones;
Building the Temple and the Levite vesting,
Turning to altar yonder quarried stones.
The prophecy has found fulfillment clear;
The house of God, in three days built, is here![*42]

For Durward, God's promises to the people of Israel about restoring the Land were transferred to Christianity. In *Holy Land and Holy Writ* he relates a conversation near Nablus. The Philosopher, quoting *Genesis*, asks whether his fellow travelers think the promise to Israel was fulfilled since the Jews are scattered, no more a nation, and Muslims rule the Land.[†] The Artist, thinking it was, because "the Jews may come into their own again," cites evidence in *CA*: at the Frankfurt Zionist convention, Otto Warburg (1859-1938) had described immigrant Jews starting industries in Palestine that could be promoted by agricultural settlements, and Franz Oppenheimer (1864-1943) reported the establishment of a new colony; Jews already possessed the best parts of the Land, with 90,000 in Jerusalem, 20,000 in Jaffa, 8,000 in Safed, 7,000 in Tiberias, and 1,000 in Hebron—an overall increase of 300 percent over the last 10 years.[43] "We are surprised by this admission from the Franciscan paper, and will be on the lookout for confirmation of its truth—or the contrary." A third participant concludes the conversation: "These promises were made to the chosen people of God and were kept as long as they were faithful. When they ceased to be the true church, they would be fulfilled in favor of their successor the kingdom of Christ."[44]

Once Christ appeared and the Jews rejected and murdered Him, Durward writes, they were accursed. "They are not allowed inside the Basilica of the Sepulcher and resurrection of Him Whom they slew. Their living are exiles in every land, and their dead are on the western looking slope of Olivet. Indeed, the malediction they called down on themselves has been fulfilled: 'His blood be upon us and upon our children.'"[‡] Because they were cursed they continued to live in misery. In Jerusalem their dwellings were the dirtiest, and their places of worship other than the Ashkenazi synagogue on Mount Zion were insignificant.[45] In appearance the Jews were silent, haggard, fearful, and ashamed,

---

*See, for example, *Mark* 14:57-58: "And there arose certain, and bare false witness against him, saying, We heard Him say, I will destroy this temple that is made with hands, and within three days I will build another made without hands."

†"For all the land which thou seest, to thee will I give it, and to thy seed for ever." *Genesis* 13:15.

‡*Matthew* 27:25.

unable to look one another in the face. They were still the sordid money changers they were in the days of Christ.

There was, nevertheless, much that Durward appreciated about Jews. He was touched by their extraordinarily long history and by their ritual, especially Passover. While Christian history was interrupted and at points even lost in obscurity, Jewish history was traceable to Abraham, Noah, and Adam himself. It was lamentable "that such nobility should have the curse upon it of a rejected Messiah! Of a crucified Redeemer! . . . However much the world despises and hates the Jewish people, there is something in this nation that touches the heartstrings." Chosen by God, they had kept the law of Sinai engraved in their human nature for 2,500 years. Indeed, the Jews "were the true church through which Jehovah made His revelations and bestowed His favors." Durward reconciled their accursed condition with their great history and special tie to divine revelation by anticipating Jewish atonement for sin and return to the true, Christian fold.

At the Wailing Place on 12 April 1889—where he recognized "the Hebrew Jew by the lovelocks on his temples, the Polish Jew by his ragged dirtiness, the Spanish Jew by his blackness, the Russian Jew by his long hair and intense piety"—he composed a sonnet in response to the Jews' litany.*[46]

The moaning sea against a rocky shore;
Such art thou, Israel, in thy awful woe,
With palm and forehead pressed forevermore
Upon those blocks that raised thy Temple's glory;
Or swaying palsied gray hairs to and fro,
And giving to the winds thy anguished story:
"Oh for our palace walls in desolation—
Temple and bucklered tower now o'erthrown;
Oh for the perished glories of our nation,
Oh for our priesthood fat and lazy grown,
Oh for our king and pontiffs gone astray,
We sit alone and weep." Oh restless sea!
Return, return, Jerusalem, and stay
The sobbing of thy mournful litany.[47]

Durward offered an interesting interpretation of circumcision. He said it had the same function as baptism did in the "new law": a symbolic renewal of the profane, it removed original sin and admitted one to the community of the elect. It was performed not by the priest but sometimes by the mother, more often by the father, and with stone rather than metal because that was considered more

---

*"For the palace that lies waste," supra, Chapter 4.

sanitary. The practice had fallen into disuse among contemporary Hebrews, but the Muslims still practiced it widely. Durward participated in a Seder ("Jewish Easter") and observed that "after the Catholic Mass there is nothing so fine, at least from the literary standpoint—though some say it is often carried out with much distraction of intervening talk." He thought the celebrants misread the psalmist's phrase during the Hallel section about the rejected stone becoming the cornerstone: they interpreted it to mean that Israel would be built again into God's Temple, whereas in fact the cornerstone was Christ.*[48]

Andrew E. Breen

Andrew E. Breen's *Diary of My Life in the Holy Land* is not so much a pilgrim's experience of the sacred as it is a clinical portrayal of the geography, customs and history of the Land, with extensive citations from scholarship about the Holy Land.[49] He shared the Catholic's romanticism, reflected in his attitude toward archaeology and Jews of the Land. In his 1899 interpretation of *Luke* 4:28-29 Breen says that instead of recognizing their defects which Christ identified, the Jews became "fired with fanatical hate" against Him:[†]

> They saw their pretensions ridiculed. They saw that the Savior, instead of excusing His action, based it upon celebrated precedents in Israel's history. All their national pride was set aside by Him and the worst elements of their natures obtained ascendancy in them. Smarting from the just rebuke of their infidelity, they cry that He is a blasphemer, that He has made Himself the son of God. A wild tumult seizes the assembly, they rush upon Him, and lay hands upon Him, and drag Him from the synagogue.[50]

Presumably, Breen felt Jewish antagonism toward Jesus caused their subsequent misery. He considered Jewish life in Palestine miserable, the result of a divine curse. Jerusalem was "sickened by the foul odors, and the palpable evidence of a degradation of man which has passed all bounds." In the Jewish quarter "all is squalor and dust, and the strange unnatural faces of the Jews themselves make an unpleasant impression." At the Wailing Wall, "The expression of their

---

*"The stone which the builders refused is become the head stone of the corner." *Psalms* 118:22. "Jesus saith unto them, Did ye never read in the scriptures, The stone which the builders rejected, the same is become the head of the corner: this is the Lord's doing, and it is marvelous in our eyes?" *Matthew* 21:42.

†"And all they in the synagogue, when they heard these things, were filled with wrath, And rose up, and thrust Him out of the city, and led Him unto the brow of the hill whereon their city was built, that they might cast Him down headlong." *Luke* 4:28-29.

countenances is most repulsive." The scene at the Wall was "one of the saddest, weirdest sights" in Jerusalem:

> At Jerusalem one cannot fail to distinguish the Jew from all other races of men. His dress is distinctive; but most of all what distinguishes them is their peculiar countenances, mysterious, hopelessly sad. There is here no miscegenation of the Jew with any other race. They are a people apart, a mystery of the human race.

The misery of Jerusalem was God's curse: "There is a peculiar, desolate character attached to the ruins; they are ruins upon which rest the anathema of God. The desolation predicted by Daniel remains.* A strange air pervades the city; it is haunted by so many awful memories . . . the curious history of this, the holiest and the unholiest of cities" typified the human soul that God wanted to love but which by sinning could become "the object of God's eternal hate. No man who closely observes the misery of this city will deny that God's curse still hangs over it." At the Wailing Wall the Jews themselves gave voice to their condition in their litany and prayer.† When Breen participated in the Seder at the home of Lazar Gruenhut (1850-1913)—a scholar of Midrash and of Palestinian geography, then director of Jewish Boys' Orphanage in Jaffa—he noted, as had Durward, the misinterpretation of the psalmist's phrase about the rejected stone becoming the cornerstone:‡ He found it pitiable that they identified Israel with the rejected stone which would be the cornerstone of the new Zion.[51]

What patterns emerge in the nineteenth-century thought and activity of American Catholics vis-à-vis the Holy Land? Deep attachment to the Land is evidenced by pilgrimage to and concern for the holy places of Christ's life and death. American Catholics translated the Land's space and time into Christian Scripture—for Bergan and Durward disjunctions between the two were easily overcome. The Land as Christ's necessarily evoked a condemnation of Jews as killers of Christ. Bergan, the Franciscans, Durward, and Breen all found the results of deicide in the spiritual and physical condition of the Jews of Jerusalem; those dismal conditions reconciled Jewish space with Christian Scripture. Formerly Jews had been blessed with divine *shekhina*, but since the crucifixion

---

*"In the first year of his [Darius'] reign I Daniel understood by books the number of the years, whereof the word of the Lord came to Jeremiah the prophet, that he would accomplish seventy years in the desolations of Jerusalem." *Daniel* 9:2.

†"For the palace that lies waste," supra, Chapter 4; "We beseech Thee to have pity on Zion," supra.

‡*Psalms* 118:22, supra.

they were abandoned by it. Their internal and external daily life confirmed their loss.[52]

Political Ramifications, 1917-1948

Early expressions of Catholic theology vis-à-vis the Holy Land were later brought forward into the political arena.[53] In the period of the Balfour Declaration and the San Remo Conference, American Catholic concerns continued to revolve around holy places and Jewish sin but with the addition of Arab interests.

The Franciscans were concerned with the political identity of the Land in order to secure the safety of the holy places. Jerusalem was the area where Jesus lived, suffered, and died, where He "sealed His doctrine by His glorious resurrection and admirable ascension." They trembled when they heard about Turkish threats to destroy the holy shrines in October 1917. If the holy places were destroyed the Franciscans would "mourn over their ruins, as the Jews do every Friday and Saturday at their Wailing Place." Franciscans objected to sending a Jewish regiment to Palestine, for "millions of Christians throughout the world are naturally opposed to the thought of the Jews eventually becoming the political guardians of the most precious monuments of the Christian religion."[54]

The entry of General Edmund H. H. Allenby (1861-1936) and Allied forces into Jerusalem on 9 December 1917 was celebrated as the "most momentous event in history of the Holy Land since the Crusades." *CA* reported that Archbishop James Gibbons (1834-1921) of Baltimore was grateful to God for placing earthly places hallowed by Christ's footsteps in the control of Christian nations.[55] With Palestine dragged into the war zone, anxiety that Christ "become the permanent prisoner of Mohammed" was eased when the English—the Franciscans saw them as the descendants of Crusader Richard the Lion-Hearted—broke the spell of centuries and returned Christianity's most precious legacy. After generations of "bondage and profanation," Jerusalem was liberated from the "hands of infidels" to become once again the Holy City of Christians, the "City of God *par excellence,* the capital of the divine mission, the leading star of the pilgrimages, the source of faith irrigating the oasis of the world." As Jews had once rebuilt their Temple, Christians would now beautify their sacred places. "A new era is dawning on the Holy Land and God has visited His people."[56]

The hopefulness surrounding the Christian takeover appeared again in a January 1919 report about the Basilica of the Nativity in Bethlehem. In 1847 Greeks had built a "hideous" wall across the church, cutting off the sanctuary. The Basilica had become a rendezvous point for Arabs, a lounging place for their soldiers:

Perhaps now that the Holy Land has passed into the hands of a Christian power, it will be possible for the faithful to restore once more to its former beauty that once grand temple, that stands over the spot which was sanctified by the events of the first Christmas night, and which has been so appropriately called the "marvel of Palestine."[57]

When the San Remo Conference of 18-26 April 1920 awarded a mandate over the Land to Great Britain, the *Catholic Historical Review* published a statement from Jerusalem by English Dominican Reginald Ginns (b. 1893), a former student of Marie J. LaGrange (1855-1938) at the École Biblique. Ginns said the mandate's forced introduction of Jews into Palestine breached the justice of immigration laws. The inhabitants of Palestine had as much right to determine who settled there as any native nation had with its land, and they considered the Jew a "most undesirable alien." Given Arab sentiment, the arrival of the Jews could in fact precipitate a massacre. The notion that Arab and Jew would live side by side was a chimera. Zionists thought of the land as Jewish, bestowed by God, the scene of Jewish national history, the place toward which Jews had turned their eyes with sorrow and yearning for centuries. They wanted Palestine to become "as Jewish as England is English," and Arabs were the intruders. Already they were buying up land and beginning to outflank the Arabs commercially, and Arabs were no match, steeped as they were in their ancestors' habits. People were already being interrogated as to whether they were Jewish or not (*"Ata Yehudi?"*), and soon the situation would be reminiscent of the era of Muslim Caliphs, when Christians had to wear large crosses slung from their necks as a mark of scorn. Ginns felt the money- and western-minded Jews were alien to the Land.[58]

The subject of deicide resurfaced in July 1922 when Cyprien Jourdin, rector of the Passionist Retreat at Bethany, wrote in *The Sign* that killers of Christ were desecrating Jerusalem. The city should be filled with pilgrims pressing forward to venerate the cross, but instead the "Zionist Jewish republic" was spreading pornography and prostitution and holding dancing parties in front of Calvary. Jourdin reported that Jewish students would cover their eyes with their hands and spit on the ground when someone passed wearing a cross, or make the sign of the cross with their fingers and spit on it. He quoted the French philosopher-priest Hugues Lamennais (1782-1854): "Everywhere oppressed, they are yet everywhere. Every nation has seen them pass; all have been seized with horror at their aspect; they are marked with a sign more terrible than that of Cain: on their foreheads a hand of iron has written: 'Deicides!'"[59]

In following years the themes of safety for Christian holy places, Arab welfare and Jewish sinfulness assumed new forms. When the Shaw Commission report of 1 April 1930 recommended limiting Jewish immigration, Vincent Sheean (b. 1899) commended it for sounding the "death knell of Zionism," a movement he considered a disastrous mistake from the beginning. As far as he was concerned, even a race for whom history was "one long disappointment" could not be expected to place its money on such a "doped horse" forever.[60] *CA* also supported the Shaw Commission report:

While the Wailing Wall question, especially the unusual political demonstration held there on 15 August [1929] by the Jews, is considered the immediate cause of the outburst of Arab feeling, the real cause frankly is admitted to be the Zionist policy of the Jews. The Arabs fear that, because of the wealth, immigration, and extensive land purchases of the Jews, they themselves will soon be deprived of a livelihood and be placed economically and politically at the mercy of the Jews.

The commission urges that the Balfour Declaration be once more defined and that the mandate of 1919 be clarified. It also suggests that a garrison be maintained in Palestine; that Jewish immigration be placed under a quota; that the land question be carefully studied both as to ownership and methods of improving the soil; that the rights of the Wailing Wall and other shrines be settled. The idea of a representative government is treated very favorably.

The *CA* editor observed that the Labor Party member of the Shaw Commission, Harry Snell, blamed the Grand Mufti of Jerusalem for failing to take measures to prevent the clash at the Wall, claimed that Arabs were misinformed about the land question, and considered Zionism a "noble experiment" despite its failure. The editor felt these positions indicated Snell's "Zionist tendencies" and so were not to be taken seriously:

Naturally, the Jews are bitterly disappointed. They have received a severe jolt, and if the recommendations of the Shaw Commission should be carried into effect, they would paralyze Zionism. It is highly significant, moreover, that the government has not for the first time prohibited all immigration, including Jewish, into Palestine.[61]

In May 1936 the editor of *America* explained that the British Mandate was failing because it ignored the fact that the overpowering interest in the Holy Land's welfare was neither Jewish nor Islamic but Christian. "And as its soil was trodden by the incarnate word Who formed His church there, the welfare of Palestine is inextricably bound up with the Catholic and Apostolic Church of Christ."[62] In September 1936 David H. Hickey wanted Jewish immigration stopped, opposed the "unhealthy increase in population," and approved a position enunciated in the London *Spectator* that Palestine's economic capacity was ignored in evaluating recent immigration. Palestine could not support all the shopkeepers, merchants and professionals coming in. "The solution seems to be to return to 1922, to put the policy then laid down [in the White Paper] into practice, in spirit and in the letter." Hickey thought that building the Land would mean tragic oppression of the native Arabs: "The situation is enough to make one weep. Here we see the power of capital committing the same crime of unfair racial discrimination against which all Jews protest so vigorously when applied to their race in other lands."[63]

In June 1939 the editor of *America* supported the White Paper of 1939, "an honest attempt to act justly, as far as justice is possible in conflicting and contradictory claims." He explained that the Palestine problem had partly to do with

> the force and vehemence of the attack of international Jewry. The union of sentiment, the similarity of method, the use of propaganda, the moral pressure of Jews in every nation, particularly in the British Commonwealth and the United States, all manifest that Jewry is an international power, that it is aggressive and may be ruthless, and that it is determined to champion its interests against all and any who would question its aims.

Particularly in the United States there was "a new Jewish consciousness characterized by militancy and acumen," and it would require "a new American evaluation and orientation."[64]

In August 1939 the editor of *The Sign* rejected Jewish claims to Palestine:

> We Americans hear very little of the Arab side to the quarrel in Palestine, but we do hear a great deal about the Jewish side. American Jews have been extremely active in their efforts to enlist the aid of the State Department in Washington to bring pressure to bear on Britain to modify the White Paper on Palestine in favor of the Jews. They have attempted to enlist Catholic support in this undertaking—in some cases successfully. Sympathy for the Jews should not blind us Catholics to the fact that the Jews have less right to Palestine than the Indians have to Manhattan. Catholics should remember too that their fellow Catholics in Palestine have sided with the Arabs in resisting what can only be termed a Jewish invasion.

At the same time he was concerned about the Jewish plight in Europe:

> Some solution for this situation and for the distress of the persecuted Jews of other nations must be found. No Christian worthy of the name can be indifferent to the awful plight in which these people find themselves in many countries which consider themselves not only highly civilized, but even Christian.[65]

During and after World War II, Catholic opposition to a Jewish state involved separating compassion for Jewish suffering from the issue of Jewish political sovereignty. In May 1943, while the Warsaw ghetto revolt was being finally smashed, Archbishop Francis J. Spellman (1889-1967) of New York spoke in Jerusalem of Christ weeping over the whole world as once He wept over

Jerusalem, of the entire human race undergoing the passion and the crucifixion.* The archbishop did not say that the Land could help alleviate the suffering of the Jews.[66]

In May 1944 *The Sign's* editor—Ralph Gorman (1897-1972), C.P. (College of Preachers) a student of Hugues Vincent (b. 1872) at the École Biblique—observed that although, as often repeated, the Balfour Declaration spoke of a "home" and not a political commonwealth, still it was mistaken for an "Atlantic Charter of political Zionism." He feared that if political Zionism was successful in pressuring "our government to implicate itself in obtaining Palestine for the Jews, despite the British White Paper of 1939 limiting Jewish immigration," America would be drawn into "a foreign commitment we have neither inclination nor means to implement." There was sympathy "in every decent heart" for the unparalleled persecution of Jews, but "the distinction between the humanitarian and the political aspect can not be too strongly emphasized." It was an international responsibility to provide refuge for the four million Jews left, but to conclude that Palestine should therefore become a "national Jewish state" was to incorrectly shift from humanitarian to political terms. What of the "fundamental rights" of the Arab inhabitants of Palestine? Jerusalem was their Holy City as well. Before the Zionist influx, the Arab/Jewish ratio was 10:1; now it was 2:1, and the Arabs who had lived in Palestine for centuries naturally resented "these European strangers." If there was to be a Jewish homeland, he suggested Madagascar or some unpopulated land in central Africa. Americans needed to ask themselves this: "Are we willing to embroil our country in the establishment of a Jewish nation in an Arab land and to protect it by force from the dispossessed owners? Just what can be gained by removing Jews from the prejudices of Europe only to place them in an environment equally hostile?"[67]

In *The Sign* of June 1945 church historian Thomas J. McMahon, S.T.D., (1909-1956) of New York expressed anxiety over the holy places. The presence of Franciscan hospices, "from the depths of Gethsemane to the heights of Tabor, amid the sweet memories of Bethlehem and Nazareth, in the polyglot clamor of Jerusalem," proved that "even the murderous trek of Islam could not expel Jesus from His homeland." Would this now be done by Jews? A Jewish "commonwealth could hardly be expected to respect the holy places." Along with plans for partition, "enclave" of the holy places, or larger Arab federation, a commonwealth threatened the sacred character of Christ's homeland. The pages of the New Testament are a Christian historical geography of Palestine, and no part of the Land should be "without Christ." McMahon distinguished between the issues of Jewish suffering and political identity. Jews needed a place of refuge:

---

*See, for example, *Luke* 13:34, supra.

For nearly a hundred years, the Jews have been looking to Palestine as a possible homeland. Their claims lie deep in the dim recesses of biblical history. Not even their tragic exiles and their dispersion over the face of the earth could erase from their memories their Land of promise. The bitter persecution which they have been forced to endure in Hitler's Germany and elsewhere made more actual the need of a place of refuge.

But the Arabs had their rights as well, and for McMahon the plight of the Jews did not neutralize them.[68]

After the war, in February 1946, John E. Uhler wrote that he was reluctant and fearful to deny Jewish aspirations in view of the painful two-millennial history of the Jewish people and the Land, "stressed a thousandfold by the recent persecution of the Jews in Europe." But many Jews themselves were opposed to the Zionist movement as harmful to Judaism—for instance, the American Council for Judaism and Elmer Berger (b. 1908) in *The Jewish Dilemma* (1945). While American sentimentalism was stirred by the litany of Jews gathered on Friday evenings at the Wailing Wall, the prayer call of the Muslim muezzins that had sounded for thirteen centuries went unheard.* Uhler predicted that "if Zionism imposes a political state on (Muslim) Holy Land, a cataclysm of blood will begin again to drench the earth."[69]

In September 1946 Gorman wrote that the survivors of Jewish Holocaust were "a problem of human suffering and misery that should appeal to the Christian conscience." Immigration laws were no excuse, and he recommended dividing the refugees among many countries. At the same time, the sufferings should not blind anyone to the facts about Palestine. The Arabs were "united in their undying opposition to the establishment of a Jewish state in Palestine." The historical reasons to justify the right of the Jews to Palestine were "patently absurd": Jews had not ruled Palestine for two thousand years, while Arabs had occupied the Land for 1300 years. To Gorman, "Zionist efforts to make Palestine an independent Jewish state in spite of Arab opposition are acts of aggression, and the Arabs would be justified in meeting them as such."[70]

In May 1947 Gorman described the holy places and the Christian minority in Palestine as vital Christian interests. Political "realism" must not "be allowed to exile Jesus Christ from his homeland and ignore the rights of His followers."[71] The next month he distinguished between the plight of Jewish refugees and the question of Palestine once again:

Sympathy for the suffering Jews is being played for all it is worth to arouse public opinion and to use that opinion as a lever in forcing the decision to make Palestine a Jewish state. There are two distinct problems . . . They

---

*"For the palace that lies waste," supra, Chapter 4.

should be kept distinct in spite of the deliberate attempt to merge them. The one is the problem of displaced European Jews. The other is the Arab-Zionist problem of Palestine. The one is a humanitarian problem. The other is a purely political problem.

Gorman rejected Abba H. Silver's joining of the two when he spoke to the UN Special General Assembly, urging immediate relaxation of immigration restrictions to relieve human suffering:

> The Jewish claims on the Holy Land as their national home and as a Jewish state are legally doubtful at best and morally without foundation. In seeking to oust from control a people who have dwelt in Palestine for centuries, to gain as their own a Land only a portion of which they ruled some two thousand years ago, merits little sympathy. But when Zionists capitalize on the sufferings of their own European brethren in their mighty, well-endowed effort toward a political objective, they merit no sympathy at all—only rebuke.[72]

As the Jewish state became a reality, America's self-interest became more pronounced in the mixture of Catholic opposition. In March 1948 Uhler said that America's "attempt to wrest a large part of Palestine from Islam for the sake of Zionism" was reminiscent of the failures of the medieval Christian Crusades "after several hundred years of bloodshed." The immediate motive for the partition plan—persecuted European Jews were Hitler's enemies and therefore America's friends—did not strike Uhler as sufficient grounds for American support. Uhler again cited Jewish opposition: "thousands of Jews are opposed to the Zionists"; the American Council was organized "to combat the logic of Zionism"; Berger's *Jewish Dilemma* was "an attack on a Jewish political state"; Morris S. Lazaron (1888-1979) feared the consequences of Zionism and opposed U. N. support. Uhler also claimed that the Stern Gang was largely Communist and included Moscow agents and that Moscow was letting thousands of Jewish Communists out of Eastern Europe into Palestine and giving them arms to become "the nucleus of a Communist movement in the new state." Further, since America was responsible for Zionist agitation and the UN partition resolution, she would have to send her "boys to fight in Palestine for a foreign state, artificially created, against people who have never done us any harm."[73]

In April 1948 Gorman claimed that American backing for Zionism came from politicians out for the Jewish vote or from "a laudable sympathy for the sufferings of the Jewish people but a meager knowledge of history and geography." They looked to Palestine only as a refuge for persecuted Jews, ignoring reality: "unless the Arabs are willing to give up a territory rightfully theirs, rivers of blood—much of it Jewish blood—will redden the sacred soil of the Holy Land." He feared that if American military forces became involved, "the first casualties among our boys fighting in Palestine would enkindle a flame of antisemitism in this country." Gorman recommended a UN trusteeship to "protect the fundamental rights not only of Jews and Arabs but also of the millions of Christians who look to Palestine as the birthplace of their religion, a Land made sacred by the life and death of Jesus Christ."[74]

In May 1948 the editor of *Commonweal* divided Holocaust from Jewish state in a new way. All had to share responsibility for the deaths of the six million Jews killed by the Nazis and for those who had survived in European camps. "Yet the fate of the Jews was nothing to all who passed by from 1933-1939, and it is only something today to most people and peoples because of its horrid nuisance value. It is utterly tragic that the only way the Jews can be satisfied is at the expence of a hardly less tragic people, only recently liberated." He reiterated Gorman's earlier point that Jews had less historical claim to the Land than the Muslims, who had possessed it for over 1300 years: "Equitably, spiritually, culturally, even economically, they have equal if not greater rights." But he concluded with an awareness of the impossibility of bifurcation: "Nationally, the case for Arab sovereignty seems clear; internationally, the need for a Jewish homeland in Palestine is imperative. And may God have mercy on our souls."[75]

Catholic concern for political aspects of the Holy Land during the twentieth century reverberated with nineteenth-century theological motifs: protection of holy places; antipathy for the Jews, whose ancestors murdered Jesus; and belief in Palestine as Christ's Land, never to be controlled by Muslim or Jew. In the Balfour years there was deep anxiety over what the Turks might do to the holy places in case of war. The British entry was conceived as ordained by God, a victory of Christianity over Islam. A poignant comparison was drawn between threatened loss and subsequent securing of holy places for Catholics, with the destruction and hoped-for recovery of the Temple for the Jews. The Land was not considered Jewish and the Jews had no absolute right to it. Sympathy for Arabs—notwithstanding Catholic antagonism to Islam—was such that Jewish entry into the Land vis-à-vis indigenous Arabs was compared to medieval Muslim persecution of Christians. Jerusalem's Jews were still identifiable with the ancient perpetrators of the crucifixion. With the San Remo Treaty and Shaw Commission, Christian humanistic concern for the Jewish plight was neutralized by attention to the Arab plight vis-à-vis Jewish immigration. There was an antisemitic tone to descriptions of the activities of "international" Jewry.

During World War II American Catholics expressed Christian concern for Jewish suffering but isolated it from political solutions involving Palestine. There was concern on a Christian and humane level but not on a Jewish and national one: there was compassion for Jews as human beings but not as Jews, at least Jews as identifiable with their Land. After World War II there was renewed concern for Arab (as distinct from Muslim) suffering—here too, on a Christian and humane level. It was considered sinister to link Holocaust and Zionism. While Jewish national interests were isolated from Jewish suffering, the anti-Zionist effort of the American Council for Judaism was considered a valid argument against Jewish sovereignty. In spring 1948 the schism between Jews as human beings and Jews as nationalists continued; the fact that Jews were the enemies of Hitler did not mean that they should be supported politically. Concern for America was expressed in terms of alleged Communist leanings of Russian Jews in the Land. Jews were still denied a priori right to the Land, and there was an unwillingness to respond to Jewish tragedy by possibly creating an Arab one.

Observations

There are constant elements in the variety of American Catholic perspectives on the Holy Land, from the time Vetromile went there in 1870 through the creation of the Jewish state: desire to preserve the holy places; resistance to undermining the identity of traditional holy spots through archaeological and historical study; belief in the Land as a reflection of the life of Christ—and in the New Testament as historical geography; romantic longing for the Land as it existed in Christ's lifetime; and living memory of the crucifixion and its Jewish perpetrators in the mind of the pilgrim. Once the idea of Jewish sovereignty became reality, concern for Arab welfare—perhaps rooted in the identification of Arabs with the Land in the time of Christ—became major. With the Holocaust, human compassion in Christ's name was separated from the idea of Jewish refuge in a sovereign Land. The source of that separation lay in commitment to Christ's suffering for mankind, fear of what a Jewish government would do to the holy places, and the incongruity of Jewish sovereignty in the Land where Jews killed Christ.

Notes

1. Eugene Fisher and Gerard Sloyan, "American Catholics and Holy Land," Colloquium on America and the Holy Land (Pollin Center for Study of Judaism in America, Washington D.C., 19 September 1979).

2. William H. Bergan, *Notes of Hand: Drawn at sight by William H. Bergan. Busy Thoughts of a Traveler in the Orient. A Record of Observations, Impressions, and Feelings, Simply and Candidly Expressed in His Correspondence to "The Catholic Standard" of Philadelphia. Experiences Began with Departure from the City of Trieste at the Head of the Adriatic Sea, on 28 February 1874* (Philadelphia 1908):23-24.

3. "Crusade for the Holy Land: The crusader's prayer. 'O divine eternal Father! I offer Thee the precious blood of Jesus Christ, in reparation for my sins, for the wants of the holy church, for the wants of the Holy Land, for the conversion of poor sinners and for the release of the suffering souls in purgatory'. . . The good work of the Holy Land," *CA* 26 no. 1 (1 October 1917):9-15.

4. I have run across the term "Wailing Place" among Catholics, Episcopalians, and Presbyterians but have been unable to determine the significance, if any.

5. Eugene Vetromile, *Travels of Europe, Egypt, Arabia, Petraea, Palestine, and Syria* (New York 1871):2:187-189.

6. Bergan, *Notes of Hand,* 57, 62, 74, 78, 79, 80.

7. Svendsen traveled to the Holy Land on the steamer *Daphne* and took the train from the port of Jaffa to Jerusalem. Charles C. Svendsen, "Easter Scenes at Jerusalem," *Catholic World* 67 (April 1898):79-93.

8. Bergan, *Notes of Hand,* 23-24.

9. I have been unable to identify the Cicero quotation. John T. Durward, *Holy Land and Holy Writ* (Baraboo, Wis., 1913):xii-xiv.

10. Andrew E. Breen, *A Diary of My Life in the Holy Land* (Rochester, N.Y., 1906):281-290. Earlier, Breen was alleged to have had "an astonishing scepticism about all sacred sites." Thomas K. Reilly, O. P. (Dominican Order of Preachers), in *The American Ecclesiastical Review* (June 1907):596, review of Andrew E. Breen, *A Harmonized Exposition of the Four Gospels,* 4 vols. (Rochester, N.Y., 1899-1908), cited in Benjamin J. Blied, "Rev. Andrew E. Breen, D.D.: Priest, Professor, Author," *Salesianum* 48 no. 4 (October 1953):172-179.

11. Bergan, *Notes of Hand,* 38, 39, 41, 69, 76.

12. See David Klatzker, "American Christian Travelers to the Holy Land, 1821-1939" (diss., Temple University, 1983); Joseph G. Kelly, "American Catholic Interest in the Holy Land: 1880-1980" (Rochester, N.Y., 3 April 1978); and G[odfrey] K[loetzli], "The Franciscans in the Holy Land," *Holy Land Review: Illustrated Quarterly of the Franciscan Custody* 1 no. 1 (Spring 1975):16-21.

13. Vissani, who arrived in America in 1868, was the fifth president of Saint Bonaventure College (1874-1877). Cf. Walter Hammon, "Fr. Charles Vissani . . .," in *The First Bonaventure Men: The Early History of Saint Bonaventure University and the Allegheny Franciscans* (Saint Bonaventure, N.Y., 1958):156-175. Vissani founded *The Pilgrim of Palestine* in 1884, which became *The Pilgrim of Palestine and Messenger of Saint Francis* in 1888, *The Advocate of the Good Work of the Holy Land* in 1889, and *The Crusader's Almanac* (sometimes called *The Pilgrim of Palestine*) in 1892. "The V. Rev. Chas. A. Vissani, O.S.F. (Order of St. Francis)," *CA* 5 no. 2 (1897):2. Godfrey Schilling, O.S.F., the Vice-Commissary of the Holy Land Commissariat, succeeded him as Commissary.

14. On Holy Land, Columbus, and the Franciscans, see John L. Phelan, *The Millennial Kingdom of the Franciscans in the New World*, 2nd ed. (Berkeley, Calif., 1970); Leonard I. Sweet, "Christopher Columbus and the Millennial Vision of the New World," *The Catholic Historical Review* 72 no. 3 (July 1986):369-382; and Hector Avalos, "Columbus as Biblical Exegete: A Study of the *Libro de la profecias*," Symposium on Religion in the Age of Exploration, Creighton University, Omaha, 26 October 1992.

15. Brother Joseph, archivist at the Franciscan monastery in Washington, D.C., informed me that the priests and brothers who edited *CA* and its predecessors were not identified in print and that feature articles and contributed material often did not carry the author's name. The staff of *CA* included Charles A. Vissani, Godfrey Schilling; Charles Conti, O.S.F.; and Isidore Germiat from Belgium. All material required ecclesiastical permission (*imprimatur*) or permission of the superior (*nihil obstat*) for publication. I am indebted to Brother Joseph for his help in verifying sources. Some *CA* editions were not numbered, and in some cases the numbers are unavailable (indicated by a question mark).

16. "Christopher Columbus and the Holy Land," *CA* 1 (1893):29-30. Cf. "Franciscan Mission of Palestine," *CA* 7 no. 1 (1899):16 (?). Vissani, "The Holy Places in Palestine," *Pilgrim of Palestine and Messenger of Saint Francis* 4 no. 2 (April 1887):46-77; "To Our Promoters, *CA* 7 no. 2 (1899):2.

17. "The V. Rev. Chas. A. Vissani, O.S.F.," *CA* 5 no. 2 (1897):2.

18. "A New Crusade: The army of the cross or the association of the Holy Land," *CA* (1893):3 (?).

19. "Memorial Church of the Holy Land in Washington," *CA* 27 no. 1 (1919):62.

20. Vissani, *Pilgrim of Palestine and Messenger of Saint Francis* (5 February 1888):81-82, cited in Mary J. Huth, "Charles Vissani, O.F.M. [Order of Friars Minor] and the First American Catholic Pilgrimage to the Holy Land," *Holy Land Review* (Jerusalem) 10 no. 1 (Spring 1990):7-25.

21. James Pfeiffer, *First American Catholic Pilgrimage to Palestine, 1889* (Cincinnati 1892); John T. Durward, *Sonnets of the Holy Land: With an Introduction on the Pilgrimage to Palestine* (Baraboo, Wis., 1900) and *Holy Land and Holy Writ* (Baraboo, Wis., 1913); Vissani, "First Catholic American Pilgrimage to Palestine," *The Advocate of the Good Work of the Holy Land: A publication devoted to the interests of the sanctuaries of the Catholic church in Palestine* (New York [1890?]). Seton recorded that they used Lievin de Hamme, *Guide-indicateur des Sanctuaires et Lieux Historiques de la Terre-Sainte*, 3rd ed. (Jerusalem 1887). Robert Seton, "Excelsior Diary: And miscellaneous jottings 1889," New York Historical Society.

22. Leo XIII, *"Ea ad loca, pretioso Humani Verbi sanguine purpurata"*; *"De Eleemosynis pro Locis Sanctis Colligendis,"* in *Pontificis Maximi Acta* (Rome 1887-1888):7:244-247. The full text follows:

Vicar on earth, although unworthy, of our Lord and savior Jesus Christ, Who delivered Himself up for the redemption of the world by becoming obedient unto death, even the death of the cross, we, in the midst of the grave and multiplied cares of the supreme Apostolate, which absorb us, still desire to apply our special vigilance and our pastoral solicitude to the preservation and safe-keeping, with all possible care and veneration, of all the monuments which remain of so great and holy a mystery in the city of Jerusalem and the neighboring country, and also to watch that the orders and instructions wisely given on this matter by the Roman Pontiffs, our predecessors, shall be fully carried out.

Indeed, for a long time, and from the earliest days, the sovereign Pontiffs, turning their eyes towards those places crimsoned with the precious blood of the God-Man, urged the Catholic nations to take possession of the Tomb of Christ; when these holy places had again fallen under the control of the infidels, and the Friars Minor of the Order of Saint Francis alone had permission to be their guardians, the Popes never ceased to look, as much as they possibly could, after their preservation, and to provide, according to circumstances, for the needs of those religious, who could not be driven from their glorious work by persecutions, by vexations or by the most cruel tortures.

Repeatedly the Popes have urgently recommended, either by word of mouth or by Letters Apostolic, to the Patriarchs, Bishops and other Ordinaries of the entire world, to prevail on the faithful confided to their care to collect alms for the preservation of the holy places. On this very point they laid down special rules in several Apostolic Letters, sometimes under the form of Bulls, sometimes under the form of Briefs, and with unanimous accord they directed all the dioceses of the world, under precept of obedience, to set apart certain days every year for the collection by the faithful, of alms for the holy places.

Finally, Pius VI, of happy memory, our predecessor, in his Bull *Inter caetera divinorum judiciorum abdita arcana,* of 31 July 1778, ordered all the Bishops to recommend four times a year to the charity of the faithful, the wants of the Holy Land.

In our days, our beloved son, Bernardin of Portogruaro, Minister-General of the Order of Friars Minor of the Observance, has laid before us the facts that the necessities have increased of late years, and that the resources received recently from the faithful have not been sufficient to keep up the holy places, especially because, a hundred years having passed since the constitution of Pius VI, a number of bishops let it go unheeded as if it had fallen into disuse, and no longer exhort the faithful, with the solicitude that is becoming, to contribute to the fund for the Holy Land. He has also addressed to us an humble and urgent entreaty that we, in the plenitude of our apostolic authority, should make some new directions on this subject.

Therefore, desiring to grant this petition, and on account of the particular interest which we feel for the preservation of the holy places, in virtue of our apostolic authority, we decree, by these presents and forever, that our venerable brethren, the Patriarchs, Archbishops, Bishops and other Ordinaries of the whole world shall be bound, under holy obedience, to see that in every parochial church in their respective dioceses the needs for the Holy Land be recommended to the charity of the faithful, at least once a year, that is, on the Friday of Holy Week, or on some other day every year, at the choice of each Ordinary.

By the same authority, we expressly prohibit and interdict any one from changing in any manner the destination of the alms collected for the Holy Land, to apply them to other purposes. Besides, we ordain that the proceeds of the collection, made as has been ordered, shall be sent by the parish priest to the Bishop, and by the Bishop to the nearest Superior of the Order of Saint Francis, who is a Commissary for the Holy Land. Finally, we desire that this Superior shall, according to custom, forward as soon as possible the alms to Jerusalem to the Father Custodian of the Holy Land.

Given at Rome, near Saint Peter's under the ring of the Fisherman, the 26th of December 1887, in the tenth year of our pontificate, Leo P.P. XIII.

The Pilgrim of Palestine and Messenger of Saint Francis (4 March 1888):145-146, quoted in Huth, "Charles Vissani." Seton wrote in his "Excelsior Diary" that "a collection was taken up in the very presence of the Pope and most shocking."

23. Seton, "Excelsior Diary." Seton also recalled this incident involving Consul Gilman:

On our way from Ramle to Jerusalem a horseman, riding fast, met us at the place where we had stopped for lunch, and spoke excitedly to Father Vissani. Between them in a corner, like conspirators, the flag was detached from its staff and hidden inside the carriage. I was informed that, to be prudent, we would enter the Holy City in small groups. I felt ashamed of the cowardice and protested, but bided my time, and when we arrived at the Jaffa Gate, got out quickly and ran to the consul Mr. Gilman, whom I saw standing with some of his friends waiting for us, having been advised of our coming. I told him what had happened, and he was very indignant. We went back to the carriage, where he bent "Old Glory" to the pole, which I held. We then formed processionally, and advanced like honest people. Our silver cross was carried at the head by one of the priests of the party, and the American flag was borne behind it by a layman who had served on the right side in the Civil War. Next came our energetic consul in full uniform, with pride in his port, accompanied by dragoman and kavass [guard], and supported by Bishop Rademacher and myself in our purple costumes. The other pilgrims, walking two and two—ladies wearing black veils—brought up the procession. We went directly through a large and respectfully inquisitive crowd of natives and other people down to the Church of the Holy Sepulcher, where we knelt and said our Prayers of Thanksgiving.

Seton, *Memories of Many Years: 1839-1922* (London 1923):198-199. See also "American Pilgrims in Jerusalem," *CA* 5 no. 3 (1897):3.

24. Durward, "The Holy Sepulcher," in *Sonnets*, 25.

25. Vissani, "First Catholic American Pilgrimage," 10.

26. Pfeiffer, *First American Catholic Pilgrimage*, 123. In his more condensed version, ("First American Catholic Pilgrimage," 11) Vissani was unclear about the use of an actual human corpse:

When they ascended Calvary the Father with the crucifix placed himself on the rear of the altar facing the people. Then a brother approached the front of the altar and removed the nails, one after the other, from the hands and feet. As the nails were

318 / Holy Land and Religious America

removed from the hands, the hands bent down and swung as if it had been a dead body, presenting a touching, realistic picture of the sacred act performed on the same spot nineteen centuries ago.
For a description of the Church of the Holy Sepulcher and the fourteen Stations, see Eugene Hoade, O.F.M., *Guide to the Holy Land*, 4th ed. .(Jerusalem 1971):102-177.

27. Seton, typed version of diary, New York Historical Society.

28. The Catholics cited various versions of the litany and the prayer, but the differences are not substantive.

29. Pfeiffer, *First American Catholic Pilgrimage*, 137-139.

30. Seton, typed version of diary.

31. See, for example, "American Pilgrims in Jerusalem," *CA* 5 no. 3 (1897):3.

32. "Privileges Granted to Crusaders by Our Holy Father Leo XIII," *CA* 4 no. 1 (1896):16; "A Special Blessing for Crusaders: Our Holy Father Leo XIII has deigned to recommend the good work of the Holy Land and to renew his blessing to all crusaders, granting them the following spiritual benefits, by rescript, 26 June 1894," *CA* (1895):3, 16; Vissani, "The Holy Places in Jerusalem," *CA* 4 no. 2 (April 1887):46-47; "The Crusade for the Holy Land," *CA* 5 no. 1 (1897):3; "Our Medals," *CA* 5 no. 1 (1897):2-3; "Indulgences Attached to the Crusaders' Medal," *CA* 4 no. 1 (1896):2; "Privileges Granted to the Crusaders and Benefactors of the Holy Land," *CA* 27 no. 1 (1919):49.

33. Godfrey Schilling, "Life at the Holy Sepulcher," *north American Review* 159 no. 452 (July 1894):77-87. Cf. Frederick Joseph, "Holy Sepulcher through the Ages," *Holy Land Review: Illustrated Quarterly of the Franciscan Custody* 1 no. 1 (Spring 1975):6-15.

34. Cf. Durward, *A Primer for Converts: Showing the reasonable service of the Catholics* (New York 1892).

35. Durward, *Holy Land and Holy Writ*, x-xiv, 103, 107.

36. Durward, Introduction, in *Sonnets*, 20-21.

37. *Ibid.*, pp. 6-7.

38. See Charles Coueasnon, O.P., "The Holy Sepulcher from 1009 to the Present Day," *The Church of the Holy Sepulcher in Jerusalem* (London 1974):54-62.

39. Durward, *Holy Land and Holy Writ*, ix-xiv, 89, 534.

40. Durward, Introduction, in *Sonnets*, 11-13.

41. Durward, "Bethany House of Mary and Martha," ibid., 29.

42. Durward, "The Real Presence in the Temple Area, Jerusalem," ibid., 28.

43. I have been unable to identify the Zionist convention in Frankfurt. The author may have meant the ninth Zionist Congress, held 26-30 December 1909 in Hamburg.

44. "Is Palestine to Become a Jewish Kingdom?" *CA Pilgrim of Palestine* 20 no. 1 (1912):46. Durward, *Holy Land and Holy Writ*, 92.

45. See Joseph Schwarz, "The Synagogue of the Ashkenazim—Arabic, Dir Ashkenazim," *A Descriptive Geography and Brief Historical Sketch of Palestine*, trans. Isaac Leeser (Philadelphia 1850):277-283.

46. Durward, *Holy Land and Holy Writ*, 531-544.

47. Durward, "The Wailing Place," in *Sonnets*, 40; idem, *Holy Land and Holy Writ*, 536.

48. Durward, "Litany," in *The Building of a Church* (Baraboo, Wis., 1902):76-78:
"Thou hast chosen the lowly, O God my God;"
    (Happy the soul elect.)
"The head of the Temple's corner, behold!
    Is the stone that the builders reject."
"They are planted secure in the house of the Lord;"
    (Happy the soul that with God is content.)
"I had rather be abject and poor in Thy courts
    Than dwell in the sinners' gilt tent."
Idem, *Holy Land and Holy Writ*, 536-539.

49. Breen, *A Dairy of My Life,* 473, offered this observation about Selah Merrill:
The American Colony has been bitterly opposed, especially by the American consul, Dr. Merrill. This is not strange. Dr. Merrill is himself a clergyman of one of the sects of the Protestant church. His chief business in Jerusalem is in looking after the interests of the Protestant missions here. Naturally he is not in sympathy with an association which declares the sects to be effete. In effect the American Colony is one of those meteoric crystallizations of religious thought which has thrown off subjection to the proper religious authority instituted by Christ. In professing to follow Christ they contradict Christ; for Christ certainly established the principle of religious authority in the world.

50. Breen, *A Harmonized Exposition of the Four Gospels* (Rochester, N.Y., 1899):1:502-503. Cf. idem, *A General Introduction to Holy Scripture* (Rochester, N.Y., 1897). Breen, "Jews in Socialism," in *Sociological Essays*, 2 vols. (Rochester, N.Y., 1922), speaks of Jewish involvement with Marxism.

51. Breen, *A Dairy of My Life,* 4-5, 118, 244, 359, 382, 491. Breen provided a detailed description of the Seder at Gruenhut's home as well as of the Samaritan Passover. Durward, *Holy Land and Holy Writ*, 491-501, 621-624.

52. Other early travelers to the Holy Land were Timothy Birmingham of Charleston, S.C.; Stanislas Buteux of Natchez, Miss.; and Bishop James R. Bagley of Newark, N. J.; see Klatzker, "American Christian Travelers."

53. See Esther Y. Feldblum, *The American Catholic Press and the Jewish State, 1917-1959* (New York 1977).

54. "Conditions in the Holy Land," *CA* 26 no. 1 (1 October 1917):31-33.

55. In 1891 Gibbons signed the Blackstone petition. William E. Blackstone, "Baltimore," in *Palestine for the Jews: A copy of the memorial presented to President Harrison 5 March 1891* ([Chicago?] 1891):12. On 15 April 1919 he wrote President Wilson in Paris, asking him to take an interest in the holy places on behalf of the Catholic Church. John T. Ellis, *The Life of James Cardinal Gibbons, Archbishop of Baltimore, 1834-1921* (Milwaukee 1952):2:282n.

56. "Jerusalem Delivered! Most momentous event in history of the Holy Land since the crusades. Capture of the Holy City brings joy to every Christian heart. British forces enter Jerusalem on 9 December 1917. Capture of City effected without damage to the sacred places. The history of this great event drawn from authentic sources," *CA* 26 no. 3 (1 April 1918):2-15; reprint, *CA* 27 no. 1 (1 October 1918):29-43.

57. "The Marvel of Palestine: A Glance at the History of the Basilica of the Nativity in Bethlehem," *CA* 27 no. 2 (1 January 1919):5-12.

58. Reginald Ginns, "Palestinian Problems," *Catholic Historical Review: For the Study of the Church History of the United States* n.s. 1 no. 3 (October 1921):394-395, originally published in *Blackfriars: A Monthly Review Edited by the English Dominicans* (September 1921).

59. Cyprien Jourdin, "Zionism in Palestine," *The Sign: A National Catholic Magazine* 1 no. 2 (July 1922):19.

60. Vincent Sheean, "The Palestine Report," *Commonweal* 11 no. 26 (3 April 1930):737-739. Cf. Sheean, "Holy Land," *In Search of History* (New York 1935):368-442.

61. "Holy Land News: Palestine Government Report," *CA* 38 no. 4 (1 July 1930):10.

62. "The New Jerusalem," *America: A Catholic Review of the Week* 55 no. 8 (30 May 1936):172.

63. D. Harold Hickey, "The Palestinian Arab Cause," *Catholic World: A Monthly Magazine of General Literature and Science Published by the Paulist Fathers* 143 (September 1936):684-689. I could not verify the *Spectator* citation. Cf. William Brumberg, "The Arab and Zionist Policy," *The Spectator* no. 5638 (17 July 1936):96.

64. "Palestine Homeland," *America* 61 no. 8 (3 June 1939):180.

65. "Jews and Arabs in Palestine," *The Sign* 19 no. 1 (August 1939):5-6.

66. Francis J. Spellman, *Action This Day: Letters to My Father* (New York 1943):119. Cf. Jakob Rosenheim, "Defeat on the Road to Messianic Victory," *Ha'derekh: Bitaon mercazi shel ha'histadrut* 115 (29 May 1947, Hebrew):1.

67. [Ralph Gorman], "The Zionist Movement in America," *The Sign* 23 no. 10 (May 1944):564.

68. Thomas J. McMahon, "Threat to the Holy Places: Peace Planners Must Safeguard the Sacred Character of Ancient Christian Sanctuaries," *The Sign* 24 no. 11 (June 1945):594-596.

69. John E. Uhler, "Is America Fair to Islam?" *The Catholic World* 162 no. 971 (February 1946):396-402. Cf. Elmer Berger, *The Jewish Dilemma* (New York 1945).

70. Gorman, "The Jews and Palestine," *The Sign* 26 no. 2 (September 1946):2. On Jews and Jesus, see also Gorman, *The Last Hours of Jesus* (New York 1960).

71. [Gorman], "Christians in Palestine," *The Sign* 26 no. 10 (May 1947):20.

72. See Abba H. Silver, "Jewish National Home in Palestine: United Nations Should Uphold International Commitments of the League. By Abba H. Silver, Representative for the Jewish Agency for Palestine. Delivered before the Political and Security Committee of the United Nations General Assembly, Lake Success, N.Y., 8 May 1947," in *Vital Speeches of the Day* 13 no. 15 (15 May 1947):453-456; [Gorman], "Palestine and Jewish Refugees," *The Sign* 26 no. 11 (June 1947):5-6.

73. Uhler, "America and the Party of Palestine," *The Catholic World* 161 no. 996 (March 1948):493-501.

74. Gorman, "Palestine Dilemma," *The Sign* 27 no. 9 (April 1948):4.

75. "King Cyrus and the Coats[?]," *Commonweal* 48 no. 4 (7 May 1948):69.

13 Judaism: Centrality of the Land

The Land of Israel was a primary concern in the religious life and thought of twentieth-century Judaism through 1948.[1] Some in the Reform movement continued to affirm Zion-as-America, but most spoke of the cultural, political, or spiritual importance of the Land. Conservative Jews spoke of the Land as the source of vitality for moribund diaspora Judaism. The Orthodox were committed to restoring the Land but differed about how (by divine or human initiative) and when (before or after Tora was established there). The secularists saw the Land either as a means toward trans-Jewish ideals such as democracy or as a necessity, given antisemitism in the diaspora.

Reform's New Positive Attitude

In the nineteenth century the scales of Reform Judaism were tilted heavily in favor of the idea of Zion-as-America. In the twentieth, as the political reality of the Jewish state grew more likely, the balance shifted. A number of thinkers who had been anti-Zionist became non-Zionist: they now spoke of restoring the Land as a cultural and spiritual center and Jewish refuge, although not as a sovereign state.

Thus Hyman Enelow, who had rejected the centrality of the Land for Judaism before the turn of the century, wrote directly after the Balfour Declaration that Reform was not anti-Zionist or opposed to the restoration of Palestine. Jerusalem should be restored as a center of Jewish vitality, though not as the capital of a Jewish state.[2] Earlier, Max Margolis (1866-1932) had attacked Zionism for conceding to (presumably American) antisemitism by leading Jewish immigrants away from the United States. But in 1903 he wrote, "Reformed Judaism, insofar as it is a religious, spiritual movement, has points of affinity with spiritual Zionism, [even while] spiritual Zionism looks forward to the political independence of Palestine Jewry as an ultimate goal."[3] In 1905 Margolis joined the Zionist movement.[4] In 1903 Kaufmann Kohler (1843-1926) told the HUC Board of Governors that American Judaism stood for American thought and spirit, not "Zionistic neo-Hebraism," and in 1916 he spoke against selling American citizenship for a "land in the clouds."[5] But in 1919 there was a shift. While Kohler did not await a Zion brought about through diplomacy, for Zion remained a spiritual category, he did want "our ancient home . . . to become a center of Jewish culture and a sole refuge for homeless Jews."[6] While Leo M. Franklin was a student at HUC he attacked Zionism. After becoming president of the CCAR he supported the April 1920 San Remo Conference's confirmation of the Balfour Declaration, and he thought of Palestine both as refuge and context for a special expression of Jewish spiritual genius.[7]

Other Reform thinkers were Zionists Maximilian Heller (1860-1929), David Neumark (1866-1924), Henry Malter (1864-1925), and Abba H. Silver.[8] Heller, a New Orleans rabbi, was vice-president of the Federation of American Zionists (1906) and CCAR president (1909-1911).[9] In 1901 he identified the Land as the definitive separation between Israel's submergence and emergence, between assimilation and antisemitism on the one hand and national resurrection on the other.[10] In 1910 he looked forward to the exodus of American Jews to Palestine.[11] In August 1918 he believed that the ripened "soil of a resurrected Palestine" was needed to carry out Israel's prophetic mission of sending forth the law from Jerusalem, a development to be accomplished through social justice and action according to the highest standards of rectitude and humanity in the Land.[12] At the April 1919 CCAR convention Heller urged his listeners to "be a little more temperate about bending our knee before America." He paid homage to Americanism but would not exalt it into a perfect ideal transcending other national loyalties. He also did not consider Zionism a function of Jewish failure, e.g., only for disadvantaged Jews of Russia, but as an expression of the vital forces in Judaism, a counterforce to assimilation: "We have lost our Sabbath and our Jewish feeling toward the Sabbath. I, a child of the ghetto, who have seen a ghetto Sabbath know what it means spiritually, that it supplies something solid and Jewish—it is because I want to live where I can have a Sabbath that I want to go to Palestine."[13]

Neumark, professor of philosophy at HUC, wrote in 1906-1907 that "our people possesses no capacity or attitude which is not rooted in its faith and its religion"; Judaism's nationality was essentially its religiosity. In turn, the "national religion" required an independent political framework. Insofar as Reform Judaism and Zionism were together rooted in religion, they implied one another. Zionists affirmed the Jewish religion while Reformers stressed prophetic morality tied to a particularist concept of God. In 1916 Neumark wrote that Zionists Ahad Ha-am (1856-1927), Joseph Klausner (1874-1958), and Nahum Sokolow (1859-1936) were good Reform Jews, committed to the idea of secularized redemption.[14] Malter, professor of medieval philosophy and Arabic at HUC until 1907 and of Talmudic literature at Dropsie College thereafter, believed that Judaism's survival and salvation could not come from religion alone but depended upon reviving the national feeling, culture, and ideal of Judaism.[15]

In his address on 2 May 1943 to the National Conference for Palestine, Abba H. Silver, national chairman of the United Palestine Appeal and future president of the Zionist Organization of America (ZOA), catalyzed American Jewry to unified action on behalf of Zionism. He quoted Marshall Ferdinand Foch's declaration at the second battle of Marne (summer 1918): "We have been beaten on the right; we have been shattered on our left; our center is broken. I have issued orders to advance on all fronts." Silver cautioned against beguilement by empty words of sympathy for the Jewish plight and denunciations of Nazism, as if the massacre of two million Jews was not already known as something horrible. The tragic problems of Jewry could not be solved by Rosh Hashana greetings from government officials. Instead, the Jews would have to struggle for survival as Jews always had—with their own resources, however diminished, with their own unbroken will and confidence in their destiny, and with God's help. The struggle centered on a Jewish state.

Silver said there was an inescapable logic to events. Israel's rebirth as a nation in her historic home would take place, as surely as God's word accomplishes its mission. The hour was near when all the doors of the world would be closed to Israel, but the "hand of destiny" would open Palestine's door by force. The situation was volcanic. After the war, masses of Jews would have to emigrate from Europe, and there would be no viable place ready to welcome them—except one. In the Land of Israel, decades of labor and initiative had prepared the country for just such an emergency. The Jewish problem was a world problem in the war—Nazis used the defenseless position of Jews as a weapon to disintegrate Europe and expand their empire. As Europe forced its Jews out, with nowhere for them to go, the situation would become so explosive as to threaten rehabilitation after the war. Silver considered the world's treatment of Jews an index for international prospects of rebuilding, quoting Nahman of Bratslav (1772-1811): "The reconstruction of the world will be patterned after Palestine." If the world's most ravaged and defenseless people were treated with justice, vision, and statesmanship, there was hope that the whole world could be healed.

There was also a mandate from *midrash*. When the children of Israel went through the desert to the Promised Land they were led by two arks: the ark of death containing Joseph's corpse and the ark of life of the covenant.* Both arks

---

*"The ark of Joseph went with the ark of everlasting life. Those who passed by asked, What is the benefit of these two arks? This is the ark of the dead person, and this is the ark of everlasting life. And they said to them, What is the benefit in having the ark of the dead person go with the ark of everlasting life? And they responded, The one who rests in this ark kept what is written in what rests in this ark." Pesikta 24b, *Mekhilta Beshallah*.

were equally real in 1943. In the ark of death were the memories of two million victims, leading Israel through the "wilderness" of the European catastrophe to Palestine. The horror, pathos, and "crushing logic of their needless deaths" led Israel on:

> This vast ghostly company from the slaughter-pens of Warsaw, Cracow, and Lemberg now join up with the older companies of the last war from Galicia and the Ukraine, and from Kishinev and Bialystock of the earlier years, and with those tortured hosts of the foregoing generations—all the way back to the universal holocaust in the days of Chmielnitsky and with their brothers from other parts of Europe in almost every century and every land. It is their spirits which give us no rest, which admonish us against all vain illusions and false hopes. It is their innocent blood which will not be covered up, until out of their martyrdom a new life is born—the free and redeemed life of their people.

In the ark of life of the covenant the Land of Israel rested. Silver invoked the memory of Hussite leader John Ziska (1360-1424) and the religious wars in Bohemia. As Ziska lay dying he exhorted his followers to remove his skin to use for a drum to lead his troops into battle. He had the faith to use his death for victory and life, and so did the people of Israel—a faith in their destiny, their peoplehood and their God. "Exiles are never terminated and peoples are never freed except through faith."

Silver called for Jewish initiative. Jews must not put off working for a Jewish state until the Allies won. The difficulties would not diminish in the interim, for there was no sign that the world's ideals would change, that justice would oblige the world to try to save Jews, that in an effort to avert future tragedies the world would take measures to ensure Jewish a national rehabilitation in Palestine. The Balfour Declaration and Palestine Mandate implemented Israel's historic claims to Palestine as national homeland, the existence of the people was being recognized, and between the wars the Jews had invested life, energy, and substance in building the Land. He asked for an active Israel:

> The hammer of destiny is even now fashioning a new world, and Israel is, again, the anvil which bears the strokes of humanity. It is a noble role, but we are a little tired of this role. We have been noble and beaten for so long. We now wish to be noble and free and, as a free people in its own land, to work together with all other free peoples for a just and peaceful world.[16]

Reform's Negative Attitude

Reform's earlier resistance to reviving the Land, however, did not disappear. On the institutional level, resistance was voiced in response to the Balfour

Declaration and the San Remo Treaty. At its 1918 conference the CCAR responded to the Declaration. It appreciated the goodwill toward the Jews behind the Declaration. It favored immigration to the Land, whether out of economic necessity or political or religious persecution, and considered Jews in Palestine entitled to political, civil, and religious equality. On the other hand,

We do not subscribe to the phrase in the Declaration which says, "Palestine is to be a national homeland for the Jewish people." This statement assumes that the Jews, although identified with the life of many nations for centuries, are in fact a people without a country. We hold that the Jewish people are, and of right ought to be, at home in all lands. Israel, like every other religious communion, has the right to live and assert its message in any part of the world. We are opposed to the idea that Palestine should be considered *the homeland* of the Jews. Jews in America are part of the American nation. The ideal of the Jew is not the establishment of a Jewish state—not the reassertion of Jewish nationality which has long been outgrown. We believe that our survival as a people is dependent upon our historic religious role and not upon the acceptance of Palestine as a homeland of the Jewish people. The mission of the Jew is to witness to God all over the world.[17]

In 1919 the Union of American Hebrew Congregations (UAHC) reaffirmed its 1898 resolution:

We are unalterably opposed to political Zionism. The Jews are not a nation, but a religious community. Zion was a precious possession of the past, the early home of our faith where our prophets uttered their world-subduing thoughts and our psalmists sang their world-enchanting hymns. As such it is a holy memory, but it is not our hope of the future. America is our Zion. Here, in the home of religious liberty, we have aided in founding this new Zion, the fruition of the old. The mission of Judaism is spiritual, not political. Its aim is not to establish a state, but to spread the truths of religion and humanity throughout the world.[18]

UAHC opposed Jewish statehood, supporting instead the universal religious mission of Judaism, the principle that Israel should be at home everywhere. In May 1920 the HUC Board of Governors responded negatively to the San Remo Treaty. No single land, not even Palestine, it said, could be a "national home for the Jews . . . Palestine is not our national home, since we are not now and never expect to be citizens of that Land." Jews had their "national home" in whichever land they were loyal citizens.[19]

On the individual level, a radically Zion-as-America position was publicized by layman Isaac W. Bernheim (b. 1848) in his May 1921 proposal for a "Reform Church of American Israelites" which he claimed found support from thousands of "liberal laymen."[20] Bernheim supported emigration to Palestine from ravaged Eastern Europe. but he rejected any attempt to create "a so-called 'Jewish state' . . . Here is our Palestine." Bernheim would "demonstrate by every adequate means that we are Americans by nationality, that our longings are not for an Oriental Palestinian homeland, that our hearts are here, our homes are here—here in America." He protested "the slightest imputation . . . that we or our children are anything but one hundred percent Americans and ready in the future as we have been in the past to defend our rightful possession with our lives." Nor was it possible to be both an American and a Zionist: "Zionism and Americanism are not now and never will be synonymous." Indeed, Zionism was a danger for American Jews, as the influential liberal *World's Week* pointed out:

> Americans see in the Zionistic movement a menace to American solidarity. For anything that tends to make any section of the population transfer a modicum of its allegiance, even a sentimental and religious allegiance, to foreign soil, is an impediment to that individual devotion which true Americanism demands. Americanism, after all, is a jealous mistress and can brook no rivals.[21]

Bernheim even objected to the way Zionists employed the term "Jewry." Jews did not form a "separate entity, a state within a state, a closed corporation of unpractical dreamers and foreign reactionaries." Such a category was as repugnant as "Methodistry" or "Baptistry." Jews in America enjoyed the fullest measure of religious liberty, and they had no right to constitute their own grouping or raise a barrier between themselves and other citizens. For that matter, he did not like the term "Judaism" either:

> In the mind of the gentiles this name indissolubly associates our religion, which is universal in its deepest sources, and universal in its scope and tendency, with the Jewish race, and thus stamps it as a tribal religion. Worse still, the Jews themselves, who have gradually come to call their religion Judaism, are most of them misled to believe that their faith is bound up altogether with the Jewish race, and that it is a "religion for Jews alone and not for people of any other race or nationality."[22]

Bernheim would follow Isaac M. Wise and "convert into actuality our reiterated creed that we are a religious body," using the term "Israel" instead of "Jewry" and "Israelite" instead of "Judaism."[23]

The 1923 *Union Haggada* closed with "My Country 'Tis of Thee" instead of the traditional "Next Year in Jerusalem."[24] The vestiges of negative attitudes toward Zionism were still present in June 1942: 96 Reform rabbis, including Leo M. Franklin, organized the American Council for Judaism to support Palestine as a refuge for needy Jews but to reject "the political emphasis in the Zionist program, which diverts attention from the historical Jewish role as a religious community and which confuses people as to the nature of Judaism."[25]

Conservative Judaism: The Land of Israel as Revitalizing Center

For Conservative Judaism's leading spokesman, Solomon Schechter (1847-1915), Zionism embodied the essence of Judaism.[26] In December 1905 he joined the Federation of American Zionists, explaining to Bernhard Felsenthal that "theological reasons kept me from joining the movement. But I see that it is a genuine manifestation of the deeper Jewish consciousness, deeper perhaps than several of its leaders realized."[27] In December 1906 Schechter explained that while the ideal of Zionism was undefinable, Zionism was empirically demonstrable by the fact that it was absolutely necessary to recover Palestine. For Judaism this was a life-and-death matter. Zionism provided the antidote to assimilation and the loss of Jewish identity. It removed despair over the loss of sacred memories, institutions and self-respect. It ended the atrophy of the Jewish soul that *galut* (exile) brought about.

What Schechter feared was not the use of English, the learning of American history and literature, or the commitment to American citizenship but rather the disintegration of Jewish identity caused by the rejection of Jewish thought, history, and mission. In Germany this took the form of public apostasy; elsewhere it meant severing synagogue affiliation and replacing it with "eclectic religiosity." Schechter saw that in *galut* a great and ancient people distinguished by loyalty to religion and devotion to sacred law was losing thousands daily by attrition; ancient and sacred institutions, for which Israel had sacrificed itself for millennia, were being destroyed and exchanged for institutions of hostile religions; a language that was universally held sacred, which contained Israel's Holy Writ and thought, was forced out of the synagogue and doomed to oblivion; descendants of those who brought revelation to the world were slavishly accepting interpretations of Israel's religion made by her opponents. Julius Wellhausen (1844-1918) had captured the essence of the process in his remark about Spinoza's views on absorption:

The persisting of the race may, of course, prove a harder thing to overcome than Spinoza has supposed. But nevertheless, he will be found to have spoken truly in declaring that the so-called emancipation of the Jews must inevitably lead to the extinction of Judaism wherever the process is extended beyond the political to the social sphere. For the accomplishment of this, centuries may be required.[28]

Schechter felt that Israel in *galut* would either acquiesce to slow death or "live continually dying" until death came as a merciful coup de grâce.

Zionism was the counterforce. It declared to the world that Judaism would preserve its life by not losing its life; that Jewish life would be healthy, have its own policy, its own religion invigorated with sacred memories; that it would be a tower of strength and unity not only for the remnant in the Holy Land but for those who by choice or necessity constituted the diaspora. Once Zionism regenerated Jewish consciousness the political goal of a Jewish state could and would be implemented. And once Israel so effectuated her own redemption she would be instrumental in redeeming the world. Zionism was Israel's Declaration of Independence, signaling the independence of the Jewish soul from material and spiritual slavery to be followed by establishing the Jewish nation. Once the Jewish soul was redeemed from *galut* and the national idea was realized, Judaism's universal mission to the world could be resumed. It could then bring forth God's word from Jerusalem.* God, the Sages said, would "not enter the heavenly Jerusalem until Israel shall come to the earthly Jerusalem."† After Israel established "divine institutions in their full integrity in God's own Land" the kingdom of heaven would triumph in all its glory.[29]

Israel Friedlaender (1876-1920) carried Schechter's themes further. In 1913 he described the state as a material and political means toward a spiritual end. A Jewish center in Palestine would evoke Israel's history. It would be "the root and fruit of Jewish national genius," a rallying point for its scattered endeavors, and as such it would be a check against the disintegration of diaspora Jewry.[30] In 1917 Friedlaender spoke about loyalty to America vis-à-vis loyalty to the Land: "Our love for America is purer, our devotion to her is deeper, because at the same time we may love and may be devoted to Palestine, to which as Jews we owe our birth and the best that is in us." He understood Zionism as the true response to the Emancipation's implication that dispersion was the final aspiration of the Jewish people. Emancipation addressed the "material" issues of discrimination and persecution, which depended upon other nations, but the internally dependent "spiritual" problems of Judaism awaited a Jewish state. There, by reconnecting with preexilic history, the exile of *shekhina* would end, the shackles of *galut* would be broken. A unified purpose, a fellowship within Jewry, could be established there to end the dissipation of Israel engendered by diaspora life: "A portion of our people settled in the Holy Land will prove a focus which will gather the efforts of all the Jewries in the world, and it will prove at the same time a powerhouse which will send forth its energies to the whole house of Israel." Then "rejuvenated Zion, by gathering the scattered energies of Israel, will prove again a great spiritual focus which will send out its vivifying rays to the stiffening limbs of the Jewish national organism throughout the diaspora, and

---

*"For out of Zion shall go forth the law, and the word of the Lord from Jerusalem." *Isaiah* 2:3.

†I have been unable to locate the source.

will make Judaism shine forth once more as the luminous bearer of a religious message to humanity."[31]

Mordecai M. Kaplan (1881-1983) also continued Schechter's themes, in *Judaism as a Civilization* (1934). Kaplan argued the inseparability of Jews, Judaism, and Land on the basis of biblical, rabbinic, and medieval sources. Judaism conceived of its life and destiny in terms of collective existence tied to the Land. For example, the Pentateuch was a "recorded deed" to the possession of the Land of Israel. From Abraham through Joshua Israelites were trained to be a people of the Land, and appropriate laws were provided. The Israelites' single irrevocable sin was the spies' negative report about the Land.* Jews were always a civilization, and land was the medium for a civilization's self-expression. Jewish continuity required an environment in which to mold the coming generations. Moreover, Jews earned their right to Palestine not simply by their achievements there but by uninterrupted devotion to it after exile. Kaplan believed that once established, the "primary" civilization of Palestine would assure Jewish "ancillary" or "coordinate" stability elsewhere. Indeed, the Jewish realities of Palestine in 1934 were already stimulating the cohesion of Jewish diaspora communities.[32]

Conservative Judaism carried Schechter's themes through the Holocaust. In 1938 Solomon Goldman (1893-1953) said that the void in American Jewish life was responsible for the lack of response to Israel's suffering in Europe: "The countless suicides of Vienna and the tortures of little Jewish children in Berlin have not persuaded us to give up for a brief period of five or ten years our night clubs, mink coats, visits to Miami Beach." He traced the void to *galut* and believed it could be filled and Jewry regenerated only with a Land for the people, one in which they were no longer alienated.[33] He reiterated Friedlaender's stress on the ideal, Israel-centering dimension to a Jewish state, beyond the material and political aspects. Goldman also said Jewish loyalty to the Land would reinforce loyalty to America, quoting Louis Brandeis as well as Albert Einstein (1879-1955). In 1926 Einstein had stated:

> The German Jew who works for the Jewish people and for the Jewish home in Palestine no more ceases to be a German than the Jew who becomes baptized and changes his name ceases to be a Jew. The two attachments are grounded in realities of different kinds. The antithesis is not between Jew and German, but between honesty and lack of character. He who remains true to his origin, race, and tradition will also remain loyal to the state of

---

*"And the men, which Moses sent to search the Land, who returned, and made all the congregation to murmur against him, by bringing up a slander on the Land, Even those men that did bring up the evil report upon the Land, died by the plague before the Lord." *Numbers* 14:36-37.

which he is a subject. He who is faithless to the one will also be faithless to the other.[34]

The following year Goldman added that since Zionism did not mean that all Jews would return to the Land, dual loyalty should not be an issue.[35]

Between 1937 and 1939 Israel Goldstein (1896-1986) spoke of the Land of Israel as the source of revival in the face of growing tragedy in diaspora, clarifying that it would be "unreasonable to expect" that all 17 million Jews would congregate there. As Jeremiah wanted to build up his own land in the face of Jerusalem's fall, so now the Land should be built in the face of the "world of *Hurban* [Holocaust]."[*] The "prostrate" Jacob, the contemporary trouble, was a "necessary transition" which strengthened Israel's will and would subsequently yield to a Jewish homeland.[†] The separate identity lost with the Emancipation would be restored in the Land, and spiritual life would flow therefrom the world over to assure survival of Judaism amidst democracy and freedom. The Land would overcome the submissiveness, passivity, and loss of self-respect induced by *galut*: "Like the reviving limbs of a sick man whose heart has begun to function normally again, the members of the worldwide body of Israel" have already, with the half-century of reunion in the Land of Israel, "taken on new life."[36]

As the war ended, Goldstein spoke of American Jewry as a *she'erit ha'pleta* (surviving remnant), as the "strongest surviving brother in the ravaged household of Israel," with the obligation to build in America "some compensations for the spiritual *Hurban*" of Europe. Those compensations would be Tora and modern Hebrew letters. Palestine, however, remained at the depths of Jewish consciousness. Even amidst the creativity of exilic life in rabbinic and medieval times, while "Jews were not in Erets Israel, Erets Israel was in them." The sole source for creative Judaism in America was Palestine. The only antidote to lack of dignity remained the Jewish state: "Our destiny is to be a people among peoples, standing on our feet and resting our feet upon the hallowed soil of our fathers."[37]

---

[*]"Behold, Hanameel the son of Shallum thine uncle shall come unto thee, saying, Buy thee my field that is in Anathoth: for the right of redemption is thine to buy it." *Jeremiah* 32:7. "For thus saith the Lord of hosts, the God of Israel; Houses and fields and vineyards shall be possessed again in this land." *Jeremiah* 32:15.

[†]"Art thou the Jacob whose image is engraved in the heavenly throne? Art thou the Jacob of whom the divine voice spoke, 'Israel, in whom I will be glorified' [*Isaiah* 49:3]. Art thou that Jacob who art now lying prostrate on the ground?" *Midrash Bereshit Rabba* 68:12. "And, behold, the Lord stood above it and said, I am the Lord God of Abraham thy father, and the God of Isaac: the land whereon thou liest, to thee will I give it, and to thy seed." *Genesis* 28:13.

Orthodox Support for Zionism

Orthodoxy during the first decades of the twentieth century had intense desire to restore the Land of Israel as the Jewish homeland or state.[38] Spokesmen before the Balfour Declaration included Joseph M. Levin, who arrived in America in 1891 and served as rabbi in Wilkes-Barre, Atlanta, and Cincinnati. In 1905 he spoke of American Jews as being on a burning ship: if they stayed aboard they would die in the flames of antisemitism, while if they leapt into the ocean they would drown in assimilation. At the last moment the rescue vessel of Zion appeared on the horizon. American Jews should rush to board it. They had the freedom to take action, nor should they wait passively for enlightened nations to lead them. Although comprehensive redemption depended on God, when natural means were available, Israel should not wait. Levin urged American Jews to unite in body and soul around the goal of Zion.[39] The effort, he pointed out in 1916, had begun with Herzl, who had revived the nation's soul, integrated its different parts, and provided hope amidst despair.[40] Tsevi H. Masliansky (1856-1943), expelled from Russia for Zionist activity, promoted Zionism from the time he arrived in America in 1889 as the "Moses"—so he called himself—for contemporary exiles. He addressed himself to assimilation, which split Judaism into twos—two languages, holidays, calendars, names—and identified the antidote as Jews in their own Land.[41] Tsevi H. Orliansky (1864-1940), who arrived from England in 1917, spoke of America as a "pot of salt," a place empty of *shekhina* where Israel was threatened with heresy and perversion. Settlement in the Holy Land, where Tora and redemption were accessible, was the answer.[42]

Following the Balfour Declaration, Shemaryahu L. Hurwitz (1878-1938), who was born in White Russia and came to New York in 1908, expressed his Zionism in terms of the current Passover. The candles were really memorial candles for the Judaism ending with American Jewish children. When the prophet Elijah appeared at the Seder he felt the emptiness of parents alone, and he rushed away to the Land of Israel. There the Seder was joyous, and after it Jews walked freely through fields of aromatic flowers under beautiful skies. During the intermediate days of the festival Maccabi athletes paraded with the Hebrew flag. Hurwitz was convinced that American Jews had no alternative but to forsake their exile in America for freedom in the Land.[43] Abraham I. Hurwitz (b. 1857 in Lomza) of Cincinnati explained that before the Balfour Declaration he awaited God's initiative, believing that God would inspire the enlightened nations to return Jews to their Land. He rejected both secular and revisionist Zionism for acting independently of Tora and God. But with the Declaration and the victories by God-fearing Jewish Legionnaires he came to believe that God had entered history, and Hurwitz became a Zionist.[44] Gedaliah (George) Silverstone of Washington, D.C., (b. 1873), who came to America in 1907 from Belfast, Ireland, drew from the Sages to say at the end of 1918 that World War I constituted the messianic suffering which preceded redemption; the

Balfour Declaration was Elijah's shofar.* He predicted that resurrection of the dead and collective return to the Land were imminent.[45] Soon after he arrived in New York from Manchester, England, in 1921, Abraham A. Yudelovitch (1850-1930) wrote that the Jew had to start building Jerusalem for God to finish. When the love for the Holy Land was intense enough, the redemptive process would assume its own momentum; if the Jew pulled on the feet of the messiah, the messiah would come and the mending (*tikkun*) of the Land would begin.† Yudelovitch supported secular and liberal Zionists who went to the Land because they added strength to the human effort.[46]

Perhaps the outstanding representative of Zionist Orthodoxy was Haim Hirschensohn, who came to America in 1903.[47] He explained that once the Emancipation in Europe shattered Jewish communal strength and precipitated religious decline, the Land of Israel became the only place for national strength—the expression of covenantal unity—to be actualized.[48] Hirschensohn thought of the restoration dialectically: (1) While England and her allies brought about temporal political resurrection, Tora and *halakha* provided eternal reality for the Jewish homeland. (2) While the people of Israel actively pursued redemption through natural means and developed a *halakhic* structure for the state, the messianic process unfolded from above. (3) The "marriage canopy" awaited Israel, but to enter it Israel had to "dress" properly. Because she had failed to prepare herself in earlier times, many messianic ends to history were lost. This time she must "build the Temple," i.e., develop the Land and become the majority, whereupon transhistorical forces could take effect. Hirschensohn considered America the ideal planning area for the human part to restoration. American Jews had the intellectual distance to establish a comprehensive structure, and the American political system provided a living example for the covenantal democracy of Scripture desirable for a Jewish state.[49] By 1934, however, while serving as honorary president of the Federation of Palestine Jews in America, Hirschensohn despaired over the disjunction between the Zionist movement and the spiritual realities in the Land. Yehudah Halevi's plaint— "Where, where is the Holy Land? My spirit longs for it"—still remained unanswered. The Zionist movement provided an active response, but within the Land itself the soulful, holy atmosphere needed to ease the longing was absent. Sadly the soul was cast down in the Land; the spiritual Tora-ideals of Babylon and Volozhin were being crushed by materialism.[50]

---

*See, for example, *Sanhedrin* 97a: "Thus hath Rabbi Johanan said: In the generation when the son of David will come scholars will be few in number, and as for the rest, their eyes will fail through sorrow and grief. Multitudes of trouble and evil decrees will be promulgated anew, each new evil coming with haste before the other has ended."

†"How beautiful upon the mountains are the feet of him that bringeth good tidings, that publisheth peace; that bringeth good tidings of good, that publisheth salvation; that saith unto Zion, Thy God reigneth!" *Isaiah* 52:7.

Orthodox Resistance to Zionism

Orthodoxy in the twentieth century, however, was not all positive toward Zionism. The anti-Zionist position was enunciated as well. In 1910 Shalom Israelson (1861-1931) of Chicago, who arrived in America in 1894, bemoaned the vitality of Jewish nationalism in America vis-à-vis the moribund Tora-religion that had provided hope for Judaism in the past. He believed that God's spirit, not the sword, would miraculously overcome Israel's enemies.* Only when God poured His spirit into the people of Israel, so that they served Him totally, would there be eternal salvation.[51] In 1916-1917 Ephraim Deinard (1846-1930), who came to America in 1897, distinguished the ideals of Zionism—which presumably he supported—from reality, which lacked national-religious substance. Zionism as practised came down to cash profits and commerce. Zionism in the Land itself was dominated by merchants, procurers, socialists, anarchists, Bundists, and Hebraists; there were "no Zionists in Zion."[52]

In 1918 Barukh M. Klein, who arrived in New York from Hungary in 1909, attacked the hypocrisy of American Zionists. The wealthy talkers were not about to leave to become observant Jews in the Land of Israel; neither Reform leader Stephen S. Wise nor his intermarried Free Synagogue congregants were yearning to recite psalms at the Western Wall. There was also a sinister aspect to their free advice: it jeopardized the scholarly and pious Jews in the Land, the very Jews who prayed for the welfare of their brethren, should the Turks retaliate for American Jewish support of English control. Klein also criticized secular Zionists in the Land, for they rejected Tora in favor of vocational training, separated Tora from nation, ridiculed ritual (forbidden food was eaten in Jerusalem itself), and tried to undermine Orthodox schools. Klein was convinced they would be punished, that God would have the Land repel them as a prince vomiting rotten food.†

The Zionist movement, Klein explained, violated classical Jewish theology. According to the classics, redemption was a transnatural phenomenon. Human action was not to attempt to precipitate it, whether through immigration,

---

*"Not by might, nor by power, but by My spirit, saith the Lord of hosts." *Zechariah* 4:6.

†"'And the Land is defiled: therefore I do visit the iniquity thereof upon it, and the Land itself vomiteth out her inhabitants' [*Leviticus* 18:25]. [Rashi:] This is comparable to the son of a king who was fed a loathsome thing which does not remain in the intestines, but he vomits it out. Likewise the Land of Israel does not retain transgressors."

speculation about the timing or excessive prayer.* Religious revival, however, was a prerequisite for settlement; exiled Jews had to return to God, the Temple had to be rebuilt.† As Meir L. Malbim (1809-1879) explained, only the pious would be eligible for entry into the Land.‡ When the exile ended, the world would be filled with knowledge of God and worthy leaders would be available.# Certainly, Klein observed, Israel Zangwill (1864-1926) was no messiah, Max S. Nordau (1849-1923) no Elijah, Stephen S. Wise no high priest. Klein was content to remain in America, where gentiles allowed Jews to be Jewish and study Tora. Better to live in exile among gentiles than in exile in the Land among antisemitic Zionists.[53]

The outstanding representative of Orthodox anti-Zionism in America was Joel Teitelbaum, who arrived in 1947. On 29 March 1948 he described the imminent establishment of a Jewish state as tragic. Like the "heroes" who were responsible for the destruction of the First and Second Temples because they acted by themselves, the Zionist "heroes" today were endangering Israel; Zionism's effort to establish a sovereign state was a Satanic act, blocking redemption. But Zionists were in total control, and pious Jews who objected were disgraced. Teitelbaum was left with the truth and the pain: "I am sick at heart over the condition of our generation. Woe to those who rise up today in this manner. I cannot describe the destruction. I have such great fear for the Holy City of Jerusalem, may it be rebuilt speedily in our day [from above]. I fear for all the residents of the Holy Land. I fear at the plight of all Israel."

---

*See, for example, *Sanhedrin* 97b: "Rabbi Samuel ben Nahmani said in the name of Rabbi Jonathan: Blasted be the bones of those who calculate the end. For they would say, since the predetermined time has arrived, and yet he has not come, he will never come."

†"The Temple is prior to the ingathering of exiles. The ingathering of exiles is prior to the resurrection of the dead, and the resurrection of the dead is the last of all." *Midrash Hane'elam, Zohar Toldot.*

‡"'And the Lord thy God will bring thee into the land which thy fathers possessed, and thou shalt possess it; and he will do thee good, and multiply thee above thy fathers' [*Deuteronomy* 30:5]. [Meir L. Malbim:] It states in *Ezekiel* 'And I will bring you into the wilderness of the people . . . And I will purge out from among you the rebels, and them that transgress against me: I will bring them forth out of the country where they sojourn. And they shall not enter into the Land of Israel: and ye shall know that I am the Lord' [*Ezekiel* 20:35-38]. In principle, you do not hear that He will bring the pious ones to the Land . . . He will gather them, i.e., into one place, then He will bring them to the Land. For He will gather them in one location and then 'the Lord thy God will bring thee into the Land.' It means that He will bring only the pious ones who [are with] God into the Land. But not those who rebel and transgress."

#"And the spirit of the Lord shall rest upon him, the spirit of wisdom and understanding, the spirit of counsel and might, the spirit of knowledge and of the fear of the Lord." *Isaiah* 11:2.

Teitelbaum drew upon traditional texts to denounce human, political initiative. If Jews accepted the yoke of dispersion, then God, the *midrash* explained, would rescue the lone sheep from the wolves.* Instead, Zionists were violating the scriptural oath about waiting for God to decide when redemption would take place.† Obadiah Sforno (1475-1550) had explained the matter in terms of submissiveness and deep roots. When Jacob became submissive to Esau, Esau stopped his aggressiveness (*Genesis* 32-33). It was possible to be rescued from the prideful children of Esau by surrender and tribute.‡ Johanan ben Zakkai, for example, said that if Israel's heroes had not stopped him he could have come to Vespasian in time to prevent the destruction.# Meanwhile, Israel was to be as the reed, whose many roots resist the wind.** Similarly, Solomon ben Akiva Eger (1761-1837) explained the Sages' point that Israel's assertive overtures to the nations caused exile. If the people had submitted to Nebuchadnezzar during the First Temple era and to Titus during the Second, God would not have dispersed them.††

As stated in *Ketubot*, Teitelbaum continued, Jews were under oath not to emigrate en masse to the Land before God directed, not to revolt against the nations which held them prisoners of war, while God was under oath not to let the nations of the world oppress them too much.‡‡ The matter could also be explained in terms of slavery. The prophet Isaiah differentiated between the world to come, when the moon would be confounded and the sun ashamed while God reigned, and the messianic era, when the light of both moon and sun would

---

*"Adrianus said to Rabbi Joshua, Great is the sheep who stays among seventy wolves. The rabbi told him, Great is the shepherd who rescues and guards the sheep, and destroys the wolves before her." *Toldot* ch.5, *Midrash Tanhuma*.

†"I charge you, O ye daughters of Jerusalem, by the does, and by the hinds of the field, that ye stir not up, nor awake My love, till he please." *Solomon's Song* 2:7.

‡"That saith in his heart, Who shall bring me down to the ground?" *Obadiah* 3.

#"As for your question, Why if you are a king I did not come to you till now, the answer is that the heroes among us did not let me." *Gittin* 56b.

**"'For the Lord shall smite Israel, as a reed is broken in water' [*I Kings* 14:15]. The reed grows by the water and its stock grows new shoots and its roots are many. Even though all the winds of the universe come and blow at it, they cannot move it from its place, for it sways with the winds and as soon as they have dropped the reed resumes its upright position." *Ta'anit* 20a.

††"What caused Israel to be scattered among the nations? The approaches [to the nations] which she desired." *Pesahim* 118b.

‡‡"One, that Israel shall not go up [all together]; the second, that whereby the Holy One, Blessed be He, adjured Israel that they shall not rebel against the nations of the world; and the third is that whereby the Holy One, Blessed be He, adjured the idolaters that they should not oppress Israel too much." *Ketubot* 111a.

grow sevenfold.* Rabbi Samuel explained that the eras were distinct, for in the messianic era slavery would disappear in a transhistorical manner.†

It was, for Teitelbaum, Satanic to try to initiate the messianic realm by ending slavery, and the consequences would be severe. According to *midrash*, God would provoke vile nations against such heretics.‡ An example was that of Titus, who committed a sin with a harlot in the Holy of Holies. When he slashed the curtain and blood spurted out, he thought that somehow, miraculously, he had killed God.# Rashi (1040-1105) explained that God allowed this so as to let Titus continue to defile himself. Similarly, God allowed the Zionists to establish a state and consider it miraculous so they could go on defiling themselves. Before the messiah would come every vestige of sovereignty had to be removed. Rabbi Hama ben Rabbi Hanina declared that the son of David would not come until Israel eliminated her political structures. Rashi added that this included even the most insignificant forms.** Political sovereignty and redemption were mutually exclusive; the appropriate complement to redemption was expectation for heavenly action.[54]

---

*"Then the moon shall be confounded, and the sun shall be ashamed, when the Lord of hosts will reign in mount Zion, and in Jerusalem, and before his ancients gloriously." *Isaiah* 24:23. "Moreover the light of the moon shall be as the light of the sun, and the light of the sun shall be sevenfold, as the light of the seven days, in the day that the Lord bindeth up the breach of his people, and healeth the stroke of their wound." *Isaiah* 30:26.

†"Rabbi Hisda opposed *Isaiah* 24:23 and *Isaiah* 30:26. No problem. The latter refers to the messianic era, the former to the world-to-come. And according to Samuel, who maintained, This world differs from the messianic era only in respect of the servitude of the diaspora, it is still no problem; the latter refers to the camp of the righteous, the former to the camp of the divine presence." *Sanhedrin* 91b.

‡"'They have moved Me to jealousy with that which is not God; they have provoked Me to anger with their vanities: and I will move them to jealousy with those which are not a people; I will provoke them to anger with a foolish nation' [*Deuteronomy* 32:21]. *They* refers to the heretics, [equivalent to] the stupid one [who said in his heart, There is no God." *Sifre* to *Deuteronomy*.

#"This was the wicked Titus who blasphemed and insulted Heaven. What did he do? He took a harlot by the hand and entered the Holy of Holies, and spread out a scroll of the law and committed a sin on it. He then took a sword and slashed the curtain. Miraculously, blood spurted out, and he thought he had slain [God] Himself." *Gittin* 56b.

**"'Rabbi Hama ben Hanina said, The son of David will not come until even the pettiest kingdom ceases [to have power] over Israel' [*Sanhedrin* 98b]. [Rashi:] That is, until even the pettiest rule ceases among Israel."

Nonreligious Zionists and the American Ideal

Secular Zionists thought that America had failed to fulfill the scriptural principles brought by the Puritans, and they turned to the Land of Israel, where those principles originated.

The philosopher and educator Horace M. Kallen regarded the San Remo Treaty as the synthesis between ideal and real Zions, enabling the "metaphysical transvaluation" of Zion from symbolic vision of otherworldly future salvation into coercive fact. Kallen made his contribution to the change by delineating an ideology or philosophy of Zion for institutional implementation. His political ideal of Jeffersonian liberal, just, socialist democracy had not been realized in America. He turned to the Land, whose ancient prophets once proclaimed social justice; his undergraduate study of American Puritan involvement with Scripture interested him in the prophets and their Land. Kallen spoke of a "Hebraic" state which was secular, where Hebrew was the spoken language. State Hebraism would encompass the totality of national Jewish history and ethnic solidarity. Religion, including the soul's commitment to the Land, was one of the state's components. In his 1918 *Pittsburgh Program* he explained that the new Zion would be based upon social justice that secured individual life, liberty, and happiness. Controlled natural resources and free public education, including instruction in Hebrew, would yield economic and social democracy. The state would preserve free expression and abolish private ownership and privilege. There would be political and civil equality, equality of opportunity, land ownership not for speculation but for long-range development and cooperative undertakings. The state would be a model of democratic, Jewish nationality and fulfill the prophetic and legal transformation of the Jewish people.[55]

Louis Brandeis was influenced by Kallen's idea that a Jewish state could provide a new and just social order, one which implemented the equality in difference and so could realize American ideals.[56] Brandeis rooted his Zionism in the American values of the citizen's overwhelming sense of duty, intellectual achievement, submission not to authority but to leadership, and advanced sense of community. In turn, he recognized that American democracy and justice were brought to America by Puritans who imbibed Hebrew Scripture. Thus one could be a good American by being a good Jew, and one could promote American ideals by becoming a Zionist. During 1914-1916 Brandeis identified the themes of his Zionist commitment:

1. Nationalities had individualistic characters which were impossible to obliterate, and each had as much right to develop the character as the individual person did. Principles of individualistic nationalism were indispensable to liberty, and civilization flourished with the differentiations.

2. The fourteen million Jews of the world were not expected to go to Palestine—which in any case could accommodate no more than one-fifth that number. Brandeis was committed to the free choice between Palestine and other countries, in the name of freedom as well as in the name of equality; the Irish and Greeks, for example, had that free choice. Accordingly, Zionism must not try to compel anyone to go to Palestine.

3. Zionism realized the hope that had nourished Jews in the face of persecution for two thousand years—as Giuseppe Mazzini (1805-1872) Giuseppe Garibaldi (1807-1882), and Camillo B. Cavour (1810-1861) had realized Italian hopes in the nineteenth century.

4. The establishment of a homeland would stop the current disintegration of Jewish life and fully develop the Jewish spirit—for which a majority population in the Land, but not a greater number than Jews outside, was required.

Zionism, Brandeis stressed, was not incompatible with patriotism. To the contrary, given the principle of pluralism and the special Jewish tie to America's original scriptural values, the American Zionist was the better patriot. The Jewish spirit, indeed, coincided with the American: "Not since the destruction of the Temple have the Jews in spirit and ideals been so fully in harmony with the noblest aspirations of the country in which they lived." For example, the brotherhood of man which America sought to realize was a fundamental Jewish law more than 2500 years ago. America's striving for social justice had been present among Jews for ages; persecution had imbued Jews with deep sympathy for others and intense passion for righteousness. The centrality of Jewish principles to American identity was such that loyalty to America even demanded that each American Jew become a Zionist.

Brandeis drew attention to demoralization among American Jews. The remedy was self-respect, possible through the restoration of the Jew's ties to his noble past and the glorious future it implied. Zionism was the source of this renaissance. In Palestine itself there was already a new pride, a sense of Jewry's glory and new commitment to ideals—Brandeis pointed to the great accomplishments of scientist Aaron Aaronsohn (1876-1919), educator David Yellin (1864-1941), and craftsman Boris Schatz (1866-1932). This self-respect would spread through the diaspora. Henry W. Steed (1871-1956), for example, observed that Zionism inspired glory in the Jewish race, traditions, and resistance to suffering. It enabled the Jew to confront the world with pride in Israel's contributions to religion (Christianity in particular), to modern commerce and art. Before Zionism, Jews at Austrian universities were despised, able to enter the professional world only by dint of mock humility, mental acuteness, and clandestine protection. Zionism gave them courage:

The best fencers of the fighting German corps found that Zionist students could gash cheeks quite as effectively as any Teuton, and that the Jews were in a fair way to become the best swordsmen of the university. Today the purple cape of the Zionist is as respected as that of any academical association. This moral influence of Zionism is not confined to university students. It is quite as noticeable among the mass of the younger Jews outside, who also find in it a reason to raise their heads, and, taking their stand upon the past, to give straightforwardly into the future.[57]

Justice Felix Frankfurter (1882-1965) believed that Palestine would rescue Jewish national identity. It would replace those Jews who were "so pathetic and so devoid of erect manhood" with Jews living with their ancient grandeur and beauty. Frankfurter believed that a Jewish state would reinforce principles of America and the World War I Allies by realizing a life of freedom, liberal and democratic. He contrasted the freedom espoused by America or Zionism with the absolute self-definition of Germanic theory. Frankfurter did not expect American Jews to move to Palestine, but he did expect them to use the opportunity of the Balfour Declaration, the Magna Charta of Jewish life, to develop the state. Since American Jewry was the last reservoir of Jewry in the world, the realization of the dream for Palestine depended upon its efforts.[58]

Secularist Realism

In December 1945 the political philosopher Hannah Arendt (1906-1975) enunciated her overriding concerns about Zionism and the Land. First, she did not believe that antisemitism was endemic to mankind, or that Jewish history was naturally and ontologically separated from the rest of the world; the 1933 Transfer Agreement between Germany and Palestinian Zionists was one example to the contrary.[59] The Zionist view of emancipated Jewry was too dark:

Compared with the earthquake that has shaken the world in our time, those predictions read like prophecies of a storm in a teacup. The fierce outburst of popular hatred which Zionism predicted, and which fitted well within its general distrust of the peoples and overconfidence in governments, did not take place. Rather, in a number of countries it was replaced by concerted government action, which proved infinitely more detrimental than any popular outburst of Jew-hatred had ever been.

A Jewish state should therefore not be viewed as the necessary response to an ontic division.

Second, Arendt sought increased sensitivity on the part of Jews in Palestine to Jews outside—to American Jews in particular, who nourished those in Palestine and were the most significant force for a Jewish commonwealth. They were important to the World Zionist Organization and a political power vis-à-vis Zionism when it came to national elections. American Jews were able to either support their mother country in these ways or even move there because of American pluralistic values. Revisionists ignored the realities of pluralism in America and pushed for categorical and massive *aliya*. This subjected American Jews to attack for undermining pluralism; it evoked the issue of dual loyalty more violently than elsewhere because of America's multinational structure. The same American tolerance which fostered nationalistic identities and supported Jewish commitment to the mother country would oppose removing one constituent nationality. By contrast, Europe with its "national states" did not tolerate pluralism and so would not be concerned about upsetting a multinational balance.

Third, Arendt rejected potential exclusion of Arabs from the legal structure of a Jewish state. She wanted to ease the alienation between the future state and its Arab neighbors—an alienation that the superpowers would welcome as grounds for involvement and increased power in the region. It was extremely dangerous for a small people to be sucked into sphere-of-interest politics, and foolhardy to entrust a distant imperial power with protection while alienating neighbors. A working agreement with Arabs was needed, in the binational spirit.

Finally, Arendt was concerned with the consequences of a Jewish state for diaspora Jews. If 100,000 Jews were to leave Europe, what of those left behind? If the Jewish position reverted to status quo ante, would they ever want to leave for Palestine? Would the status quo ante renew dual-loyalty charges? If the autonomous entity were established in opposition to Arab will, would American Jewry not be called upon for long-term financial and political support?[60]

When he wrote to the Central Association of German Citizens of the Jewish faith on 3 April 1920, Albert Einstein first thought that Zionism's value consisted of educating and unifying Jews, not in establishing a state so that Jewry could become worldly. He wrote to Haim Weizmann (1874-1952), after their 1921 tour for Keren Hayesod and Hebrew University, that he was interested in maintaining the healthy national feeling of Jews wherever they were living.[61] In 1923 Einstein supported settlement in terms of a spiritual center and doubted that the Land could ever receive a large proportion of Jews.

After he met German Zionist Kurt Blumenfeld (1884-1963) in 1929, Einstein spoke about the necessity of a state. Jews were regarded as foreigners even while they sought to harmonize with the peoples of the world. Without the solid foundation of their own community they could never have moral stability. Once there was a living Jewish society in the Land of Israel for diaspora Jews to be involved with, they could bear the inevitable hatred and humiliation; absent the "right arm" of vigorous Judaism in the diaspora, the Jew needed the "left arm" of a state. From the human perspective Einstein opposed the idea of subsuming Judaism into a political entity, but from the perspective of Jewry's current reality Zionism was necessary. In 1933 Einstein explained that the Jews' social health required participation in the nation as a whole and that Jewish life in Palestine could embody the awakening of this corporate spirit.

In 1944 Einstein reiterated that strong international solidarity among the Jews would enable the independent inner life able to cope with the growingly hostile environment and that Zionism made solidarity possible. Ten days before political independence was declared, he wrote to the Hagana that the Jews of Palestine must not wait for the great powers and the United Nations, they had to take their destiny into their hands and fight for their rights. In his very last working hours Einstein drafted greetings to the Jewish people on the anniversary of their "modern liberation."[62]

Observations

In twentieth-century Judaism through 1948, concern for the Land of Israel revolved around whether it should have centrality for Jewish life and thought, and if so in what form. Some Reformers continued to deny its centrality either nationalistically or politically and even spoke of Zion in America, but most made it central, either culturally and spiritually or politically. For the latter, human initiative was expected, and the role of divine—but not *midrashic*—oversight was deemphasized. Conservative Judaism, in contrast to Reform and Orthodoxy, did not subdivide vis-a-vis the Land but developed cohesively. It viewed the Land as the counterforce to the death of diaspora Judaism. That is, the assertion of the Land of Israel's centrality was accompanied by reviving life in exile. The discussion in Reform over choosing America or the Land of Israel was sublimated into a "both." In its new vital role, the Land was seen as cultural-spiritual and political reality together. The Orthodox were split. Some supported restoration culturally and politically and viewed it as a joint effort by God and man. Others considered restoration exclusively divine, possible only after all human initiative was removed, both in America and in Palestine. Some were convinced that diaspora Judaism was dying and believed Jewish life was possible only in the Land; others believed that Tora Judaism was being suffocated in the Land and that Jewish life for the present was possible only elsewhere. Unlike Conservative Judaism and, with the exception of Silver, Reform as well, Orthodoxy's tie to the Land had apocalyptic currents. For those outside the three denominations of Judaism, universal principles which America espoused or realized were central. For some, Zionism was the receptacle for trans-Jewish ideals; the restored Land's cultural and political identity was part of the greater category of democratic absolutes. Other secularists looked to the Land as realists and saw it either as supplementing Jewish life in America and Europe or as a necessity given the fact of antisemitism.

Notes

1. See Abraham J. Karp, "Reaction to Zionism and to the State of Israel in the American Jewish Religious Community," *Jewish Journal of Sociology* 8 no. 2 (December 1960):150-174.

2. Hyman G. Enelow, "Palestine and the Jews, 1 December 1917," in *The Allied Countries and the Jew* (New York 1918):63-75.

3. Max L. Margolis, "The Theological Aspect of Reformed Judaism," *CCAR Yearbook* 13 (Philadelphia 1903):294n, 302-305.

4. Naomi W. Cohen, "The Reaction of Reform Judaism in America to Political Zionism (1897-1922)," *PAJHS* 40 no. 4 (June 1951):361-394.

5. Kaufmann Kohler in *American Hebrew* 73 no. 18 (18 September 1903):562, cited in Cohen, "Reaction"; idem, "The Faith of Reform Judaism," *Menorah Journal* 2 no. 1 (February 1916):8-15.

6. Kohler, "The Mission of Israel and Its Application to Modern Times," *CCAR Yearbook* 29 (Philadelphia 1919):265-305. See Ya'akov Ariel, "Kaufmann Kohler and His Attitude towards Zionism: A Reexamination," *American Jewish Archives* 43 no. 2 (Fall/Winter 1991):207-223.

7. Leo M. Franklin to Zionist Organization of America Secretary Louis Lipsky, 3 May 1920, in "Message of the President to the 31st Annual Convention of the CCAR," *CCAR Yearbook* 30 (1920):162-188. Cf. Cyrus Arfa, "Attitudes of the American Reform Rabbinate toward Zionism, 1885-1948" (diss., New York University, 1978):70-71.

8. Other representatives were Max Schloessinger (1877-1944), Judah Magnes (1877-1948), Barnett R. Brickner (1892-1958), and Stephen S. Wise (1874-1949).

9. The Federation of American Zionists, or American Zionist Federation, was organized 4 July 1898 and succeeded by the Zionist Organization of America. See Gary L. Zola, "Reform Judaism's Pioneer Zionist: Maximilian Heller," *American Jewish History* 73 no. 4 (June 1984):375-397.

10. Max[imilian] Heller, "Our Salvation," *Menorah: A Monthly Magazine for the Jewish Home* 31 no. 6/186 (December 1901):417-423 and 23 no. 2/188 (February 1902):74-102.

11. Heller in *Maccabaean* 18 (February 1910):47-48, cited in Meyer, "American Reform Judaism and Zionism: Early Efforts at Ideological Rapprochement," *Studies in Zionism* 7 (Spring 1983):49-64.

12. Heller, "A Realized Pattern of Social Justice," *Menorah Journal* 4 no. 4 (August 1918):236.

13. [Heller], "Rabbi Max Heller," *CCAR Yearbook* 29 (Philadelphia 1919):299-300.

14. David Neumark in *Ha'shiloah* 1 (1906:1907, Hebrew):366 and *American Jewish Chronicle* 1 (22-29 September 1916):635-637, cited in Meyer, "American Reform Judaism."

15. Henry Malter, "Backward, Then Forward," *HUC Journal* 7 (October 1902-June 1903):185, cited in Cohen, "Reaction." Alexander Marx reported that "the final article which was to give the author's own solution of the inner Jewish problem was not permitted to appear." *Studies in Jewish History and Booklore* (New York 1944):413.

16. I have been unable to find the Nahman of Bratslav citation. See Nahman of Bratslav, *Editions of Our Teacher Rabbi Nahman* (Ostrog 1808, Hebrew):section 47; Abba H. Silver, "The Conspiracy of Silence," in *Vision and Victory* (New York 1949):1-12. See Aaron Berman, "American Zionism and the Rescue of European Jewry," *American Jewish History* 30 no. 3 (March 1981):310-330.

17. "Report of Committee on President's Message," *CCAR Yearbook* 28 (1918):132-138.

18. *UAHC Proceedings* 5 (1898):4002, and 9 (1919):8520-8521, cited in Cohen, "Reaction."

19. *Minutes of the Board of Governors 25 May 1920*, cited in Cohen, "Reaction."

20. Isaac W. Bernheim, *The Closing Chapters of a Busy Life* (Denver 1929):100-101.

21. [Arthur W. Page], "The March of Events: An Editorial Interpretation," *World's Week* (May 1921):1.

22. I could not find the source for the Moses citation. Cf. Adolph Moses, "Ethnological Fictions: Read at the Jewish Denominational Congress, Chicago, August-September 1893," *Yahvism and Other Discourses* (Louisville 1903):216-239.

23. Bernheim, *The Reform Church of American Israelites* (Buffalo, N.Y., 1921). Cf. Bernheim to the CCAR, *CCAR Yearbook* 28 (Philadelphia 1918):141-144.

24. *The Union Haggada: Home Service for the Passover* ([Cincinnati?] 1923):120.

25. Howard R. Greenstein, *Turning Point: Zionism and Reform Judaism* (Chico, Calif., 1981):43.

26. Other important Conservative Zionist statements include Abraham M. Hershman (b. 1880), "Zionism," in *Israel's Fate and Faith* (Detroit 1952):254-278; Israel H. Levinthal (1888-1982), "Palestine and the New World," in *A New World Is Born: Sermons and Addresses* (New York 1943):263-281; idem, "The Place of Palestine in Judaism," in *Judaism: An Analysis and an Interpretation* (New York 1935):245-256; idem, "The Religion of Israel and the Land of Israel [delivered 31 May 1943]," in *Judaism Speaks to the Modern World* (London 1963):143-149. See Arye Gartner, "Conservative Judaism and Zionism: Rabbis, Laymen, Philanthropists," in *Zionism and Religion: International Conference 1-4 April 1990 at Brandeis University* (Waltham, Mass., forthcoming).

27. Norman Bentwich, "Zionism," in *Solomon Schechter: A Biography* (Philadelphia 1946):309-331.

28. Julius Wellhausen, "Israel: Reprinted from the *Encyclopaedia Britannica*," *Prolegomena to the History of Israel* (Edinburgh 1888):548. The relevant passage in Barukh Spinoza, *Tractatus Theologico-Politicus* [1670], Samuel Shirley, trans. (Leiden 1989):99-100 reads: "[That Jews] are preserved largely through the hatred of other nations is demonstrated by historical fact. When King of Spain formerly compelled the Jews to embrace the religion of his kingdom or else to go into exile, a considerable number of Jews accepted Catholicism. Now since all the privileges of native Spaniards were granted to those who embraced their religion, and they were then considered worthy of civil rights, they were so speedily assimilated to the Spaniards that after a short while no trace of them was left, nor any remembrance."

29. Solomon Schechter, "Zionism: A Statement," in *Seminary Addresses and Other Papers* (Cincinnati 1915):91-104, originally published in pamphlet form on 28 December 1906.

30. Israel Friedlaender, "The International Zionist Congress," in *Past and Present: A Collection of Jewish Essays* (Cincinnati 1919):451-468.

31. Friedlaender, "The Significance of Palestine for the Jewries of the World," *American Hebrew and Jewish Messenger* 100 no. 26 (4 May 1917):887-888, 915, 469-478; Idem, "Zionism and Religious Judaism," in *Past and Present*, 445-450.

32. Mordecai Kaplan, "The Land of Israel," in *Judaism as a Civilization* (New York 1934):264-279, 320-321.

33. Solomon Goldman, "*Galut*," in *Crisis and Decision* (New York 1938):46-51.

34. On Brandeis, see infra. I was unable to find the source for Albert Einstein's 1926 statement. Goldman, "Anti-Zionism Tries a Comeback," in *Crisis and Decision*, 52-61.

35. Goldman, *Land and Destiny* (New York 1939).

36. Israel Goldstein, "Zionist Orientation [7 September 1937-8 December 1938]," "Realism Plus Vision [3 August 1939:20—May 1940]," "Bialik-The Hebrew Poet Laureate [20 July 1938]," "Palestine at the World's Fair [3 July 1938]," in *Toward a Solution* (New York 1940):165-193, 197-201, 221-228.

37. Goldstein, *The Road Ahead* (Washington, D.C., 1944); idem, *Zionist Program and Implementation, Atlantic City, 17 November 1945* (Washington, D.C., 1945).

38. See Gershon Greenberg, "Division and Reconciliation: American Jewish Orthodox Response to the Balfour Declaration," in *Proceedings of the Ninth World Congress of Jewish Studies* (Jerusalem 1986):125-132. Arthur Hertzberg, "*Trefene Medina*: Learned Opposition to Emigration to the U.S.," *Proceedings of the Eighth World Congress of Jewish Studies* (Jerusalem 1984):1-30.

39. Joseph M. Levin, "Discourse on Zion," in *Gleanings of Joseph* (New York 1906, Hebrew):74-76.

40. Levin, "Eulogy for Theodor Herzl, Which I Presented Here in America," in *To the House of David* (Cincinnati 1916-1917, Hebrew):100-104.

41. "Rabbi Tsevi Hirsch Masliansky, Nationalist Preacher," in *Encyclopaedia of Religious Zionism* (Jerusalem 1958, Hebrew):1:480-481. See Tsevi H. Masliansky, *Sermons for Sabbaths and Holidays* (New York 1909, Yiddish):2:3-12, 48-63, 84-91. On Masliansky's ties to Elhanan Spektor and *Hibbat Tsiyon*, see "Tsevi H. Masliansky," in *Masliansky's Sermons for Sabbaths and Holidays* (New York 1908, Yiddish):1:v-xii.

42. "The Rabbi Tsevi Orliansky," in *Encyclopaedia of Religious Zionism,* 1:480-481. On Orliansky's ties to *Hibbat Tsiyon* and Elhanan Spektor, see Tsevi H. Orliansky, "Story of My Life," in *Sermons of Rabbi Tsevi H. Orliansky* (New York 1922, Hebrew):5-22.

43. Shemaryahu L. Hurwitz, *Holidays and Seasons* (New York 1918, Hebrew):55-57.

44. Abraham I. Hurwitz, *Valley of Jehoshaphat* (St. Louis 1918, Hebrew):4-5, 56-58, 135-136.

45. Gedaliah Silverstone, "Sermon on Zion," in *Sweetness from Honey* (Baltimore 1918, Hebrew):3:9-19.

46. Abraham A. Yudelovitch, "Sermon on Zionism," in *Fundamental Exposition* (New York 1925, Hebrew):5:190-194.

47. See Eliezer Schweid, *Democracy and Halakha* (Tel Aviv 1978, Hebrew).

48. Haim Hirschensohn, *Novellae on Tractate Horayot* (Jerusalem 1914-1926, Hebrew):1:preface.

49. Hirschensohn, *My King into the Sanctuary* (Saint Louis 1919, Hebrew):1:125; ibid., (St. Louis 1923, Hebrew):4:233.

50. I have been unable to find the citation in Halevi's poetry. Haim Hirschensohn, "Where, Where Are You, Land of Holiness? My Spirit Longs for You," in *Yearbook of the Federation of Palestine Jews of America: Second Annual Convention,* 13-14 June 1931 (New York [1931?], Hebrew):20-23. Founded in August 1929 in New York City, the Federation worked towards reconstructing the Jewish homeland and assisted Jews to return to Palestine.

51. Shalom Israelson, "The Future of Israel," *Ha'mitsape* 4 (September 1910, Hebrew):9-12; "War Between Matter and Spirit," *Ha'mitsape* 5 (April 1911, Hebrew):5-9. Cf. his 1923 letter to Hirschensohn in *My King into the Sanctuary* (Sinai, Romania, 1928, Hebrew):6:70-74, and his Introduction in *Words of Peace* (St. Louis 1920, Hebrew):iii-xiii.

52. Ephraim Deinard, *Glorious Zion in Unclean Hands (Isaiah 30:13)* (Arlington, N.J., 1917, Hebrew):preface.

53. Klein's sources included Moshe ben Nahman, *Book of Calculating the End* (1342; reprint, Jerusalem 1959 as *Book of Redemption,* Hebrew); Yonatan Eybeschuetz (1690-1764), "*Haftara* of *Ve'ethanan*" and "*Haftara* of *Nitsavim*," in *The Love of Jonathan* (Hamburg 1766, Hebrew):2:1-5, 24-28; Don Yitshak Abravanel (1437-1508), "Portion *Atem Nitsavim* [*Deuteronomy* 29:9-30:20]," *Interpretation of the Tora* (Jerusalem 1963-

1964, Hebrew):273-287; Israel ben Benjamin (17th century), "Messiah," in *New Commentary* (Lublin 1648, Hebrew):153; Boaz R. Rothschild, "Gate of Redemption," in *In the Depths of the Sea* (Fürth 1766, Hebrew):1:70-73; Meir L. Malbim, "Bursting towards the End [commentary on *Daniel* 12:11-12]," in *Prophets and Writing . . . Holy Scriptures* (Warsaw 1874, Hebrew):49; Klein, *Pray for the Peace of Jerusalem.*

54. Joel Teitelbaum, *Concerning Israeli Government Prior to the Coming of the Messiah* (Brooklyn, N.Y., 1980, Hebrew):87-89. See idem, *On Redemption and on Change* [*Ruth* 4:7] (Brooklyn, N.Y., 1966-1967, Hebrew):12, 79, 85.

55. Horace M. Kallen, "Facing the Facts of Palestine," *Menorah Journal* 7 no. 3 (August 1921):133-143; ibid. no. 4 (October 1921):238-245. See idem, "Constitution Foundations of the New Zion," *Maccabean* (April 1918):97-100 and May 1918):127-129; "Zionist Ideals and Palestinian Realities," in *Frontiers of Hope* (New York 1929):93-118; Sarah Schmidt, "Messianic Pragmatism: The Zionism of Horace M. Kallen," *Judaism* 25 no. 2 (Spring 1976):217-229; idem, "Toward the Pittsburgh Program: H. M. Kallen, Philosopher of an American Zionism," *Herzl Yearbook* 8: *Essays in American Zionism, 1917-1948* (New York 1978):18-36; idem, "The Parushim: A Secret Episode in American Zionist History," *AJHQ* 65 (1975-76):121-139. Representative Albert H. Vestal of Indiana, responding to the 11 June 1918 ZOA inquiry to Congress, said of Kallen's Pittsburgh Program:

> I am in entire accord with the principles laid down by the Zionists of the world at Basle and especially with those ideals enunciated at the last convention of the Zionists of America held in Pittsburgh. These principles and ideals are, in my opinion, based to a great degree upon those laid down by the founders of this Republic, and I venture to state that it will be these very principles upon which the Republic of Judea will be founded.

Reuben Fink, ed., *The American War Congress and Zionism: Statements by Members of the American War Congress on the Jewish National Movement* (New York 1919):103.

56. Sarah Schmidt, "The Zionist Conversion of Louis D. Brandeis," *Jewish Social Studies* 37 no. 1 (January 1975):18-34.

57. Henry W. Steed, *The Hapsburg Monarchy* (New York 1913):175-176; Louis D. Brandeis, "Why I Am a Zionist [delivered at the Free Synagogue of New York, 21 October 1914]," *Opinion* 17 no. 11 (September 1947):12-13; idem, "A Call to the Educated Jew," *Menorah Journal* 1 no. 1 (January 1915):13-19; idem, "The Jewish Problem: How to Solve It [1916]," *Jewish Frontier* 8 no. 10 (October 1941):23-26.

58. Felix Frankfurter, "The Statesmanship of the Balfour Declaration," *Menorah Journal* 4 no. 3 (August 1918):195-203.

59. The Transfer Agreement (*Ha'avara*) facilitated emigration of German Jews to Palestine by transferring their capital through German exports. See Edwin Black, *The Transfer Agreement: The Untold Story of the Secret Agreement between the Third Reich and Jewish Palestine* (New York 1984).

60. Hannah Arendt, "Zionism Reconsidered," *Menorah Journal* 33 no. 2 (October-December 1945):162-196. See idem, *The Jew as Pariah: Jewish Identity and Politics in the Modern Age*, Ron H. Feldman, ed. (New York 1978); Stephen J. Whitfield, *Into the Dark: Hannah Arendt and Totalitarianism* (Philadelphia 1980):166-177.

61. The Karen Hayesod Palestine Foundation Fund was established in 1920 at the London Zionist Conference.

62. Yosef Gottlieb, "Einstein the Zionist," *Midstream* 25 no. 6 (June-July 1979):43-48; Isaiah Berlin, "Einstein and Israel," in *Personal Impressions* (New York 1980):146-155. See also idem, "Einstein and Israel"; Yitshak Navon, "On Einstein and the Presidency of Israel"; Uriel Tal, "Jewish and Universal Social Ethics in the Life and Thought of Albert Einstein"; Fritz Stern, "Einstein's Germany," all in G. Holton and Y. Elkana, eds., *Jerusalem Einstein Centennial Symposium: Albert Einstein, Historical and Cultural Perspectives* (Princeton 1982):281-343; Solomon Goldman, "Is Einstein Religious?" in *Crisis and Decision* (New York 1938):100-119.

Conclusion

My goal has been to present the data on the Holy Land as a religious topic among the major religions of America until 1948 and thereby point to the symbiotic character of the involvement. Judaism (Sephardic, Reform, Conservative, Orthodox, secular), Protestantism (Puritan, pilgrim, black, literalist, liberal), Catholicism, and Mormonism were drawn together by the spiritual and physical soil of the Holy Land. All sought a territory in which to deposit and invest their hopes, and if their hopes were to have ultimate meaning the territory had to carry absolute validity. The scriptural Land was the obvious space. The data indicate two sources for the attraction. One was the a priori concept of the Holy Land, a source within collective American consciousness. The other was the a posteriori product of empirical experiences—a distinction which could explain the prevailing disjunction between ideal and real which I have found.

At the same time that American religions anchored themselves in the common ground of scriptural territory and shared concerns, they had differences. Confined within a single boundary, they found themselves involved in frontal encounters from which there was no escape. Each religion was obliged to define itself, to show that the others were different and of lesser value. Thus missionaries, consuls, literalists, blacks, Catholics, and Mormons all devalued Judaism and Jews in Palestine. Puritans who identified America as Zion considered Judaism regressive and alien to the American (Christian) future. On the other hand, messianic Judaism asserted its ultimacy in world history, leaving Christianity to fold itself into its Jerusalem-centered kingdom at the end of time. Among Jews, those who identified America as Zion devalued Jews who identified it with the Land of Israel, while Jews who identified Zion with the messianic future devalued those who drew it into the present. The few exceptions to the process of self-definition cum denial of the other, namely secularist Jews and liberal Protestants, identified universal principles that transcended any spatial Holy Land, although those principles were associated with American values. Mutual respect was possible when the spatial boundaries of the Holy Land were broken and purportedly transcendental values were established.

As an example, let us look at the symbiotic relationship between religious America and Holy Land vis-à-vis the final end to religious history. Puritans identified the *eschaton* with a Christian America, beyond and excluding Judaism. Protestant pilgrims in the Land of Israel, hoping to find the imagined transcendental territory of the Bible intact, inevitably became involved in the disjunction between real and ideal; they found it "difficult to make the transition from a transcendental, incorporeal perception of the 'Holy Land' to a realistic, physical one."[1] Some (Melville, Twain) were disenchanted or even crushed by the experience and lost hope. Others (Prime, Fulton, Talmage) overcame the disjunction and felt assured that the Land of Scripture would stage the Christian end to history.

Congregational missionaries (indirectly Puritan) sought to precipitate the Jerusalem-centered Christian kingdom by changing the minds of the Jews of Palestine, those who denied Christ. Several of the consuls could be considered this-worldly missionaries, for they saw the Holy Land in Christian terms and viewed Jewish existence there negatively. Degrading the Jew helped clear the Christian path toward the *eschaton* through the Holy Land. Cresson stood out for his personal involvement as a Christian become Jew. His experiences encapsulated world history according to Jewish messianism, whereby Christianity will ultimately pay tribute to Israel and the Land of Israel will be restored.

Some Protestant literalists retreated from the Millerites' uncompromising call for Jewish conversion as a condition for the beginning of restoration. Clorinda S. Minor wished to restore the Land to prepare for Christ, Who would transform the universe, Jews included. Blackstone wished to facilitate Jewish ingathering and sovereignty as a prelude to Christian apocalypse. Conversion was not required within the historical process: in the Christian kingdom of God, which Jews would help to precipitate, conversion would happen by itself.

For blacks the sacred territory of Scripture was identifiable with the Land of Israel, but it was more than the Land alone. Whether their eschatology related to the individual's life in history or to mankind's life at the end of history, it excluded Jews. Protestant liberals drew the *eschaton* into the present, expecting that God's kingdom could be founded within the principles of democracy.

Mormons were a crucible of various attitudes. Like the Puritans, they were committed to *eschaton*-America. Like the Congregational missionaries, they rejected the reality of postcrucifixion Judaism in the Land, anticipating the *eschaton* centered in old Jerusalem. Like the Protestant literalist Blackstone, they encouraged Jewish sovereignty even while they prayed for the Mormon culmination to history. The Mormon crucible also produced a unique product: a universal Mormon kingdom of God, a spiritual universe in which the two centers combined into an America-dominated synthesis, a new Jerusalem with a geographical reflection where land masses reconnected to restore geography to its configuration before Peleg.

Significantly, the distinctive, mutually exclusive eschatological positions found common ground when it came to American Indians as descendants of the Ten Lost Tribes. Protestants of various hues (Puritans, Congregationalists, missionaries, millennialists) and Mormons all took the Ten Lost Tribe connection seriously.[2] The theme simultaneously added scriptural identity to America, brought America into Jerusalem-centered Christian eschatology, and removed native Americans of Hebrew origin from America. In such a theology all Christ-centered religions could share. From this perspective, Mordecai M. Noah's sublimation of the notion into the Jewish value system was remarkably defiant.

Catholics did not speak of Zion-as-America, nor did they concentrate on restoring the Land of Israel in preparation for Christ's coming. For American Catholics the sacred territory of the Land of Israel was concentrated into the biography (life-death-life) of Christ. The Land was important because of the places made sacred by Him, it became significant as His "garment." Their interest was not in the future but in preserving the eternity that was already in place with the life of Christ. Accordingly, the physical and religious presence of Christ deniers (Jews) was disturbing; the idea of their having sovereignty over the holy places was frightening. The absolute value of the holy places—holy because they retained the biography of Christ—was such that rather than possibly endanger them by the presence of Judaism and Jews, hundreds of thousands of Holocaust Jews should be separated from the religious universe. That is, the sacred life-death-life of Christ as contained in the holy places was more important than the life of man (Jewish), for whom Christ had suffered and died.

The Jewish views of history and its end were radically different from one another. The Sephardim discovered ramifications for Zion in post-Revolutionary America but thought they implied ultimate Zion in the Land of Israel. Reform Jews of the nineteenth century were primarily against the restoration of the Land—whether culturally, nationally, or politically—and (like Puritans) were for Zion in America. In the twentieth century they first supported the Land for cultural and rescue reasons and eventually as a sovereign state. As with the Sephardim, there was a connection between their growing security in America and turning their eyes toward Zion. But unlike their Sephardic predecessors, messianism was essentially absent in any Reform support for the Land of Israel.

The Orthodox did relate to the Land in messianic terms. In a division strikingly similar to premillennialism versus postmillennialism, some were against restoration and statehood because they compromised the messianic realm, some thought human initiative was the legitimate partner to the divinely arranged messianic drama, and some thought it was up to the Jewish people to precipitate the onset of the messiah. Historical and Conservative Judaism maintained the outlook of the Sephardim, that Jewish life in America should be a foundation for building the Land, and added another: unless a vibrant source for Jewish life was established in the Land, life outside would die. Finally, the secular idealists thought in terms of universal ("American") ideals, and pragmatists in terms of security for Jews in the face of antisemitism; neither type dwelled on the holiness of the Land.

There were some broader differences among the Judaisms of America as well. While for Reform (Silver) and Orthodoxy the Holy Land had apocalyptic ramifications, for Conservative Judaism it did not. For early Reform the Land had no special status, for Orthodoxy—whether this-worldly or other-worldly—it was always central, and for Historical-Conservative Judaism it was indispensable. For Reform and secular Zionists, Conservative Judaism, and some Orthodox, the Land was needed right away. For the Sephardim and the remaining Orthodox, it could and should wait for the future.

Still, from a collective perspective—here I am still speaking of the final end to religious history—Jews differed from Christians. First, Christians—whenever they were involved with the Land of Israel, whether theologically (missionaries, literalists, Mormons), historically (diplomats, pilgrims) or spiritually (Catholics)—were concerned with Jews. For Jews, on the other hand, the reality of Christian life barely entered the debate; their discussions were internal to Jewry. Thus, Christians were not required to change their religion for Jews to cope with their Land. Second, Jewish concern for particular holy places, including even the Western Wall, did not reach the intensity of the Catholic. Jews were concerned with the totality of the Land—culturally, politically, theologically. Third, most Christians considered the Land of Israel an important ingredient of their religious lives. For some (Catholics, Episcopalians, Protestant liberals, blacks) the Land was a circumscribed dimension of religious life; for others (missionaries, literalists, Mormons) it was central. But it did not determine Christian identity per se—with the notable exceptions of the Minor colonists and Adams' Church of the Messiah. In all of Judaism (proto-, anti-, counter-, non-, pro-Zionist; messianic, amessianic, quasimessianic) the Land did determine religious identity; it was always on the Jewish mind.

As a parting note, I would point to some of the many themes that have yet to be explored. Some general areas of concern are these: To what extent was the America-as-Zion theme as enunciated by the Puritans used by Reform Jews or Mormons? Did the Sephardic concept of messianism by stages influence Historical Judaism? Were there historical connections between the anti-Zionism or pro-Americanism of ultra-Orthodox Jews and that of Reform? How did views of the Holy Land relate to specific religious contexts? And what were the ramifications for those religions' *Weltanschauungen*? Some specific areas that should be researched follow:

1. Samuel Langdon's theology of history and America's Holy Land.
2. The significance of Elias Boudinot's millennialist theology for his view of American Indians.

3. The historical validity to the claims of James Adair concerning the Hebraic origins of the Indians.
4. The role of the Holy Land in John Fulton's Christian theology.
5. The theological ramifications (especially messianic issues) in the 1822-1823 debates between Congregational missionaries and the *Kollel Perushim*.
6. The reaction of Jews in Palestine to nineteenth-century American missionaries.
7. Warder Cresson's theology of history and his method of scriptural interpretation.
8. Daniel Seaton's religious thought and the biblical Holy Land.
9. The existential religious factors in Clorinda S. Minor's transformation from Millerite to Holy Land colonist, or George W. J. Adams' from Mormon leader to Church of Messiah colonist in the Holy Land.
10. The impact of Isaac Elhanan Spektor on American Orthodox Zionist thought.
11. The representation of the Holy Land in the nineteenth-century American Catholic press.
12. Franciscan archival sources for the Catholic pilgrimage of 1889.
13. The impact of the Holocaust on American Catholic thought about the Land of Israel (1938-1948).
14. Orson Hyde's theological encounters with Jewish and ex-Jewish religious thinkers in Europe and the Holy Land.
15. Avraham Ashkenazi and Mormon pilgrims of 1872.
16. American Christian perceptions of Muslims in the Holy Land.
17. Gedaliah Silverstone's theology of history and its significance for a Jewish state.
18. Millennialist method of scriptural interpretation in the nineteenth century concerning restoration of the Jews.
19. Interactions between Cresson, Minor, James T. Barclay and Edward Robinson in the early 1850s in the Holy Land.

Final judgment on the symbiotic relationship between American religion and the Holy Land (in America and for the Land of Israel) as well as of the suggested a priori and a posteriori correlative development awaits many years of research into themes such as these.

Notes

1. See Yehoshua Ben-Arieh, "Perceptions and Images of the Holy Land," in Ruth Kark, ed., *The Land That Became Israel: Studies in Historical Geography* (Jerusalem 1989):37-53.

2.   See also Isaac P. Labagh, "The Restoration of the Ten Lost Tribes," in *Twelve Lectures on the Great Events of Unfulfilled Prophecy: Which still await their accomplishment and are approaching their fulfillment* (New York 1859):41-60.

Acronyms

ABCFM	American Board of Commissioners for Foreign Missions
ACMS	American Christian Missionary Society
ACPC	American Christian Palestine Committee
AHBA	*Advent Harbinger and Bible Advocate*
AJHQ	*American Jewish Historical Quarterly*
AME	African Methodist Episcopal Church
ATS	Andover Theological Seminary
CA	*The Crusader's Almanac*
CCAR	Central Conference of American Rabbis
DS	*The Day-Star*
HUC	Hebrew Union College
ICJ	Institute of Contemporary Jewry
JEFI	*Jewish Expositor and Friend of Israel: Containing monthly communications respecting the Jews and the proceedings of the London Jewish Society*
LC	*The Living Church: A weekly record of its news, its work, and its thought*
LDS	Latter-day Saints
LDSMA	*The LDS Messenger and Advocate*
LDSMS	*LDS Millennial Star*
LJS	London Society for Promoting Christianity amongst the Jews (more familiarly known as the London Jews' Society)
MC	*Midnight Cry*
MCA	*Magnalia Christi Americana*
MH	*Missionary Herald*
MI	*Monthly Intelligence of the Proceedings of the London Society for Promoting Christianity amongst the Jews*

OAJA	*The Occident and American Jewish Advocate: A monthly periodical devoted to the diffusion of knowledge on Jewish literature and religion*
PAJHS	*Publications of the American Jewish Historical Society*
STHP	*Sword of Truth and Harbinger of Peace*
TS	*Times and Seasons*
UAHC	Union of American Hebrew Congregations
VH	*View of the Hebrews*
ZOA	Zionist Organization of America

Index